AF660284

Essentials of

International Marketing

Essentials of

International Marketing

Donald L. Brady

JAICO PUBLISHING HOUSE

Ahmedabad Bangalore Bhopal Chennai
Delhi Hyderabad Kolkata Lucknow Mumbai

Published by Jaico Publishing House
A-2 Jash Chambers, 7-A Sir Phirozshah Mehta Road
Fort, Mumbai - 400 001
jaicopub@jaicobooks.com
www.jaicobooks.com

Published in arrangement with
M.E. Sharpe, Inc.
80 Business Park Drive
Armonk, NY 10504, USA

Authorized reprint edition, for sale in
India, Pakistan, Bangladesh, Nepal, and Sri Lanka.

ESSENTIALS OF INTERNATIONAL MARKETING
ISBN 978-81-8495-230-8

First Jaico Impression: 2011

Printed by Pashupati Printers (P) Ltd., Delhi-95

This book is dedicated to
my loving wife, Patricia,
and our two sons, Eric and Theron.

Brief Table of Contents

Detailed Table of Contents

Preface and Acknowledgments

Numerous factors make this book unique. Perhaps the most significant is that the content is presented in a brief manner. Only the most important information is included and then in a straightforward manner. Discussions omit content that is unessential to the concept and simply fills up space. Information that tends to change rapidly and become dated quickly is kept to a minimum. Up-to-date information can easily be obtained from the Internet, when needed, by interested students.

Chapter objectives are presented at the beginning of each chapter. The chapter objectives allow the reader to know what information should be derived from the chapter so that reading can be better focused on the important concepts the student should understand.

Each chapter starts with a dedicated vignette. It describes a company situation intended to introduce the chapter content and stimulate the reader's interest. The vignette provides an interesting illustration of how the chapter topic relates to the business world. Most of the vignettes are based on factual information about specific companies. Liberties were taken in some instances to create situations that did not occur in the companies so that the content of the chapter could be better illustrated. The basic facts about the companies presented in the vignettes are otherwise accurate.

Key words are listed at the end of each chapter. The definition of each word can be found where the word is printed in bold in the chapter and in the glossary at the back of the book. Every discipline involves vocabulary that the reader should know to be conversant in that field of study. Emphasizing key words will help the student make these terms a part of everyday terminology.

A chapter on the metric system is included (chapter 2). Since most of the world uses the metric system, international marketers will encounter metric measures in normal business activities. Simply knowing what a kilometer and gram are is inadequate. International marketers need to appreciate the relationship of metric units to one another. Understanding how to work with the metric system is an important first step in learning about other cultures and showing an interest in understanding foreign business associates. Instructors may skip this chapter without affecting the basic content or structure of their course. However, the mathematical technique presented in this chapter for making conversions among metric and American units of measure is the same technique used to make currency conversions in the financial chapter.

Therefore, if students are unfamiliar with that technique, referral to that material in chapter 2 is recommended.

An entire chapter is devoted to countertrade (chapter 16). The serious international marketer will encounter requests for countertrade. Without knowledge of countertrade, some business opportunities will be lost.

International marketing managers manage and direct their firm's international efforts. Therefore, basic management concepts applicable to directing the marketing function have been integrated into the book where appropriate. After all, developing an effective international marketing strategy involves and requires knowledge of how to apply certain managerial skills to marketing situations.

Business examples are used throughout the book where possible. The business examples should help the reader comprehend and appreciate the important facts and concepts presented, and provide a practical application of course content to the real world.

The book contains seventeen chapters, a manageable number to fit nicely in most semester-long academic programs. Each chapter is designed to fill approximately a week of teaching time.

I hope you will find the approach interesting and motivating. Enjoy the book.

* * *

I thank my wife, Patricia Brady, for giving me the time to write this book. Many days were spent researching and writing instead of being with Pat and helping her. Also, because Pat is especially good at editing, she read and offered suggestions for each draft once I became serious about the project. She devoted many days of arduous work to improving the readability, punctuation, and grammar of the final manuscript. I am lucky to have a loving and supportive wife who gives much more to our marriage than she takes. Without her understanding, support, and encouragement, this book would not have been possible.

Thanks are extended to Kimberly Taylor, who was a student at Millersville University. Kim proofread the first draft of the manuscript. She spent many hours reading, rereading, and suggesting grammatical revisions. Kim's assistance with the initial efforts was invaluable. Students in my International Marketing classes also deserve a thank-you. My students served as the sounding board for many of the ideas that eventually became part of the book and made innumerable comments regarding content and presentation. I appreciate all the input my students provided when writing this book was only an idea in its infancy.

I thank the sabbatical leave committee members and administration of Millersville University for approving my yearlong leave in London. During my time in London, I significantly revised and updated the manuscript and added current business examples to illustrate the concepts being presented. The time the sabbatical leave provided to do in-depth research and add personal experiences improved the book. Thanks also go to Dean John Short of Millersville University for his support and for believing that he would have a copy of my book on his office shelf someday.

Special thanks belong to Radica Kasirska, a former student at the American University in Bulgaria, for doing all the legwork for updating content, verifying the accuracy of content, and locating new and improved examples for possible inclusion in the book. Because of her help, appropriate revisions that were necessary to make content and examples as current as possible were accomplished.

Also, I want to recognize Sylvia Zareva of the American University in Bulgaria for her assistance with structuring and formatting the pictures. She helped make my poor-quality photos acceptable. Her photography skills made most of the pictures included in the book possible.

Finally, the editors and production staff of M.E. Sharpe, Inc. deserve recognition and thanks for the many suggestions that improved content and readability. Working with them was really a pleasure.

Essentials of International Marketing

1 The International Marketing Phenomenon

The largest company in the Republic of Kazakhstan is КАТЕЛКО, ZAO (Katelco). Katelco was formed in 1995, when Kazakhstan's National Satellite System of TV/Radio Broadcast and Data Transmission (NSST & DT) was introduced as an alternative method to transmit state television programs. In 2002, the division Katelco Plus was created to provide commercial multichannel direct-to-home reception (DTH) satellite service. After the dissolution of the former Soviet Union, management's philosophy and approach to controlling the company were slow to change. Managers, who had grown up with communist ways, were reluctant to adapt new management styles.

Lack of marketing emphasis, hierarchical structure, and communist methods of control adversely impacted the company's image and contributed to increased customer dissatisfaction. Also, management had no clear vision of what the company's market position should be, how marketing activities should be directed, and as a result, no well-defined marketing strategy. In fact, until the late 1990s no marketing efforts existed. Another problem was that employees did not know their responsibilities and were treated as units of production. As a result, middle-level managers were not concerned about motivating employees and trying to achieve the company's objectives.

Because of the influence of the old communist way of doing business, managers were not motivated to improve the company. These managers were primarily concerned with keeping their own positions and therefore prevented subordinates from demonstrating their full capabilities by restricting their contact with top management. In the area of marketing, a simple sale of a standard set of equipment required the customer to obtain three signatures. Only one person was designated the authority to sign in each of the three areas where signatures were required. Thus, customers had to locate the authorized signers, and, if any were unavailable, they had to return at a later time. Top management was aware of the problems and was initiating efforts to make improvements. To do so, however, a new corporate philosophy had to be instilled and an effective marketing strategy developed.

To expand business in 2002, the management of Katelco Plus began offering multichannel direct-to-home (DTH) satellite service with equipment purchased from Motorola, Inc. in 2001. The management of Motorola, with headquarters in Schaumburg, Illinois, was prepared to work with the management of Katelco Plus to satisfy the firm's equipment needs. However, because of the potential impact of the lack of marketing in the past, Motorola's management could possibly have had trouble assessing the future growth rate for equipment. The opportunity for future business could not be assumed with any certainty, which may have increased the business risk for Motorola's management. However, in 2004, Motorola was selected again to supply digital video encoders and satellite set-top equipment and service to increase the number of available channels that could be offered to forty-eight.

Source: Based in part on information from Katelco's Web site, http://www.katelco.kz; "Katelco Selects Motorola Technology to Expand Digital Services in Kazakhstan," *Space Newsfeed,* April 29, 2004, http://www.spacenewsfeed.co.uk/2004/2_5_2004/2May2004_7.html.

CHAPTER OBJECTIVES

After reading this chapter, you should

- be able to appreciate the importance of international marketing as a business endeavor;
- understand what international marketing is all about;
- understand in what ways international marketing and domestic marketing are similar and different;
- know how international marketing relates to international business;
- appreciate why studying international marketing is important;
- understand why international marketing opportunities are growing;
- understand what the international environment is and why that environment affects decision making and risk in the organization; and
- understand the orientations management may take toward international marketing.

INTERNATIONAL MARKETING IN PERSPECTIVE

All a person has to do today is look around to see the impact of international marketing on our lives. You can scarcely avoid seeing the evidence of international marketing, regardless of where you look. "Made in Taiwan" is written on the label inside your shirt or blouse. The bananas you eat boldly display stickers stating that the fruit comes from Honduras or Ecuador. The tires on your vehicle are embossed "Made in Korea," and your TV is emblazoned with the declaration that it was made in Japan.

Many of the products that we use regularly and consider necessities either were made outside of the United States or contain foreign-made components. Whether we are aware of it or not, international marketing touches almost every aspect of our lives.

Exhibit 1.1 **Minerva Greek Extra Virgin Olive Oil**

This bottle of olive oil is from Greece. The words *Greek* and *Product of Greece* and the Greek flag are displayed on the label to help make buyers aware of that fact.

Hardly a day goes by that we do not embrace some aspect of international marketing. The presence of international marketing is all around us and is growing year by year and day by day—a presence that will influence our lives more and more in the future.

THE IMPORTANCE OF INTERNATIONAL MARKETING

Today, international marketing has become an essential part of business activity. Without international marketing, many of the products we enjoy would either be unavailable or the quantity available for purchase would be significantly reduced. For example, people living in colder climates would have no bananas to eat. People living in the United States would have no television sets. All of the television sets purchased in the United States are produced in foreign countries. Not one TV is produced in the United States anymore.

As we can see, without international marketing our world and our lives would be much different. The availability of some products would be curtailed, and the prices of those products would certainly be higher. International marketing enriches our lives and contributes to an improved standard of living.

Because international marketing is so important, career opportunities in the field are increasing. Employment prospects are good and will probably increase in the future. Opportunities exist for qualified people in a variety of positions in this exciting and challenging area of business.

THE CHALLENGES OF INTERNATIONAL MARKETING

As we have just seen, we cannot escape an involvement with international marketing, because the process affects our lives so significantly whether we realize that fact or not. Being involved with so many of the products we buy, international marketing is becoming an increasingly important component of American business life. Every day, the opportunities for involvement in international marketing increase. The international aspects of marketing are exciting, challenging, expanding, and glamorous to a certain extent. At the same time, international marketing unfortunately suffers from a shroud of mystery, misunderstanding, and fear. This occurs because of the tendency for businesspeople and the public, in general, to lack knowledge about the topic or have a negative bias resulting from inaccurate information, a domestic orientation, or both. In fact, a survey of 11,700 managers in twenty-five countries revealed a rising desire for trade protectionism. In the United States, 60 percent of managers wanted their government to buy from domestic firms and 38 percent favored restrictions on the movement of domestic facilities to foreign countries.[1]

Managers who understand and appreciate the potential impact of international marketing on the future of their firms are the managers who stand to profit from the growing opportunities in foreign markets. Managers who lack this perception and appreciation are spurning tremendous opportunity. Fortunately, however, regardless of the size of the firm being managed, type of products produced, or other considerations confronted, most managers possess the capacity for joining this expanding area of business activity if desired. Comments by the chairman and chief executive officer of Caterpillar, Inc., that illustrate an understanding of the importance of international marketing to the future of the firm are shown in Exhibit 1.2.

Hardly a day goes by without some reference to international marketing in the news media. Such exposure is indicative of the growing prominence and significance of this area of business. Examples of newsworthy international marketing successes occurring recently include Lockheed Martin Corporation's receiving a contract to sell forty-eight F-35 Lightning II Joint Strike Fighter jets to the country of Norway, a purchase that will bring the company US$2.5 billion.[2] Another example is that the Boeing Company was selected by the government of India to provide eight P-8I long-range maritime reconnaissance and antisubmarine warfare aircraft to the Indian Navy. India is the first international customer for the plane, which is a modification of the P-8A Poseidon that Boeing developed for the U.S. Navy.[3] Also, Boeing, which has about a 65 percent market share of the growing

Exhibit 1.2

Comments from the Management of Caterpillar, Inc.

If there was ever a year that proved the strength of Caterpillar's global business model, it was 2007. . . . As predicted, our North American sales and revenues dropped significantly. . . . But customer demand for Caterpillar products in the rest of the world—particularly the emerging markets—was explosive. Sales and revenues were up 28 percent in Asia-Pacific, 34 percent in Europe, Africa, the Middle East and The Commonwealth of Independent States (CIS) and 18 percent in Latin America.

Source: James W. Owens, chairman and CEO, "To Our Stakeholders," Caterpillar, Inc., *2007 Annual Report*, 26.

Chinese commercial aircraft market, received an order for eighty Boeing 737 jets priced at US$4.6 billion. Boeing executives predict China will need about 2,600 additional aircraft over the next twenty years and expect to be one of the country's primary suppliers.[4]

Although international marketing is a growing area of business for many firms, mere involvement does not guarantee success. Business risk also exists in international markets. Therefore, knowledge of the marketing process is important to a successful marketing program regardless of where marketing occurs. This fact is particularly pertinent as the number of businesses engaged in international marketing and the extent of their involvement grows. The marketer's initial international experience must be a good one, and the expansion of international endeavors favorable, if the growth trend in international marketing is to continue.

WHAT IS INTERNATIONAL MARKETING?

International marketing as a discipline is related to the broader activity of international business. Therefore, an interrelationship exists with international marketing and the other aspects of international business. These related areas contribute to and have an impact directly or indirectly on international marketing activities. Out of necessity, an appreciation of these other areas is needed if an understanding of the scope and involvement of international marketing is to be appreciated.

INTERNATIONAL BUSINESS DEFINED

International business is, perhaps, the broadest perspective for explaining the involvement of business firms in foreign business endeavors. The broadness of international business is reflected in the following statement: "Inasmuch as international business operates within the broad context of the world environment, it must of necessity draw on the contributions of a number of basic disciplines including geography, politics, law, economics, and anthropology. In addition, international business covers the functional business fields of marketing, management, and finance."[5]

International business can be considered to consist of five distinct areas of activity:[6]

- comparative analysis of business operations in different economic systems
- comparative analysis of management in similar firms in different markets
- export and import trade efforts
- the analysis of the functions of business occurring among different markets
- the operations of a domestic firm relative to its overseas branches

Actually, international business does not involve everything that management embraces in worldwide activities, as initial impressions might suggest. Rather, the focus is on the structural framework of the institutions and organizations that produce international transactions. The concern is more with the realities involved in the motivation, functioning, and behavior of business firms engaged in business activities beyond their home countries.[7]

International business can be defined as the study of firms that are involved in business-related endeavors more than one country. Since marketing is a business function, by this definition international marketing must be considered as a specialty area of study within the broader field of international business.

INTERNATIONAL TRADE DEFINED

International trade, sometimes referred to as foreign trade, is the vanguard discipline in the field of international business. International trade is, perhaps, the first formalized study of activities involved with international business. The field of international trade involves only export and import operations.

This discipline is, therefore, limited to aspects of selling domestically made products in foreign markets and procuring foreign-made products for use in the domestic market. Why and how products and services are moved from sellers in one country to buyers in another country is studied. Incentives and restrictions governments impose on the movement of these products and services are also of concern. **International trade** may be defined as the activities of firms relating to the production of products domestically for the purpose of shipment to buyers in foreign countries and the procurement of foreign-made products.

INTERNATIONAL ECONOMICS DEFINED

Another area related to international marketing is international economics. International economics embraces a variety of topics associated with international finance and trade relations.

This area of study, while addressing product movements among nations, is more concerned with the financial undertakings and obligations resulting from those movements. Attention is directed to business activities only as those activities relate to international payments.

International economics is theory centered and, therefore, tends to be concerned with abstract principles and concepts that may or may not explain the realities in international business activities.[8] International economics also tends to be macro oriented and therefore concentrates more on international business relationships among nations than among firms and individual customers. Attention is always focused on the role economic factors play in determining the direction of trade activities around the world. Currency policies of governments are considered important because of the significant influence those policies are perceived to have on determining the direction of worldwide trade. **International economics** can be defined as the analysis of financial and trade policies that describe the movement of products and investments among nations and help develop individual national economies.

INTERNATIONAL CROSS-CULTURAL MANAGEMENT DEFINED

International cross-cultural management is a comparative analysis of the profiles of managers in different countries. Because conditions confronting management differ from country to country, the techniques and procedures used by managers will differ. An assessment of similarities and differences among these managers is desirable if management is to function successfully outside of the domestic environment.

Of concern in international cross-cultural management is the equivalence of the phenomena and conditions being examined across nations. Activities that are similar across nations may be performed for different purposes. For instance, Chinese women are willing to pay for premium cosmetic products but tend not to be brand loyal. For cosmetics, the Chinese market is extremely promotion driven. Therefore, promotional incentives become a more important marketing-mix component in China than in the United States.[9] Thus, a study of foreign management procedures is necessary to determine how those procedures differ from our own. **International cross-cultural management** may be defined as the comparative study of the management process in more than one country at similar points in time.

INTERNATIONAL MARKETING DEFINED

Marketing is most frequently defined as the activities of firms that are designed to bring about exchanges and build relationships with customers. In other words, marketing consists of everything done to satisfy the needs and wants of a group of potential buyers. Marketing is usually considered to involve the development of necessary strategies and programs to profitably facilitate and expedite the exchange process.

International marketing involves the marketing process and therefore is also an exchange process. International marketing is marketing in the true sense of the concept and differs only because exchanges that transcend national boundaries are involved. Thus, international marketing involves everything done to satisfy customers, only the customers are located in foreign countries. The exchange process must involve at least one marketing activity that crosses national boundaries and also include participants in two or more sovereign nation-states.

International marketing, therefore, involves two unique yet related aspects. That is, international marketing consists of two distinct ways for using marketing activities to facilitate the exchange process. One aspect utilizes marketing functions and processes to move products produced in one country to another country. The product must cross national boundaries. This aspect of international marketing is what was previously defined as international trade.

In one respect, then, international marketing involves the marketing discipline as related to international trade. But also involved are marketing activities that occur primarily in foreign countries but that originate in firms with facilities or a physical presence located in another country. Thus, any marketing activity that results from investments and facilities (operations) of firms in countries outside the home country (domestic market) is also international marketing. International marketing can, therefore, involve marketing not only *to* but also *in* foreign countries.[10] For example, by manufacturing vinyl flooring in the United States and shipping to buyers in Canada, Armstrong World Industries, Inc., is conducting international marketing. When flooring products are sold to English buyers from a plant that Armstrong owns in England, international marketing is also being conducted. As long as marketing functions occur outside the domestic country and the domestic parent company is involved, international marketing results.

International marketing, then, involves an internationalization of the exchange process and has no regard for national boundaries. From this perspective, **international marketing** may be defined as the performance of marketing activities that facilitate and expedite exchanges and build relationships with buyers in foreign markets. This definition means that international marketing involves everything done to satisfy the needs and wants of buyers who reside outside the boundaries of the firm's domestic country.

INTERNATIONAL AND DOMESTIC MARKETING COMPARED

International marketing must be considered independent of domestic marketing. All marketing activities that take place within the confines of a single country are referred to as domestic marketing. The marketing process is limited by the boundaries of the country. Exchanges cannot occur outside the boundaries of the firm's home country if those exchanges are to be considered domestic marketing. For example, tires produced at the Gadsden, Alabama, plant of the Goodyear Tire & Rubber Company and sold to a wholesaler in Pennsylvania constitute domestic marketing. Similarly, domestic marketing occurs when a German woman buys a dress created by German designer Beate Heymann at the Valini clothing store in Düsseldorf, Germany.

As soon as exchanges occur outside the boundaries of the home market or involve a foreign national, the marketing process is no longer domestic and becomes international in perspective. For the marketing process to be referred to as international, the exchange cannot occur domestically, but must involve one or more marketing functions embracing locations outside the domestic country. Therefore, whether the marketing process is classified as domestic or international depends on where the buyer resides or the location of the organization the buyer represents. For example, if the Goodyear tires produced at the Gadsden plant are sold to a buyer in Saudi Arabia, the transaction becomes international marketing. This is true even if the Saudi buyer travels to the United States to conclude the sale, as long as the tires will be delivered and used in Saudi Arabia or some other location outside of the United States. Or, if a Swiss woman buys the Beate Heymann–designed dress from the Stomeo Uomo Moda store in Zürich, the sale must be considered international marketing.

TERMS USED TO DESCRIBE INTERNATIONAL MARKETING

A variety of terms are employed in the literature and among businesspeople to explain the process of marketing beyond the domestic country. Five of the most frequently encountered terms are the following:[11]

- **Cosmopolitan marketing** is marketing between sovereign nation-states without a nationalist frame of reference. Cosmopolitan marketing is a mélange of the international and multinational concepts.
- **Global or world marketing** is marketing that takes place in a global perspective where the world is the market and no domestic references exist. No distinction is made between local and foreign markets.
- **International marketing** extends marketing activities beyond national borders to support international transactions. The term is often used with a wider connotation, which includes activities between and in foreign countries.
- **Multinational marketing** is doing business in foreign markets rather than between domestic and foreign markets.
- **Supranational marketing** is considering marketing in terms of supranational markets (conglomerates of nations providing harmony of business practices among participating countries) such as the European Union. Supranational markets tend to develop their own political, legal, and economic constraints and opportunities.

Although each of these terms has a slightly different meaning, all are essentially describing the same concepts. In fact, the individual differences in the terms are frequently ignored and the five terms are often used almost interchangeably. Thus, the common practice among businesspeople is to employ these terms as though they all have the same meaning. Although technically incorrect to do this, discriminating among the differences does not seem to be extremely important in practice. For this reason and because of the broad interpretation, the preferred term used in this book to describe this subject matter is **international marketing**. Throughout the book the term *international marketing* will be employed even though one of the other terms could sometimes be used more appropriately.

INTERRELATIONSHIP OF DISCIPLINES

As is easily seen, international marketing is related to all of the international areas previously discussed. Although each of these international areas, including international marketing, is unique and considered as a separate subject or discipline, a certain amount of overlap is unavoidable and even desirable. The overlap occurs because common subject matter is addressed in each. For instance, for international trade to be conducted a knowledge of currency exchange is necessary. Knowledge of currency exchange is also necessary for international economics to help explain the direction of world trade. The overlap is desirable because it strengthens each area individually and permits an appreciation of the interrelationships.

WHY STUDY INTERNATIONAL MARKETING?

The chances of becoming involved in international marketing at some time during a business career are greater today than ever before. Thus, knowledge of international marketing is desirable to prepare businesspeople to adapt more easily should they encounter international involvement. Certainly broad business knowledge that includes international marketing should help anyone be a better, more well-rounded, employee or manager.

At least four basic reasons exist for having businesspeople study international marketing:

- An awareness of the opportunities afforded by foreign markets is growing among businesspeople.
- The demand for foreign-made products is increasing.
- Governments are increasing efforts to promote and stimulate the involvement of businesses in foreign markets.
- Unique conditions are encountered in international marketing.

GROWING AWARENESS OF OPPORTUNITIES

Today's executives tend to be more world oriented than their predecessors. Increasingly, managers are realizing that markets extend beyond national boundaries and that foreign markets represent increased sales possibilities. Business schools are emphasizing the international aspects of business subjects and increasingly internationalizing the curricula. Therefore, graduates possess a better understanding of international aspects of business and are increasingly more comfortable confronting and discussing the uniqueness and nuances of the topic. More and more managers are considering the possibilities that their products and services will do a better job of satisfying foreigners than the products those consumers are currently buying locally.

Management will continue to increase its exploration of foreign market opportunities for at least three reasons:[12]

- Corporate executives favor projects that provide growth. Foreign sales add to marginal revenue and can expand profits.
- Few countervailing forces exist in foreign countries among consumers and governments to thwart or minimize foreign business involvement. Government officials tend to not want to interfere when foreign firms are helping to improve the nation's economic welfare. Government leaders are happy when their citizens are happy.

- Foreign governments in lesser-developed countries seek foreign business to help develop their nations economically. Foreign businesses can help expand the business base, increase employment, and raise the standard of living.

Management tends to be more keenly aware of the existence of foreign markets than ever. Managers are also recognizing the potential of these markets and their importance to fulfilling organizational goals.

INCREASING DEMAND

People everywhere are demanding more foreign-made products. As a result of improving technology and increasing travel, cultural exchange proliferates. Cultural exchange allows people around the world to learn how others live and about the products and services they use. Also, as the world shrinks in terms of cultural exchange, the differences in the way people live and the products they purchase diminishes. Because of this, managers will receive more solicited and unsolicited orders from foreigners in more and more countries around the world.

The purchasing power of people in foreign nations is also increasing as economies expand, which is making the purchase of more foreign-made products possible. For instance, gross domestic product (GDP) in the People's Republic of China grew an average of 10 percent a year from 1978 to 2007 (in excess of 11 percent between 2006 and 2007), contributing to significant increases in per capita income.[13] Underdeveloped countries such as India are increasingly trying to transition to more developed economies. Thus, as the citizens of a country become more affluent and their market economy grows, the demand for all kinds of products increases. Not only are more and better-quality products sought, which frequently can only be obtained from foreign sources, but also foreign-made products that were previously unattainable or unavailable are desired.

GOVERNMENT ENCOURAGEMENT

Most governments, including that of the United States, recognize the importance of international marketing to a strong and healthy economy. International business is good not only for the growth of the firm involved but also for the prosperity and security of the nation. International marketing can contribute to the improvement of a country's balance of payments. Also, international marketing helps create jobs for workers directly involved in producing and marketing products for foreign markets and workers indirectly involved in supplying and supporting those businesses.

In the United States, for example, international marketing is encouraged and supported by federal, state, and local governments. The primary agency entrusted with supporting international marketing at the federal level is the Department of Commerce. Trade Advisory Centers, trade missions and centers, publication of various foreign trade statistics, and the president's E Award for excellence in exporting are all indicative of this emphasis. Many state governments have created special departments to encourage international marketing. International trade efforts can also be found within the chambers of commerce of larger cities.

UNIQUE CONDITIONS

The marketing executive can expect international marketing to exhibit both similarities and differences to domestic marketing. Both are undertaken for the same end—building relationships with and satisfying customers profitably. Both involve the same kinds of functions and apply the same marketing principles. Yet, the environment in which these similarities occur may differ significantly from country to country and market to market.

Marketing domestically or internationally embraces a technical element and a human element. The nature of these elements accounts for the similarities and differences between domestic and international marketing. The technical aspects (mechanical element) of marketing, which include all the strategic elements, such as distribution and pricing procedures, are considered to have universal validity and potential for universal application. The mechanical aspects are approached in a similar manner regardless of the country in which marketing takes place. The societal and physical environments surrounding the consumer influence the human aspect (behavioral element) of marketing. This is the element of international marketing that can differ significantly from country to country.[14] Thus, the differences between domestic and international marketing are primarily in the application of the marketing mechanics to the behavioral and social uniqueness existing in foreign countries. Therefore, the feasibility of applying the **marketing concept** to international marketing should be no different than in domestic marketing.

Because of behavioral differences in international marketing, managers should be prepared to encounter new problems that do not exist in domestic marketing and employ different techniques for managing the various kinds of problems that are common to both domestic and international marketing. Problems unique to the international market and not occurring domestically may be encountered. For instance, the foreign government may require the performance of certain activities not encountered domestically such as completion of forms and standardization of product content. Also, the foreign government may restrict or prohibit certain activities, such as the use of comparative advertising, that are normal business practice domestically. When this happens, the marketing manager must be prepared to make appropriate adjustments in **marketing strategy**. Adjustments in marketing strategy may also have to be made to facilitate different approaches required to handle the same problems faced in domestic markets. For example, the size of trucks may vary from one country to another, causing loading difficulty. These kinds of situations require the marketer to make adjustments to the domestic approach to the problem.

Differences in marketing technique may be required because of the way needs are satisfied. Consumers in different countries may buy different products to satisfy identical needs or buy identical products to satisfy different needs. For example, the need for sports entertainment may be satisfied in the United States by attending a baseball game. Attending a cricket match in Great Britain may satisfy that same need. The same product may also satisfy different needs. For example, a bicycle may be purchased in the United States to satisfy the need for recreation or exercise. The need satisfied by a bicycle in Malaysia, however, may be basic transportation. Marketing strategy will differ in each case.

Exhibit 1.3 **Oreo Cookies**

A smaller package made from plastic instead of cardboard may be appropriate in the foreign market. Note the use of the British spelling for flavoured.

These new problems and differences in technique between domestic and international marketing result in part from operation in

- conditions that cover large geographical distances;
- countries that are in different stages of industrial development;
- economic conditions that vary widely;
- national markets that vary considerably in population and area;
- national sovereignties that possess different legal, political, and monetary systems; and
- societies that hold different value systems.[15]

For example, distribution concerns are much different in the outback of Australia, where the population density is low, than in Hong Kong, where the population density is high.

The unique conditions confronted in international markets make knowledge of international marketing essential if the manager expects to be able to compete successfully. The manager must possess knowledge of world markets, not only to compete successfully internationally but also to remain competitive in the domestic market when foreign competition increases there.

PUTTING INTERNATIONAL MARKETING IN PERSPECTIVE

In domestic marketing the manager confronts two broad categories of variables—those that can be controlled and those that cannot be controlled. The **controllable variables** comprise what is often referred to as the **marketing mix**, which the manager can manipulate and change. The **uncontrollable variables** result from the **marketing**

environment in which the firm operates and are fixed in the short run. Uncontrollable variables act as constraints on or impediments to the manager's decision-making freedom and place limitations on what the manager can do with the marketing mix. That is, the marketing mix can be adjusted only to the extent permitted by the uncontrollable environment. For example, producing automobiles that can go 200 miles per gallon of gas is not possible because the technology required for obtaining that kind of mileage does not exist.

FOREIGN UNCONTROLLABLE ENVIRONMENT

The variables that are controllable domestically are also controllable in international markets. The marketing manager has the ability to adjust the components of the marketing mix internationally in the same way as is done in the domestic market. Regardless of where marketing occurs, the marketing mix may be developed in the most expedient manner consistent with the uncontrollable environment to build marketing relationships and satisfy the needs of the firm's target market.

However, since the international marketer operates in more than one country, more than one market environment is encountered. Thus, the marketing manager confronts uncontrollable variables in both the domestic and foreign countries. The ability to adjust the marketing mix is constrained not only by the uncontrollable environment of the domestic country but also by the uncontrollable environment of the foreign country. For example, an American exporter's marketing strategy must conform to provisions of the Foreign Corrupt Practices Act and U.S. antiboycott laws as well as import and product control regulations of the foreign country.

The variables comprising the uncontrollable environment internationally are the same as those comprising the domestic uncontrollable environment. These are usually considered to include forces in at least six areas:

- competitive environment
- cultural and social environment
- economic environment
- political and legal environment
- technological environment
- the firm's organizational environment

Obviously, differences encountered in areas such as economic, cultural, social, political, and legal conditions in foreign markets can influence marketing-mix decisions. Competition involves the marketing strategy of all other firms operating in the foreign market that are attempting to satisfy the customer's need. The technological environment refers not only to the level of technological development in the foreign market but also to the market's ability to assimilate new technology. The firm's organizational environment includes personnel, financial, and resource constraints confronting management. Management cannot venture beyond the acceptable objectives established for the firm. The additional uncontrollable environment introduces more factors for consideration and complicates the development of a marketing

Exhibit 1.4 **Example of an Outdoor Store**

Lower incomes and the need to keep prices low may cause different marketing methods to be encountered. Inventory in this outdoor store is kept in boxes for easy movement at closing time and to keep overhead costs low.

strategy. The restrictive relationship among the environments and management's decision-making ability regarding the marketing mix can be visualized as shown in Exhibit 1.5. As shown, the decisions the international marketing manager can make are influenced by the nature of the foreign customer and the conditions existing in the uncontrollable part of the foreign environment. Decisions that are consistent with conditions in the foreign uncontrollable environment must also conform to accepted practices within the domestic uncontrollable environment. Therefore, both the domestic and foreign uncontrollable environments combine to affect decision making. One or more unique uncontrollable environments can exist in each country in which business is being done.

THE FOREIGN MARKETING ENVIRONMENT AND RISK

Since more factors must be considered when developing an international marketing strategy rather than a domestic one, decision making must be approached with deliberation and care. Also, the manager may be less familiar with the variables present

Exhibit 1.5 **The Marketing Environment Confronted by the International Marketer**

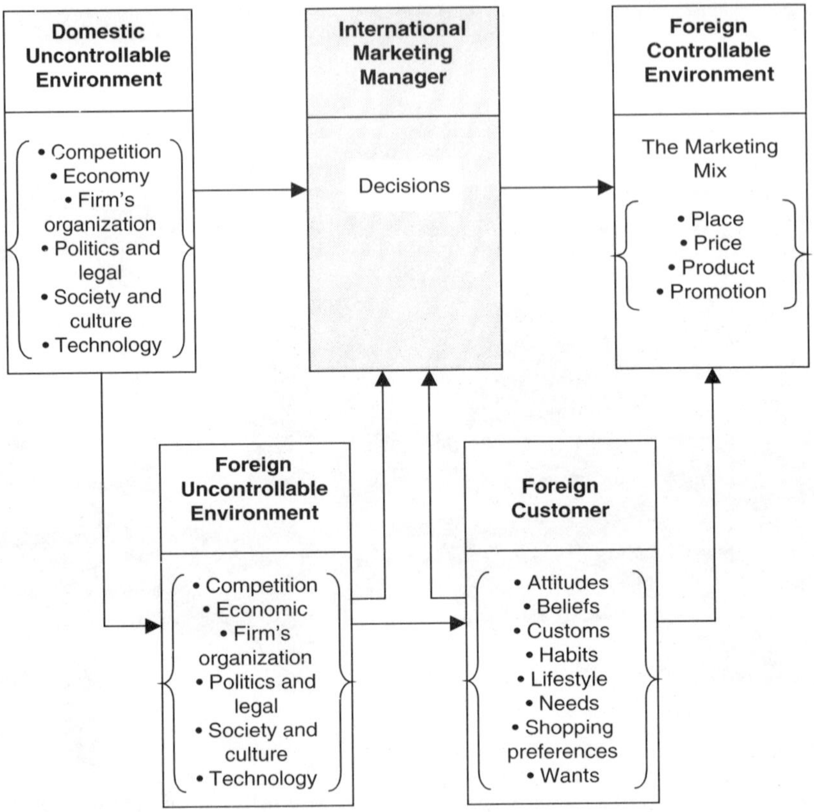

in the uncontrollable international environment than with those in the uncontrollable domestic environment. Because of these considerations, risk associated with decision making is usually greater in the international market than in the domestic market. In general, the greater the risk associated with any business venture, the greater must be the return. As a result, the financial implications of international marketing endeavors must be considered appropriate to justify the risk. This is important because international marketing investment needs to be commensurate with profit possibilities.

International Orientations

Managers may have different orientations or attitudes about the role of international marketing in the firm's business operations. The orientation is influenced by the commitment and importance ascribed to international activities. Managers can be classified into one of four categories based on their view of the scope and extent of international marketing activities and their willingness to adjust to the unique conditions encountered in the foreign environment:[16]

- ethnocentric approach
- polycentric approach
- regiocentric approach
- geocentric approach

An **ethnocentric** manager is home-country oriented and not acclimated toward international aspects of the business. This manager approaches international marketing opportunities with marketing policy similar to domestic policy. Foreign sales are all right as long as the buyer will accept the same product produced for domestic customers and no significant changes in marketing strategy are required. The international market is viewed similarly to the domestic market and is considered simply as an extension of it, albeit in a remote location. The manager will not make any special effort to accommodate the foreign buyer. The attitude is "if you want what we have to offer, we will supply, but don't ask for any special adaptations." Therefore, international marketing is secondary to domestic operations and is viewed primarily as a way to dispose of capacity not absorbed by domestic demand. Uniqueness in the foreign market is either not recognized or simply ignored.

A manager who is **polycentric** in orientation is host-country oriented. Each foreign market is viewed as unique and different and requiring individualized attention. Each country in which business opportunities exist is considered independent of all others. Although management may be considered to be internationally oriented, no coordination of international marketing strategy among countries is sought. Unique products and marketing strategies are developed for each foreign market. Markets are perceived as being autonomous and therefore require individualized attention and marketing efforts. The marketing mix is adapted to the uniqueness of each foreign market in which business is conducted.

A **regiocentric** manager views markets as being distinct, yet capable of being grouped according to location. Countries within regions of the world exhibit sufficient commonality to permit the grouping of these countries together for marketing efforts. Regions are usually consistent with some natural boundaries such as continents (Africa), areas (Asia-Pacific), or integrations of nations (European Union). Standardization of marketing strategy within regions is sought although the regions remain autonomous. Therefore, responsiveness is localized region by region.

A manager who is **geocentric** in orientation holds a global perspective. This manager sees the world as one big market and does not necessarily consider the international markets separately from the domestic markets. Differences in markets from country to country are recognized; however, those differences are not considered significant enough to prevent centralized control and coordination of all marketing efforts worldwide. Decisions are made within an overall corporate strategy and not individually from country to country. Uniqueness in foreign markets is recognized; however, accommodations to the marketing mix are standardized where possible.

Obviously, the orientation the manager embraces will influence international marketing strategy decisions. The approach the manager favors will influence decisions about concerns such as product, brand, and organizational structure. For example, an ethnocentric manager is likely to engage in limited and perhaps sporadic exporting, while, the geocentric manager is more likely to commit considerable resources to establishing production and distribution facilities in foreign markets.

CHAPTER SUMMARY

International marketing is becoming an increasingly important business activity. Businesspeople who are knowledgeable about international marketing procedures have the best chance to benefit from this growing business area.

International marketing is related to the broader study of international business but deserves special attention as a discipline because the strategies that make possible the exchange process and development of business relationships in foreign markets are complex and can differ from those encountered in domestic marketing. Related areas such as international trade and international economics contribute to the development of the theory and practice of international marketing.

Even though similarities exist in marketing techniques between domestic and international marketing, sufficient behavioral differences are encountered that necessitate the study of international marketing be separate from the study of domestic marketing. Although a variety of terms are used to describe the subject, international marketing is the most appropriate.

Studying international marketing is desirable because of its growing importance to business in general and the increased chances of international involvement during a business career, and because it will help to make a manager a better all-around businessperson. In addition, demand for foreign-made products is increasing, governments encourage foreign involvement by businesses, new marketing problems are encountered internationally, and different marketing techniques must often be used.

When operating in a foreign country, a new uncontrollable marketing environment in addition to the domestic marketing environment is confronted. The ability to develop a marketing mix and strategy is affected by this additional foreign environment. As a result, additional risk is possible in international marketing.

Managers may embrace different orientations toward the importance of international marketing to the firm's business operations. The orientation held will influence management's decision making regarding the role and scope of international marketing. This, in turn, has implications for marketing strategy development.

KEY TERMS

Controllable variables
Cosmopolitan marketing
Ethnocentric
Geocentric
Global Marketing
International business
International cross-cultural management
International economics
International marketing
International trade
Marketing concept
Marketing environment
Marketing mix
Marketing strategy
Multinational marketing
Polycentric
Regiocentric
Supranational marketing
Uncontrollable variables
World marketing

REVIEW QUESTIONS

1. What is international marketing?
2. Why is international marketing becoming a more important business activity?
3. In what ways is international marketing related to international trade? To international economics?
4. Why are marketing managers becoming more aware of the existence of international markets?
5. Why is the demand for foreign-made products increasing around the world?
6. How does international marketing differ from domestic marketing?
7. Give an example of a product that is purchased for a different reason by a buyer in a foreign market than by a buyer in the United States and explain why.
8. Why can the marketing manager expect to encounter new marketing problems in international markets?
9. Why does the foreign uncontrollable marketing environment increase risk for the international marketer?
10. Developing a marketing strategy is no different internationally than domestically. Do you agree or disagree? Discuss.

NOTES

1. "Bring Me Free Trade, Lord, But Not Yet," *The Economist,* May 11, 1991, 68.
2. "Norway Opts for F-35 Lightning II Over Gripen NG as Future Fighter." *Defense Update*, June 2009, http://defense-update.com/newscast/1108/221108_lightning2_norway.html.
3. Boeing Company, "Boeing P-8I Selected as Indian Navy's Long-Range Maritime Patrol Aircraft," news release, January 6, 2009, http://www.boeing.com/news/releases/2009/q1/090105a_nr.html.
4. "Boeing Sells 80 Planes to China," *Chicago Business*, April 12, 2006, http://www.chicagobusiness.com/cgi-bin/news.pl?id=20171&seenIt=1.
5. John D. Daniels, Ernest W. Ogram Jr., and Lee H. Radebaugh, *International Business: Environment and Operations*, 2nd ed. (Reading, MA: Addison-Wesley, 1979), 3.
6. Richard N. Farmer and Barry M. Richman, *International Business*, 3rd ed. (Bloomington, IN: Cedarwood Press, 1980), 15–17.
7. Endel J. Kolde, *International Business Enterprise* (Englewood Cliffs, NJ: Prentice-Hall, 1968), 5, 11.
8. Ibid., 5.
9. "'What Are You Giving Away?' The Challenges of Marketing in Asia," *Knowledge@Wharton*, January 9, 2008, http://knowledge.wharton.upenn.edu/article.cfm?articleid=1872.
10. P.J. Hovell and P.G.P. Walters, "International Marketing Presentations: Some Options," *European Journal of Marketing* 6 (2) (1972): 70.
11. Hugh Kramer, "Approaches to the Study of Marketing: A Three-Dimensional Evaluation Grid," *Management International Review* 12 (1972): 19.
12. William R. Hoskins, "The LDC and the MNC: Will They Develop Together?" *Columbia Journal of World Business* 6 (September–October 1971): 62.
13. "China's GDP Growth Stays Above 11%," *Los Angeles Times,* January 24, 2008, C-4; and Central Intelligence Agency, "China," in *The World Factbook*, December 18, 2008, https://www.cia.gov/library/publications/the-world-factbook/goes/ch.html.

14. Robert Bartels, "Are Domestic and International Marketing Dissimilar?" *Journal of Marketing* 32 (July 1968): 56–61.

15. Roy Blough, *International Business: Environment and Adaptation* (New York: McGraw-Hill, 1966).

16. Howard Perlmutter, "The Tortuous Evolution of the Multinational Corporation," *Columbia Journal of World Business* 4 (1) (January–February 1969): 9–18; and David A. Heenan and Howard V. Perlmutter, *Multinational Organization Development: A Social Architectural Perspective* (Reading, MA: Addison-Wesley, 1979).

2 International Measures and Conversions

Armstrong World Industries, Inc., with headquarters in Lancaster, Pennsylvania, is a leading producer of flooring, ceilings, and cabinets for the home and commercial use. Armstrong competes for the flooring market in the United States with firms such as Congoleum Corporation and Mannington Mills, Inc., and internationally with firms such as Gerflor, Tarkett, Torlys, and Domco. The company's flooring products are classified into five categories: hardwood, ceramic, linoleum, laminate, and vinyl. Armstrong floors are recognized as being among the best in the industry and are frequently preferred by builders and flooring installers.

In the late 1960s, vinyl floors produced by Armstrong were of two types. One was a foam or solid substrate with a design continuously printed on the surface and covered with a clear wear surface. The second utilized a positioned pattern process in which different-colored plastic granules were deposited into piles next to each other by a series of screens in a stop-and-go manner before being heated and solidified in large presses. The positioned pattern products were superior in quality to the surface printed products; however, they were more expensive to produce because of the slowness of the stop-and-go process.

To improve the production process, management experimented with a new positioned color process that could be printed with a rotogravure printer like those used to print fabrics. With a series of circular screens, different-colored liquid plastics were positioned into a previously prepared, porous, clear plastic substrate designed to receive and hold them. The product was finished by heating the plastics and pressing them in circular mills. The advantage, of course, was that the process was continuous, permitting more flooring to be produced in a shorter time and at a lower cost. The finished product was similar to the product made by the stop-and-go process because the pattern ran all the way through the product and was not located just on the top as with the surface-printed products.

When the decision was made to implement the new production process, the rotogravure printer to be installed in the production line to manufacture this new product was purchased from J. Zimmer Maschinenbau, GmbH, Klagenfurt, Austria.

When the boxes containing the parts of the printing machine arrived at Armstrong's factory, the distances, measurements, and tolerances specified for assembly and installation were all listed in meters and centimeters.

Source: Based in part on information from the Armstrong Web site, http://www.armstrong.com/; "How is Armstrong Vinyl Flooring Produced?" Armstrong Vinyl Flooring, Contempo Floor Coverings, Inc., http://contempofloorcoverings.com/blog/armstrong-vinyl-flooring.html.

CHAPTER OBJECTIVES

After reading this chapter, you should

- know the differences between the American and metric methods of measure;
- know the units of measure most commonly employed in the metric system;
- be able to make conversions from one metric measure to another;
- be able to make conversions from American to metric units of measure and vice-versa; and
- be able to make conversions from degrees Fahrenheit to degrees Celsius and vice-versa.

MEASUREMENT SYSTEMS

What is the temperature? You look at your thermometer and read 80°. A woman in Italy looks at her thermometer and reads 27°. If the temperature is the same in both locations and the thermometers are not broken, why do the temperatures differ? The answer is that you are reading degrees Fahrenheit and the Italian woman is reading degrees Celsius. Two different systems are being used to measure temperature.

Unfortunately, a common system of measure does not exist throughout the world. As a result, the international marketer is likely to encounter different forms of measurement during the conduct of normal business activities. This contributes to additional costs of doing business, wasting of time to make conversions, and the potential for misunderstandings. Business problems ranging from minor inconveniences to confusion and disagreements in contract provisions can occur if the international marketer does not understand these differences. Consider the malaise of an American exporter who contracts to ship 5,000 tons of scrap iron to an Indonesian buyer and is informed by the Indonesian buyer that the shipment received is 464.9 tons short when it arrives. The reason for the discrepancy is in how each party to the contract understood the meaning of a ton. The American was thinking in terms of American short tons, while the Indonesian was thinking in terms of metric tons. The difference of about 205 pounds per ton has the potential for initiating an international legal dispute. To be successful, the international marketer needs to be aware of differences in measurement and be able to work in the units of measure that are employed in any market in which business is conducted.

Two basic systems of measurement are found in the world. One is the United States' customary system (also known as the English or **American system**), which is used primarily in the United States. The other is the **metric system,** which is used elsewhere. Prior to standardization, two nonmetric measurement methods prevailed. One was the British Imperial system of measurements, and the other was the American system. The American system derived from the Imperial system, which is based on ancient Norse, Celtic, and Roman measures. Standardization of the Imperial and American systems has occurred, and today both are essentially the same with a few notable differences, particularly in volume measures such as the gallon and the ton.

The metric system originated in France in June 1799. The units of measure in the metric system are known as the Système International (SI). Today, the basic units of measure in the American system are defined in terms of the SI basic measures, so some conversions from one system to the other are exact equivalencies. To a certain extent, then, the world has been standardized, although different units of measure still exist. The metric system is used by approximately 90 percent of the world's population. Although the metric system was designated as the preferred U.S. system of measure in the Omnibus Trade and Competitiveness Act of 1988, resistance to change has been encountered from business and consumer markets. However, use by the military, medical, and scientific sectors of American industry is extensive. In fact, NASA has employed the metric system of measure since as far back as the flight of Apollo 14 on January 31, 1971.

THE METRIC SYSTEM

In their day-to-day activities, managers are sometimes confronted with metric units and must work with these measures. Order forms, machine specifications, tolerances, and travel and transportation rates are all examples of business activities that can be encountered in metric units. Thus, every manager should have an understanding and working knowledge of the metric system. This is especially true if the manager should ever become involved with business in foreign countries.

The metric system is a logical method of relating units of measure and is easy to use. The basis of the metric system is the division of each unit of measure into ten equal subunits so easy manipulation of conversions from one unit to another is possible.

The standard unit of weight, or mass, in the metric system is the **kilogram**. A kilogram is the quantity of matter present in a cylinder of platinum-iridium alloy measuring 39 millimeters (approximately 1.535 inches) in diameter and height, which is kept at the International Bureau of Weights and Measures at Sèvres, France.

The fundamental unit of length in the metric system is the **meter** (metre). Although the definition of the meter has changed over time, the exact length has not. The definitions have been changed to improve the precision of the measure. Since 1889, a meter has been defined as the distance between two lines engraved on a platinum-iridium bar that is kept at 0° Celsius, also at Sèvres. Today, that distance is defined as the length light travels in a vacuum during 1/299,792,458 of a second.

The **liter** (litre) is the fundamental unit of volume in the metric system. The liter is not an official SI unit of measure. The SI unit of volume is the cubic meter. However, the liter is compatible with the cubic meter because the cubic meter equals 1,000 liters. Thus, a liter is equivalent to one cubic decimeter (0.001 cubic meters).

Temperature is measured in degrees **Celsius** (°C) in the metric system. The freez-

Exhibit 2.1 **Frequently Used Metric Units of Length**

Unit		Equivalency
1 kilometer (km)	=	1,000 meters
1 hectometer (hm)	=	100 meters
1 decameter (dam)	=	10 meters
1 meter (m)	=	1 meter
1 decimeter (dm)	=	.1 meter
1 centimeter (cm)	=	.01 meter
1 millimeter (mm)	=	.001 meter

ing point of water was arbitrarily set at 0°C, and the boiling point was set at 100°C. The distance between boiling and freezing is divided into 100 units with each unit being classified as one degree Celsius.

Each of the fundamental units in the metric system is divided into smaller units and grouped into larger units by brackets of ten. Each one of these classifications is given a specific name. The name is composed of two parts: (1) a prefix, which indicates the size of the measure, and (2) a root, which indicates the unit of measure being considered. In the case of the measure of length where ten meters are laid end to end, the combined length is called a decameter. The prefix is **"deca,"** meaning ten, and the root is "meter," to indicate units of length are being considered. If 100 meters are grouped together, the distance is called a hectometer. The prefix **"hecto"** means 100, and the root is again "meter," indicating length. The frequently used units of length in the metric system are listed in Exhibit 2.1.

If the unit of measure to be considered is volume, the root is simply changed to liter; the prefixes and size relationships remain the same. Thus, 10 liters = 1 decaliter, 100 liters = 1 hectoliter, and so forth. The relationships are also the same for the measure of weight; 10 grams = 1 decagram, 100 grams = 1 hectogram, and so forth.

The metric units may be abbreviated as shown in the parentheses in Exhibit 2.1. In the case of units of volume, an (l) is substituted for the (m), and milliliter is abbreviated ml, decaliter is abbreviated dal, and so forth. Because the kilogram is relatively heavy, the **gram** (one thousandth of a kilogram) is more practical to use as the basic unit of measure for weight. Thus, for weight, a (g) is substituted for the (m), and milligram is abbreviated mg, decagram is abbreviated dag, and so forth. The prefix *deca* may also be written *deka* and abbreviated dk if desired.

METRIC-TO-METRIC CONVERSIONS

By looking at the equalities in Exhibit 2.1, you will notice that the next larger unit in every case is ten of the preceding smaller units and that the next smaller unit is 1/10 (.1) as large as the preceding larger unit. Therefore, 10 decameters = 1 hectometer, 10 millimeters = 1 centimeter, and 1 decameter = 0.1 hectometer, 1 millimeter = 0.1 centimeter. Because units of ten are involved, obviously every unit is related to the other units by some power of 10. For example, 1 kilometer = 10^2 (or 100) decameters. This is so because 1 kilometer = 10 hectometers and 1 hectometer = 10 decameters.

Exhibit 2.2 **Sole Classico Milk**

As indicated on the package, this box contains 1,000 milliliters or 1 liter of milk.

Therefore, 1 kilometer = 10 hectometers times 10 decameters (10 × 10) or 100 decameters. Likewise, 1 kilometer = 10^3 meters or 10 hectometers × 10 decameters × 10 meters (10 × 10 × 10) or 1,000 meters.

$$\begin{aligned} 1\text{ m} = 10\text{ dm} &= 100\text{ cm} = 1{,}000\text{ mm} \\ 1\text{ dm} &= 10\text{ cm} = 100\text{ mm} \\ 1\text{ cm} &= 10\text{ mm} \end{aligned}$$

The relationships of one metric unit to another are more obvious as shown in Exhibit 2.3 on page 29. To convert one measure to another, consult the left-hand column for the known length; then go to the right to the column headed by the unit desired. For example, how many millimeters are in one hectometer? Locate hectometer in the left-hand column; then follow the hectometer row over to the millimeter column and read 100,000. How many decameters are in one centimeter? Locate centimeter in the left-hand column, then follow the centimeter row over to the decameter column and read .001.

Now that an understanding of the relationship of metric units one to another has been obtained, some simple conversions will be examined. Suppose you desire to convert 256 l to ml; how is this done? Referring to Exhibit 2.3, and substituting "liter" for "meter" and "l" for "m," you find that 1 l is equal to 1,000 ml. To find the number of ml in 256 l, simply multiply by the factor of 1,000 and obtain 256,000 ml (256 × 1,000). How many kl are equal to 256 l? Referring to Exhibit 2.3, you find that 1 l is equal to .001 kl. Multiplying the number of liters by the factor of .001 gives the number of kl (256 × .001 = .256 kl). By an alternate rationale, it takes 1,000 l to make 1 kl, so 256/1,000 = .256 kl. By this time, obviously, you need to become familiar enough with the relationships presented in Exhibit 2.3 so that the correct conversion factor will be employed.

To reduce the risk of error in mathematical calculations, for example multiplying when dividing should be done or dividing when multiplication is appropriate, a mechanical ratio method can be employed. The logic followed is that of equalities. Take the equality $a = a$. According to the rules of algebra, both sides of the equation can be changed by the same quantity and the equality remains. Dividing both sides by "b" the equality becomes $\frac{a}{b} = \frac{a}{b}$. Again, if both the numerator and denominator are changed by the same amount, the equality remains. Thus multiplying the right side of the equality by "c" gives $\frac{a}{b} = \frac{ac}{bc}$. If the equation is cross-multiplied (the numerator of the left side is multiplied by the denominator of the right side, and the denominator of the left side is multiplied by the numerator of the right side), the equality is seen to remain and $a(bc) = b(ac)$. Rearranging the terms, the equality becomes $abc = abc$. Substituting numbers for the letters makes the equality more evident.

If $a = 2$, $b = 3$, and $c = 4$, then $bc = 12$ and $ac = 8$.

If $a(bc)$ = b(ac), then 2(12) = 3(8) or 24 = 24.

Applying the ratio technique to the previous liter problem, 2561 equals X ml, it follows that:

$$\frac{256l}{1l} = \frac{X}{1000ml}$$

or $1(X) = 256(1{,}000)$ and $X = 256{,}000$ ml.

The important points to remember are: first, put the conversion factors in the denominator (1 l = 1,000 ml) and second, keep the units of the same type on the same side of the equal sign. In other words, place the given quantity (256 l) in the numerator of the liter side of the equation (left side in this case) and the unknown quantity X (what is to be found) in the numerator of the milliliter side (right side).

Another example should help clarify the technique. How many decimeters are equivalent to 53.621 decameters? The conversion factor from Exhibit 2.3 is 1 dam

Exhibit 2.3 **Metric Unit Conversion Factors**

	The amount of the desired unit						
One unit below equals	**mm**	**cm**	**dm**	**m**	**dam**	**hm**	**km**
millimeters (mm)	1	.1	.01	.001	.0001	.00001	.000001
centimeters (cm)	10	1	.1	.01	.001	.0001	.00001
decimeters (dm)	100	10	1	.1	.01	.001	.0001
meters (m)	1,000	100	10	1	.1	.01	.001
decameters (dam)	10,000	1,000	100	10	1	.1	.01
hectometers (hm)	100,000	10,000	1,000	100	10	1	.1
kilometers (km)	1,000,000	100,000	10,000	1,000	100	10	1

Exhibit 2.4 **Determining the Conversion Factor for Converting Decameters to Decimeters**

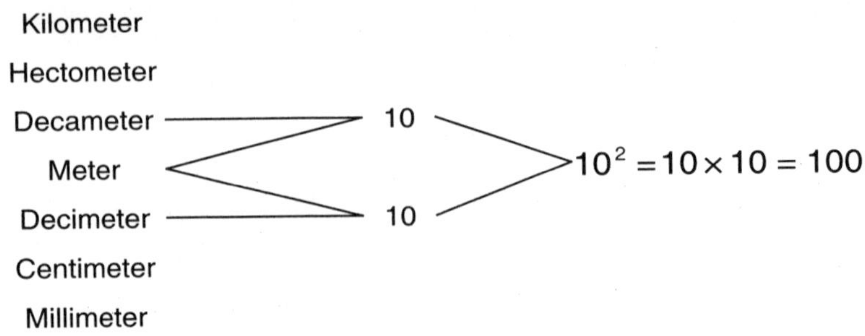

1 decameter = 100 decimeters

= 100 dm. The conversion factor can also be easily determined as shown in Exhibit 2.4. One decameter equals 10 meters and 1 meter equals 10 decimeters; therefore, 1 decameter equals 10 times 10, that is, 10^2 or 100 decimeters.

Then substituting into the ratio gives:

$$\frac{53.621 dam}{1 dam} = \frac{X}{100 dm}$$

or $1(X) = 53.621(100) = 5{,}362.1$ dm.

Since Exhibit 2.3 may not always be available to facilitate the determination of the conversion factor, memorizing the prefixes in Exhibit 2.5 makes the process easy. Once the order and names of the prefixes are learned, the conversion factor can be quickly ascertained as was shown in Exhibit 2.4. All you have to do is locate the two units in question and multiply by the appropriate multiples of 10. For example, the conversion factor for converting from centigrams to hectograms or from hectograms to centigrams is $10 \times 10 \times 10 \times 10 = 10{,}000$. Obviously, the conversion factor will be the same regardless of the root involved. Thus, the conversion factor for centimeters to hectometers or hectometers to centimeters is also 10,000. Therefore, regardless of the root, the conversion factor is determined the same way. See Exhibit 2.5 for the process of determining the conversion factor from hectograms to centigrams.

The following problems can be worked to help gain skill, speed, and confidence with metric-to-metric conversions.

Review Set 1

	Answer
1. 22.2 mm = __________ cm	2.22 cm
2. 476 g = __________ dag = __________ kg	47.6 dag and .476 kg
3. 3.122 hl = __________ l = __________ dl	312.2 l and 3,122 dl
4. How many centimeters are in 652 decameters?	652,000 cm
5. 32.7 hectograms is equivalent to how many grams?	3,270 gm

Exhibit 2.5 **Determining the Conversion Factor for Converting Hecto-units to Centi-units**

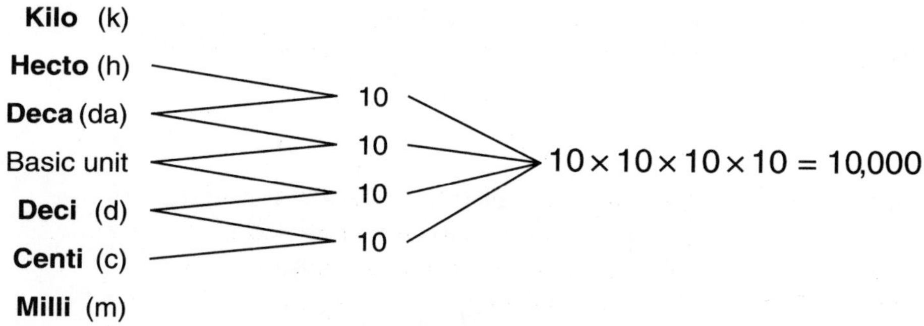

1 hecto-unit = 10,000 centi-units
For example:
1 hectogram = 10,000 centigrams

METRIC-TO-AMERICAN AND AMERICAN-TO-METRIC CONVERSIONS

Often, the manager will find changing a measure from one measurement system to another necessary. For instance, how far is the distance between two cities in miles when the road sign is printed in kilometers, or how many pounds should be shipped if a customer requests kilograms? The same ratio technique as is employed for metric-to-metric conversions can be used; however, different conversion factors must be applied. Some common conversion factors are listed in Exhibit 2.6.

Suppose a distance written in a blueprint is 12.7 centimeters and you want to know how many inches are involved. The number of centimeters is divided by the 2.54 conversion factor (2.54 centimeters = 1 inch, obtained from Exhibit 2.6) to determine the inch equivalent and 12.7 cm/2.54 cm per inch = 5 inches.

Using the same ratio approach as used for metric-to-metric conversions, place the 1 inch = 2.54 cm conversion factors in the denominators. Then place the unknown and given data in the numerators, being careful to keep like terms on the same side of the equal sign, and solve. In this case:

$$\frac{X}{1in} = \frac{12.7cm}{2.54cm}$$

Cross multiplying gives 2.54 cm(X) = 1 inch (12.7 cm). Solve for X by dividing both sides of the equation by 2.54 cm.

$$\frac{2.54cmX}{2.54cm} = \frac{12.7incm}{2.54cm}$$

Exhibit 2.6 **Metric-to-American Conversion Factors**

Length

1 meter = 39.37 inches = 3.281 feet = 1.0936 yards

2.54 centimeters = 1 inch

1 kilometer = 0.6214 mile

Volume

1 liter = 1.0567 quarts (liquid) = 2.1134 pints (liquid)

29.57 milliliters = 1 ounce (liquid)

1 hectoliter = 2.8378 bushels

Weight (Mass)

1 kilogram = 2.2 pounds avoirdupois

453.59 grams = 1 pound

28.35 grams = 1 ounce avoirdupois

1 metric ton = 0.98425 long tons = 1.1025 short tons

1 liter = 0.2642 gallons (U.S.) = 0.22 gallons (UK)

Temperature

0° Celsius = 32° Fahrenheit

100° Celsius = 212° Fahrenheit

The left side reduces to X, and the centimeters cancel out in the right side.

$$X = \frac{12.7in}{2.54}$$

$$X = 5in$$

If the need was to convert 5 inches to centimeters, the same conversion factor applies. Therefore, the conversion factors placed in the denominators are identical to the previous problem. The known and unknown data simply exchange places (keep like terms on the same side of the equal sign). Thus the equation becomes:

$$\frac{5in}{1in} = \frac{X}{2.54cm}$$

Cross multiplying gives 1 inch (X) = 5 inches (2.54 cm). Solve for X by dividing both sides of the equation by 1 inch.

$$\frac{1inX}{1in} = \frac{5in(2.54cm)}{1in}$$

This reduces to X = 5(2.54 cm) and X = 12.7 cm.

For another example, convert 68.7 pounds to kilograms. Proceed by placing the 1 kg = 2.2 lbs conversion factor in the denominator and the known quantity (68.7 lbs) in the numerator on the pounds side of the equation and *X* in the numerator on the side of the equation for the units desired. Thus:

$$\frac{X}{1kg} = \frac{68.7lbs}{2.2lbs}$$

Cross multiplying, 2.2*X* = 68.7 and *X* = 31.2 kg.

To gain additional skill making metric-to-American and American-to-metric conversions, the following problems can be solved.

Review Set 2

1. You want to know if the crane in your warehouse, which has a maximum lifting capacity of 2.5 tons, can be used to relocate equipment received from a supplier in Switzerland with an indicated weight of 2,010 kg.

Solution: The problem can be solved in either of two ways. (1) Convert the lifting capacity of the crane to pounds and then to kilograms and compare with the equipment weight. (2) Convert the equipment weight to pounds and then to tons and compare with the lifting capacity of the crane.

Solution 1.

$$\begin{array}{c} 2.5 \text{ tons} \\ \underline{2{,}000 \text{ lbs/ton}} \\ 5{,}000 \text{ lbs} \end{array}$$

The crane will lift a maximum of 5,000 lbs. The conversion factor from Exhibit 2.6 is 1 kg = 2.2 lbs.

Convert 5,000 lbs to kg:

$$\frac{X}{1} = \frac{5{,}000}{2.2}$$

and 2.2*X* = 5,000, so *X* = 2,272.7 kg.

Since the 2,010 kg weight of the equipment is less than the 2,272.7 kg lifting capacity of the crane, the crane can be used to relocate the equipment received from the Swiss supplier.

Solution 2.

Convert 2,010 kg to lbs:

$$\frac{2{,}010}{1} = \frac{X}{2.2}$$

and $X = 2.2(2{,}010)$, so $X = 4{,}422$ lbs.

$$\frac{4{,}422 lbs}{2{,}000 lbs / ton} = 2.211 tons$$

Since the 2,211 ton weight of the equipment from the Swiss supplier is less than the 2.5 ton lifting capacity of the crane, the crane can be used to relocate the equipment.

2. The following order was received from a German clothing manufacturer.

Quantity	Stock No.	Description
50,000 running meters	B-126	Black watch plaid wool cloth (6 m wide)
90,000 running meters	C-133	White lace trim cloth (5.08 cm wide)

A. How many running yards of black watch plaid cloth is the German firm ordering? (A running meter is 1 meter in length regardless of the width.)
B. How many inches wide is the white lace trim?
C. The average weight of the cloth is 1 pound per running yard. If 10 cubic feet of shipping space is needed for every 500 pounds of cargo, how much space should you reserve in the ship for the black watch plaid cloth?

Solution to Question 2A.

Convert 50,000 meters to yards. The conversion factor from Exhibit 2.6 is 1 m = 1.0936 yds, and

$$\frac{50{,}000}{1} = \frac{X}{1.0936}$$

and $X = 50{,}000(1.0936)$, so $X = 54{,}680$ yds.

Solution to Question 2B.

Convert 5.08 cm to inches. The conversion factor from Exhibit 2.6 is 1 inch = 2.54 cm.

$$\frac{X}{1} = \frac{5.08}{2.54}$$

and $2.54X = 1(5.08)$, so $X = 2.117$ inches.

Solution to Question 2C.

Since 54,680 running yards of cloth was ordered, the weight will be 54,680 lbs (1 lb per running yard).

To find the required space:

$$\frac{54{,}680}{500} = 109.36(10) = 1{,}093.6\,ft^3$$

TEMPERATURE CONVERSIONS

To convert degrees Fahrenheit to degrees Celsius, the formula °C = 5/9(°F – 32) can be employed. To convert °C to °F, the formula °F = 9/5°C + 32 can be used. Either formula can be converted to a more useful formula with algebra so that temperature conversions can be made easily in either direction with the use of only one formula. Take the formula for converting degrees Fahrenheit to degrees Celsius.

$$°C = \frac{5(°F - 32)}{9}$$

Divide both sides of the equation by 5 to get $\frac{°C}{5} = \frac{°F - 32}{9}$

Cross multiply to get $9(°C) = 5(°F - 32)$

Expand to get this useful formula $9°C = 5°F - 160$

Suppose you are planning a trip to Paris, France, and learn that the temperature forecast for the day of your arrival is 26°C. What clothes should you wear to be dressed appropriately for the expected temperature? The problem requires the conversion of 26°C to °F. Substituting into the temperature equations gives:

$$9(26) = 5°F - 160$$

→ $234 = 5°F - 160$

Adding 160 to both sides of the equation gives $394 = 5°F.$

Dividing both sides of the equation by 5 gives $°F = 78.8.$

Exhibit 2.7 **Automat Compact Grand Maximo**

The label of this washing detergent indicates the package contains 3 kg and is suitable for washing at 30°, 60°, or 95° Celsius.

Since 26° Celsius is equal to 78.8° Fahrenheit, you can dress comfortably for spring-like weather.

To change degrees Fahrenheit to degrees Celsius, the same formula can be used. What temperature in °C is the same as 52°F?

$$9°C = 5(52) - 160$$

Expand to get $9°C = 260 - 160$

and $9°C = 100$

and dividing both sides of the equation by 9 gives $°C = 11.1.$

Review Set 3

The following problems will provide additional practice with temperature conversions.

		Answer:
1.	Change 150°C to °F.	°F = 302
2.	How many degrees Celsius is 46.4 degrees Fahrenheit?	°C = 8
3.	On the television weather channel, the temperature in Rome, Italy, was shown as 33°C. What is the temperature in degrees Fahrenheit?	°F = 91.4
4.	Convert –40°C to °F. (This is the only temperature at which degrees Fahrenheit and degrees Celsius are the same.)	°F = –40

CHAPTER SUMMARY

A universally employed (common) system of measures does not exist. The American system of measures is found primarily in the United States. The metric system is employed in most of the rest of the countries of the world. Therefore, the international marketer must be prepared to encounter and use the metric system of measures in day-to-day business activities.

The basic unit of length in the metric system is the meter. The liter is the basic unit of volume, and the gram is the basic unit of weight. The temperature scale in the metric system is based on degrees Celsius. Freezing is arbitrarily set at zero degrees and boiling at 100 degrees. The metric system is a convenient measurement system because every unit is always composed of ten of the next smaller unit and grouped together in tens to form the next larger unit. Therefore, conversions from one metric unit to another are done by simply multiplying or dividing by some power of ten. Unlike with the American system in which every conversion is unique, requiring the memorization of multiple conversion factors, only the unit names need to be learned to convert from one metric unit to another.

Since the two systems of measurement exist, the international marketer also needs to know how to convert from one system to the other. When business operations in countries using the American system are expanded into countries using the metric system, appropriate conversion of units is necessary. In travel and contact with foreign markets, the international marketer will encounter the two measurement systems. Also, manufacturing, product, and other decisions will require that conversions from one system to another be made. International marketers cannot avoid the metric system and, therefore, must be able to understand and work with metric units of measure.

KEY TERMS

American system
Celsius
Centi
Deca
Deci
Gram
Hecto
Kilo
Kilogram
Liter
Meter
Metric system
Milli

REVIEW QUESTIONS

1. How does the metric system of measure differ from the American system of measure?
2. Explain why 1 kg is equal to 1,000 mg.
3. What is the metric unit of measure for volume? Distance? Mass?
4. Why are conversions from one unit to another in the metric system of measure easier to make than similar conversions in the American system of measure?
5. Explain how to convert ounces into liters.
6. Explain how degrees Celsius differ from degrees Fahrenheit.
7. Explain how the international marketer might encounter metric units of measure on the job.
8. Describe a marketing situation in which the international marketer may need to convert measurements from the metric system to the American system or vice versa.
9. Do you think the metric system of measure will ever completely replace the American system of measure in the United States? Why or why not?
10. What would be the advantage of listing the weight of a product in grams and ounces on the product's package?

3 The Scope of International Marketing

Osman Ozan, owner of a small firm that manufactures plastic castings for the automobile industry, was sitting at his desk and contemplating the declining share of the market held by the big three U.S. auto firms. Foreign sales were continuing to increase at the expense of domestically produced vehicles. The share of the market held by the big three was nearing 50 percent and was projected to decline to a percentage in the low 40s within the next decade. He knew that Ford Motor Company and General Motors Corporation were particularly vulnerable; and if the trend continued, either a merger or the collapse of one or both firms was a real possibility. Since these two companies represented a significant percentage of his firm's sales, Ozan was worried about how the uncertain future of the U.S. auto industry might ultimately affect his company's future.

Ozan had been thinking about the possibility of expanding sales to foreign auto producers or to another industry that uses molded plastic parts, such as the furniture industry. He knew that something would have to be done eventually if sales did not improve for the big three. Already, sales for plastic auto parts had stagnated, and Ozan knew he could be facing a decline in business, since a shakeout of the parts suppliers would be inevitable. He thought to himself, "I'm not going to just sit around and wait; I've got to plan ahead for the worst."

Ozan had in front of him a copy of the *World Trade Report 2008,* prepared by the World Trade Organization. The report contained a wealth of information, and as he perused the pages, he became increasingly confused about how to explore the foreign market for auto parts. His attention was drawn to the statistics concerning recent developments in the structure, volume, and value of international trade, and he wondered about the trade prospects for 2008. He noted that the growth in world output and trade decelerated in 2007 to 3.4 percent, which was lower than the 3.7 percent growth averaged over the previous decade. The reason for the decline was the slowdown in economic activity in the developed nations. He also noted that the growth in the developing regions was nearly three times the rate for the developed regions. This raised the contribution of developing countries to global output growth to over 40 percent. He also read that world merchandise trade decreased to a 5.5 percent growth rate, which is lower than the growth rates for 2004, 2005, and 2006 but still about the average growth rate for the last decade.

Other interesting facts emerged about merchandise imports—where the trade was directed. In 2007, South and Central America increased merchandise imports by 20 percent and the Commonwealth of Independent States, countries that had been Soviet republics, such as Georgia, Belarus, and Ukraine, sustained an 18 percent growth. These growth rates were more than three times the 2007 global average of 5.5 percent. Africa and the Middle East had a growth rate of 12.5 percent. On the other hand, the United States and the European Union experienced dismal growth rates of 1 and 3 percent, respectively.

But most interesting to Ozan was the information about China and India. Both countries experienced rapid increases in merchandise imports. China's increase was 13.5 percent, and India's increase was 13 percent. He also saw that the growth rate was 7 percent for the newly industrialized countries. China and even India could be potential markets for his firm's products. Ozan remembered reading that Wang Chuan-Fu, chairman of the Chinese car maker BYD Auto, had predicted that the firm would start selling cars in the United States and Europe in 2011. Ozan believed the reports were credible because Warren Buffett had acquired a 10 percent holding in BYD Auto recently. Also, news reports had claimed that the management of the Indian firm Mahindra & Mahindra, Ltd., planned to market cars in the United States through a Georgia-based distributor. The trade statistics indicated that both markets were open to receiving components and parts from foreign sources. Ozan was also aware that geographical indications can play an important role in markets for differentiated products because of the reputation buyers associate with a product's origin.

Ozan thought this information looked promising. He wondered if regional data was sufficient for his analysis or whether the potential markets should be investigated in other ways.

Sources: Based in part on information from the "World Trade Report 2008: Trade in a Globalizing World," World Trade Organization, http://www.wto.org/english/res_e/reser_e/wtr08_e.htm; "Chinese Automaker Plans US Sales by 2011," *U.S. News & World Report*, January 13, 2009, http://usnews.rankingsandreviews.com/cars-trucks/daily-news/090113-Chinese-Automaker-Plans-U-S-Sales-by-2011; and Saritha Rai, "Indian S.U.V. Maker Plans to Enter United States Market," *The New York Times, World Business*, November 17, 2006, http://www.nytimes.com/2006/11/17/business/worldbusiness/17auto.html?1321419600&en=92d66a2f39bb3afd&ei=5088&partner=rsnnyt8&emc=yss.

CHAPTER OBJECTIVES

After reading this chapter, you should

- know various ways markets can be grouped;
- understand why different market grouping arrangements may be desirable;
- appreciate the benefits of grouping markets in various ways;
- know how to classify nations based on income levels;
- be aware of the trends that are occurring in world exports; and
- appreciate the magnitude and direction of world trade.

ORGANIZING TRADING NATIONS

Since the world is a large and dynamic place, managers must target the areas where the greatest chances for success lie. In spite of advances in communication and transportation that shrink the world, over 195 unique and distinct countries with different cultures, mores, and distribution and consumption habits exist.[1] Trade barriers imposed by governments along with traditional trading habits further serve to separate and differentiate these nations. Understanding these conditions, and their differences and similarities, will help the international marketer focus attention properly. Grouping nations and making various comparisons is often a useful way for the manager to better understand and appreciate uniqueness and affinities among these nations for strategy purposes.

REGIONS

Perhaps the most convenient way to divide up the world geographically is by continents. This, however, is not a good way to regionalize a marketing strategy. Various areas of the world have trading cohesion through tradition, treaty, or pact. This is probably a better way to divide the world in general terms. Using this method, the world can be conveniently divided into nine regions. These nine regions are listed in Exhibit 3.1.

Exhibit 3.1 **Trading Regions of the World**

Africa
Arab World
South Pacific
China
Europe
Far East
Latin America
North America
Southern Asia

Economically, the nations of the North American, European, Far Eastern, and South Pacific regions are primarily capitalist. They tend to be market-oriented economies and emphasize ownership of private property, free enterprise, and open competition. Politically, the nations of these regions follow rule by law and are mainly under representative governments following democratic procedures.

The remaining regions tend to have no basic economic structure or philosophy. Politically, nations in these regions are under personal dictatorships or pseudo-democracies. China is one of a few nations that are politically communist. However, since Hong Kong was returned, reunification with Taiwan is desired, and status as a world-trading partner is sought, the Chinese market is opening. As a result, the Chinese economy is growing at yearly rates in excess of 11 percent.[2]

Of course, exceptions occur within each region. For instance, the trade of Cuba is more direct with Europe than with neighboring states, and many African nations keep close trade links with their colonizing countries. Yet, this regional perspective is one worthwhile approach for segmentation purposes.

TRADITIONAL TRADING PREFERENCES

The British East India Company, Genghis Kahn, Marco Polo, mountain ranges, and sea-lanes have had an influence on trading between countries (areas) over the years. Some traditional relationships formed centuries ago still exist and form trade bonds that will undoubtedly remain far into the future. Other relationships have ended due to new trade routes or political shifts, opening doors to new relationships. For example, prior to the Vietnam War, the countries of Eastern Europe were Vietnam's major trading partners. In 2008, the European Union surpassed the United States as the recipient of the greatest value of Vietnamese exports.[3] Still, the strength, commitment, and trust in traditional relationships should not be underestimated. Some of the major traditional bonds that stand today are listed in Exhibit 3.2.

Just as strongly as traditional trading preferences hold, so do traditional animosities. Even where geographic and cultural similarities exist, deep-rooted feelings can interfere with trade. Some examples are shown in Exhibit 3.3.

The international marketer must be aware of these influences to avoid poor market planning. Numerous businesspeople have made major and costly errors that could have been avoided with a little understanding of trade preferences. At the same time, the intelligent manager uses these established trade preferences in a trading strategy to aid in the flow of products on a global basis.

Exhibit 3.2 **Traditional Trading Partners**

Region	Countries Included
Italian Pact	Italy, Tunisia, Ethiopia
Portuguese-Speaking World	Portugal, Brazil, Angola, Macao
The Dutch Colonial Ties	Netherlands, Netherlands Antilles, Indonesia
The French Empire	France, French West Indies, countries of the former French West Africa, New Guinea, Algeria, French South Pacific
The Old British Commonwealth	United Kingdom, Canada, India, New Zealand, South Africa, British West Indies, Hong Kong, Kenya, Malaysia, Bahrain, Egypt, Trinidad and Tobago, Nigeria, Belize, Costa Rica, Jamaica
United States Protectorates	Puerto Rico, Liberia, South Korea, Philippines, Taiwan, Pacific Trust Territories

Exhibit 3.3 **Traditional Nontrading Nations**

Nations	Predicament
Chile and Peru	A 100-year-plus dispute keeps borders restricted
Greece and Turkey	Geographically contiguous but emotionally separate
India and Pakistan	Border disputes
Israel and the Arabic World	Religious differences cloud trade

PREFERENCE OF POLITICAL SYSTEMS

Though managers in individual companies create trade, countries' political influences have become more and more a factor of trading in the modern world. The political sector legislates or imposes trade barriers and negotiates trade agreements. Also, with socialist development, the political and commercial forces in the country can be one and the same. This obviously leads to an encouragement to trade with countries that share a common political perspective. Frequently, trade can be imposed through colonial or military control where the political system is dictated and trade directed. Exhibit 3.4 presents the major political trade blocs existing today. The classifications are often defined with a thin line of difference, and sometimes a country can be reclassified with a change in government.

Exhibit 3.4 **Major Political Trading Blocs**

Political Perspective	Representative Countries
Democratic Bloc	United States, United Kingdom, Australia, New Zealand, Canada, Belgium, Switzerland, Japan, Germany, Denmark, Sweden, Norway
Government-Controlled Bloc	Azerbaijan, Kazakhstan and most of the former Soviet Union, Cuba, Vietnam, Angola, North Korea, Yemen
Socialist Bloc	France, Italy, Spain, Portugal, Burundi, Zimbabwe

GEOGRAPHIC ADVANTAGES

Certain countries are fortunate to be located near an important consuming or producing country. This advantage properly structured can lead to national prosperity. If improperly structured, a dependent bilateral trade system can be created that diminishes the lesser nation to a vassal state.

Numerous countries are strategically located and receive a geographic advantage. Listed in Exhibit 3.5 are examples of the major trading country and the benefiting trading partner.

Also, a number of nations such as Singapore, Panama, and Bahrain lie on preferred trade routes and can prosper from location alone. Finally, other nations have developed a specialized role due to their size amidst trading giants. These countries have remained neutral in conflicts and have prospered by maintaining commercial ties with neighbors who might otherwise be hostile. Examples of such countries include Uruguay, Kuwait, Switzerland, and Luxembourg.

Exhibit 3.5 **Nations Benefiting from Geographic Proximity to a Major Trading Neighbor**

Benefiting Nation	Major Trading Neighbor
Channel Islands	Great Britain
Denmark	Germany
Finland	Russia
Mexico	United States
Monaco	France
Paraguay	Brazil

IMMIGRATION AND COLONIAL EFFECTS

Colonial ties create long-standing bonds, as already discussed. This is due to generations being aware of another country's habits and brand preferences. These ties are not a national circumstance but rather a personal factor. Immigration is an even more direct way to create new trade routes. As people move to other countries, they bring their own customs and preferences with them. Often these are satisfied only by the importation of products from their native countries.

This natural phenomenon can be viewed easily in the United States, where numerous people have settled and maintained trading and sympathetic ties to their homelands. For instance, Polish, Italian, Slovenian, and Chinese people all move about the globe and maintain parts of their culture that can be satisfied only through the importation of products. At the same time, luxury items or specialty items are bought by immigrants and sent to relatives in their home country. This eventually creates demand for these items in their home countries. For example, Turkish workers in Germany bring back cars, televisions, and other products. Even tourists can have a similar effect, especially in clothing styles and accessories, but to a lesser degree.

NORTH-SOUTH VERSUS EAST-WEST

A much less scientific or characteristically explainable phenomenon is a tendency for north-south trade to take preference over east-west trade. The most natural trading routes move up and down the globe longitudinally. The trade history between the United States and Latin America, and more recently the North American Free Trade Agreement among the United States, Canada, and Mexico, are prime examples. The European and African trading relationship and the Japanese and Australian marriage are other examples.

No simple explanation can be offered for this directional trading propensity. It is one of the natural phenomena that an international marketer must consider in the long-range outlook.

NATIONAL WEALTH—GNI

Very simply stated, the wealthier the country the more its people will import and consume. That means an international marketing planner should be conscious of which countries have the money to buy products and services. The amazing thing is that once you get past the most obvious of the wealthy nations (also the most hotly competitive markets), the next layer has a tendency to come and go. Mexico once looked like the next Saudi Arabia; Lebanon was a small, wealthy, consuming nation in the early 1970s and a war-torn country in the late 1970s and early 1980s. Numerous other examples exist, and those countries with wealth may be pursued as long as the possibility of movement in and out of the money circles is taken into account.

Countries can be ranked by **gross national income (GNI)** per capita, formerly gross national product (GNP) per capita, and then grouped into categories. Although the cutoff point for each category is somewhat arbitrary, classifying nations in this way can help managers target international marketing strategy. One conveniently employed categorization developed by the World Bank includes the four categories of high-income countries, upper-middle-income countries, lower-middle-income countries, and low-income countries. The World Bank income classification is shown in Exhibit 3.6. Countries are classified according to 2008 GNI per capita, calculated using the World Bank Atlas method. The U.S. dollar classification equivalencies are: $975 GNI or below is classified as a low-income country, $976 but under $3,855 is classified as a lower-middle-income country, $3,856 but under $11,905 is classified as an upper-middle-income country, and $11,906 and above is classified as a high-income country.

Another similar categorization essentially combines the low-income countries and lower-middle-income countries under the category of **less-developed countries (LDCs)** and classifies the upper-middle-income countries as **developing countries** and the high-income countries as **industrialized countries.**[4]

The industrialized or high-income countries represent the largest consuming market but the slowest growth in GNI per capita because their demand for products and services has become saturated. These countries are characterized by technology-dominated economies, and at least half of their GNI is derived from the service sector. Most of the population is employed in the market economy, and few people engage in agriculture, although their output per capita of foodstuff is large.

The developing countries are important because of their high growth rate of income and limited population growth. These countries are striving to improve the standard of living for their citizens and join the industrialized nations. Their market economy is growing rapidly, and the percentage of the population engaged in agriculture is declining. The demand for more and higher-priced products is increasing rapidly in these countries since GNI per capita is growing rapidly allowing disposable income to increase. Countries in this group that have experienced rapid economic growth and present expanding opportunities for international marketers are often referred to as **emerging markets.** If the rapid growth can be sustained, emerging markets can quickly reach the status of industrialized countries. Such countries are characteristically referred to as **newly industrialized countries (NICs)**.

The LDCs, however, possess about two-thirds of the world's population, and may in the long run present the greatest future marketing opportunities. These countries are characterized by highly agrarian populations with little market economy, low GNI per capita, high birth and low literacy rates, political unrest, and governmental instability. Products that can be sold in mass in the LDCs are normally restricted to necessities and basic discretionary items such as cigarettes. Because of the conditions encountered in these countries, the business risk is often substantial.

POPULATION

People are consumers. Therefore, one might presume that the larger the population of a country, the greater will be the potential consumption. Taking this view literally

Exhibit 3.6 **Country Classification Based on Income**

Low-income countries	Afghanistan, Bangladesh, Benin, Burkina Faso, Burundi, Cambodia, Central African Republic, Chad, Comoros, Congo Dem. Rep., Eritrea, Ethiopia, Gambia, Ghana, Guinea, Guinea-Bissau, Haiti, Kenya, Korea Dem. Rep., Kyrgyz Republic, Lao PDR, Liberia, Madagascar, Malawi, Mali, Mauritania, Mozambique, Myanmar, Nepal, Niger, Nigeria, Rwanda, Senegal, Sierra Leone, Somalia, Tajikistan, Tanzania, Togo, Uganda, Uzbekistan, Vietnam, Yemen Rep., Zambia, Zimbabwe
Lower-middle-income countries	Albania, Angola, Armenia, Azerbaijan, Belize, Bhutan, Bolivia, Cameroon, Cape Verde, China, Congo Rep., Côte d'Ivoire, Djibouti, Ecuador, Egypt Arab Rep., El Salvador, Georgia, Guatemala, Guyana, Honduras, India, Indonesia, Iran Islamic Rep., Iraq, Jordan, Kiribati, Kosovo, Lesotho, Maldives, Marshall Islands, Micronesia Fed. Sts., Moldova, Mongolia, Morocco, Nicaragua, Nigeria, Pakistan, Papua New Guinea, Paraguay, Philippines, Samoa, São Tomé and Principe, Solomon Islands, Sri Lanka, Sudan, Swaziland, Syrian Arab Republic, Thailand, Timor-Leste, Tonga, Tunisia, Turkmenistan, Ukraine, Vanuatu, West Bank and Gaza
Upper-middle-income countries	Algeria, American Samoa, Argentina, Barbados, Belarus, Belize, Bosnia and Herzegovina, Botswana, Brazil, Bulgaria, Chile, Colombia, Costa Rica, Cuba, Dominica, Dominican Republic, Fiji, Gabon, Grenada, Jamaica, Kazakhstan, Latvia, Lebanon, Libya, Lithuania, Macedonia FYR, Malaysia, Mauritius, Mayotte, Mexico, Montenegro, Namibia, Palau, Panama, Peru, Poland, Romania, Russian Federation, Serbia, Seychelles, South Africa, St. Kitts and Nevis, St. Lucia, St. Vincent and the Grenadines, Suriname, Turkey, Uruguay, Venezuela RB
High-income countries	Andorra, Antigua and Barbuda, Aruba, Australia, Austria, Bahamas, Bahrain, Barbados, Belgium, Bermuda, Brunei Darussalam, Canada, Cayman Islands, Channel Islands, Croatia, Cyprus, Czech Republic, Denmark, Equatorial Guinea, Estonia, Faeroe Islands, Finland, France, French Polynesia, Germany, Greece, Greenland, Guam, Hong Kong China, Hungary, Iceland, Ireland, Isle of Man, Israel, Italy, Japan, Korea Rep., Kuwait, Liechtenstein, Luxembourg, Macao China, Malta, Monaco, Netherlands, Netherlands Antilles, New Caledonia, New Zealand, Northern Mariana Islands, Norway, Oman, Portugal, Puerto Rico, Qatar, San Marino, Saudi Arabia, Singapore, Slovak Republic, Slovenia, Spain, Sweden, Switzerland, Trinidad and Tobago, United Arab Emirates, United Kingdom, United States, Virgin Islands (U.S.)

Source: Reprinted with permission of the International Bank for Reconstruction and Development, World Bank, creator and copyright holder of this classification method. Accessible at http://go.worldbank.org/D7SN0B8YU0.

would mean a total concentration in a global plan on India and China and little emphasis on the rest of the world's countries. Since both of these countries are poorer nations, another factor has to enter into the international marketer's equation—that of disposable personal income. People who can hardly afford bread should not be counted as customers for even the most basic of products. Yet, highly populated countries that are poor today should be watched for longer-term potential. These nations will spend resources to create jobs and, therefore, are prime candidates for labor-intensive industries and technology collaboration. History shows that in almost all underdeveloped nations, the first stages of industrialization begin in textiles, which are labor intensive.[5] Thus, these nations will import equipment and may be considered for serving a vital supply role in a global marketing plan. Also, as LDCs and developing nations become more industrialized, their middle-class populations grow. Middle-class people represent the bulk of consumers in a society. Thus, both economically and psychologically, the size of the middle class makes the difference between a nascent and a consuming society.

MAKING DECISIONS

All the factors discussed thus far indicate whether or where a market exists. Now two fundamental questions must be answered. Is the identified market appropriate? Does your product or service fit the identified market?

The relationships presented are only historical relationships. These relationships do not guarantee any identified market is a viable location for the firm's product or service. Additional research must be conducted to determine the size of the particular market, the feasibility of successfully penetrating that market, and the appropriate marketing strategy that will assure the desired response from that market. These concerns will be discussed more fully in chapter 6. Currently, the important consideration is that the various characteristics of and relationships among nations afford opportunities and risks to the international marketer. An awareness and understanding of these characteristics and relationships will give the international marketer a definite advantage in the market assessment process.

CURRENT WORLD TRADING CONDITIONS

The freest trading environment in modern history was experienced during the last quarter of the twentieth century. The nations of the world developed and fine-tuned the **General Agreement on Tariffs and Trade (GATT)** and its successor, the **World Trade Organization (WTO)**, by continually negotiating lower trade restrictions. In 1989, the fall of the Berlin Wall led to a further opening of Eastern European markets as the Soviet Union's control over its satellites crumbled. With the Soviet coalition dissolved, capitalism began to be embraced. Overall, economies remained healthy and continued to grow. Freer trade among nations seemed to be an objective most countries sought.

New transportation systems were introduced, which included the wide-bodied cargo jet and ocean containerization. Together these developments revolutionized global freight transportation. Communications systems took advantage of advanced electronic satellite breakthroughs, thus greatly improving and reducing the cost of transmission.

The Japanese showed the world that aggressive trading could result in huge market share gains anywhere in the world. American farm exports did extremely well and the doors to China were reopened. E-commerce evolved and provided a boost to international trade by offering ease of shopping and alternative sources of products. The U.S. economy sustained the longest uninterrupted growth period in history. Things looked good for the continued expansion of global trading.

Not everything was perfect however, because these advances were offset by periodic weaknesses. The quarter began under the influence of the 1973-74 Arab oil embargo. A few years later, a global recession caused numerous countries to suffer from hyperinflation and others from high unemployment. The resulting shortage of world capital caused offset trade agreements and reciprocity (countertrade—see chapter 16) to gain momentum. Barter trade became fashionable, with hard currency being scarce and expensive. Government subsidies for export became prevalent. A feeling of animosity grew in many corners of the world toward Japanese export success. Increases in trade momentum grew and waned and grew again as trading conditions fluctuated. In spite of these problems, unprecedented growth and expansion of international sales characterized the last quarter of the century.

The potential for the first quarter of the new century remains equally bright even though early into the quarter two significant events have had a detrimental effect on world trade. First was the 2001 terrorist attack on the World Trade Center in New York City. More recently was the global financial crisis that began in 2007. This was precipitated by the subprime mortgage crisis and the loss of investor confidence in mortgages repackaged into securities, which created a liquidity crisis that led to the failure of a number of well-known banks, mortgage lenders, and insurance companies, and a stock market crash. Both of these events contributed to and were followed by recessions that adversely affected world trade growth.

TRENDS IN EXPORTS

Exports are important to the individual firm for at least five reasons. They

- expand the firm's markets and revenues;
- smooth production cycles;
- are a source for new product development;
- are a source of profit and company growth; and
- utilize manufacturing downtime.

Government leaders look to exports as an expansion of their influence abroad, a means of growing employment, and perhaps most importantly, a source of hard currency. The need to stabilize a country's own currency by having a positive balance of trade has become a major objective of all nations. Government leaders enthusiastically look at exports in terms of the prosperity and employment they generate. Unfortunately, in their eagerness to achieve these goals, government leaders often interfere with free trade and begin to alter the rules of supply and demand toward their own perceived end.

Trends in recent years have been for increased global export activity in numerous sectors such as automobiles, construction equipment, vehicle spare parts, farm products, raw materials, chemicals, machine tools, and a variety of consumer products. Almost every product made has export potential somewhere. For example, U.S.-made sheets and pillowcases are selling briskly in France, and French perfume is in great

Exhibit 3.7 **Value of World Exports**

Year	Millions of US$	% Change
1990	3,425,960	
1996	5,110,378	49.2
1997	5,298,054	3.7
1998	5,217,133	−1.5
1999	5,409,483	3.7
2000	6,066,873	12.2
2001	5,828,631	−3.9
2002	6,100,946	4.7
2003	7,074,122	16.0
2004	8,566,994	21.1

Sources: Statistical Yearbook, no. 43 (Department of Economic and Social Affairs, United Nations, 1998), 687; *Statistical Yearbook,* no. 50 (Department of Economic and Social Affairs, United Nations, 2006), 613.

demand in Singapore. The most unusual products properly marketed can be sold in the most unlikely places.

Total world exports tend to exhibit an increasing trend. The value of world exports for selected years is shown in Exhibit 3.7 along with the year-to-year rate of change. The value of world trade in current U.S. dollars increased over 49 percent between 1990 and 1996, an average of 8.2 percent each year. For the eight-year period 1996 to 2004, the average annual increase in the value of worldwide trade was slightly higher, at 8.5 percent, in spite of two significant events that had adverse impacts. The Asian financial crisis contributed to a negative change between 1997 and 1998. The terrorist attacks on the World Trade Center in New York City contributed to the decline in trade in 2001. Despite the trading difficulties caused by localized recessions and unemployment, which were discussed previously, and the occasional world crises, world trade has continued to expand. Growing trends in exports are expected to continue in the future.[6]

The global trends are for producers to concentrate activities toward the major consumption markets. Today, this means most sellers want a part of the markets in the United States, the European Union, and other developed countries or areas.

Exports by region of the world are listed in Exhibit 3.8. From 1990 to 1996, the value of exports from the developed market economies increased by 44.4 percent. During the same period, the developing and LDC market economies realized a 61.2 percent increase in exports. During the period 1996 to 2004, the developed market economies increased the value of their exports by 54.2 percent. The developing and LDC market economies increased the value of their exports by 144.7 percent during the same period. The nations in the developing and LDC market economies are increasing their rates of export activity faster than the developed market economies. These figures show that the developing and LDC market economies are increasing exports at a faster rate, causing the real difference between the two groups to decrease.

Exhibit 3.8 **Exports by Region** (Millions of US$)

Year	Developed Market Economies	Developing and LDC Market Economies
1990	2,455,142	970,818
1996	3,545,561	1,564,817
1997	3,631,086	1,666,968
1998	3,699,412	2,422,162
1999	3,756,622	2,419,352
2000	4,018,950	2,505,579
2001	3,902,776	2,532,808
2002	4,035,762	2,698,222
2003	4,641,211	3,205,839
2004	5,467,252	3,828,634

Sources: Statistical Yearbook, no. 43 (Department of Economic and Social Affairs, United Nations, 1998), 687; *Statistical Yearbook,* no. 50 (Department of Economic and Social Affairs, United Nations, 2006), 613.

Exhibit 3.9 **Imports by Region**

Year	Received by Developed Market Economies	Received by Developing and LDC Market Economies	Imports Going to Developed Market Economies (in %)
	Millions of US$		
1990	2,573,572	983,185	72.4
1996	3,543,988	1,634,448	68.4
1998	3,799,158	2,370,610	61.6
2000	4,386,109	2,523,929	63.5
2002	4,339,109	2,595,308	62.6
2004	5,991,344	3,761,422	61.4

Sources: Statistical Yearbook, no. 43 (Department of Economic and Social Affairs, United Nations, 1998), 687; *Statistical Yearbook,* no. 50 (Department of Economic and Social Affairs, United Nations, 2006, 613.

Exports have a tendency to go to developed market economies, which are the primary consuming markets. As shown in Exhibit 3.9, the value of all imports consumed was 72.4 percent for the developed market economies in 1990 and 27.6 percent for the developing and LDC economies. The percentage of imports received by developed market economies in 1996 was 68.4, and in 2004 it was 61.4. For the same years, the developing and LDC market economies received 31.6 percent and 38.6 percent of all imports. These figures indicate that the developed market economies are slowly decreasing their share of the consumption of the world's products while the developing and LDC market economies are slowly increasing their share. Between 1990 and 2004, the developing and LDC market economies increased their share of imports by 282.5 percent while the developed market economies increased their imports by only 132.8 percent. During that time, the developing and LDC market economies increased their share of the world's imports approximately twice as fast as the countries comprising the developed market economy. Thus, the developing and LDC market economies are narrowing the gap with the wealthier nations as they strive to improve their economies, become more affluent, and eventually achieve developed-nation status.

CHAPTER SUMMARY

Since the world is becoming a smaller place because of technological advances in communications and transportation, differences among nations are disappearing. Still, the world is comprised of about 195 countries, each with its own uniqueness, which the international marketer must understand to be successful. The differences and similarities existing among nations, however, permit the international marketer to divide and categorize countries for marketing strategy purposes. Understanding and appreciating trading preferences based on geographic, cultural, political, and economic considerations can help improve strategic planning.

Trading conditions today are freer than ever. In spite of the advances toward freer trade that have been made, other factors such as changing economic conditions and policies of government leaders can inhibit progress. The overall trend, however, has been for a continuing expansion of world trade. A small number of wealthy countries with developed economies are responsible for most of the world's trade. These nations are responsible not only for creating the greatest amount of foreign trade but also for consuming the greatest amount of products and services. However, the developing and LDC economies are slowly narrowing the gap as their economies strengthen and grow.

KEY TERMS

Developing countries
Emerging markets
General Agreement on Tariffs and Trade (GATT)
Gross national income (GNI)
Industrialized countries
Less-developed countries (LDCs)
Newly industrialized countries (NICs)
World Trade Organization (WTO)

REVIEW QUESTIONS

1. Which of the world's nine regions do you expect to exhibit the fastest growth in the next twenty years? Why? Which regions do you expect to have the slowest growth in the next twenty years? Why?
2. As China opens its market to foreigners, what kinds of problems and risks should the international marketer consider before trading there?
3. Suggest a strategy the international marketer could embrace to simultaneously have a marketing presence in Israel and neighboring countries of the Arab world.

4. As the United Kingdom strengthens its affiliation with the European Union countries, what is likely to happen to its traditional trading ties with former British Commonwealth nations?
5. Develop a rationale for marketing your firm's product in politically unstable countries such as Sudan and Sri Lanka.
6. Why does knowing that Finland is a trading partner of Russia make Finland a more attractive market than otherwise would be the case?
7. Explain how GNI per capita can affect the decision to enter or not enter a market.
8. Why does the fact that a country possesses a large population not necessarily make that country an attractive international market?
9. The freest trading environment in modern history exists in the world today. Why are the world's markets likely to become even freer in the years to come?
10. In what ways does management benefit from expanding the firm's exports?

NOTES

1. Matt Rosenberg, "The Number of Countries in the World," About.com, March 18, 2008, http://geography.about.com/cs/countries/a/numbercountries.htm.

2. Central Intelligence Agency, "China," in *The World Factbook,* December 18, 2008, https://www.cia.gov/library/publications/the-world-factbook/goes/ch.html.

3. "EU Remains Vietnam's Premier Trading Partner in 2008," Communist Party of Vietnam online newspaper, January 6, 2009, http://www.cpv.org.vn/cpv/Modules/News_English/News_Detail_E.aspx?CN_ID343016&CO_ID=30105. Also see "EU Remains Vietnam's Largest Export Market," Cambodia-Laos-Vietnam Development Triangle Portal, May 30, 2009, http://www.mpi.gov.vn/portal/page/portal/clv_en/819138?p_page_id=&pers_id=823667&folder_id=&item_id=2686602&p_details=1.

4. John A. Weber, "Worldwide Strategies for Market Segmentation," *Columbia Journal of World Business* 9 (Winter 1974): 31–37.

5. James Kurth, "The Political Consequences of the Product Life Cycle: Industrial History and Political Outcomes," *International Organization* 33 (Winter 1979): 5.

6. World Trade Organization, "World Trade Report 2004: Exploring the Linkage Between the Domestic Policy Environment and International Trade" (Geneva, Switzerland: World Trade Organization, 2005), 13.

4 The Importance of International Marketing

Boots Group, PLC, is the leading health and beauty retailer and one of the best-known company names in the United Kingdom. Through Boots Healthcare International, the company's brands are sold in over 130 countries around the world. Boots is the developer and marketer of innovative over-the-counter (OTC) products and health care brands for the global self-medication market. The company is benefiting internationally from the growing trend toward self-medication. International sales are rooted in three core product categories: analgesics such as Nurofen, cough and cold remedies such as Strepsils, and skin care products such as Clearasil.

Retailing operations in Thailand began in 1997. By 2007 over seventy-three stores had been opened in various Thai cities. Thailand's OTC health care market has experienced accelerated growth since the economic crisis of the late 1990s.[1] Management was attracted to the Thai market because of the country's expanding economy. However, the balance of payments problem that ultimately contributed to the country's financial debacle could have adversely affected the future for Boots. The financial crisis that began in Thailand significantly affected the currencies, stock markets, and other asset prices of other Asian countries, including South Korea and Indonesia. Although less severely, the impact of the crisis was felt worldwide and even forced the shutdown of the U.S. stock market after a sell-off of stocks resulted in the second-largest percentage decline ever in the Dow Jones industrial average, on October 27, 1997. The Thai baht lost about half of its value, and the severe price inflation that resulted adversely affected business. The economies of the affected countries became depressed. Retailers were hurt as local demand dropped. The declines in demand affected all kinds of products, including those sold in Boots stores.

The International Monetary Fund arranged financing to help bail out and stabilize the Thai economy. Eventually, the economy recovered. A potential disaster for Boots management was averted. However, the changing conditions in Thailand's balance of payments could have had a debilitating impact on the company's future in that country. Today, the number of Boots' branded products in Thailand is being increased, and management has started the manufacturing of selected products in Thailand to shorten the supply chain and avoid import duties.

Sources: Based in part on information from Wikipedia, "1997 Asian Financial Crisis," http://en.wikipedia.org/wiki/Asian_financial_crisis; Malcolm Falkus, "Historical Perspectives of the Thai Financial Crisis," *Journal of the UNE Asia Center, UNEAC Asia Papers* 1 (1999), 10–20.

CHAPTER OBJECTIVES

After reading this chapter, you should

- know the position of the United States in export and import activity;
- understand how imports are changing as a percentage of total business activity in the United States;
- appreciate the role exports play in the economies of various countries;
- be able to explain why international trade occurs;
- define and explain the various theories that have been advanced to explain why international trade occurs;
- know what a country's balance of payments is;
- know the components of the balance of payments; and
- understand the impact the balance of payments can have on international marketing.

TRADE POSITION OF THE UNITED STATES

World trade refers only to products that are produced in one country and shipped and sold in another country. Thus, world trade concerns only exports and does not include sales from a nation's investments in other countries.

Although growth in **world trade** has increased substantially in the last quarter of the twentieth century and the beginning of the twenty-first century, not all countries have shared equally in this growth. Between 1988 and 2002, world trade increased by approximately 203 percent, from US$2,826 trillion to US$8,567 trillion, or approximately 12.7 percent on average per year.[2] As a percentage of total world exports, the U.S. share increased slightly between 1988 and 2000 before dropping below the 1988 level in 2004. Between 1988 and 2004, the Japanese and United Kingdom's shares, for example, have declined. The German share declined until 2000 and increased after that. Exhibit 4.1 shows the trend of these four countries' share of exports.

The United States has historically been the world's leading exporter and importer of merchandise. The United States reached a high of about 13.0 percent of all world trade in 1998, but declined steadily to about 10 percent in 2004. Germany surpassed

Exhibit 4.1 **Exports as a Share of World Exports for Selected Countries**

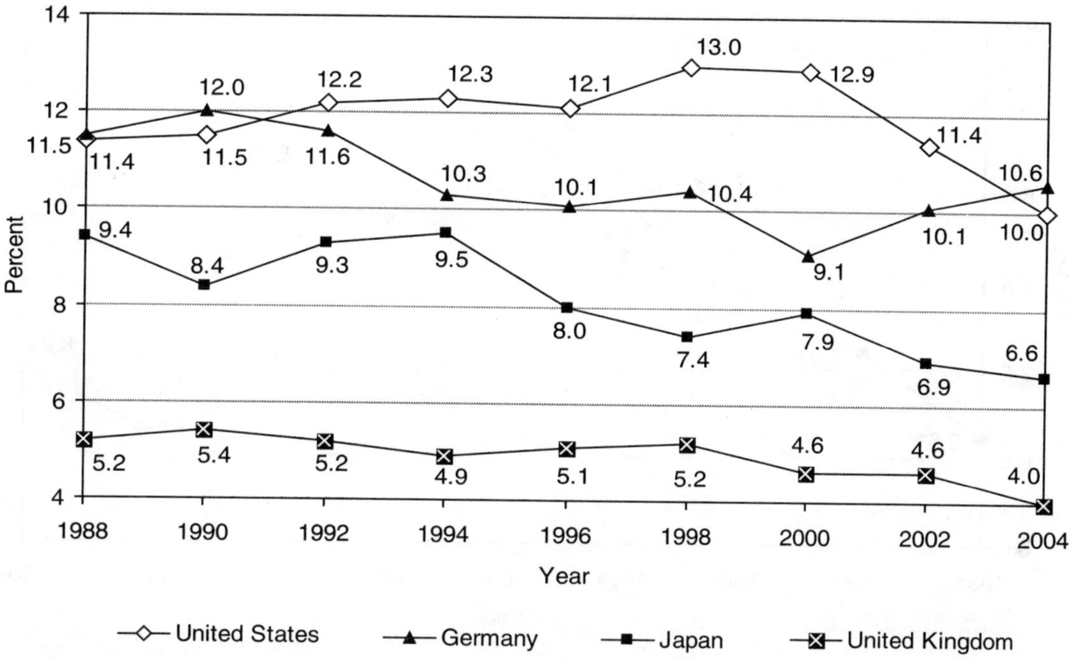

Sources: Statistical Yearbook, no. 43 (Department of Economic and Social Affairs, United Nations, 1999), 687, 691, 699; *Statistical Yearbook,* no. 50 (Department of Economic and Social Affairs, United Nations, 2006), 613–615.

the United States in 2004 to regain the distinction of being the world's leading exporting country that it lost in 1992. The United States accounted for about 15.8 percent of all imports in 1988, compared to 17.4 percent in 2002.[3] Between 1988 and 2004, the value of U.S. exports increased by about 155 percent and the value of U.S. imports increased by about 233 percent. The trend has been for the value of imports to grow faster than the value of exports, contributing to a balance of payments deficit (see the balance of payments discussion later in this chapter).

Although the United States is one of the leading exporters in absolute terms, relatively speaking the value of exports is a small part of the nation's total business activity. That portion experienced an increasing trend until 2000 as interest in international marketing increased. Since then, however, a downward trend has occurred. Still, this means that the U.S. economy is not very dependent on exports and most (about 90 percent) of business activity results from domestic sales. Exhibit 4.2 shows the portion of the **gross domestic product (GDP)** accounted for by exports in the United States. GDP is the market value of all products and services produced in a country in a year and is equal to the sum of the values of consumption, investment, and government spending, and the difference between exports and imports.

In relative terms, many other countries are much more dependent on exports to support their economies than is the United States. The Netherlands, for example, produces almost 60 percent of its business activity from exports. The reason for

Exhibit 4.2 **U.S. Exports as a Percentage of U.S. GDP**

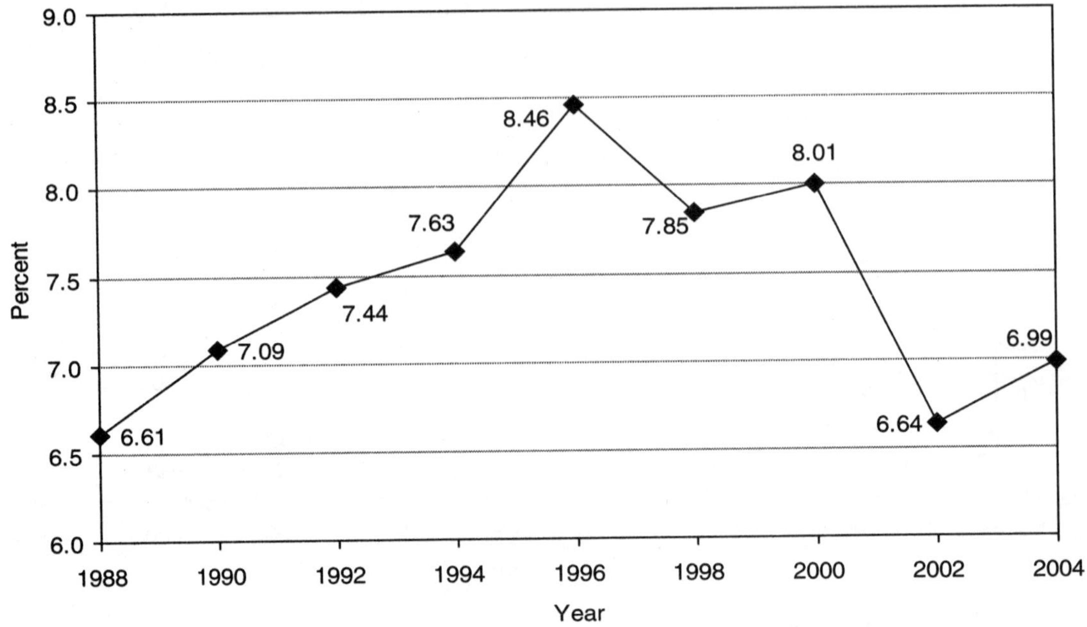

Sources: Statistical Yearbook, no. 43 (Department of Economic and Social Affairs, United Nations, 1999), 162, 687; *Statistical Yearbook,* no. 50 (Department of Economic and Social Affairs, United Nations, 2006), 153, 615.

this is that the domestic population of the Netherlands is small and able to consume less than one-half of the nation's output. The United States, on the other hand, has a large population that consumes over 90 percent of the nation's output. The value of exports for 2004 as a percent of GDP for selected countries is shown in Exhibit 4.3.

Since U.S. domestic business activity is so large, why should the U.S. government be concerned with exports and international business? Even though the amount of export sales is small in relative terms, the total dollar value is large. US$819 billion (2004) is no small number, and if exports were completely eliminated the impact on the U.S. economy would be substantial. Additionally, exports are a significant component in the profit structure of certain U.S. companies. International marketing is extremely important to some companies and industries. The sales and profits of these firms would be adversely affected if exports were eliminated. The proportion of earnings resulting from foreign sales in selected companies is shown in Exhibit 4.4.

Exports alone do not indicate a nation's total involvement in international marketing. Exports are only a portion of the total financial value of international marketing activity. For the United States, approximately four times as many dollars in sales are generated by foreign investments of U.S. firms located in foreign markets as by exports. Foreign investment refers to business that results from all other forms of international involvement excluding exporting (see chapter 5 for a discussion of

Exhibit 4.3 **Exports as a Percentage of GDP for Selected Countries in 2004**

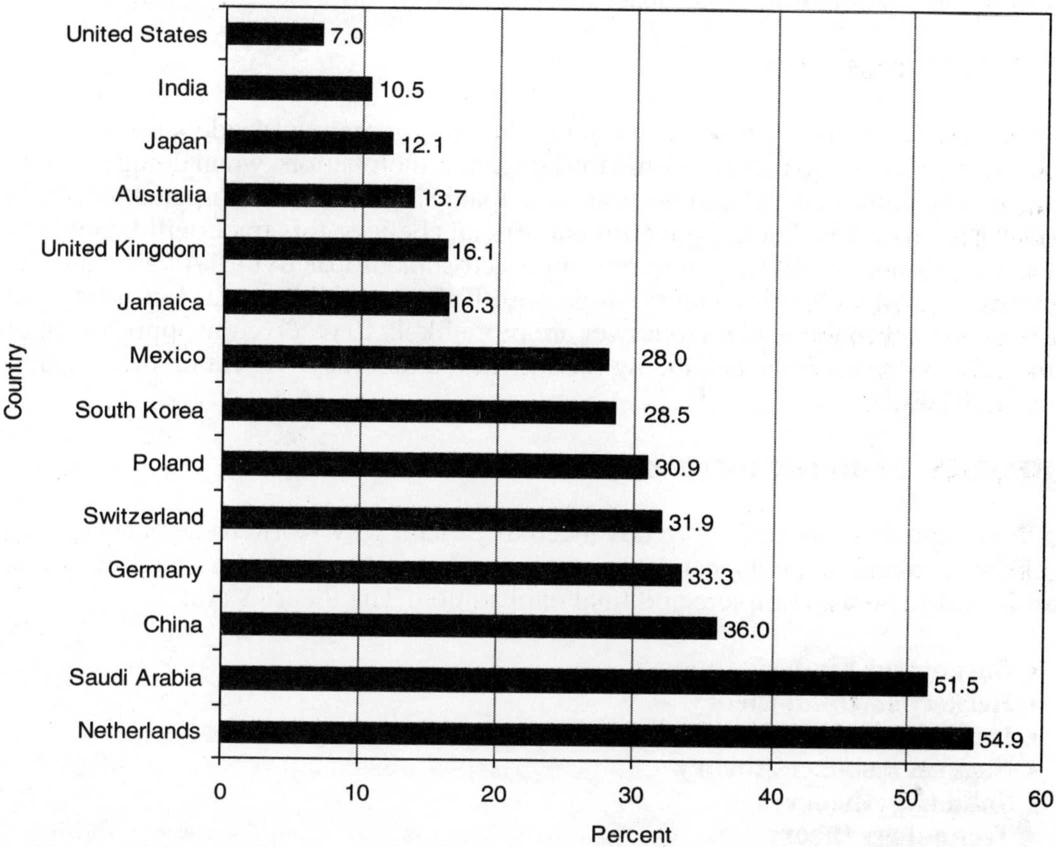

Source: Statistical Yearbook, no. 50 (Department of Economic and Social Affairs, United Nations, 2006), 140, 143–145, 147–150, 152–153, 613–615, 621–623, 625.

Exhibit 4.4 **Percent of Earnings Derived from Foreign Sources for Selected Companies**

Company	Percent
Procter and Gamble Company	38.9
General Motors Corporation	44.5
Goodyear Tire & Rubber Company	62.3
McDonald's Corporation	65.4
The Coca-Cola Company	65.9
Hewlett-Packard Company	66.6

Sources: 2006 and 2007 Annual Reports of the indicated companies.

foreign investment). Exporting then contributes only about 20 percent of the total dollar value of all U.S. international business activity.

WHY NATIONS TRADE

Why do nations trade with other nations? Why do government leaders permit firms from other countries to market within the borders of their nations when doing so could conceivably reduce sales from domestic companies? What is the impetus for world trade? The answer is that the government officials believe this trade will benefit the nation's citizens by offering them an improved standard of living. As a result, the citizens' overall well-being can be improved. If the people's standard of living can be improved, then the leaders in power are more likely to receive the approbation of a majority of the citizens, enhancing the likelihood that they will retain their leadership positions.

THEORIES OF INTERNATIONAL TRADE

At least eight theories have been advanced to explain why world trade occurs. Each probably explains some aspect of the phenomenon; however, none is definitive and considered to be the complete and final explanation. The theories are:

- **Burenstam Linder's theory**
- **Heckscher-Ohlin theory**
- **International product life cycle theory**
- **Natural resources theory**
- **Solidarity theory**
- **Technology theory**
- **Theory of comparative advantage**
- **Trade creation theory**

BURENSTAM LINDER'S THEORY

Staffan Burenstam Linder, a Swedish economist and politician, developed this theory. According to this theory, great domestic demand for a product leads to increasing world demand, creating a large export market. As production capacity increases domestically, exporting becomes feasible. Managers look overseas to find a market for the excess capacity.

HECKSCHER-OHLIN THEORY

Two Swedish economists, Eli Heckscher and Bertil Ohlin, developed this theory. The theory focuses on the two important factors of production: capital and labor. The basic premise is that firms in capital-abundant countries will export capital-intensive products (computers and automobiles, for example), and firms in labor-abundant countries will export labor-intensive products (textiles and handpicked agricultural

Exhibit 4.5 **Lace Making**

This Bulgarian woman is making lace by hand, the traditional way.

products, for example). Firms in a country that have a lot of labor and little capital (machinery) will tend to produce labor-intensive products. Firms in a country that have an abundance of capital will tend to produce products that use machinery in their production. The price of the labor-intensive product in the labor-abundant country will be bid down relative to the price of that product in the capital-intensive country because of the extra supply. Likewise, the price of the capital-intensive product in the capital-abundant country will be bid down relative to the price of that product in the labor-intensive country because of the extra supply. Profit-seeking firms in the labor-abundant country will export their products to the capital-abundant country, and firms in the capital-abundant country will export their products to the labor-abundant country because of the relatively higher prices the products will bring. The amount of capital per worker and not the absolute amount of capital is the important consideration in determining which products are traded. Although a small country like the Netherlands has less capital in total than India, it has more capital per capita. According to the theory, then, firms in the Netherlands will export capital-intensive products to India, and Indian firms will export labor-intensive products to the Netherlands.

International Product Life Cycle Theory

According to this theory, new products are developed and introduced first by firms in the high-income developed nations. As sales grow and the product reaches the maturity stage, foreigners eventually become aware of the product. In the beginning, foreign demand for the product is small and is satisfied by exports from the developed nation that introduced it. Eventually, a point is reached at which the foreign demand increases sufficiently that production outside the domestic market becomes attractive and economically feasible. Lower labor costs in the foreign country, and its import tariffs, transportation costs, and increasing demand all contribute to the impetus to move production abroad. As the product continues to mature in the developed nation that introduced it, production there declines in line with stagnating or declining demand. Exports also decrease as production increases abroad. Eventually, production abroad will increase to the point at which output is large enough to permit exports. At this time, the foreign firms begin to export the product to the developed nation that first introduced it. Eventually, production ends in the developed nation that introduced the product, and all demand there is satisfied by imports from foreign producers. The production of television sets in the United States is a good example of the application of this theory. In the early days of television, all sets were manufactured in the United States. Today no TV sets are produced in the United States, and every TV has to be imported for buyers in that country.

Natural Resources Theory

Firms in countries that are richly endowed with a particular natural resource will tend to export that product to countries that have a scarcity of it. Firms in countries with plentiful resources can generally produce or harvest those resources less expensively than firms in countries with a dearth of the resource. Therefore, because of its abundance and the cost benefits, exporting the resource becomes attractive and essential. This theory explains why firms in Middle Eastern countries export oil, firms in Canada and other countries with expansive forests export large amounts of lumber, and firms in Central American countries export coffee beans and bananas.

Solidarity Theory

Managers in developed countries recognize their moral obligation to assist the developing and LDC nations to improve their economies. Therefore, the decision making of these managers is virtuous in that they want to help provide for the needs of the less fortunate people in these countries. Trade results from assisting these nations to achieve commercial independence and a higher standard of living for their citizens. Products that can help develop the infrastructure are exported to these countries.

TECHNOLOGY THEORY

Technology is always advancing. Thus, firms in nations with a technology advantage will export their technology to countries needing that technology. Because new technologies are always emerging, countries can lose their technological lead quickly, causing shifts in the direction of exports. Japan is a good example. In the last fifty years, Japanese firms advanced to a position of technological superiority in the automobile industry, surpassing the U.S. leadership. Japanese automakers quickly changed the direction and size of world automobile trade.

THEORY OF COMPARATIVE ADVANTAGE

The underlying supposition of the theory of comparative advantage is that world trade occurs because the number and variety of products and services available to consumers is increased. Trading will make a nation's supply of products greater than what would be available if all the same products were produced domestically.

To explain the theory of comparative advantage, a simple hypothetical example will suffice. A two-country/two-commodity world must be assumed to illustrate the basic precepts of the theory, which will hold true for a multicountry, multiproduct situation but is difficult to explain. Once a simple two-country/two-product example is provided, grasping the theory's application to the real world should be easily appreciated.

South Korea and the United States will be the two countries, and the two products will be tires and computers. If the resources in each country are employed solely in the manufacturing of tires, U.S. firms will be assumed to be able to produce 125 and South Korean firms will be assumed to be able to produce 100. If the same resources are employed only in the production of computers, U.S. firms will be assumed to be able to produce 50 and South Korean firms will be assumed to be able to manufacture 25. If the resources in each country were reorganized so that both tires and computers would be made, then one possible production arrangement could be 50 tires and 30 computers from U.S. firms, and 40 tires and 15 computers from South Korean firms. These production alternatives are shown in Exhibit 4.6.

These are only three of the unlimited production arrangements that are possible if each nation's resources are slowly shifted from the manufacturer of tires to the manufacturer of computers. The production alternatives can be depicted in a graph known as a "production possibility curve" or "production frontier." By redistributing a nation's resources between the production of tires and computers, any combination of the two products that is represented by a point on the production possibility curve is possible. The production possibility curves for both countries are shown in Exhibit 4.7.

The production possibility curve shows what output is possible with full employment of the resources. Any combination of tires and computers located to the right of the curve is impossible with the existing resources. Combinations of products to the right of the curve are possible only if the resources increase. Combinations of products to the left of the curve are attainable but will be produced only if some of

Exhibit 4.6 **Production Possibilities**

Product	Production possibility (units) A	B	C
United States			
Tires	125	50	0
Computers	0	30	50
South Korea			
Tires	100	40	0
Computers	0	15	25

Exhibit 4.7 **Production Possibility Curves**

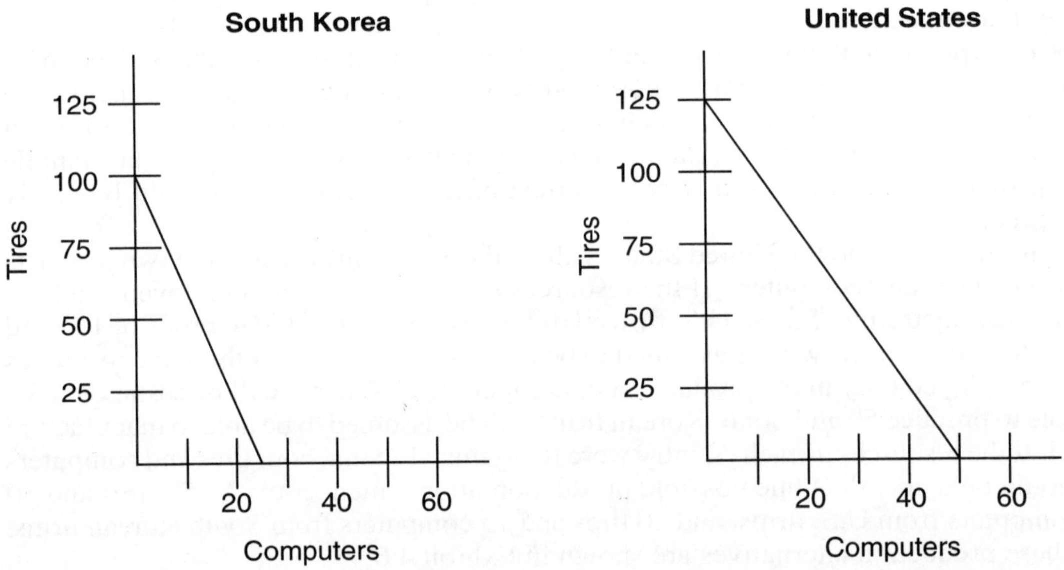

the available resources are either underemployed or unemployed. Thus, with full employment of the resources in the United States, if 100 tires were produced, only 10 computers could be produced. The resources needed to produce more tires require that resources be diverted from the production of computers. Obviously, the resources are not completely interchangeable and equally efficient at making both products. To make one more tire, more than one computer must be sacrificed.

The exchange of resources from the production of one product to make the other is known as the **opportunity cost**. Thus, the rate of exchange of one product for the other equals the opportunity cost. In the United States, the opportunity cost is 2.5 tires for each computer. To move from production possibility A in Exhibit 4.6 to production possibility B, the resources needed to make 75 (125–50) tires must be reallocated to the production of 30 (0–30) computers. Therefore, 1 computer is equal to 2.5 (75/30) tires. In South Korea the opportunity cost is 4 tires for 1 computer. Moving from production possibility A to production possibility B redirects the resources for making 60 (100–40) tires to the production of 15 (0–15) computers. Thus, 1 computer is equal to 4 (60/15) tires.

These opportunity costs indicate that although each country can use its resources to better advantage to produce tires, the United States can use its resources better than South Korea to make both tires and computers. Therefore, the United States is said to have an **absolute advantage** in the production of both products. However, relatively speaking, the resources in South Korea are employed better to make tires and the resources in the United States are employed better to make computers. This is true because the resources are employed four times better in making tires in South Korea and only two-and-one-half times better in the United States. As a result, firms in South Korea can produce tires more efficiently than firms in the United States. On the other hand, firms in the United States can produce computers more efficiently than firms in South Korea. In the United States, if the resources required to make 2.5 tires must be reallocated to make 1 computer, then 1 tire is equal to .4 computers (1/2.5). In South Korea, 1 tire equals .25 computers, since the resources required to make 4 tires must be reallocated to produce 1 computer (1/4). Thus, firms in the United States can employ their resources 1.6 times better (.4/.25) than firms in South Korea to manufacture computers.

Since the resources in South Korea can be used more efficiently to make tires, South Korean firms are said to have a comparative advantage in their production. Comparing the efficiency of production, South Korean firms are superior to U.S. firms for making tires. On the other hand, U.S. firms have a comparative advantage in the production of computers. The resources in the United States are employed more efficiently in producing computers in relative terms. A **comparative advantage** exists when the firms in one country can produce a product more efficiently (at a lower opportunity cost) than firms in another country. The country in which the product can be produced more efficiently has the comparative advantage. The other country, which is less efficient, is said to possess a **comparative disadvantage** in the production of that product. Thus, the United States has a comparative disadvantage in the production of tires, and South Korea has a comparative disadvantage in the production of computers.

The theory holds that the firms in each country should specialize in the production of the products for which the resources can be used most efficiently. That is, they should produce the comparative advantage products (those with the lowest opportunity costs). By specializing in the production of the products the firms in a nation can produce best, the world's supply of products will be increased. This is true because efficient use of resources allows optimum productivity. Efficiency always assures greater productivity than inefficiency. The production data in Exhibit 4.6 illustrate this phenomenon. If both products are produced in both countries (production possibility B), 90 tires and 45 computers, or 135 total products, are produced and consumed. The pre-trade production and consumption for production possibility B in both countries are shown in Exhibit 4.8.

If the firms in each country specialize in the production of the product in which

Exhibit 4.8 **Pre-trade Production and Consumption**

	Tires		Computers	
South Korea	40		15	
United States	50		30	
Totals	90	+	45	= 135 products

Exhibit 4.9 **After-specialization Production**

	Tires		Computers	
South Korea	100		0	
United States	0		50	
Totals	100	+	50	= 150 products

the country has a comparative advantage—for example, U.S. firms produce only computers and South Korean firms produce only tires—more of both products can be produced. U.S. firms would produce 50 computers (move to production possibility C in Exhibit 4.6), and South Korean firms would produce 100 tires (move to production possibility A in Exhibit 4.6)—a total of 150 products. The after-specialization production is shown in Exhibit 4.9.

The number of tires and computers available in the world is larger than what was available when firms in both countries produced both products. Total output was increased by 11 percent (10 tires and 5 computers). The problem, however, is that all the tires are in South Korea and all the computers are in the United States. Consumers in South Korea would like to buy computers as well as tires, and consumers in the United States would like to buy tires as well as computers. Therefore, trade must occur if both products are to be made available for consumption in both countries. But how many tires should be traded with the United States, and how many computers should be traded with South Korea?

South Korean firms must get more than 1 computer in return for every 4 tires shipped to the United States. To accept less would be unwise, because it would be more effective to switch South Korean resources to making computers domestically. Likewise, U.S. firms must receive more than 2.5 tires for every computer exported to South Korea. To accept less would be unwise because U.S. resources could be switched to produce more tires. Therefore, the acceptable terms of trade must lie between:

1 computer = 4 tires and
1 computer = 2.5 tires

Let us assume that the terms of trade acceptable to firms in both nations are 1 computer = 3 tires. Then, one option would find South Korean firms willing to ship

Exhibit 4.10 **After-trade Consumption**

	Tires		Computers	
South Korea	46		18	
United States	54		32	
Totals	100	+	50	= 150 products

54 tires to the United States if U.S. firms will ship 18 computers to South Korea. As a result, after-trade consumption of both products in both countries is increased. The after-trade consumption for this trading option is shown in Exhibit 4.10.

Comparing the after-trade consumption with pre-trade consumption (Exhibit 4.8) shows that the consumers in each country have more of both products available to buy. The welfare of the citizens in both countries has been improved as a result of trade. Living standards have improved because people can enjoy more products of a better quality. All of this is possible as a result of firms in each country specializing in the comparative advantage product and trading with firms in other nations. Thus, government leaders will encourage world trade because of the economic benefits that can accrue to their nations and their citizens.

According to the theory of comparative advantage, the economic impact of world trade is to transfer resources to countries that have a comparative advantage in their use and away from countries that have a comparative disadvantage in their use. This theory helps explain the flows of raw materials and finished products. Most of the oil pumped is not consumed by the producing nations but goes instead to firms in the developed nations that have a comparative advantage in its use. For the same reason, the United States is no longer the major producer of textiles and shoes. The textile industry has moved to other countries such as India and China that have a comparative advantage in their manufacture. Likewise, the shoe industry has moved to countries such as Italy and Mexico.

The theory of comparative advantage is not entirely applicable, because of interference by governments. Government leaders justify imposing various trade restrictions that constrain the movement of resources to the countries that have a comparative advantage in their use for at least three reasons:

- national defense
- protection of domestic industry
- protection of jobs

When trade restrictions, such as tariffs and quotas, are imposed for whatever reason, specialization cannot occur. Resources that would otherwise flow to firms in countries with a comparative advantage in their use are restricted from leaving the original country. Thus, those constrained resources are used by less efficient producers. Because of this inefficiency, output produced with the constrained resources is reduced and poorer quality and higher prices result. This occurs because those resources are not being used as efficiently as possible. As a result, the theory of comparative advantage has been used as an argument against protectionism and in support of the concept of free trade.

Another problem with the theory of comparative advantage is that people of one nation may value a particular product so much that they are unwilling to trade it for another product. Even though another country has a comparative advantage in the production of some other product, a trading partner cannot be found. Therefore, the firms in that country are forced to produce the comparative disadvantage product, so it is available to the local consumers who want it.

TRADE CREATION THEORY

Profit-oriented managers always prefer to buy the lowest-priced components, parts, and products available. Therefore, purchases will be made from lower-priced foreign suppliers when feasible. So, as trade restrictions are reduced and eliminated in foreign countries, lower-priced foreign sources of supply are sought to replace higher-priced domestic sources.

BALANCE OF PAYMENTS

When a product is sold to a foreigner, payment must be made to the seller. This causes money to flow from the buyer's country to the seller's country. An accounting of these transactions must be made so the flows of currencies can be monitored and a country's financial health determined. A government's accounting of currency flows between its country and all other countries is known as that country's **balance of payments**. Every country has its own balance of payments. A nation's balance of payments condition can have implications for the strength of its currency and ultimately investment decisions.

What is a balance of payments?

- "Balance of payments" is a misnomer. A nation's balance of payments is rarely balanced. That is, the amount of currency coming into a country is unlikely to be equal to the amount of money flowing out. Since inflows are separate from outflows, a balance of payments that is balanced (inflows equal outflows) could occur only by accident.
- A balance of payments is a statement of all international transactions for a country. Since currency flowing in and out can vary over time, a nation's balance of payments can fluctuate from surplus to deficit or deficit to surplus from year to year, month to month, and any one period of time to another.

COMPONENTS

The balance of payments is composed of all activities that cause money to flow into and out of a country. Examples of activities that influence the U.S. balance of payments are shown in Exhibit 4.11.

Exhibit 4.11 **Examples of U.S. Balance of Payments Activities**

Cause inflows of currency	Cause outflows of currency
Exports	Imports
Foreigners investing in the United States	Americans investing in other countries
Americans repatriating profits from foreign investments	Foreigners repatriating profits from investments in the United States
Foreigners vacationing in the United States	Americans vacationing in foreign countries
	U.S. military expenditures in foreign countries
	Economic aid to foreign countries

A nation's balance of payments is composed of two basic accounts:

- A **current account** is the difference between the value of the import and value of the export of products and services. A special part of this account is the **balance of trade**, which excludes services and considers only merchandise transactions.
- A **capital account** is the difference between the value of capital flowing into and out of the country for any reason other than for products and services.

The balance of payments condition for the United States in 2004 is outlined in Exhibit 4.12. As indicated, the United States recorded a balance of payments deficit of US$85.4 billion in 2004. The balance of trade was responsible for a US$662 billion deficit. Although the overall balance is what is of concern, the U.S. balance of payments deficit could be completely eliminated by increasing exports by US$85.4 billion, reducing imports by the same amount, or some combination of both resulting in a US$85.4 billion improvement. Similarly, changes in the capital account could easily erase the entire deficit. Since the United States is becoming a service-oriented economy, increases in the sale of those services to foreigners might be expected in the future, which might continue to help offset the balance of trade deficit being experienced.

Exhibit 4.13 lists the 2004 balance of payments for a few trading partners of the United States. Exhibit 4.14 shows the balance of payments position of the United States between 1991 and 2004.

IMPACT ON MARKETING STRATEGY

Why should the manager be concerned with a nation's balance of payments? What are the implications of the balance of payments for an international marketer's strategy? The manager needs to be alert to countries that continuously run deficits in their balance of payments or are experiencing deepening deficits. Marketing in these countries is more risky. The problems that deficits present should not necessarily inhibit investment and sales, but make the manager cautious, careful, and prepared for quick action to respond to the variety of marketing problems that may be encountered.

Exhibit 4.12 **U.S. Balance of Payments in 2004** (billions of US$)

Current Account			
Goods: Exports	811.0		
Goods: Imports	–1,473.0		
Total		–662.0	
Service and Income: Credit	719.9		
Service and Income: Debit	–645.2		
Total		74.7	
Current Account Balance			–587.3
Capital Account			
Transfers: Credit	17.9		
Transfers: Debit	–98.9		
Total		–81.0	
Capital account: Credit	1.1		
Capital account: Debit	–2.8		
Total		–1.7	
Financial account	581.8		
Reserves and related items	2.8		
Total		584.6	
Capital Account Balance			501.9
Balance of Payments Balance			–85.4

Source: Statistical Yearbook, no. 50 (Department of Economic and Social Affairs, United Nations, 2006), 732.

Exhibit 4.13 **Balance of Payments for Selected U.S. Trading Partners in 2004**

Country	**Millions of US$**
Argentina	131.1
Canada	–4,651.0
Germany	32,454.8
Japan	–28,904.6
Mexico	–2,227.5
Poland	1,955.6
Saudi Arabia	0.0
Switzerland	9,123.2
United Kingdom	11,125.6

Source: Statistical Yearbook, no. 50 (Department of Economic and Social Affairs, United Nations, 2006), 701, 706, 712, 716, 720, 724, 727, 730, 732.

Exhibit 4.14 **United States Balance of Payments, 1991 to 2004**

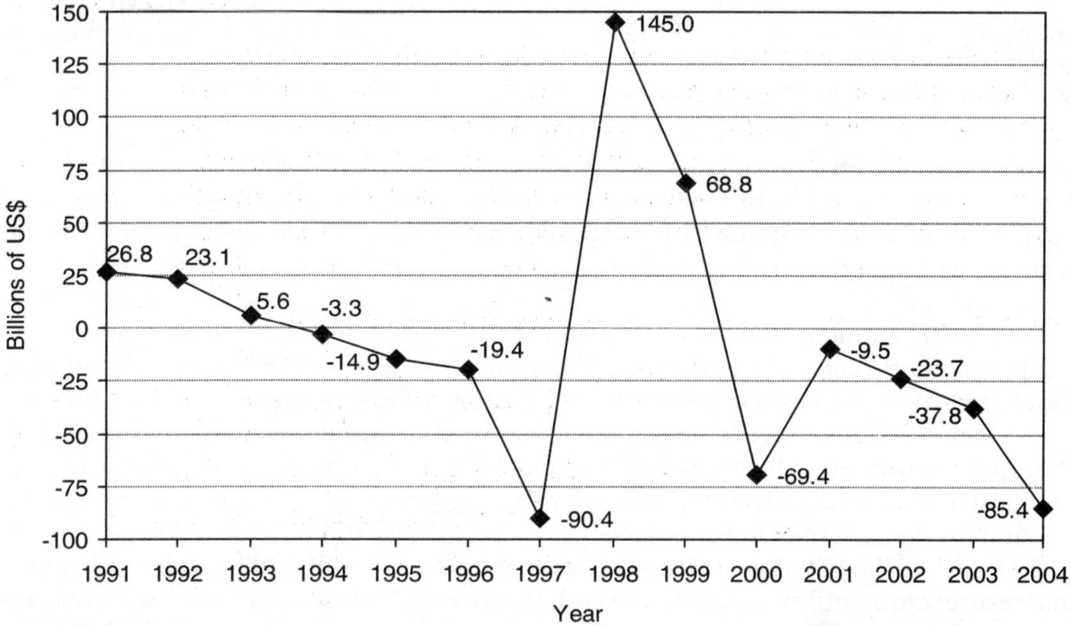

Sources: Statistical Yearbook, no. 43 (Department of Economic and Social Affairs, United Nations, 1999), 792; *Statistical Yearbook,* no. 50 (Department of Economic and Social Affairs, United Nations, 2006), 732.

The risks that may be encountered fall into four areas:

- currency inflation and devaluation
- foreign exchange restrictions
- influence on foreign investments
- trade barriers

When deficits in a country's balance of payments persist, the government will suffer from a shortage of hard currency. This occurs because more money continues to leave the country than is received. Therefore, the money needed to buy imports is inadequate. As a result, the government may impose various exchange restrictions in an effort to ameliorate the shortage. Exchange restrictions, which will be discussed in detail in chapter 9, can include the imposition of unfavorable exchange rates that make the exchange of currencies unattractive. Governments can even restrict the amount of currency that can be taken out of the country in an effort to retain money. This means that the manager will have a difficult time repatriating money to the firm's domestic headquarters if that is desired. Therefore, exchange restrictions can have an adverse impact on cash flows. Also, governments may restrict import purchases until sufficient foreign exchange is available to pay for them. That means the international marketer may have identified a buyer that is unable to make the purchase until authorized by the government. In these cases, sales may be allocated to a queue, requiring the waiting of long periods until the country's central bank obtains enough currency to authorize the sale. If sales are desired more quickly, the manager may be forced to engage in countertrade. Countertrade, which will be discussed in chapter 16, means that the manager will be required to accept all or part of the payment in merchandise instead of money. That, of course, means the problem of disposing of the countertraded products must be addressed.

Persistent deficits may cause government leaders to impose trade barriers as a means of saving currency. Trade barriers, which will be discussed in chapter 5, are intended to make importing merchandise into a country plagued by balance of payments deficits more difficult. By restricting imports, the available currency can be retained and spent on the highest priority imports. Examples of trade barriers are tariffs and quotas.

Foreign investments the firm may have in the country are not exempt from potential problems balance of payments deficits may cause. If components and parts are purchased by the investment from sources outside the country plagued by balance of payments deficits, government policy may be changed in ways that interfere. For example, restrictions placed on imports may force components and parts normally purchased from foreign sources to be purchased from local suppliers. Being required to purchase locally may have adverse price and quality implications.

To improve the balance of payments picture, governments can implement policies that restrict cash outflows, accelerate cash inflows, or both. Foreign exchange restrictions, trade barriers, countertrade, and limitations on foreign investments work to limit cash outflows. Cash inflows can be encouraged by changes made to the country's currency value. To pay for imports, more currency can simply be printed. The printing of more currency causes the currency to experience price inflation and a subsequent loss in value relative to other currencies. As a result, foreigners find the price of exports from the country experiencing balance of payments deficits to be relatively less and thus the sale of these products is increased. A government may unilaterally adjust the value of the nation's currency relative to other currencies by devaluing it. **Devaluation** is the most severe adjustment government leaders can take in an attempt to correct a balance of payments problem. The problem for the international marketer is that money held in the devaluing currency loses value when repatriated. Of course, the same impact results from price inflation, only more slowly. The impact of price inflation and devaluation will be discussed more fully in chapter 9.

The international marketer must exercise care when exporting to or investing in countries with balance of payment problems. The risks just discussed may or may not occur depending on the severity of the balance of payments problem and the inclination of government leaders. Before increasing exposure in the country, management may want to thoroughly examine and understand the risks and prepare contingency plans.

CHAPTER SUMMARY

The United States is the world's leading exporter and importer of merchandise. However, the value of exports to total U.S. business activity is small. The economies of many other countries rely more heavily on exports. Even though the percentage of business activity resulting from exports is small in the United States, the total dollar value is still large, and decreases would affect the economy. Exports contribute significantly to the profits of many large U.S. firms.

An analysis of exports provides an understanding of why government leaders permit foreign firms to sell products in their country. The theory of comparative advantage is one explanation of why trade occurs. International trade occurs because it permits improvements in living standards by providing a bigger variety of better-quality products in larger quantities and at lower prices than can be produced domestically. Trade improves the welfare of all people in the trading nations. Other explanations such as the international product life cycle theory and the Heckscher-Ohlin theory are also popular. In actuality, no one theory completely explains why trade occurs; however, in their totality, the theories provide useful insight into the phenomenon and a deeper understanding of the contingencies involved.

When contemplating doing business in a foreign country, international marketers need to be aware of the balance of payments condition of that country. Countries that suffer from consistent and deepening deficits in their balance of payments can present additional risks for the manager. Governments experiencing balance of payments problems may undertake efforts to retain existing foreign currency or increase inflows of new foreign currency to lessen deficits. The actions governments may take can adversely affect the business environment in those countries for the international marketer. As a result, the manager needs to exercise care and discretion prior to entering these markets and be prepared to adjust and protect against inauspicious government action.

KEY TERMS

Absolute advantage
Balance of payments
Balance of trade
Burenstam Linder's theory
Capital account
Comparative advantage
Comparative disadvantage
Current account
Devaluation
Gross domestic product (GDP)
Heckscher-Ohlin theory
International product life cycle theory
Natural resources theory
Opportunity cost
Solidarity theory
Technology theory
Theory of comparative advantage
Trade creation theory
World trade

REVIEW QUESTIONS

1. Why is the United States' share of total world exports remaining fairly level around 12 percent?
2. How can the value of the United States' exports as a percentage of U.S. GDP increase when its share of total world exports is remaining almost constant?

3. Could exports as a percentage of GDP in the United States ever reach the level found in the Netherlands? Why or why not?
4. What is a comparative advantage?
5. Why do resources flow to countries with a comparative advantage in their use?
6. What is a comparative disadvantage?
7. Explain the concept of opportunity cost.
8. How does the international product life cycle theory differ from the trade creation theory?
9. What does a country's balance of payments measure?
10. Why does the international marketer need to be concerned about a country's balance of payments?

NOTES

1. Thailand had experienced economic growth averaging 9 percent from 1985 to 1995. This contributed to a highly developed industrial economy but a poorly developed financial market. As a result, large current account deficits occurred, which encouraged external borrowing and led to excessive exposure to foreign exchange risk. The Thai baht came under pressure and ultimately was devalued in July 1997, causing depreciating financial and real estate asset values.

2. *Statistical Yearbook,* no. 43 (New York: Department of Economic and Social Affairs, United Nations, 1999), 686; and *Statistical Yearbook,* no. 50 (New York: Department of Economic and Social Affairs, United Nations, 2006), 613.

3. *Statistical Yearbook,* no. 43, 686; and *Statistical Yearbook,* no. 50, 613, 615.

5 International Market Entry Methods

In April 2008, Scottish & Newcastle, PLC, was acquired by Heineken N.V., the world's most international brewer. Scottish & Newcastle, PLC, is now known as Scottish & Newcastle UK (S&N) and has become the United Kingdom operating company within Heineken's Western European region.

Tony Froggatt is the chief executive of S&N. Froggatt and the management of S&N are responsible for the expansion of the firm's products to new markets. They were well aware that the beer markets of Western Europe, North America, and other developed regions were relatively mature and not expected to grow by more than 1 percent next year. The real growth was expected in the developing nations, especially China and Eastern Europe.[1] In some markets, such as the United Kingdom, beer and cider sales declined an average of almost 1 percent per year between 1979 and 2007.[2] Expansion into the developing nations might be desirable for the firm to continue to grow.

S&N is one of the top four brewers in Europe and has the number one market position in four core markets—the United Kingdom, France, Russia, and India. Also, S&N is ranked among the top ten brewers in the world by sales volume. The firm's products enjoy a leading market position in fourteen European and Asian countries and are exported to more than sixty countries around the world. Three of the top ten beer brands in Europe—Foster's, Kronenbourg, and Baltika—belong to S&N. In 2007, sales of £4.2 billion and an operating profit of £535 million were recorded.

Sales of S&N products are made through direct exports, trading subsidiaries, and licensed brewing. Beer is exported from company-owned breweries in the United Kingdom, Ireland, France, Belgium, Portugal, and Finland. Joint venture investments have been used to enter China and India, two of the fastest-growing beer markets in the world. Subsidiaries have been formed in Switzerland, Germany, Italy, and Spain. A joint venture was used to enter the Greek market. Russia, Ukraine, Latvia, Lithuania, Estonia, and Kazakhstan are served by Baltic Beverages Holding, a joint venture with Carlsberg. Newcastle Brown Ale, one of the fastest-growing import beers in the United States, is exported to the United States from England. In the United Kingdom, five breweries and a cider production plant are operated by S&N.

Cider might be one of the products management could use to expand to new markets. Cider is an alternative alcoholic beverage to beer and is popular in the United Kingdom. Strongbow, one of three brands of cider produced by S&N, enjoys the number one market position in the United Kingdom. Strongbow is exported from the H.P. Bulmer brewery, where it is made for markets across Europe, Scandinavia, the United States, Australasia, and the Far East. One of the possible growth markets Froggatt could evaluate is Serbia.

People living in Serbia accept social drinking in bars and cafes. The population is becoming more receptive to new tastes and has an increased desire to experiment with a wider range of drinks. The Serbian economy is still unstable following years of political mismanagement. The country is going through a process of transition to privatization. A trend exists for foreign firms to expand into Serbia, and those that are willing to take the risk should benefit from the advantages of being the first entrant into the market. Were management to cultivate Strongbow's entry, doing so would be consistent with one of the firm's growth strategies of brand development. Additionally, such a move should contribute to the S&N mission of sustained revenue growth leading to improved returns on invested capital. However, if S&N were to enter the Serbian market with cider, careful consideration and analysis about how to best enter the market would be needed. Such evaluations would certainly be important to Gary Guthrie, head of marketing at S&N.

Source: Based in part on information from the Heineken UK Web site at http://www.scottish-newcastle.com.

CHAPTER OBJECTIVES

After reading this chapter, you should

- understand what motivates managers to enter international markets;
- know how attitude influences the international market entry decision;
- be aware of the factors affecting international market entry form;
- comprehend and know when to use the various international market entry forms;
- explain the difference between equity and nonequity joint ventures;
- appreciate the managerial implications of the international market entry forms;
- know why the international market entry form tends to be an evolutionary process; and
- understand and explain various trade restrictions the international marketer may encounter.

MARKET ENTRY MOTIVATION

Why nations trade was examined in Chapter 4. However, those reasons do not explain the motivation for an individual manager to seek international involvement for the

Exhibit 5.1

A Partial List of Reasons for Entering International Markets

- Acquire factors of production
- Be close to new technology and trends in customer desires
- Build market share
- Create a foreign market for components
- Increase profits
- Increase the firm's size
- Keep foreign sellers from gaining a competitive advantage
- Keep up with competitors
- Locate near a source of supply
- Maintain the firm's image
- Obtain a foothold in foreign markets for the future
- Protect the firm's profit-making opportunities and capabilities
- Reduce overhead
- Replace lost domestic sales
- Respond to a request for the firm's products from foreign sources
- Respond to competition from foreigners in the domestic market
- Become more international in scope
- Have business become more diversified
- Utilize lower costs in manufacturing
- Utilize old machinery

firm. What is the impetus for involving the firm in international marketing? Why should management consider marketing abroad? Many reasons motivate the decision. The specific incentive may depend on the firm's situation and management's unique circumstances. A few of the reasons managers may seek international involvement are listed in Exhibit 5.1.

The specific reasons are essentially unlimited and determined by the situations managers confront. However, a close examination of the reasons listed in Exhibit 5.1 will lead to the conclusion that the profit incentive is the underlying reason and the basis upon which all other reasons depend. Regardless of the reason management gives, that reason is ultimately profit motivated. Entry into an international market will never occur only for philanthropic reasons or because it seems like a nice thing to do. The decision must be profit oriented from one of two perspectives:

- profit improvement
- profit retention

Profit improvement occurs when management is drawn into the foreign market because of the inviting opportunities perceived to exist there. A need is recognized in the foreign market that is not currently being satisfied or that management believes the firm's offering can satisfy better than the offerings presently available. In this case, management is enticed into the foreign market because of its perceived ability to increase the firm's sales and profits. Profit improvement is an offensive reason for entrance. For example, Commercial Sheering, Inc. (name changed to Commercial Intertech Corporation in 1994; acquired by Parker Hannifin Corporation in 2000), a

U.S. firm, entered the European market with a pneumatic pump because management observed that users were unhappy with the quality of available pumps. Management believed users would prefer Commercial Sheering's higher-quality, more reliable pump despite a slightly higher price. Thus, Commercial Sheering's management was pulled into the European market because of the perceived opportunity to increase sales and improve profits.

Conversely, profit retention occurs when management is pushed into the foreign market because of the lack of domestic business. Management is forced to look for foreign markets to absorb the slack in the domestic market. In this case, failure to move into the foreign market means production cuts, employee layoffs, and reductions in sales and profits. Management's motivation is the need to sustain profits, which is a defensive reason for entrance. For example, U.S. cigarette makers are experiencing declining domestic sales as the number of smokers declines. Sales hit a fifty-five-year low in 2005, falling more than 21 percent in the previous eight years, while population more than doubled during the same time.[3] Management has been forced to find foreign markets to sustain the company's business. Growing demand exists for cigarettes in places like China and Eastern European and third world countries, which more than replaces the loss in domestic business.[4] Thus, the management of these cigarette makers was pushed into the international market because of the lack of domestic sales and the need to retain profits. Whether the stated reason for entering international marketing is for profit improvement or profit retention, the underlying motivation for any decision is always profit oriented.

MANAGEMENT ORIENTATION

The profit motivation and specific reasons managers have for becoming involved in international marketing do not tell us why the management in some firms experiencing favorable stimuli to market abroad become involved while others experiencing the same favorable stimuli do not. If the profit incentive was the entire answer, every company that could market internationally would. Statistics indicate that although two-thirds of the world's purchasing power is outside the United States, only one-fourth of U.S. companies that have the capacity to export actually do so. And those firms, on average, meet only one-fourth of their overseas trade potential.[5] Obviously, something besides profit affects the decision. What is this driving force? When managers in two comparable firms face equal opportunities in a foreign market, why would one manager involve the firm and the other manager not? The answer is the attitude of management.

The management of all firms engaged internationally have a strong interest in and commitment to international marketing. At least one manager in the firm must possess a strong desire and resolve for international marketing and act as the driving force. The management of firms that are not involved do not show that same high interest or commitment. In particular, managers who become involved in international marketing have higher profit and lower risk perceptions of the market opportunity than those managers who do not become involved.

Attitudes influence the propensity of management even to consider the international

Exhibit 5.2

A Partial List of Reasons for Unfavorable Attitudes toward Entering International Markets

- A fear exists that control will be lost
- Apathy exists
- Documentation and paperwork are considered too laborious
- Expectations are unfavorable
- Export sales are considered marginal business
- Information about the foreign market is inadequate
- Barriers or obstacles are thought to exist
- Presumption of inability to compete in the foreign market
- Cost considered excessive
- Firm deemed to lack qualified personnel
- Small size of firm believed to be a detriment

Exhibit 5.3

A Partial List of Characteristics of Managers with Favorable Attitudes toward Entering International Markets

- Favor an aggressive and competitive marketing strategy
- Had favorable international exposure
- Have a belief that the firm has a competitive advantage in the foreign market
- Have a belief that the firm possesses high-quality management
- Have a high propensity for risk taking

option. Management will not investigate foreign opportunities unless the perceived benefits are greater than the costs of involvement. Attitudes may be unfavorable for a variety of reasons. Exhibit 5.2 lists some of these reasons.

On the other hand, favorable attitudes are more likely to exist among managers who possess certain characteristics. Some of these characteristics are listed in Exhibit 5.3. In general, the more international experiences managers have had, the more likely their attitudes will be favorable. International experiences can include a variety of activities such as international travel, studying a foreign language, collecting stamps, and corresponding with someone from a foreign country. If their attitude is unfavorable, for whatever reason, consideration of international opportunities will be forgone, even if great opportunities exist. Therefore, the cultivation of favorable attitudes should be a high priority in training and management education programs. The inability to expand internationally is usually due to a lack of international education among employees.[6]

THE MARKET ENTRY DECISION

The decision to engage in international marketing is not impulsive. Some stimulus is generally encountered that is associated with either pushing or pulling management into considering international involvement. Management possessing a favorable attitude will investigate the feasibility of the opportunity when this stimulus is encountered. Assuming the opportunity is favorable and a decision is made to engage

Exhibit 5.4

A Partial List of Factors Affecting International Market Entry Form

- Control desired over international sales
- Flexibility needed to change to another entry form
- Foreign competition
- Investment payback period
- Investment requirements
- Long-term profit objectives
- Market feedback required
- Nature of the firm's products
- Number of markets to be covered
- Operating costs of entry form
- Organizational goals regarding the extent of international involvement
- Penetration desired within markets covered
- Personnel requirements
- Profit potential of entry form
- Risk factors
- Size of foreign sales volume potential
- Size of the firm in sales and assets
- Speed of market entry desired

in international marketing, management must select the most appropriate way to enter the foreign market. The decision will be influenced primarily by the degree of commitment management wants to make to international marketing, the nature of the opportunity, and the extent of the firm's resources that can be allocated. A number of considerations can affect the form-of-market-entry decision. Some of these factors are shown in Exhibit 5.4. Management's assessment of the factors considered important to the entry-form decision will ultimately influence the specific way the foreign market will be entered.

Basically, two different approaches to producing products for international markets are available, depending upon where the product is produced:

- The product can be produced domestically and shipped to the foreign market.
- The product can be produced in the foreign market.

The first approach is known as **exporting** and can be undertaken separately or in conjunction with the second approach. When exporting is involved with production of a product in a foreign market, the purpose is usually to supply a raw material, component, or part that is utilized in the manufacturing process.

The second approach, producing the product in a foreign country, can be subdivided into two basic alternatives:

- The international venture can be wholly owned.
- The ownership or involvement in the venture can be shared in some way with other participants.

A **wholly owned** international venture takes the form of a 100 percent owned subsidiary or branch of the domestic firm that is located in a foreign country. The foreign operation is an extension of the domestic company even though the foreign entity may operate independently and be separate from the parent. This kind of arrangement is usually referred to as a **foreign direct investment (FDI)** because the investment is made outside the domestic firm's country. Occasionally the terms direct foreign investment (DFI) or direct ownership are used instead of FDI.

If ownership is to be shared, a variety of partnership arrangements broadly referred to as joint ventures can be developed. A **joint venture** is any business association that involves the collaboration of its participants over an extended period. All joint ventures may be divided into two categories:

- equity joint venture
- nonequity joint venture

An **equity joint venture** is also called a **joint ownership, joint venture** and occurs when the owners of a domestic firm enter into a direct investment arrangement in a foreign country with one or more foreign partners. The owners of the domestic firm may buy an interest in an existing business or share in the formation of a new operation. All parties contribute equity (money) to the venture and share in the ownership and control. An equity joint venture requires a well-written contract that elucidates the requirements and operating procedures for each party involved. Of concern to the partners are the responsibilities expected of each member. At issue, for example, are quandaries about how much of the profits should be retained in the business and how much should be distributed to the partners; how expenditures should be distributed among business activities like advertising, new product development, and shipping; and who should guide long-range strategy decisions. Without a contract listing these and other business concerns, conflict can develop among the partners when control disagreements occur. Control concerns are obviously linked to the amount of ownership of each partner. If one partner has majority ownership, that partner can make decisions even if the other partners vote together. If no partner has majority ownership, then positioning can occur among the partners for control and to the detriment of the other partners. Therefore, a written contract outlining the expectations and responsibilities of each partner is essential to the well-being of minority partners.

A **nonequity joint venture** is a partnership arrangement involving the sharing of anything other than money and ownership. The following are examples of nonequity joint ventures:

- **Construction and job performance contracts** are arrangements in which a domestic firm builds a physical plant and facilities for a foreign firm. If a complete factory is built, workers are trained to operate it, and control of the whole operation is eventually given to the foreign firm, the procedure is called a **turn-key operation**.
- **Contract manufacturing** is an agreement with a foreign firm to transfer production expertise so a product can be produced for the domestic firm. The domestic firm retains all marketing responsibilities.
- A **franchise** is an agreement in which the management of a domestic firm gives

a foreign firm permission to market a product or service according to the rules and procedures prescribed by the domestic management.

- **Licensing** is a contractual arrangement whereby the management of a domestic firm transfers production and marketing rights for a product to a foreign firm in return for royalties on each unit produced.
- A **management contract** is an arrangement whereby the management of a domestic firm supplies management expertise to a foreign firm. The foreign firm supplies the equipment and manufactures the product while the domestic management supervises production, marketing, and other business functions.
- A **rental agreement** results when the management of a domestic firm provides equipment and maintenance to a foreign firm to equip its factory in exchange for rental or lease payments.
- A **technical services contract** is an arrangement in which technical expertise and process knowledge are provided to a foreign firm to make high-tech equipment operational.

MARKET ENTRY ALTERNATIVES

Thus, depending upon where the product is produced, three basic alternative forms of market entry are available to the international marketer:

- exporting
- joint venture
- foreign direct investment

That is, the marketer can ship the product to the foreign market (exporting), cooperate with a foreign partner (joint venture), or use a wholly owned international presence (foreign direct investment). Which of the three alternatives should management select? The three market entry options can be viewed as a continuum with forms of exporting at one extreme and forms of foreign direct investment at the other. Forms of joint ventures are intermediate. This continuum is shown in Exhibit 5.6.

As Exhibit 5.6 indicates, forms of exporting require the least investment, personnel, and commitment and are therefore the simplest and least risky entry methods. Exporting can be a one-time activity if desired, and if problems arise, management minimizes the potential loss. For these reasons, most managers begin their international involvement via exporting (see chapter 11 for a discussion of the evolutionary process of the international marketing channel). As you move to the right on the continuum, the investment, personnel needs, and commitment increase, and therefore, forms of joint ventures are generally more complex and risky than forms of exporting. This means management stands to incur a greater loss if it enters the foreign market with a joint venture than if it enters the market via exporting, should problems arise. The same rationale applies to FDI. An FDI is more risky than a joint venture because the investment is greater. An evolution in the market entry method occurs.[7]

As management gains experience and becomes more committed to international marketing, a tendency exists to move from exporting to joint ventures and ultimately

Exhibit 5.5 **Logodaj Winery Bulgarian Wine**

Wine made in Bulgaria and offered for sale in another country is exporting.

to an FDI. This evolution occurs because of the profit incentive. Joint ventures are potentially more profitable than exports, and an FDI is potentially more profitable than a joint venture. Therefore, if the firm's size and financial situation permit, as time passes and international marketing experience increases, it is natural for management to seek a deeper involvement in foreign markets, because of the potential for improved profits.

The evolution process does not preclude management from following a long-term exporting strategy with no intent to move to more involved entry methods. Nor does it prevent management from entering different markets with different market entry forms or entering one market with more than one market entry form. Thus, management may find it needs to serve one target group with exports and another target group through a licensing arrangement in a particular country. Management may be precluded from exporting to some countries because of trade barriers such as high tariffs that cause the product to be noncompetitive on price. In other cases, such as in Japan, law precludes FDIs. Also, some overlap can occur in the characteristics of the market entry methods that may interfere with the evolutionary process. For example,

Exhibit 5.6 **International Market Entry Continuum**

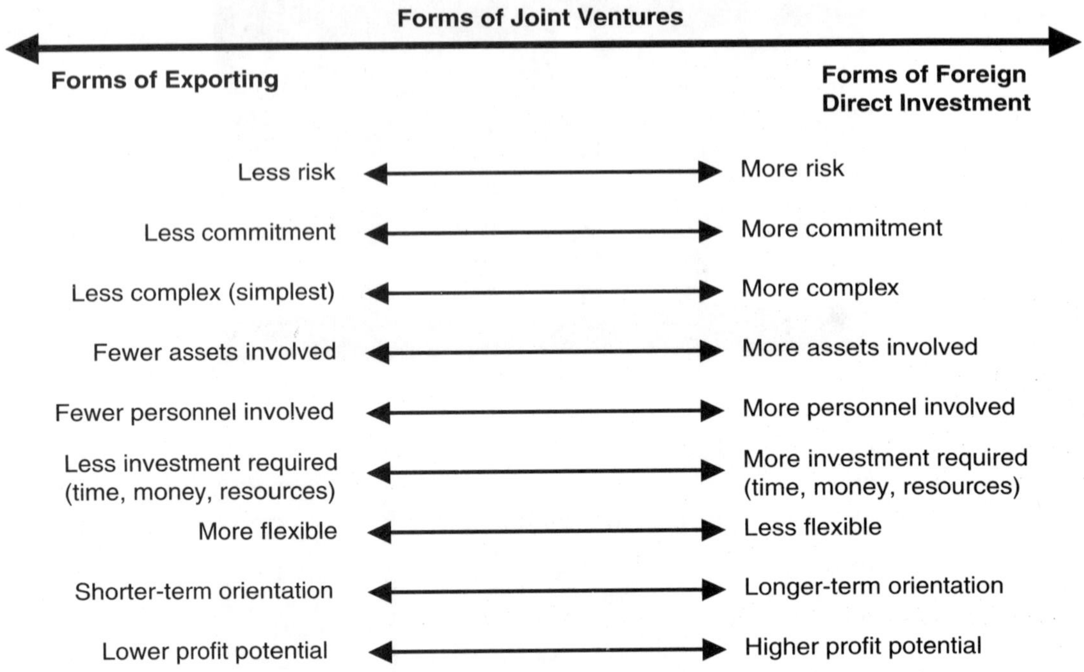

some forms of exporting (direct methods that will be discussed in chapter 11) can involve greater risk than some simple forms of joint ventures.

Because risk perceptions are involved in the foreign market entry form decision, management will take a variety of risk factors into consideration when making the market entry decision and any evolutionary change decisions. To minimize the perceived risk, management may seek to have greater control of the factors involved in the entry process or shift the risk to another involved entity. Three issues influence the degree of control management desires:[8]

- cultural differences
- management's desire for control based on prior experience
- the structure of the industry

The specific risk factors that influence the market entry decision are anything that affects the ability to enter a market, distribute products or services, and increase or maintain market share. These can include the following:[9]

- competitive rivalry risk
- customer taste risk
- market demand risk
- marketing infrastructure risk

- operating risk
- ownership risk
- political risk
- transfer risk (restrictions on the movement of products into or out of a country)

Managers tend to prefer high-control forms of market entry when risk perceptions are low and low-control forms of entry when risk perceptions are high.[10]

TRADE RESTRICTIONS

Trade barriers can interfere with the ability to enter a foreign market by means of exporting. **Export barriers** are any restrictions that will limit exporting or make it impossible. The nation from which exports originate or the nation to which exports are directed can impose trade barriers. The exporter's home nation may impose trade restrictions to prevent sensitive or strategic products from falling into the wrong hands. Thus, the U.S. government may restrict the export of products with military potential such as supercomputers and nuclear materials. The importing nation may impose trade barriers for the following reasons: to raise revenue, protect local infant industries, retain scarce foreign exchange, and political considerations. Thus, the import of microcomputers into Brazil was prohibited to protect the nation's fledgling computer industry from competition and to stimulate domestic production. And, in the United States, the import of Cuban cigars is prohibited because of the strained relations that exist between the two countries. Trade barriers can be classified into two categories:

- tariff barriers
- nontariff barriers

TARIFF BARRIERS

A **tariff** is a duty levied on exported or imported merchandise. It is a type of tax or fee that is charged for the privilege of exporting or importing the product. Three types of tariffs may be encountered:

- A **specific tariff** is a fee assessed at a flat rate per physical unit. The fee remains the same regardless of the value of the product. For example, $500 is charged per car regardless of whether it is a luxury or a compact car. Another example is $150 per ton of apples regardless of grade.
- An **ad valorem tariff** is a fee assessed as a percentage of the value of the product. Similar products that differ only in features or amenities will each receive a different fee based on the product's price—for example, 12 percent of the price of the product. In this case, a larger fee will be paid for the luxury car than for the compact car. Upon what value of the product should the tariff be assessed? This can vary depending on the country and is usually based on a shipping term used to determine the product's price, such as CIF or FOB (shipping terms will be discussed in chapter 14).

- A **combination tariff** is a fee that combines a specific and an ad valorem tariff. The item is assessed a rate per unit, and a percentage of its value is added to determine the total fee—for example, $200 per car plus 5 percent of the wholesale price of the car.

NONTARIFF BARRIERS

A **nontariff barrier**, also known as an **invisible tariff**, is any nonfinancial impediment or restriction on exported or imported merchandise. Nontariff barriers can be just as restrictive, if not more so, than tariff barriers. Five of the more commonly encountered types of nontariff barriers are the following:

- **Administrative and legal barriers** consist of a host of impediments intended to slow down importing the product or make it difficult or impossible. For example, customs officials keep losing import forms or shuffling them from one wrong office to another. The granting of licenses required to import certain products can be limited in number or selectively issued.[11] The product may be impounded or require excessive customs inspections and fees. Safety questions and health issues may be raised as a means of delaying or restricting import. Often these barriers are more frustrating than restrictive and may stem from unethical customs officials who are seeking payoffs or gifts as incentives to facilitate the transaction. The need to pay small sums of money or give gifts to low-ranking officials for lubrication purposes (to expedite) is lawful and common practice in many countries, particularly in the Middle East.
- A **boycott** is the refusal of a nation's citizens or government to purchase a product. No restrictions are placed on the import of a product; however, people prefer, for whatever reason, to avoid the product. For example, people may unwittingly boycott foreign-made products because of an inherent preference for domestically made products or because of fears about the safety of the product. A worldwide boycott of Nestlé products began in 1977 for unethical marketing practices involving its infant formula in less-developed countries. The boycott was suspended in 1984 and resumed in 1988. It continues today in some eighteen countries around the world under the coordination of Baby Milk Action, an organization affiliated with the International Baby Food Action Network (IBFAN).[12] This boycott has had an undesirable impact on Nestlé's image, reputation, and profits.
- An **embargo** forbids or prohibits any imports. Embargoes are often imposed to protect infant industry. The rationale is that if foreign competition is eliminated, the fledgling local industry stands a better chance to get established. The problem with this thinking is that without competition the fledgling industry may become inefficient, penalizing consumers with higher prices and/or lower quality. And, once in place, the embargo tends to be retained because the fledgling industry develops a financial reliance on it.
- **Exchange barriers** are restrictions that adversely affect foreign exchange transactions. Government manipulation of exchange rates makes currency conversions unprofitable. As a result, repatriating money and profits is affected detrimentally. A discussion of exchange restrictions is located in chapter 9.

- A **quota** places a limit on the amount of a product that can be imported or exported. The limit can be in physical units or monetary value and may be applied to a product category, industry, or nation. For example, the number of imported vehicles may be restricted to 100,000 per year. A quota can be an absolute limit or used in conjunction with a tariff, as, for example, if the first 10,000 cars can enter duty free, the next 90,000 are assessed an ad valorem tariff of 15 percent, and total imports are restricted to 100,000.

The General Agreement on Tariffs and Trade (GATT; 1947–95) was responsible for the significant lowering of world trade barriers. Representatives from the member nations of the GATT met periodically to negotiate mutually agreeable reductions to trade barriers. Initial successes were with tariff barriers; however, ultimately nontariff barriers were improved as well. An international organization called the World Trade Organization (WTO) replaced GATT in 1995 and is currently composed of 153 member countries, 30 observer countries, and 2 countries awaiting membership acceptance.[13] The WTO continues in the spirit of GATT by negotiating requisites for freer trade, not only in products but also in services and intellectual property. Thanks in part to the GATT and the WTO, the freest trading environment ever exists today.

CHAPTER SUMMARY

Managers have many reasons for deciding to market abroad. Underlying all of these reasons, however, is the profit incentive. The decision is ultimately driven by the desire to improve profits or the need to retain profits. Managers are either enticed by inviting foreign opportunities or forced by declining domestic demand.

A manager's attitude will influence the decision to enter or not enter a foreign market. Even though profit-driven, international marketing opportunities will be forgone if the manager perceives that the risks outweigh the potential returns. That is, even if entering the foreign market would be exceedingly lucrative, the manager will not even investigate the opportunity if an unfavorable attitude is held, because the perception of risk will be too great. Attitudes can be improved by exposure to international experiences and appropriate training and education.

Once the decision is made to enter an international market, the appropriate entry method must be selected. The three basic alternatives are exporting, joint ventures, and foreign direct investment. The method selected will depend on a variety of considerations influenced by the degree of marketing involvement and commitment management wants to make in the foreign market. Involvement in the foreign market tends to be an evolutionary process. Exporting is normally the first entry method management will employ since it is the least risky. As international marketing experience is gained and involvement and commitment increase, managers tend to move to forms of joint ventures and eventually to forms of foreign direct investment. The potential for increased profits along with lower risk perceptions resulting from increasing experience in international marketing contribute to this evolution. In the end, however, management may seek to minimize the perceived risk by exercising greater control over the factors involved in the entry process or by shifting the risk to another involved entity.

Trade restriction can interfere with management's desire to enter a foreign market via exporting. The export impediments managers may encounter are either tariff barriers or nontariff barriers. The World Trade Organization is an international organization that works to reduce trade barriers and create a freer world-trading environment.

Key Terms

Ad valorem tariff
Administrative and legal barriers
Boycott
Combination tariff
Construction and job performance contracts
Contract manufacturing
Embargo
Equity joint venture
Exchange barriers
Export barriers
Exporting
Foreign Direct Investment (FDI)
Franchise
Invisible tariff
Joint ownership, joint venture
Joint venture
Licensing
Management contract
Nonequity joint venture
Nontariff barrier
Quota
Rental agreement
Specific tariff
Tariff
Technical services contract
Turn-key operation
Wholly owned

Review Questions

1. Why do managers involve their firms in international markets?
2. Explain how the profit incentive influences the decision to enter international markets.
3. How does a manager's attitude affect the perceived risk of entering international markets?
4. How does the location where the product is produced enter into the market entry decision?
5. List and explain the three basic market entry methods.
6. What is the difference between an equity and nonequity joint venture?
7. Why does the market entry method tend to be an evolutionary process?
8. Why do most managers begin their international marketing by exporting?
9. Differentiate between tariff and nontariff trade barriers.
10. Explain how the manager can market the firm's product in a country that has imposed an embargo on the importation of that product.

Notes

1. The Freedonia Group, "World Beer Containers Market to 2005," May 2001, http://www.the-infoshop.com/study/fd7498_beer_container.html. Also available at http://www.freedoniagroup.com/World-Beer-Containers.html.

2. "Five Reasons Beer Sales Have Slumped," BBC News, November 20, 2007, http://news.bbc.co.uk/1/hi/magazine/7103268.stm.

3. Melissa McNamara, "U.S. Cigarette Sales Hit 55-Year Low," CBS News, March 9, 2006, http://www.cbsnews.com/stories/2006/03/09/business/main1384910.shtml.

4. Myron Levin, "Cigarette Makers Go Overseas to Ignite Sales: Foreign Markets Worth Billions," *Chicago Sun-Times*, November 20, 1994, http://www.highbeam.com/doc/1P2-4258421.html.

5. "Task Force Dominican Republic—Florida," Global Foundation for Democracy and Development, 2008, http://www.globalfoundationdd.org/gfdd/cpo_florida.asp.

6. Linda Gorchels, Thani Jambulingam, and Timothy W. Aurand, "International Marketing Managers: A Comparison of Japanese, German, and U.S. Perceptions," *Journal of International Marketing* 7 (1) (1999): 97–106.

7. Jan Johanson and Jan-Erick Vahlne, "The Internationalization Process of the Firm—A Model of Knowledge Development and Increasing Foreign Market Commitments," *Journal of International Business Studies* 8 (1) (Spring–Summer 1977): 23–32.

8. Zafar U. Ahmed, Osman Mohamad, Brian Tan, and James P. Johnson, "International Risk Perceptions and Mode of Entry: A Case Study of Malaysian Multinational Firms," *Journal of Business Research* 55 (10) (October 2002): 805–13.

9. Keith D. Brouthers, "The Influence of International Risk on Entry Mode Strategy in the Computer Software Industry," *Management International Review* 35 (1) (January 1995): 7–28.

10. Ahmed, Mohamad, Tan, and Johnson, "International Risk Perceptions and Mode of Entry."

11. Earl Naumann and Douglas J. Lincoln, "Non-Tariff Barriers and Entry Strategy Alternatives: Strategic Marketing Implications," *Journal of Small Business Management* 29 (April 1991): 60–70.

12. Baby Milk Action at http://www.babymilkaction.org.

13. World Trade Organization, "WTO Members and Accession Candidates," July 23, 2008, http://www.wto.org/english/thewto_e/acc_e/members_brief_e.doc.

6 Researching Foreign Markets

The French-based multinational Groupe Danone is a leader in three market sectors—fresh dairy products, beverages, and biscuits and cereal products—with brands such as Danone, Evian, Wahaha, Volvic, and Lu. With a presence in more than 120 countries, Groupe Danone is ranked number one worldwide in the sales of fresh dairy products and bottled water and number two in biscuits and cereal products.

The company's marketing research has consistently indicated an interest on the part of consumers for healthier and more nutritious foods. In the area of fresh dairy products, an interest in the future of probiotics was kindled by these findings. Probiotics are foods containing potentially beneficial bacteria and yeasts. Probiotics are the subject of ongoing research because the degree of the suggested benefits has yet to be completely decided by the scientific community. However, interest in probiotics is growing, and sales are expected to increase significantly in the future. Undoubtedly, Mr. Franck Riboud, chairman and CEO, would like Groupe Danone to be the leader in products containing bacilli believed to enhance health.

However, avoiding the mistakes the company made in the 1970s when entering the Japanese yogurt market is imperative. Because of faulty marketing research, management drew incorrect conclusions about market potential. To be polite, Japanese consumers, when interviewed, would say the yogurt tasted good even if it was disliked. Furthermore, the Japanese failed to distinguish the difference between Western health food and junk food. As a result of the flawed marketing research, management believed the growth potential for the yogurt market was high. Unfortunately, actual sales fell well short of the most conservative estimates. Research would need to be planned more carefully so such problems did not occur again.

Thanks to the Japanese probiotics pioneer Yakult Honsha Ltd., Japanese consumers are among those most interested in probiotic products. Yakult produces a fermented milk drink containing bacteria that are not killed by stomach acid and are considered beneficial for digestion. Groupe Danone researched the market, bought 5 percent of the Yakult's stock in 2000, and in 2003 increased its ownership to 20 percent.

Because of the fast-growing population and 7 percent economic growth in India in 2004, Groupe Danone and Yakult formed a joint venture to develop the Indian market for probiotics. The company, Yakult Danone India Private Ltd., is held equally by the two firms and is expected to become India's leading producer of probiotics. The joint venture began marketing Yakult-brand products in January 2006. Danone products are expected to be added to the product line in the future. Undoubtedly, the marketing research was done carefully because of the large investment Danone has made already.

Sources: Based in part on information from Danone, "Group Danone and Yakult Honsha Set Up Joint Venture in India," press release, April 26, 2005, http://phx.corporate-ir.net/phoenix.zhtml?c=95168&p=irol-newsArticle&ID=991495&highlight=; Danone, "Group Danone and Yakult Honsha Enter Into a Strategic Alliance," press release, March 4, 2004, http://phx.corporate-ir.net/phoenix.zhtml?c=95168&p=irol-newsArticle&ID=991460&highlight=; "Group Danone 2004 Final Audited Results," press release, February 11, 2005, http://finance.danone.com/phoenix.zhtml?c=95168&p=irol-newsArticle&ID=991473&highlight=; Reuters, "Japanese Dairy Now in India via French Danone," *The Financial Express,* April 26, 2005, http://www.financialexpress.com/latest_full_story.php?content_id=89061.

CHAPTER OBJECTIVES

After reading this chapter, you should

- understand the role marketing research plays in the foreign market entry analysis;
- know the steps involved in conducting the foreign market entry analysis;
- be able to explain how to research the foreign market entry process;
- recognize and avoid the problems inherent in using secondary data for international marketing research;
- recognize and avoid the problems inherent in using primary data for international marketing research;
- understand the use of ongoing research for improving international marketing strategy; and
- comprehend the international market entry process and the most commonly made entry analysis mistakes.

THE RESEARCH PROCESS

Research involves the collection and analysis of data and information that is useful for management to help reduce the risks involved in the decision-making process. Research should be undertaken internationally for the same reasons it is done domestically and should utilize the same techniques. Therefore, the international research process must be structured after the firm's domestic research procedures and will generate data from these two sources:

Exhibit 6.1 **The Research Process**

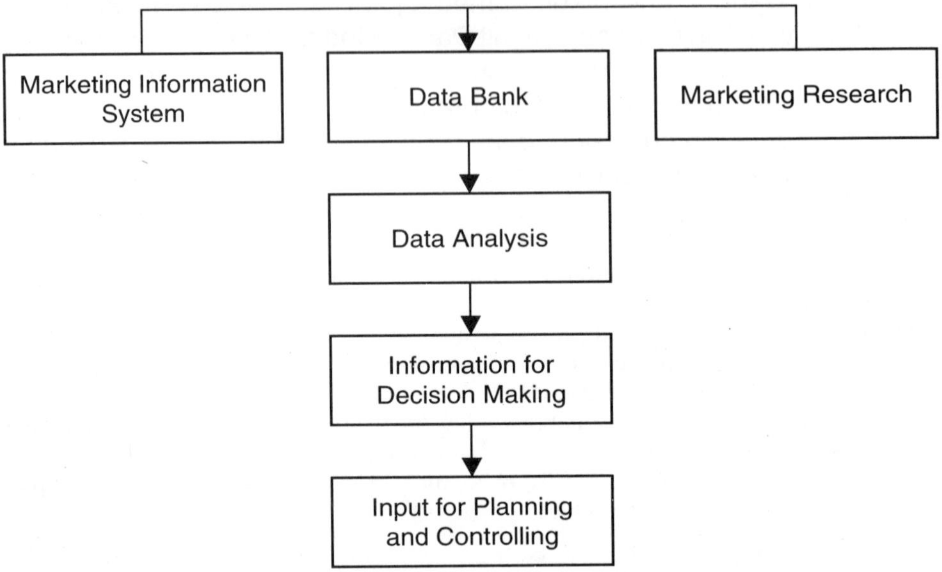

- The **Marketing Information System (MIS)** is a continuous data collection activity. Periodically (daily, weekly, and monthly) available information that is routinely gathered from internal and external sources comprises the firm's MIS. These data are generated from sales, accounting, production, other company sources, and domestic and foreign competitors, suppliers, intermediaries, and customers. Information from the firm's MIS is made available to management at regular intervals in standardized report formats. These data provide the international marketing manager with insight into routine marketing issues and problems that are of concern to the development of an effective marketing strategy.
- **Marketing research** is the one-time collection of information that is not available from the MIS and is generated for the purpose of solving specific marketing problems. Marketing research projects are initiated only when a particular need is identified that requires special attention beyond the MIS data alone.

Information from both the MIS and marketing research are stored in a data bank. Appropriate data can then be selected from the data bank and subjected to analysis as needed. The results of the analysis provide information pertinent to management's decision-making process and can be used for planning and controlling international marketing efforts. The research process is represented in Exhibit 6.1.

The international research effort, like its domestic counterpart, consists of two facets:

- market entry analysis
- ongoing research of existing markets, products, customers, and related concerns

Exhibit 6.2 **International Research**

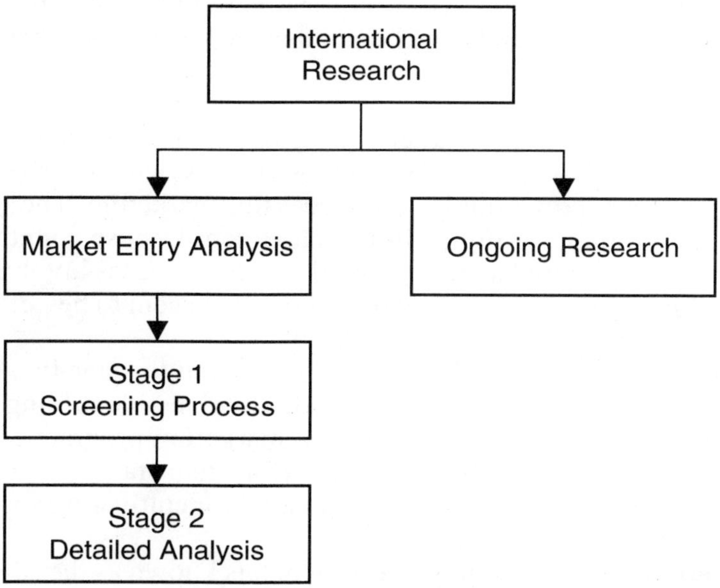

Market entry analysis is concerned with the investigation of foreign countries for the purpose of identifying appropriate expansion markets. Ongoing research includes the gamut of statistical analyses and assessments management utilizes to track and better understand marketing operations. Ongoing research helps management adjust to changes in the marketing environment and develop a more effective marketing strategy. The two aspects of international research are shown in Exhibit 6.2.

FOREIGN MARKET ENTRY ANALYSIS

Once management has made the decision to engage in international marketing, an analysis of potential foreign markets (market entry analysis) is made to determine opportunities presented. Personal and government information is used as a basis for making this decision more often than information from documented sources.[1] Surprisingly, many managers do not use a formal process when entering international markets.[2] Blunders have been made because of the failure to properly evaluate the foreign market. For example, the management of a U.S. tobacco company entered into a joint venture to sell filter cigarettes in Asia without doing research. Sales were so dismal that the cigarette was withdrawn from the market. Had research been conducted, management would have learned that smokers were unwilling to switch from unfiltered cigarettes because their attitudes toward health and smoking were different from those of U.S. smokers. The chances of contracting lung cancer were not a concern.

Improper research can be just as devastating as the failure to do research. For example, the management at McDonald's Corporation used a traffic count as one piece of information to help identify locations for new restaurants. A high pedestrian count contributed to the location selection for a new restaurant built in Hamburg, Germany. When sales were found to be poor, management learned that the restaurant was located down the street from a red-light district; passersby had no interest in eating hamburgers there.[3]

As shown in Exhibit 6.2, the market entry assessment is generally viewed as a two-stage process. The first stage is a screening process, which is used to identify a group of countries that show promise for successful marketing. The objective is to eliminate, with a minimum of time, effort, and expense, those countries that show little or inappropriate potential as foreign markets. The process involves a screening of possible candidate countries to select only those that seem to be potentially profitable and present no apparent obstacles to entry.

Countries that survive the initial screening are moved to stage two and subjected to a detailed market analysis. The second stage involves identifying the preferred country or countries and the development of a marketing program and entry strategy. This process requires considerably more effort than stage 1 and is intended to identify the countries that offer the greatest potential for cultivating appropriate entry procedures.

Most managers use this two-step process, which is known as the rifle approach, to decide which markets to enter. The idea is to fire once, identifying the best country to enter, and concentrate efforts there, like aiming a rifle to hit the bull's-eye. Some managers prefer to use a shotgun approach to make the decision. Like the broad shot pattern from a shotgun, managers will enter several markets with minimal involvement. As the most promising markets are determined, efforts are increased there while the firm's presence is withdrawn from the other, less attractive, countries. The rifle approach may be more popular because the shotgun approach is perceived to waste resources in the less-promising countries, and resources are spread so thin among many countries that successful entry is more difficult. Also, leaving a market quickly could damage the firm's reputation with customers, suppliers, and residents. Although the rifle approach permits management to focus its attention on one market, enhancing the chances of successful entry, the risk always exists that the best market gets overlooked.

Screening Process

In stage 1, the screening process, the manager should research those factors that will differentiate between the promising and unpromising countries. Obviously, because of the large number of countries, only those of interest should be examined. The number of these countries can still be quite large. Therefore, this procedure should permit a quick and inexpensive yet efficient separation. We want to be able to divide the countries into two groups, those to be discarded and a small number to be examined in more detail in stage 2. The factors that facilitate this process may vary depending on the product and management's needs, but at least the following should be included (the order in which these factors are evaluated can vary depending on management's preference):

1. Determine the need served by the product. Remember that people buy products for the benefits they provide or the problems they solve. The need people have for the product in the foreign country may not be the same as people have in the domestic country. For example, a manufacturer of women's sanitary napkins found demand in an African country to be much larger than expected. Sales were higher because miners were using the napkins as face masks to filter coal dust, a use management did not anticipate.
2. Analyze the international marketing environment and eliminate countries with unfavorable conditions. Consider these and other differences that may interfere with the ability to enter the country profitably: politics and laws, culture and society, competitors, technology, and the economy.
3. Identify trading barriers and eliminate unfavorable countries. Inquire at the consulate of the country or the U.S. Department of Commerce.
4. Identify the enterprise's competition. How are the needs being met and which firms are suppliers of the product? Talking to people from the candidate country visiting or living in the firm's domestic country can be a source of information for need identification and competition identification.
5. Estimate market potential. Use complementary indicators derived from secondary data when possible for this assessment. For example, the number of replacement tires might be estimated from the number of vehicles owned, amount of gasoline consumed, and number of miles of highway. Record the population and average income to assist the assessment.
6. Estimate sales potential. What share of the market is realistic? A check of the U.S. Department of Commerce Export Schedule B will indicate how much is exported to the country by U.S. firms. The share supplied by U.S. firms can be estimated.
7. Eliminate countries not meeting minimum sales and profit requirements.
8. Rank order the remaining countries by potential.
9. Determine geographical clusters that would favor regional expansion. A market with less potential may be preferable if it is near, because expansion into a neighboring country may be easier than into a distant or dissimilar country. Because of commonalities in business practice, economic integration of nations (see chapter 8) can also facilitate expansion.
10. Select the countries to be included in a detailed analysis in stage 2. Since considerable time and cost are involved in completing a detailed analysis, the number of countries selected should be limited.

DETAILED ANALYSIS

A risk always exists that a good market may be overlooked and a weak market may survive the screening process. If care is exercised in stage 1, this risk can be minimized. The detailed analysis is much more involved and more costly; it can involve sophisticated statistical analyses as well as trips to the foreign country. The objective at this stage is to determine which of the countries surviving the screening process are the most promising; then, develop a market entry strategy. The following are the factors to be considered:

1. Specify the marketing objectives for the country. Management has to identify goals that can be used to assess the success of the international marketing effort.
2. Prepare a detailed market analysis. Market conditions and business opportunities are assessed. Although this might be done entirely with secondary data, a need to generate primary data may occur. A thorough analysis will include the following:
   a. Assess the marketing environment presently existing and anticipated in the future.
   b. Analyze competition. Examine business conditions in the industry, including the state of technology, distribution, promotion, and pricing policy. What competitive advantages, if any, does the firm possess?
   c. Examine the nature, size, and purchasing ability of the market. Evaluate cultural and social influences. Understand consumers' lifestyles, shopping habits, and purchasing propensity. Specify target segments to be cultivated and served.
   d. Estimate sales. Determine sales potential and expected future market growth.
3. Identify the market entry method (see Chapter 5).
4. Develop the marketing strategy. Specify the marketing mix and program required for satisfying each segment identified.
5. Estimate resources required. Determine needs such as personnel, financial, materials, equipment, and time.
6. Estimate operating results. Calculate expected revenues, costs, and profits.
7. Select the market or markets to be entered.
8. Implement the marketing plan.

RESEARCH PROBLEMS

The manager or researcher conducting the research must decide whether primary data, secondary data, or both are appropriate. **Primary data** are facts the managers or researchers gather for the first time by their own endeavors. **Secondary data** are facts that have been generated previously by another source. Secondary data can be attained for free or for a fee from the originating source or from repositories such as libraries, trade organizations, governments, chambers of commerce, and Web sites. Secondary data should always be preferred over primary data as long as they are available and suitable for the research study, because secondary data are less expensive and less time consuming to acquire than primary data. However, since someone else collected the data, their correctness must be guaranteed. Consider the following in determining whether the data are unbiased, valid, and reliable:

- Data can be biased if the source selectively collected facts to support or imply a desired conclusion—advocacy research. For example, only consumers known to frequent a particular store are interviewed so that opinions about the store can be reported more favorably.
- Data can be invalid if they do not accurately reflect what they purport to measure. For example, data have been collected in an unbiased manner, but are recorded incorrectly for tabulation, causing numerical errors.
- Data can be unreliable if improper sampling procedures were used. For example, people are randomly selected from the telephone directory to be called for an interview. However, if low-income people cannot afford telephones, only the more wealthy people are contacted.

Managers and researchers needs to assure themselves that secondary data were properly generated and are accurate. If confidence can be placed in the secondary data, they may be used, otherwise primary data are indicated. Completing a market entry analysis without some primary data is uncommon. Usually, contacts with potential intermediaries and other channel members require at least one foreign trip. Because of its importance, the market entry analysis is not the place to try to save a few dollars. As the two examples at the beginning of the chapter show, a mistake in the market entry decision could spell disaster.

SECONDARY DATA COLLECTION PROBLEMS

A variety of problems can occur that are of concern when collecting data from secondary sources internationally. These problems make the data less accessible and reliable. Therefore, the manager should be more suspect of secondary data obtained from international sources. The following are some of the problems that may be encountered:

- *Data may not be comparable.* The researcher may have trouble comparing statistics from different sources because of irregular collection. Irregularly collected data means the time period represented varies, and data do not have a common base. For example, data representing twelve months cannot be directly compared with data reported for a nine-months' period.
- *Data may not be complete.* Where data collection is infrequent, there may be periods for which information is unavailable.
- *Data are dated.* Even though the desired data are available, they are sometimes not current enough to be useful. International data are frequently outdated by the time they are published. This is exacerbated by the fact that data are also collected less frequently. Although the published data were accurate when collected, conditions may have changed so much that the true nature of the current environment may no longer be reflected. Thus, if conditions change enough, the data may be useless and in fact project an inaccurate situation.
- *Data may lack detail.* U.S. data are reported with specificity. Information is itemized precisely to the six-digit North American Industry Classification System

(NAICS) codes, for example. Much foreign data lack such specificity, making precise assessments difficult. For example, data on welding equipment may be lumped together and include sales of all kinds of welders, electrodes, and accessories. Thus, specific information on electric welding machines and various categories of electric welders is unavailable. If the aggregated data is used to represent electric welders, the conditions that exist may look more optimistic than they really are.

- *Data are prejudiced.* To project confidence, data available from some countries, particularly less-developed countries, may be adjusted to reflect a more favorable situation than really exists. The sources from which the data are collected may also fabricate or modify the real situation. Data reported to the government may be changed to minimize tax liabilities or to obtain assistance. If the government accumulates these inaccurate statistics and reports them as fact, although designated as official, they are nonetheless inaccurate.
- *Desired data are unavailable.* Most countries, particularly those outside the group of developed nations, do not collect the wealth and variety of statistics provided by the U.S. government. Therefore, the information desired simply does not exist. Organizations such as the United Nations and the Organization for Economic Cooperation and Development (OECD) have helped expand the availability of international data. However, when the desired data cannot be located, primary data collection will be required.

In general, the accuracy and applicability of secondary data from international sources should be more suspect than those of similar data obtained from domestic sources. Determine who collected the data, how they were collected, and for what purpose they were collected. Only after the manager or researcher can be assured that the data are reliable and representative should they be used.

PRIMARY DATA COLLECTION PROBLEMS

Conducting primary research also presents difficulties. These data collection problems, when encountered, can cause the data to be incomplete and inaccurate. Use of these data will provide erroneous conclusions even if the research procedures are appropriate. The following are a few of the problems that may be encountered:

- Differences in language create communications difficulties.
- Lack of knowledge about the population makes probability sampling difficult.
- Respondents may not cooperate.
- Survey techniques may be inappropriate.

Differences in language are an ever-present problem. A questionnaire, which is required for survey research, must be translated into the foreign language before it can be administered. Care must be taken to assure the translated version has the same meaning that the original-language version has. Literal translation and idioms (expressions with no exact translation) in the foreign language can present problems.

Exhibit 6.3 **British and American Vocabulary Compared**

What a British Person Would Say	What an American Would Say
Mental	Gone crazy
Bomb	Expensive or going well
Brolly	Umbrella
Caravan	Travel trailer
Cracking	Stunning
Filch	Steal
Holiday	Vacation
Lift	Elevator
Right knackered	Very tired
Rubber	Pencil eraser
Subway	Underground pedestrian passage
Tube	Subway
Wonky	Shaky or unstable

Even with a careful translation, meanings can be changed. The foreigner must understand the questionnaire in the same way as it is understood in the original language. This problem arises even in the case of English-speaking countries such as Canada, Australia, and Great Britain. The English in these countries can be different than the English in the United States. Exhibit 6.3 lists a few British words and their U.S. equivalents.

In the United States, you would be admonished to "Watch your step" if there were a space between a train and the platform. In Great Britain, the announcement would be to "Mind the gap." In the United States, a person might say, "May I wake you up in the morning?" The British would say, "May I knock you up in the morning?" If differences in meaning can occur within English, imagine how more likely it is that such problems will occur from one language to another.

Two procedures can be used to minimize the chances of translation errors. Translating from the original language to the desired language and then retranslating back into the original language is known as **back translation**. Any differences between the original version and the retranslated version may mean the original translation was faulty. The second procedure is parallel translation. **Parallel translation** occurs when two people translate the same wording from the original language into the desired language. The resulting translated versions are then compared for differences. Observed differences may indicate an understanding or wording problem.

Problems in probability sampling may also arise. Randomness in sampling may be impossible to obtain because of incomplete information about the members of the population. The lack of census tract data and street maps for rural communities in some countries make cluster and area sampling impractical. Inadequate demographic information such as age and income make random sampling impossible. Without a random sample, the people selected may not be representative.

Cultural differences may result in lack of cooperation from some respondents. In

Exhibit 6.4 A **Traveling Vendor in Turkey**

Obtaining accurate data may be difficult when identifying all the roaming vendors is impossible.

some cultures personal information is considered private and will not be discussed with strangers. Getting people to complete a survey may be difficult. Participation may be reduced because people distrust strangers and are suspicious of their intentions. In Muslim societies, wives are not permitted to talk with strangers. A door-to-door personal interview with women would be impossible. Aspects of private lives are never discussed with strangers, making the collection of behavioral and attitudinal information impossible. Also, the pleasant "yes" is often a response in some societies, which really means maybe or even probably not.

Finally, what we consider normal survey procedures can be unacceptable for a variety of reasons. For example, a telephone survey would produce unrepresentative results in Tanzania or Nicaragua because only a small percentage of the population has phones. The wealthy people would be overrepresented, and the less affluent people would be greatly underrepresented. Mail surveys are a problem where mail delivery is slow and unreliable. Convenience sampling is easier to employ for personal interviews; however, such procedures always produce a non-probability sample. A non-probability sample usually results in a sample that is not as representative of the population of interest as a probability sample would be.

Because the U.S. manager may be unfamiliar with aspects of the foreign culture and what constitutes acceptable primary research procedures, seeking local help is advisable. Personnel in a local research firm will be familiar with the culture and know what research techniques are appropriate and can be used successfully. Also, people may be more open and cooperative with a native of the country who speaks the language and is not perceived as an outsider.

ONGOING RESEARCH

Once the foreign market has been entered, management will need to engage in ongoing research similar to the research conducted domestically to continually monitor and assess performance in that market. This ongoing research is necessary to help management determine if market entry objectives are being met and if any adjustments in marketing strategy are needed. The ongoing research process is not immune to the problems encountered internationally from the use of primary and secondary data. Therefore, the manager will need to take these concerns into consideration when formulating and implementing ongoing research projects.

TYPES OF RESEARCH DESIGN

Depending on the degree of problem definition, the manager can utilize one of three types of research design:

- **Exploratory research** is appropriate when the nature of the problem is unknown. The problem that exists is not immediately clear, and only symptoms are evident. Exploratory research clarifies the nature of the problem and permits an understanding of its dimensions. Once the problem is adequately comprehended, additional research is done to provide solutions. Some problems that require exploratory research before a full-blown research project is undertaken might include an explanation for declining sales, or consumer interest in a redesigned version of the product.
- **Descriptive research** is appropriate when the problem is understood and the manager needs only to describe characteristics or attributes. Decisions can be made from the results of descriptive research to improve marketing strategy; however, the manager may not appreciate why those decisions are best. "What kind of person buys our product?" and "How often do consumers view our advertising?" are problems that can be addressed with descriptive research.
- **Causal research** is appropriate when the problem is clearly defined and management needs to make forecasts or projections. Cause and effect relationships and why they exist can be understood. How will a change in price affect sales and how will changes in training influence the effectiveness of the sales force are problems requiring causal research.

RESEARCH DATA COLLECTION METHODS

Once the appropriate type of research design is determined, a feasible research data collection procedure must be selected. Depending upon the nature of the problem, one of four methods can be used to collect the data required to do the research.

Primary Data Methods

The **experimental method** permits the impact of systematically changing stimuli in a controlled environment to be determined. Various variables can be manipulated to ascertain how they influence some other variable. Experiments can be performed in a laboratory setting or in a real business situation. Environmental components can be more easily controlled in a lab setting than in a real business situation. However, in a lab setting subjects are aware that they are participating and are being evaluated, and they sometimes behave differently than they would normally. When experiments are conducted in the field, control groups are usually employed to determine the effects of variables that cannot be controlled, so their influence can be negated. A benefit of the experimental method is the ability to create a controlled situation where a particular concern of the manager can be analyzed in detail. A weakness of an experiment is that interactions of controlled factors may be overlooked. An example of an experiment would be testing the impact of different package designs on sales volume.

Observation methods are employed when the problem is simply watched by the researcher. No interference with the marketing situation occurs, and the participants may not be aware research is being conducted. The strength of observation is that the researcher can see firsthand what is being done. No chance exists for the subject to forget or make recall errors as can occur when methods that require the subject to report information after the fact are used. As a result, a true and unbiased understanding of the problem is more likely to result. Weaknesses include the inability to assess intangible factors such as a consumer's motivation and opinions and, occasionally, difficulty quantifying results for statistical analysis. Examples of observation include mystery shoppers and time-in-motion studies.

The **survey method** involves the evaluation of information gathered from people by means of interviews. Survey is the most frequently used method of generating primary data in marketing and is absolutely necessary when information inside an individual's mind such as ideas, beliefs, preferences, and attitudes is sought. Survey data are usually collected by means of interviews conducted in person, on the telephone, by mail, or with a computer. Since these data are collected by means of a questionnaire, its construction is an important issue. Care must be exercised in the wording of individual questions so respondents know what information is wanted and how to answer accurately. The questionnaire must be checked for validity. Data must be obtained in the correct form to facilitate statistical analysis. A strength of the survey method is the ability to personalize the data-gathering process. A weakness is that people may intentionally or unintentionally provide erroneous responses as they hurry to finish the questionnaire. An example of a survey would be an assessment of consumer perceptions of the quality of the firm's product.

Secondary Data Method

Secondary data are historical data that may sometimes be adequate and in sufficient quantity to do the research. If primary data are not needed, using secondary data facilitates quick and inexpensive results. The strengths and weaknesses of secondary data have been discussed previously. An example of secondary data use would be the analysis of manufacturing economic activity data provided by the United Nations to assess market share.

Sampling

Because the masses of items involved in business research are usually too large to measure by a census, sampling is necessary. A **sample** is a small group of items drawn from all the items (population) that have the information the manager needs. The sample is analyzed and, based on the observed characteristics of the sample, conclusions about the characteristics and nature of the whole population are inferred. Sampling decisions are concerned with the sample size, the sampling procedure, and the appropriateness of the sample. The sample must be large enough to make evident the true nature of the population from which it was drawn. If the sample is too small, certain members of the population may be underrepresented.

Sampling procedures embrace the method by which the sample is selected. Probability sampling procedures are preferred because they guarantee that every member of the population has a known likelihood of being selected for inclusion in the sample. This assures the items selected are more likely to be representative of the makeup of the population and that no bias is introduced into the sample.

The appropriateness of the sample has to do with non-sampling issues involved in data measuring and processing. The researcher must be careful to assure that the data obtained from the sample are accurate. Nonparticipation and interviewer bias in administering a questionnaire or recording facts introduce error. Improper verification and handling of sample data by the researcher can also introduce error.

Data Analysis

Once the appropriate data are collected, analysis can begin. The data are verified, coded, and entered into a computer data bank. Various statistical tests, data sorting, summarizing, and qualitative assessments can be applied to the data. The results of the scrutinized data are interpreted, and along with all other available pertinent information, conclusions are drawn. Implications for decision making are formed and recommendations developed for appropriate actions to be implemented to solve the research problem. The manager can expect the results of the research to be presented in written and oral reports.

INTERNATIONAL MARKET ENTRY PROCESS

Management should follow a systematic approach to making the decision to become international. A six-step **Way Station Model** can help structure the process.[4] Each step can be considered as a process that must be completed before moving onto the next. The following are the six steps comprising the model:

1. motivation and strategic planning
2. marketing research

3. market selection
4. selection of market entry mode
5. planning of contingencies
6. post-entry strategic commitment

In chapters 5 and 6, we have already discussed these six considerations and their details. Motivation has to do with exogenous and endogenous stimuli that influence management to consider international marketing. Marketing research is undertaken to assess the viability of the market alternatives. Based on the results of the research, the most desirable country or market is selected. The market entry method that will best permit development of the market is determined. A marketing strategy is established that is appropriate for the desired market entry method. Contingency plans are prepared for implementation if marketing performance is not in line with objectives. To remain successful, management needs to be proactive in its orientation once entry objectives have been achieved. Following the Way Station Model helps ensure that management is not overlooking some aspect of the market entry process and that everything involved is managed in the proper order.

Care must be taken to avoid common pitfalls managers make when expanding into international markets. The following are the seven most common mistakes managers make:[5]

- *Associating with inappropriate partners.* Regardless of how great the product and marketing strategy are, choosing an incompetent distributor or partner with incompatible goals can create problems. Any potential foreign business partner should be thoroughly examined before any commitments are made.
- *Expecting customer motivations and benefits to be similar worldwide.* Differences in culture, behavior, and motivation are likely to exist from the domestic market. Failure to research customers adequately can result in misinterpreting the correct way to appeal to consumers.
- *Failing to adequately protect the brand.* Brand positioning is important to business success. Inappropriate positioning of the brand in the foreign market can adversely influence brand position in the domestic market. If consumers in the foreign market acquire a poor perception of the brand, that perception could ultimately be transferred to the domestic market, making sales decline there as well. Failure to consider where and how the product will be sold could damage brand image.
- *Introducing the product with the wrong price.* Setting the price too high, too low, or equal to the domestic price can force management into an unwanted market position. A price acceptable to consumers and management must be determined.
- *Not considering the future.* If entry strategy is viewed as a single process and focuses only on achieving early sales to get established, future adjustments that will be required to remain competitive are likely to be overlooked. Penetration of a foreign market is not achieved in a single step. Long-run survival requires constant adjustment to changes.

- *Rank-ordering markets according to size and demand.* The ability to gain market share and outperform competition is an important consideration. A smaller market from which a large market share is obtained may be more desirable than a small market share from a larger market.
- *Underestimating existing competition.* The competition is already well entrenched, will be sensitive to attacks, and will retaliate when you enter. It is important not to underestimate its capabilities. Market entry plans must include awareness of and respect for the ability of competition.

Managers must never underestimate the complexity and degree of difficulty associated with the process of expanding into foreign markets. Entering a foreign country involves a series of new and difficult challenges not normally encountered when operating in the domestic market. To avoid these seven common entry predicaments, management must perform careful and thorough research. Solicitous planning that includes not only the immediate entry strategy but also thinking ahead for contingencies is required.

CHAPTER SUMMARY

The need to conduct research internationally is the same as the need domestically. In fact, the need internationally may be greater because of the lack of familiarity with the foreign market. When the decision to market internationally is made, research is required to assist with the market selection and entry decisions. The market entry analysis is a two-stage process. In the first stage, the potential markets are screened and the least promising eliminated. The second stage is a detailed analysis of the remaining countries. The country with the greatest potential is identified, an entry method determined, and an entry marketing strategy developed.

More problems are encountered when conducting international research than in conducting domestic research. These problems result from concerns that are inherent to the foreign country and affect both primary and secondary data. The problems encountered with secondary data make these data less abundant and reliable. The manager must verify the accuracy and applicability of secondary data and assure their validity before use. Primary data are often difficult to obtain and may be unrepresentative. Many of the problems encountered are in the data collection process because of lack of cooperation of respondents and the inappropriateness of the application of normal survey procedures. Language differences can also create troubles. Using a research firm in the foreign country may be advisable.

Once the international market has been entered, ongoing research is needed. Ongoing research is used to assess market success and assist with strategy adjustments. Therefore, ongoing research is similar to and conducted in the same manner as domestic research designed to assess market performance. As with researching the market entry process, the manager must remain cognizant of the problems that may be encountered with the implementation of primary and secondary research procedures.

The international market entry process should proceed in a systematic and structured manner. The six-step Way Station Model is one method of organizing the process. Following the model can help assure everything relevant to the market entry process is taken into consideration and done in the proper order. Care must be taken to avoid making foreign market entry mistakes. Thorough and careful marketing research is required.

Key Terms

Back translation
Causal research
Descriptive research
Experimental method
Exploratory research
Market entry analysis
Marketing Information System (MIS)
Marketing research
Observation method
Parallel translation
Primary data
Sample
Secondary data
Survey method
Way Station Model

Review Questions

1. What is the difference between the firm's marketing information system and its marketing research?
2. Describe the screening process for foreign market entry analysis.
3. How does the demand analysis of stage 2 of the foreign market entry analysis differ from the estimate of market potential done in the screening process?
4. Select a foreign country and explain which primary data collection problems a researcher would expect to encounter there.
5. Why is language such a problem for collecting primary data?
6. What should the researcher do when secondary data collection problems are encountered?
7. Is an assessment of outdated secondary data better than no assessment at all? Explain.
8. Interview a foreign student and identify three or four words that would present literal translation problems.
9. How might ongoing research in a foreign market differ from ongoing research done domestically?
10. Explain the differences among observation, experiment, and survey research methods.

Notes

1. Po-Lin Yeoh, "Information Acquisition Activities: A Study of Global Start-Up Exporting Companies," *Journal of International Marketing* 8 (3) (2000): 36–60.

2. George S.Yip, Javier Gomez Biscarri, Joseph A. Monti, "The Role of the Internationalization Process in the Performance of Newly Internationalizing Firms," *Journal of International Marketing* 8 (3) (2000): 10–35.

3. David A. Ricks, *Blunders in International Business*, 4th ed. (Malden, MA: Blackwell, 2006), 149–50.

4. Yip et al., "The Role of the Internationalization Process in the Performance of Newly Internationalizing Firms."

5. Kenneth Simmonds, "International Marketing—Avoiding the Seven Deadly Traps," *Journal of International Marketing* 7 (2) (1999): 51–62.

7 Culture and Buyer Behavior

McDonald's Corporation, a U.S. firm, is the world's largest food service provider, with more than 30,000 restaurants in more than 100 countries, serving around 52 million customers each day. McDonald's and Coca-Cola are the two most well-known brands in the world. Regardless of the market, the management of McDonald's pursues founder Ray Kroc's goal of providing quality, service, cleanliness, and value to offer customers 100 percent total satisfaction. To accomplish this goal, management must be culturally sensitive, and India and the countries of the Gulf Cooperation Council (GCC) are two excellent examples.

Over 80 percent of India's 850 million people are Hindu. Approximately another 12 percent are Muslim. Together, these two religions, comprising about 92 percent of the population, have dietary uniqueness that affects their way of life. This fact presented a real problem for McDonald's, whose primary product is a beef hamburger. Since the cow is taboo for Hindus (the cow is "aghanya," which means it may not be slaughtered), beef is not eaten. For the Muslims, beef may be eaten only if it is "halal," which means lawful or permitted. Meat must meet certain conditions established by Islamic law from the Quran before it can be eaten. These requirements include: No pork content or meat from a reptile or meat-eating animal; it must be slaughtered only by a Muslim in the prescribed Islamic manner; it must contain no blood or blood by-products and no alcohol. For the people of India, chicken and lamb are the meats of choice, and many people forgo meat completely and are vegetarians. Obviously, for Arabs in the GCC, any beef meat served must be halal.

To conform to local customs and culture in these countries, McDonald's management has tried to be as sensitive to Indian and Arab lifestyles as possible. In India, McDonald's has formed fifty-fifty joint ventures with Amit Jatia, who owns and operates all the restaurants in western and southern India, and Connaugh Plaza Restaurants, PL, which owns and operates all the restaurants in northern India. In the GCC countries, the restaurants are owned by local Arabs. For example, the twenty-five restaurants in the United Arab Emirates are owned by Emirates Fast Food Corporation with Emirati Rafic Fakic as the managing director. Menus have been modified to conform to religious practices and to accommodate the local palate and preferences. In India, nonbeef and vegetarian offerings such as the McVeggie

Burger, McAloo Tikki Burger, McCurry Pan, and the Chicken Maharaja Mac are provided. Restaurant operations have been reengineered to assure vegetable products are 100 percent vegetarian. Vegetable products are prepared using separate equipment and utensils, pure vegetable oil for cooking, and cheese and sauces completely vegetarian and eggless. Separation of vegetarian and nonvegetarian foods is maintained throughout procurement, cooking, and serving.

In the GCC, only 100 percent pure beef with no additives, fillers, or flavor enhancers is served. The beef is halal, from only prime cuts of flank and forequarters, and grilled in a double-sided hot plate. No oil or shortening is used during food preparation. Products that appeal to local tastes such as McArabia Chicken and McArabia Kofta have been added to the menu. Additionally, local sourcing is employed for all food and supplies used in the restaurants.

In India, health and safety is assured by utilizing "Hazard Analysis Critical Control Points" throughout the supply chain to monitor health and hygiene. Perishable products are maintained in a "Cold Chain" from supplier to restaurant. Community involvement is an important component of marketing strategy. McDonald's management supported the Nalanda Foundation's "girl-child" initiative because of the cultural inclination that many Indians have to favor the boy child more than the girl child. The purpose of the foundation's initiative is to assure educational benefits and other privileges young girls deserve but are frequently denied. Support was also provided for Pulse Polio, which was an initiative intended to make India polio free by 2005. In the GCC, refreshments were provided to volunteers and McDonald's restaurant employees who helped clean up beaches. A series of workshops was sponsored to help raise awareness of environmental issues such as environmental management, recycling, environmental law, corporate social responsibility, and ecotourism in the Middle East.

In March 2005, McDelivery, a home delivery service to neighborhoods that are no more than seven minutes away from a McDonald's restaurant by road, was begun in India. Although McDonald's is a fast-food business, management has positioned it as a family restaurant in India. To provide convenience to the family, particularly those who find traveling to the restaurant difficult, home delivery is an attractive service. Remaining culturally sensitive has been a business necessity at McDonald's.

Sources: Based in part on information from McDonald's USA at http://www.mcdonalds.com/; McDonald's India at http://www.mcdonaldsindia.com/; and McDonald's, "Welcome to McDonald's UAE," at http://www.mcdonalds.com/content/countries/uae.html.

CHAPTER OBJECTIVES

After reading this chapter, you should

- know what being sensitive to a culture means and involves;
- understand the role of culture in developing international marketing strategy;

- be able to define and explain the kinds of cultural knowledge the international marketer needs to know and appreciate;
- know what the self-reference criterion is and how to avoid it;
- understand the different cultural strategies management may employ;
- be able to decide and plan which cultural strategy is appropriate for various international marketing situations; and
- appreciate the impact of cultural change for international marketing strategy.

CULTURE

One of the most important considerations for success in international marketing is appreciating and understanding cultural differences between the foreign country and the domestic country. Culture has been suggested to be the root cause of most international marketing blunders.[1] Most assuredly, an optimum international marketing strategy cannot be developed without taking the foreign culture into account.

CULTURE DEFINED

What exactly is a nation's culture? The term *culture* can have multiple meanings. From a business perspective, we can consider **culture** to refer to a distinct way of life for an aggregate of people. Thus, within a single country, various segments of society can have some common and some different cultural components. The citizens from all segments may share certain characteristics that identify the entire nation, or each group may be unique. Think of culture as a society's way of living—the entirety of learned behavior that influences conduct and lifestyle. Culture is influenced by everything that affects a society's way of life. Culture determines what is acceptable and what is not. Culture includes, but is not limited to, concerns regarding beliefs, habits, customs, morals, laws, religion, education, family, cuisine, work, and art. Cultural beliefs and values are learned by living in a society and are passed on from generation to generation.

Since it is learned, culture is dynamic and evolves over time. Each new generation is influenced by the cultural value of the previous generation. And because the world is becoming smaller due to advances in technology and communications, cultures can influence each other. The desired aspects of other cultures are attractive and can be absorbed into any culture through contact. Therefore, every culture can have an influence on another culture because of the exposure caused by travel, TV, and other interactions.

IMPORTANCE OF CULTURE

Why should the international marketer be concerned with culture? Culture is basic to any society and influences how people live. Part of people's way of living is their buying behavior. Therefore, culture influences how, when, where, and why products and services are bought. Managers must be knowledgeable about culture because aspects of culture can have an impact on consumers' wants and needs and how those

Exhibit 7.1 **Malchev Supermarket**

The sign on this small neighborhood grocery store reads "Supermarket."

wants and needs are satisfied. The more thoroughly a culture is understood the greater is the likelihood that an ideal marketing strategy can be developed. The uniqueness of the culture that can influence strategy development can be taken more fully into account. With an understanding and appreciation of the culture, the likelihood of making inadvertent mistakes in decisions is minimized and international marketing errors can be reduced. Culture, then, is pervasive in all international marketing efforts and requires a high priority in management's decision making.

CULTURAL KNOWLEDGE

What kinds of cultural knowledge does the international marketing manager need to succeed internationally? Two kinds are important to the manager:

- factual knowledge
- cognitive knowledge

FACTUAL KNOWLEDGE

Factual knowledge is knowledge about a culture that can be learned. The manager can obtain the knowledge by reading a book, talking to people from the foreign country, or experiencing the culture directly by living in the foreign country. Factual knowledge is absolutely required to be successful. Without factual knowledge, the manager will make cultural blunders. Before entering any country, sufficient effort must be devoted to acquiring the factual knowledge that will influence consumer acceptance of the firm's products or services. The international marketer must understand the following major components of culture that constitute factual knowledge:[2]

- education
- language
- politics
- religion
- social relationships
- technology
- values

Education

Education is concerned with learning a culture's appropriate behavior. As people mature, they are taught appropriate ways to act as functioning members of society. Therefore, the education process is unique to each culture.

Education can be formal or informal. Informal education occurs through observation and involvement with others at home and in a variety of social settings. A child learns to take turns by observing the order in which peers are served. Older children learn what kind of respect is given to adults by interacting with them. This kind of education is acquired by living it. Daily, people assimilate information without really being cognizant of doing so. Much of a person's socialization process is realized through informal education. For example, by interacting with others in Turkey, people learn that speaking with your hands in your pockets or crossing your arms on your chest is considered rude and should be avoided.

Formal education is learning in a structured environment such as a school. A culture's approach to formal education influences its citizens' occupations and ultimately the class structure of society. Some cultures place a greater importance on formal education than others. Differences exist in terms of the emphasis on literacy, availability of education based on gender, and availability of secondary and higher education. For example, formally educating women is not considered important in India. And, the Wahabi branch of Sunni Islam, Saudi Arabia's official religion, preaches that education for girls is counterproductive.

Attitudes and availability of formal education affect workers' understanding and appreciation of technology. Therefore, care and maintenance of machines may not be considered important where formal education is not stressed. Appropriate training will not be available from local sources and must be provided within the firm. If management doesn't provide its own training, equipment will be neglected, resulting in maintenance problems, production stoppages, and expensive repairs. Education level will influence the type of people that can be hired to perform particular kinds of jobs. That in turn can affect the firm's productivity and efficiency. As a result, management may have to centralize operations to ensure that workers understand manufacturing processes and adhere to required service and maintenance schedules.

Language

Language is the primary means by which cultural awareness is communicated, and therefore it defines social life. However, language is meaningful to each culture in its own unique way. How a society understands its surroundings is determined by its use of its language. Approximately 6,900 different living languages are spoken in the approximately 230 nations of the world.[3] Each of these unique languages can constitute a unique culture. Obviously, some countries have more than one language and therefore more than one culture. An example is Belgium, which is divided into two culturally autonomous sections, with Flemish speakers in the north and French-speaking Walloons in the south. Of the world's living languages, only 347 (about 5 percent) have one million or more speakers; these few are spoken by 94 percent of the world's population.[4] Since only 6 percent of the world's people speak the remaining 95 percent of the languages, these languages tend to be of less concern to the international marketer.

Language is important to the international marketer because of the potential to misunderstand the meaning and enunciation of words, that is, what is implied by what is said and how people express themselves. In some cultures, for example in Saudi Arabia, people will say "yes" when they really mean "maybe" or "no." They agree simply to be polite. People are expected to know these courtesies are always extended so feelings are not hurt. In some cultures, such as Syria's, not being embarrassed is extremely important. Syrians often find admitting they were wrong is difficult. Thus, during business negotiations, care must be given to choosing words so that the person who forgoes the most has a comfortable way out, permitting prestige and reputation to be retained. If you do not understand the culture, you can easily unintentionally insult a foreigner by what you say. Word emphasis and voice inflection can also influence the meaning of what was said. Thus, how you state your communication is important, as well as what the actual communication is, so that the understanding is clear.

Communication can be complicated when workers speak different languages or when they speak different dialects of a language. A dialect is a variation of a language that is unique to a region or a group of people, such as American and British English, or the English spoken in Boston and that spoken in the southern United States.

Exhibit 7.2 lists a few countries and the number of languages spoken in each. When different dialects or different languages are spoken in a factory, management must hire translators, have signs printed in multiple languages, and find creative ways to coordinate understanding. In cultures lacking in technology, words may not exist to adequately explain the complexities of high-technology machines or products. Management must learn the uniqueness of a culture's language to understand and appreciate acceptable communicating behavior.

Nonverbal language is also important. How people behave and project themselves can communicate more distinctly than what is spoken. Thus, body language, gestures, and movements can project meaning. For example, the thumbs-up gesture that signi-

Exhibit 7.2 **Number of Languages Spoken in Selected Countries**

Country	Number of Languages
China	235
Germany	27
Ghana	79
India	415
Italy	33
Japan	15
Kenya	61
Mexico	298
Nigeria	510
Russia	105

Source: Raymond G. Gordon Jr., *Ethnologue: Languages of the World,* 15th ed. (Dallas TX: SIL International, 2005). Online version at http://www.ethnologue.com/.

Note: One language may be spoken in more than one country. For example, Mandarin Chinese is spoken in China and Indonesia.

fies everything is alright in the United States means "screw you" in Australia. During business meetings in Japan, displaying an open mouth is considered rude. In Germany, smiling and laughing are considered inappropriate during business meetings. A person is considered to be thinking deeply when arms are folded across the chest in Japan. Hand gestures such as the thumb and first finger forming a circle means alright in some cultures but signifies homosexuality in Turkey and "screw you" in others.[5] Syrians are known to utilize a high level of nonverbal communication during business meetings. Hand gestures are prevalent, and close association, including touching, is common. Bulgarians shake their head from side to side to indicate yes and up and down to signify no. Therefore, the manager should be aware that nonverbal language, just as verbal language, can have a different meaning from culture to culture, and what you do can communicate just as compellingly as what you say.

Politics

Politics are associated with the political system in a country and affect what is permissible for people. Politics ultimately influence economic conditions and the ability of people to achieve economic independence. Thus, the bureaucratic incentives or disincentives that surround people's lives influence behavior. Governmental and political influences will be discussed in detail in chapter 8.

Religion

Religion is people's beliefs about organizing and interpreting conditions over which they have no control or which they do not fully comprehend or understand. Religion helps people explain and confront social problems such as inequalities in status, in-

Exhibit 7.3 **The Blue Mosque**

The Blue Mosque in Istanbul, Turkey, is a place of worship for people of the Muslim faith.

come, and well-being. Religion also explains injustices and suffering and provides an incentive for doing what is socially correct instead of what is selfishly desired. Religion is not supportable with scientific or logical arguments and is based on faith. What is appropriate has been spiritually commanded and is therefore irrefutable and accepted by faith.

Formal religions such as Islam, Christianity, and Hinduism include various beliefs that regulate behavior and affect a person's underlying demeanor. Religious events, holidays, and activities influence lifestyle in ways that can affect business culture and marketing efforts. For example, Hindus do not eat beef, Muslim Ramadan limits activity, and Irish Catholics and Protestants do not interact. Formal religion can affect work schedules, which must be interrupted for prayer and religious holidays. Formal religion can also affect social behavior which, for example, may make doing business with women difficult in some countries. In Saudi Arabia, society is male dominated and women, except relatives, do not have the right to interact with men.

Informal religions also exist in many countries. Superstition, ancestor worship, spirit worship, and magic are examples. Informal religious practice, as well as formal religious activity, can disrupt business. For example, if an undesirable unexplained event, such as an accident, occurs at work, it may be considered to have been caused by some other unhappy occurrence such as the passing of a loved one or the howling of a wild animal. A shaman or spiritual leader may be consulted for guidance and

Exhibit 7.4 **Backgammon Game**

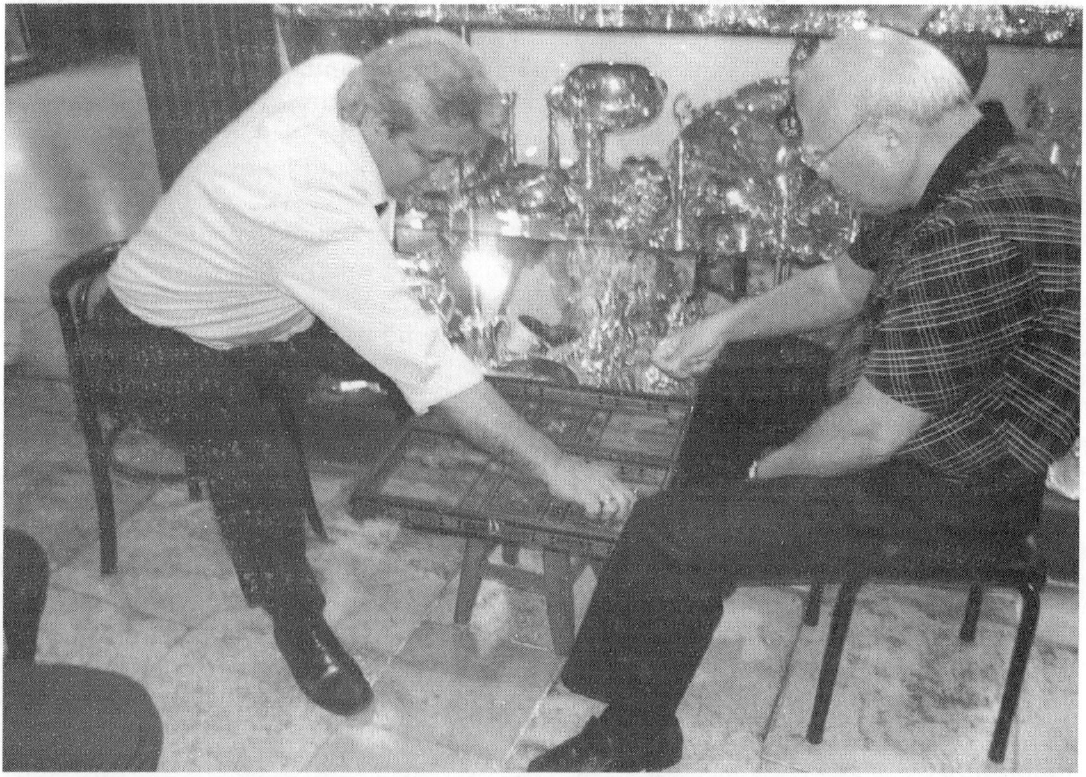

Two men playing backgammon are obscuring part of the window display of a business establishment.

performance of a ritual to remove the evil spirit. Some cultures claim to be nonreligious or atheist.

Social Relationships

Social relationships are widely varied. What is socially acceptable in a given culture depends on norms and codes of conduct developed within organizations such as the family, business, and religion. For example, the use of promotional pieces that include unmarried men and women clasping hands in public and talking about personal hygiene might be unacceptable in some cultures because such a social relationship is considered inappropriate.

Societies determine the appropriate distance between communicants. In some cultures, such as in the United States, invading another person's space is unacceptable; while in others, like Syria, people will talk face-to-face and touch each other when emphasis is required. Displaying the sole of your shoe will be considered an insult in Iran and Turkey. A youngster drinking beer in Germany or drinking wine in France is socially acceptable. Colors can have special meanings. For example, green is the traditional color of Islam, is associated with nature in the United States, and is a symbol of sickness in some Asian cultures. Men in Austria are taught to rise when a woman enters the room. The use of titles is important to Germans. Germans also shake hands at the beginning of a business meeting and again at the conclusion. Saudis do not shake hands but rather clasp hands firmly and briefly. Indians also do not shake hands, but instead hold the palms together at chin level as if praying and nod or bow slightly. In China, business cards should be presented with both hands and a slight bow. Immediately upon receipt, the card should be examined intensely for a few minutes before being placed away.

Social considerations influence whether a culture is individualistic or collectivistic.[6] **Individualistic cultures** tend to emphasize the importance of the individual over that of the group. Individuals are flexible in social settings and give precedence to their own self-interest. **Collectivistic cultures** tend to emphasize the group over the individual. Individuals are loyal to the group regardless of personal sacrifices that have to be made. As a general rule, Western countries tend to be more individualistic, and Eastern countries tend to be more collectivistic.

Social norms help determine apropos behavior. Class status, occupation, and wealth can influence a person's position in society and determine what behavior is socially appropriate. For example, in Germany, age tends to take precedence over youth. The oldest person will enter first unless a younger person holds a higher position in the firm. A positional hierarchy is important in Italian firms with little fraternization between work-position levels. Rank and status are also important for business relationships in China and Syria. The international marketer needs to learn what is considered socially acceptable behavior to avoid costly and embarrassing mistakes.

Technology

Technology refers to the infrastructure system that satisfies a society's needs for what constitutes a comfortable way of life. Included is the importance of possessing the variety of machines that may be considered necessary to provide a comfortable and happy life. Technology concerns a society's acceptance of research and development and attitude toward newness and change.

The appropriate style of life and values of a society influence the kinds of technology that are acceptable. The level of technology with which people are comfortable and that they consider important influences the kinds of products they are willing to buy, and therefore, reflects the mechanical complexity of the business environment in which people can work. New and complicated technologies may not be embraced when introduced, or considerable training will be required to acclimatize employees. Problems can be encountered during training because the native language may not have words for all of the new technology. Therefore, a literal translation is not possible, and the technical word will have to be retained from the originating language or new words created to express a comparable meaning.

A culture's level of technology will also influence the ability to introduce innovations. An electric hair curler may not be appreciated or acceptable in a culture where it is traditional to braid hair or style it with beads. Likewise, an electric frying pan may not sell well where preparing a meal requires cooking the food in direct contact with the flames. The fact that such a product can save time is not valued by the culture because personal attention and love are required during food preparation to produce an acceptable meal. The manager must learn what technology is acceptable to a culture and use that information in decision making.

Values

Values are filters used to determine priorities among alternative actions a person can take. Values determine which of several behaviors are most appropriate for a certain situation. What one culture values another may eschew. For example, punctuality is a virtue and expected by most Germans, while tardiness is of little concern to the Syrians. In countries such as the United Kingdom and Bulgaria, arriving late for engagements is socially appropriate and expected. Values usually relate behavior to underlying assumptions about power, rank, and often religion.[7]

Values can pertain to anything that influences a person's acceptable behavior. Values may include issues such as a culture's position and attitudes toward time, achievement, work ethics, adroitness, wealth, and change. Some cultures, such as the German, have a lineal view of time while others, such as most Middle Eastern and Latin nations, have a circular view of time. The lineal view holds that lost time cannot be recaptured, and a missed opportunity may be gone forever; it promotes a sense of urgency. In the circular view, time is seen as moving in a circle. What is not done now can be done later; thus a missed opportunity will return at a later time. There is not the same sense of urgency about time as in the lineal view. The international manager can learn that because of differences in values, arriving early for an appointment is impolite in Brazil, children should not look at their parents while talking to them in Tanzania, and business is not discussed before a period of socializing in Japan, Syria, Mexico, and Saudi Arabia.

COGNITIVE KNOWLEDGE

Cognitive knowledge is the ability to think and feel comfortable in a foreign culture so that the factual knowledge can be understood and appreciated. Involved is the ability to use reason, perception, and intuition to assimilate the cultural conditions. Knowing what is acceptable in the culture is not the same as knowing why that behavior is appropriate. Appreciating the culture (making it part of one's being) permits a deeper comprehension of the differences and fine points of life. A manager with cognitive knowledge can think and function more comfortably in the culture, akin to the way the local people do.

Even with cognitive knowledge, some customs should not be embraced by the international marketer. **Cultural exclusives** are behaviors from which foreigners are excluded. Cultural exclusives are only appropriate for participation by a member of that culture. People from other cultures should avoid involvement, and trying to participate, regardless of one's cultural appreciation, is considered in poor taste or offensive. For example, a Christian should not worship in a Muslim mosque.

Appropriate actions are expected and must be embraced if the international marketer is to be accepted. **Cultural imperatives** are behaviors that foreigners must observe to be successful. For example, in countries such as Syria, Saudi Arabia, and Spain, developing friendship and trust may be necessary before business can be conducted. Failure to build the personal relationships precludes the possibility of negotiating any business association.

The international marketer may selectively embrace most other cultural practices. **Cultural electives** are behaviors that foreigners may observe but are not required or expected to respect by members of the culture. Practicing elective behavior is neither harmful nor helpful. These are cultural practices that should be understood and appreciated, and embraced if the international marketer feels comfortable with them. One will not be viewed less highly or more highly for participation. For example, in some cultures, men customarily greet each other with a kiss on the cheek. The international marketer may use this form of greeting or refrain from it. A local businessperson will not feel slighted if a kiss is not offered, because they recognize that you are not one of them. The international marketer needs to realize whether an exclusive, an imperative, or an elective is involved, and be able to respond appropriately.

SELF-REFERENCE CRITERION

Why is increasing one's cultural IQ so important? Managers need to be as intimate with the foreign culture as possible to help them develop cultural empathy. **Cultural empathy** means putting yourself in the foreigners' position so you can understand and appreciate their perspective. This permits you to share the foreigners' emotions and feelings and to clearly understand them. Obtaining cognitive knowledge helps make this possible, but simply possessing cognitive knowledge does not guarantee that cultural empathy will exist. Cultural empathy requires sensitivity to perspectives different from your own so the foreign market can be objectively evaluated. Cultural empathy precludes cultural apathy and ignorance. Failure to practice cultural empathy is the cause of many international marketing mistakes.

Failure to adequately appreciate the foreign culture is known as the **self-reference criterion (SRC)**.[8] The SRC is a tendency to consciously or subconsciously view the foreign culture in terms of your own cultural experiences. Imposing your cultural values, or failing to have cultural empathy, typify the SRC. No matter how well you learn and appreciate the foreign culture, you know and understand your culture better. Therefore, you need to be constantly aware of putting your thinking in the foreign culture and discounting your own culture. Not recognizing the SRC is a common mistake made by international marketers; causing indiscretions to be easily committed unintentionally. For example, the SRC is active in the manager who, while developing marketing strategy, thinks back to familiar experiences with consumers in the home country and assumes those behaviors will be similar in the foreign country. This manager unknowingly lets familiar values override the values of the foreign culture and thereby becomes a casualty of the SRC. Making decisions without an adequate knowledge of the foreign culture, whether intentional or not, is likely to result in SRC mistakes. The SRC may provide one good argument for minimizing the involvement of expatriate managers in foreign markets.

A four-step process should be followed to help minimize the chances of committing the self-reference criterion:[9]

1. Identify the factors such as traits, values, needs, habits, and economics that contribute to the success of the marketing program in the domestic market.
2. Identify the factors such as traits, values, needs, habits, and economics in the foreign culture that may influence the success of the marketing program.
3. Compare the two lists of factors for differences. Any differences constitute potential SRC problems.
4. Pay attention to significant differences, which serve as a warning signal that the marketing program must be modified to accommodate more thoroughly those factors that are different in the foreign culture.

The idea is to isolate and identify differences between your own values and those in the foreign culture. Attention can then be centered on the recognized differences so appropriate adjustments can be made. In this way, your own cultural prejudices can be ascertained, thus reducing the likelihood of allowing them to inhibit your thinking and decision making.

CULTURAL STRATEGY

Obviously, the firm's marketing strategy must be developed with consideration for the culture in which it will operate. However, how important is it to conform to the local cultural norms and values? To what extent must management coordinate with accepted business practices? How much freedom does management have to be creative with marketing strategy? When developing marketing strategy, the manager can react with one of three responses to the foreign market's cultural environment. The manager's approach may be

- culturally congruent,
- culturally distinct, or
- culturally disparate.

CULTURALLY CONGRUENT STRATEGY

To employ a **culturally congruent strategy,** management follows a marketing program that is similar to those of the local competition. The product line will need to include: Models already on the market, distribution in acceptable outlets, standardized promotion, and a competitive price. The objective is to minimize channel and consumer resistance by not upsetting the status quo. Consumers' buying habits are not disrupted, and they do not have to learn new purchase behaviors. The philosophy followed is that of "When in Rome, do as the Romans do." Although this approach appears to offer the advantages of cultural empathy, it also provides little differentiation for the firm and for the ability of the product to better solve the customers' problem or satisfy their needs. Trying to be "Roman" may not be a good idea because Rome is already full of Romans (competitors) appealing to the customer in similar ways. Therefore, Rome may not appreciate nor need another Roman (identical competitor). Also, trying to be Roman may be difficult. The Romans are good at being Romans (successful competitors) and may outperform a foreigner in their own market. Therefore, being different, or at least distinctive in some way, may be more desirable for the outsider.

CULTURALLY DISTINCT STRATEGY

With a **culturally distinct strategy** management remains culturally similar in most of the marketing program but introduces one or a few changes that possess cultural dissimilarities. Although these differences may be contrary to acceptable cultural norms, if accepted, they offer some benefits not available from the competition. The dissimilarities allow management to differentiate the firm and its product in some manner from the local competition. No efforts are made to encourage consumers to accept the cultural differences. Management expects the benefits customers will realize from the cultural dissimilarity will be recognized and ultimately accepted. Thus, disruptions will be minimized and society will not feel pressured to change. Since management makes no concerted effort to convince consumers of the advantage of the cultural dissimilarity, the acceptance process may be slow and people may not realize or appreciate the benefits offered. If rejected by the society, an otherwise good marketing program may be unable to achieve its potential or become completely unsuccessful.

CULTURALLY DISPARATE STRATEGY

A **culturally disparate strategy** is used when management deliberately ignores the prevailing cultural norms. The cultural dissimilarities are extensive, and management undertakes intentional efforts to change the culture by convincing people that the new method is more advantageous. The intent is to accelerate the rate of acceptance by altering those aspects of the culture that are most likely to offer resistance. A considerable investment in advertising and communications with potential customers is required. No guarantee exists that the efforts to change the culture will succeed. Attempts to change parts of a culture can have negative effects on consumers' attitudes and cause them to boycott the firm and its products. However, if successful, management stands to gain considerable market share at the expense of local competition.

STRATEGY IMPLEMENTATION

Management must assess the cultural climate and decide which of the three cultural approaches is most desirable. Suppose consumers in the foreign market are accustomed to buying unsliced bread from a bakery. Would the international marketer be more successful by introducing bread that is shaped differently, sliced, and sold in a grocery store or by opening a lot of bakeries and selling the traditionally shaped, unsliced bread? Researching the market can help answer these questions. Ultimately, management must implement the strategy approach that is believed to have the greatest chance of success.

CULTURAL CHANGE

As the world grows smaller because of improvements in communication, transportation, and technology, the opportunity for cultures to touch each other increases. As a result, cultural exchange occurs and desirable aspects of other cultures are espoused and embraced. Therefore, by operating in a foreign country, management acts as a change agent influencing the dynamic nature of the culture. Your presence in the foreign culture introduces characteristics of your own culture. To the extent that the foreigners accept differences in marketing strategy, management has been responsible for changing the foreign culture. The rate of cultural change depends on the propensity of society to accept the change. As a result of cultural change, many foreign cultures are becoming Americanized as they embrace U.S. ways and values. In some instances, foreigners welcome these changes while in others, Americanization of the culture is feared and shunned. For example, in Iran the Shah was overthrown in 1979 because the American conduct he embraced clashed with religious beliefs.

One of the reasons for protectionist trade policies (tariff and nontariff barriers) is the fear of foreign intervention in the society. Fear that foreign investors will gain too much control of the economy and that their business practices will be contrary to national goals contributes to government regulation of international marketers. Therefore, the international marketer must remain flexible and be a good corporate citizen of the foreign country. Management should adapt to the foreign culture and practice cultural empathy. Appreciation of and respect for the culture should be built into the marketing strategy.

CHAPTER SUMMARY

Culture is an extremely important consideration for the international marketer. Culture influences how a group of people lives. Therefore, culture permeates people's decision-making and buying behavior. How they shop, what they buy, where they buy, and how they buy are influenced. The international marketer must learn and understand the foreign culture if the most successful marketing strategy is to be developed.

The two kinds of cultural knowledge management needs are factual knowledge and cognitive knowledge. Factual knowledge is the minimum required knowledge and can be learned. Information about a culture's language, education, religion, values, technology, social relationships, and politics comprise the factual knowledge managers must know. Cognitive knowledge takes factual knowledge one step further by permitting the manager to value and feel a part of the culture. Cognitive knowledge provides an appreciation of cultural exclusives, imperatives, and electives.

The international marketer must stay alert to avoid the self-reference criterion. The self-reference criterion is viewing the foreign culture in terms of your own cultural experiences. The self-reference criterion is responsible for many mistakes made in international marketing. To avoid this, managers need to identify factors in the foreign culture that are different than in the domestic culture and would adversely affect marketing strategy. Managers must practice cultural empathy.

When developing an international marketing strategy, management may utilize one of three cultural approaches. A culturally congruent approach is as similar to the foreign culture's accepted values as possible. A culturally distinct approach introduces strategy changes that include minor cultural differences and allows the culture to discover the benefits of the changes. A culturally disparate approach introduces strategy changes that include major cultural differences and attempts to persuade consumers to accept the changes.

The international marketer is a cultural change agent. The firm's presence introduces aspects of the domestic culture to the foreign culture. Management must be sensitive to the foreign culture's propensity to accept change and must act in a way that shows respect for the foreign culture.

KEY TERMS

Cognitive knowledge
Collectivistic cultures
Cultural electives
Cultural empathy
Cultural exclusives
Cultural imperatives
Culturally congruent strategy
Culturally disparate strategy
Culturally distinct strategy
Culture
Education
Factual knowledge
Individualistic cultures
Language
Politics
Religion
Self-reference criterion (SRC)
Social relationships
Technology
Values

REVIEW QUESTIONS

1. What is culture?
2. Why is a foreign culture important for the international marketer to understand?
3. Describe cultural empathy.
4. Is it really possible for you to perceive and understand situations from a foreigner's point of view? Why or why not?
5. Talk to a foreign student and identify three differences between that student's culture and your own.
6. Explain the difference between factual knowledge and cognitive knowledge.
7. Give an example of how the international marketer can make mistakes by communicating improperly in a foreign advertisement.
8. Explain how the international marketer can avoid becoming a victim of the self-reference criterion.

9. Select a product and country of your choice. Which of the three cultural marketing strategies is most appropriate for marketing this product in that country? Why? Provide arguments supporting your strategy decision.
10. What risks does management face when following a culturally disparate strategy?

NOTES

1. James A. Lee, "Cultural Analysis in Overseas Operations," *Harvard Business Review* 44 (March–April 1966): 106–14.
2. Vern Terpstra and Kenneth David, *The Cultural Environment of International Business*, 3rd ed. (Cincinnati, OH: South-Western Publishing, 1991). The seven components of culture presented are those listed in this source.
3. Raymond G. Gordon Jr., *Ethnologue: Languages of the World,* 15th ed. (Dallas, TX: SIL International, 2005), http://www.ethnologue.com/.
4. Ibid.
5. Roger E. Axtell, *Gestures: The Do's and Taboos of Body Language Around the World* (Hoboken, NJ: Wiley, 1998).
6. Zeynep Gurhan-Canli and Durairaj Maheswaran, "Cultural Variations in Country of Origin Effects," *Journal of Marketing Research* 3 (3) (2000): 309–17.
7. Terpstra and David, *The Cultural Environment of International Business,* 106.
8. Lee, "Cultural Analysis in Overseas Operations."
9. Ibid.

8 Governmental and Political Risks

On February 18, 2006, Orange Personal Communications Ltd. (OPC) initiated litigation against easyGroup (UK) Ltd. OPC is part of Orange SA, owned by France Telecom Group. Orange SA is an international mobile communications firm serving over fifty-seven million customers in twenty countries in Asia, Europe, Africa, and the Caribbean. The company began in 1994 with OPC's entry into the market in the United Kingdom. Since 2001, Orange has achieved the distinction of being the largest mobile phone company in the United Kingdom, with over twelve million customers.

EasyGroup is a holding company for sixteen different businesses including easyPizza.com, easyMusic.com, easyCruise.com, easyCinema.com, and, perhaps the best known, easyJet.com. In November 2004, easyMobile.com was launched by the Danish telecom company TDC A/S and T-Mobile UK Ltd. under license from easyGroup.

So, why was the management of OPC taking easyGroup to court? The problem was the color orange. Both companies utilize orange in their logos and brand marks.

The management of OPC initiated a trademark infringement suit claiming it was first to use the orange color in the United Kingdom, and by utilizing a similar-colored logo, easyMobile.com would cause confusion among customers and damage OPC's business. Citing "passing off" laws, management asserted that easyMobile.com made itself appear like OPC to customers in an attempt to take part of OPC's market. Very simply, it claimed that the color orange was synonymous with the company's name and any use of the color was an infringement of its trademark. Management claimed a trademark is protected, and any shapes, sounds, and colors that are a distinctive part of their trademark may not be copied. According to management, the company's brand is extremely important to the success of the business.

According to Stelios Haji-Ioannou, founder of easyGroup.com, and Frank Rasmussen, CEO of easyMobile.com, UK, use of the orange color is the company's right. Since the firm's inception in 1998, all easyGroup companies have used the color orange in their trademark. Maintaining the orange color would be one way the management of easyMobile let customers know that easyMobile is part of the easyGroup. Unlike OPC's products, easyMobile's products would be available only online, and no handsets or accessories would be sold. Rasmussen claimed the color was not being used to confuse customers or to try to take customers from OPC. The sole purpose was to let customers know easyMobile is part of easyGroup. Also, the two colors of orange, although close in appearance, are not exactly the same hue. And, management planned to add a disclaimer to the company's Web site to alert customers that easyMobile has no connection with OPC. Rasmussen surmised OPC was simply afraid of the competition.

Since the orange color is an established and predominate aspect of both companies' images, expecting easyMobile to change colors seems inappropriate. However, precedent may exist for a firm to own a color. For example, H. J. Heinz Company owns the rights to the distinctive turquoise color used on the labels of its canned goods. Cadbury Schweppes PLC is associated with a unique light shade of purple for its candy. The orange color was not a problem between OPC and easyGroup as long as the two firms did not compete in the same industry. The legal questions to be resolved were whether easyMobile could use its orange color in the mobile communications industry, and whether the orange color would be confusing to customers in such a way that the competitor's product would be purchased by mistake. Since the two companies' logos are not just orange, but also contain easily seen wording of the firm's name, it is difficult to comprehend how consumers would confuse the two. However, because the managements of the two firms could not resolve the dispute, the courts would have to decide.

On December 13, 2006, easyMobile ended mobile phone service in the United Kingdom, so the court did not get to resolve this case. One reason given for the decision was low customer growth in the United Kingdom. The management at easyMobile also blamed a change of ownership at TDC A/S for the problem. Could the prospects of losing the lawsuit with OPC have had a bearing on the decision also? Haji-Ioannou said easyMobile will eventually reintroduce service in the United Kingdom once another partner is located.

Sources: Based in part on information from easy.com at http://www.easy.com/features/easymobile.html; Orange.com at http://www.orange.co.uk/; Steve Ranger, "Orange Gets the Pip over easyMobile Branding," vnunet.com, February 24, 2005, http://www.vnunet.com/articles/print/2126829; Duncan Walker, "Can You 'Own' a Colour?" BBC News, August 11, 2004, http://news.bbc.co.uk/1/hi/magazine/3555398.stm; BBC News, "Orange Colour Clash Set for Court," February 20, 2005, http://news.bbc.co.uk/1/hi/business/4281845.stm; and Nancy Gohring, "EasyMobile to Close Mobile Phone Service in UK," *Info World*, November 15, 2006, http://www.infoworld.com/article/06/11/15/HNeasymobileshuts_1.html.

CHAPTER OBJECTIVES

After reading this chapter, you should

- understand why the international marketer should be aware of the political climate in a foreign country;
- know the most common political risks of marketing in a foreign country;
- be able to explain how to lessen the firm's vulnerability to political risks;
- understand how economic cooperation among governments affects the foreign marketing environment;
- be able to describe the kinds of economic integration that are possible;
- explain the European Union and its business implications;
- appreciate how law differs from country to country and can, therefore, affect marketing conditions;
- know what a jurisdictional clause is and the importance of its inclusion in a contract; and
- understand how to settle international legal disputes.

GOVERNMENTAL SOVEREIGNTY

The international marketer is a guest in the foreign country and must abide by the laws and regulations of the sovereign host government. The conditions and procedures under which business may be conducted within a nation's borders may be stipulated by the government in power because of its sovereignty. The international marketer will find many differences in laws and governmental practices affecting business conduct in the foreign market from what exists in the domestic market. Thus, many obstacles can appear when doing business in foreign countries. Trade restrictions, lack of economic cooperation, and other governmental policies can intervene negatively to slow the movement of products, people, and money.

POLITICAL CLIMATE

Before doing business in any country, management should assess the current as well as anticipated future political climate, which help indicate the attractiveness and safety of the market. Analysis of the political climate permits the nature of the business environment and its permanency to be assessed. Government stability and positive political climate are important to the international marketer because of the possibility of government intervention, regulation, and takeover of the firm's assets located in the foreign country. Investments can be lost and profits jeopardized if governmental policy changes or controls or restrictions are placed on the business. To assess the prevailing political atmosphere of a nation, the following five factors must be considered.

The Current Form of Government

The United States is essentially a democracy with a free market economy. Economic decisions are determined by consumers with governmental intervention only for the

Exhibit 8.1 **Billboard Advertisement**

A billboard advertisement for a Bulgarian political candidate.

purposes of helping assure fairness of the business environment and stability of economic conditions. Across many countries, government control varies considerably from limited to autonomous. The business climate will differ depending upon whether the government is socialist, communist, or a dictatorship. The amount of government influence and interference in business and the ease with which business changes can be made are influenced to a certain extent by the form of government.

The Current Political Party System

The United States has basically a two-party political system with fixed procedures for elections. The transition of power from one party to the other is calm, and continuity is maintained. Conditions in some countries are much more hectic and uncertain. Multiple parties make achieving a majority vote difficult, causing uncertain coalition governments to be established. Votes of "no confidence" by politicians can dissolve governments and require new elections. The political views of different parties can be quite contrasting, causing major changes and disruptions in business practice as parties go in and out of power. Political parties can vary widely in their support for business.

Financial Risks and Incentives Resulting from Political Activity

Whether political agendas are business friendly or not will influence management's decisions. An assessment of trends in business facilitation and regulation allows management to determine the politicians' attitudes toward foreign marketers. Are policies being developed to encourage or discourage foreign marketers? Are trends favorable or unfavorable?

The Stability of the Current Government

A society's dissatisfaction with the existing government can result in changes that range from minor revisions in existing conditions to replacement governments. Political unrest, a coup d'état, and the emergence of a strongman leader could result in different policies toward foreigners. For example, unrest and chaos resulted from a coup in Honduras after the Supreme Court ordered the army to remove President Zelaya from office. He had angered the judiciary, Congress, and the army by seeking constitutional changes that would have allowed presidents to seek reelection beyond a four-year term. Destabilization could also result from discontented voters who, for example could elect a reform government that would be drastically different from the existing government. Actions such as these can result in the formation of a new constitution, land reform, or, as in Venezuela and Bolivia, in democratic governments being replaced by socialist leaders like Hugo Chávez and Evo Morales. In other instances, such as in India and Nepal, elected socialist and communist parties remain prominent and influence the decisions of government.

Stability and Permanency of Government Policy

Frequent changes in policy cause disruption to long-term strategy, which complicates planning and increases the risk of doing business. Because government policies are less likely to endure, unwillingness may exist to make substantial commitments to the foreign market.

POLITICAL RISKS

Government leaders can implement a variety of policies that may affect adversely the international marketer. These policies are justified as being necessary to national interests or fiscal soundness. All can have undesirable consequences for management. The following are a few of the most common political risks that the international marketer can encounter.

Exchange Controls

Exchange controls are restrictions placed on the exchange of the country's currency to those of other countries. Exchange controls are used to conserve the nation's supply of foreign exchange and are usually employed by countries with balance of payments problems. The government manipulates exchange rates in a way that makes converting its currency unattractive and unprofitable. Exchange controls are described in detail in Chapter 9. Exchange controls affect the international marketer by making repatriation of profits difficult and interfering with the ability to pay for imports in the seller's currency. For example, in 2002 exchange controls were applied to the peso by the Argentine central bank in an attempt to stabilize exchange rates. Foreign exchange traders and banks were banned from buying U.S. dollars at the market rate, and the sale of dollars was restricted to US$1,000 for an individual and US$10,000 for a business.[1]

Expropriation

Expropriation is the acquisition of the firm's property in the foreign country by the foreign government. Expropriation or nationalization of property and equipment by the host government is one of the most devastating political risks faced by the international marketer. If investments have been made in the foreign country, financial losses can be tremendous. The foreign government may or may not provide compensation for the expropriated property. If compensation is provided, it may be less than the true worth or value of the property. Management may be offered pennies on the dollar of the actual value. For example, the Venezuelan government expropriated a slaughterhouse, an H. J. Heinz Company tomato processing plant, a wheat processing plant owned by Empresas Polar S.A. (one of the largest Venezuelan corporations), and an unfinished shopping mall in Caracas.[2] Financial assets in the foreign country's banks can also be frozen or seized. Obviously, management should not invest more in the foreign country than it can afford to lose.

What recourse does management have if the firm's property is expropriated? No recourse is possible except to ask the United Nations and the U.S. Congress to enact economic sanctions. Under Chapter VII, Article 42 of the UN Charter, sanctions may be applied to countries to maintain or restore international peace and security. Such actions require approval of the UN Security Council, generally require the severest of circumstances, and have been enacted only sixteen times in the past. Expropriation is unlikely to be considered a severe enough situation to precipitate UN action. In the United States, the Hickenlooper Amendment to the Foreign Assistance Act of 1961 grants Congress the authority to cut off foreign aid to countries expropriating U.S. businesses. This option may not be effective, however, because the leaders of nations expropriating U.S. property tend to be unconcerned about receiving U.S. foreign aid.

Import Restrictions

Import restrictions are limitations placed on the ability of the international marketer to import raw materials, components, or parts. Import restrictions are used to conserve foreign exchange or to support local business. Governments with balance of payments problems may employ import restrictions. Restricting imports has a positive influence on the balance of payments by curtailing outflows of currency, which helps reduce deficits. International marketers will be encouraged to buy needed materials and services within the country, thus stimulating local producers' sales. Import restrictions may be any trade barrier but are often quotas or embargoes that restrict the quantities of certain products that can be imported. For example, because of balance of payments problems, in January 2009 the government of Ecuador introduced import restrictions that raised tariffs and imposed import quotas on a wide range of products. Also in 2009, the Ukrainian government imposed a 13 percent import surcharge on a wide range of products.[3]

The implications for the international marketer are obvious. Diverting purchases to local suppliers may result in reduced quality and increased cost. Local suppliers may not be able to deliver comparable worth in terms of desired values such as product performance, reliability, delivery schedules, service, and standards. If local suppliers are inefficient, the prices of locally obtained items are likely to be higher than of imported items. The reason products were imported originally was because doing so offered some advantages over what was available from local suppliers. Otherwise, the purchases would have been made locally. If the materials the international marketer is forced to buy locally are assembled into the firm's product, quality as well as the firm's reputation could be adversely affected.

Labor Problems

Labor problems can occur in some countries because of laws that are favorable to employees and the influence labor unions can exert on government leaders. Strong labor can secure concessions from the government. The international marketer may be forced to follow rules initiated by labor unions and imposed by the government that restrict management's flexibility. For example, according to Belgian law, a distributor cannot be replaced without a just cause. Failure to aggressively promote the firm's product or consistently not attaining sales goals is not considered a just cause. Dismissing the distributor for not performing to expectations will be viewed by the courts as depriving the distributor of the right to earn an income. As a result, management could be forced to pay the distributor a sizable penalty for the distributor's future lost income. Dismissing employees may be more difficult in a foreign country than in the United States. Hiring must be done carefully where dismissing an employee can be difficult. In some countries, such as Germany, labor representatives participate in management decisions. Representatives of labor are placed on the board of directors or must have input before any decisions are made. The strong position of labor, therefore, causes management to modify its decision making. Failure to adequately consider labor's influence may result in management being surprised by politicians enacting restrictive policies that limit management's decision-making freedom.

Price Controls

Price controls are constraints on the price management may charge for its product. A price control is an arbitrary ceiling above which management may not raise the selling price. Price controls are used mostly by governments whose currency is experiencing rampant inflation. The controls are applied to certain essential products in an attempt to curtail inflation by limiting price rises. For example, the Venezuelan government of Hugo Chávez has set price controls on twelve basic foods including cooking oil, coffee, sugar, cheese, tomato sauce, powdered milk, and rice, which are staples of the diets of many Venezuelans.[4] The impact of price controls is to create

Exhibit 8.2 **Impact of Price Controls**

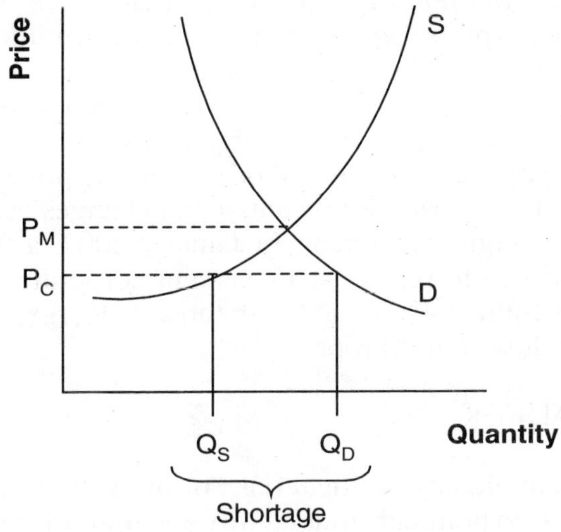

The shortage = $Q_D - Q_S$
Where: P_M is the market price
P_C is the price ceiling
Q_D is the quantity demanded
Q_S is the quantity supplied

shortages of the involved products. Since the government-imposed price ceiling prevents the manufacturer from charging what otherwise would be the market price, production is discouraged. A price ceiling permits the consumer to buy the product at a price that is lower than what otherwise would be the market price and encourages consumption. Therefore, the amount of the product demanded becomes larger than the amount producers will supply, resulting in shortages. The impact of a price control is shown in Exhibit 8.2.

The implication of price controls is that the international marketer cannot charge the price the product would normally bring. The lower than normal price that is dictated by government leaders causes the profit per unit to be reduced, so that producing and selling the product may become less profitable or unprofitable, and therefore undesirable. Once the price controls are lifted, producers will strive to regain the money that was lost when the price controls were in place. This can cause the price to rise rapidly above what the increase in market price would have been had price controls not been implemented. Although the market mechanism works best to regulate price, government leaders sometimes think they can control prices directly without affecting supply or demand.

Taxes

Taxes can be changed. Government leaders may decide that tax revenues are inadequate and arbitrarily increase tax rates or assess supplemental taxes. Or, government leaders may grant the firm a tax holiday to attract the international marketer to locate in the foreign country. A **tax holiday** is a period when low or no taxes are assessed. Before the tax holiday expires, government leaders can unilaterally change their minds and begin collecting taxes. Similarly, the government can renege on any prior agreement. For example, the government of Ghana agreed to sell Kaiser Aluminum Corporation electricity at a fixed price for thirty years. That rate was quickly raised when the Arab oil embargo in the early 1970s caused the price paid for the oil used to make the electricity to increase significantly. Tax changes can also be made as an incentive to increase foreign investment. In January 2007, a flat tax of 12 percent was adopted in Macedonia to replace a 15 percent corporate tax rate. The flat tax was reduced to 10 percent in 2008. Along with those of Kyrgyzstan and Kazakhstan, Macedonia's tax is the lowest in Europe.[5]

LESSENING POLITICAL RISK

Management wants to avoid any political risks of marketing in the foreign country. What can be done to lessen political vulnerability and minimize the jeopardy of doing business in the foreign country? No matter what actions management takes, the risk of political vulnerability is always present. However, efforts can be made to reduce the probability of their occurrence. Basically, management should not do things that will attract the unfavorable attention of a society or government. It should avoid activities and behaviors that will cause government leaders to intervene in the business. Specifically, management needs to embrace any behaviors that are consistent with these two fundamental principles:

- Treat people fairly.
- Be a good citizen.

To treat employees and the public fairly, management should employ policies in the foreign country that are similar to those employed in the domestic country. If college tuition is reimbursable to employees in the home country, then to be fair, tuition should be paid in the foreign country also. Foreign workers should not be exploited simply because doing so is possible within their laws. Although hiring women to work for twelve hours a day in sweatshop conditions for 50 cents per hour is permitted in El Salvador, doing so would not be consistent with treating people fairly. If employees are given time off from work for social causes such as helping the Red Cross in the domestic country, then employees should be encouraged to engage in social causes during working hours in the foreign country.

Being a good citizen means acting in a manner that is considered appropriate in the foreign country. For example, respecting cultural differences that affect how people dress in the workplace is appropriate. Also, if flowers are planted at the factory in the domestic country to beautify the area, then being a good citizen dictates the same behavior in the foreign country.

Good citizenship and fair treatment of others just make sense ethically. When people are treated fairly and management behaves like a good citizen, people will be more likely to view the firm favorably. Government officials will be more likely to view the firm positively and less likely to impose restrictions. Why penalize a firm that is a valuable economic asset and is contributing to the economy?

Management may do anything that conforms to these two principles or rules and should avoid engaging in activities that would be contrary or contradictory. The following are a few examples of activities that are fitting and appropriate:

- *Allow nationals to manage the business.* Place local citizens in positions of responsibility. In some cases, a period of training and indoctrination in management's philosophy at the domestic headquarters will be necessary to adequately prepare nationals to assume leadership positions. Workers will be more comfortable receiving supervision and directions from colleagues than from foreigners.
- *Employ nationals in the business.* Try not to use expatriates except in the most critical positions where local citizens cannot be found who possess the required skills. Eventually train local people for these positions. Employing nationals helps people see the firm as their own.
- *Invest in the foreign business.* Do not repatriate excessive amounts of profit. Be sure to use profits to modernize and upgrade facilities and equipment in the same manner done in the domestic country. The foreign part of the business should not be exploited.
- *Provide a comprehensive package of benefits.* Benefits such as health and life insurance, vacations, and retirement are appropriate to provide security and job satisfaction.
- *Provide fair compensation to employees.* Even though wages may be lower in the foreign country, develop an equitable salary schedule. Provide for regular evaluations and reasonable salary adjustments that are commensurate with economic conditions and improvements in productivity.
- *Provide training and a mechanism for employees to advance their careers.* An employee's self-concept must be recognized, and opportunities should be provided to help each person achieve desired goals. Promotions and movement within the firm should be structured to improve employee morale. People need to have the opportunity and support necessary to attain their work-related objectives.
- *Respect traditions and the culture.* Even though the traditional work procedures in the foreign country may be less efficient than those employed in the domestic country, do not be tempted to make major changes. If workers are accustomed to taking a siesta in the middle of the afternoon, then keep this schedule to promote good working relations. Do not fly the U.S. flag from the flagpole and Americanize the work environment. Disregarding tradition will only create resentment that may culminate in government intervention or restriction.
- *Sell stock in the company to employees if the firm is public.* A stock option program as a component of compensation will allow employees to invest in the firm. This will help people identify with the firm and view it as a local organization rather than a foreign entity. Employees who own part of the firm may be less critical because they want to see their investment grow.

Obviously, these are only a few of the many efforts that can be initiated to be fair and a good citizen in the foreign country. Treating people nicely not only lessens political vulnerability, but also improves productivity. A good rule to follow is to treat foreigners the same way people in the home country are treated. After all, the foreign aspects of the business are just an extension of the home-country business, only in a different location. Employing a different business demeanor in the foreign country than at home makes no sense. Unfortunately, good citizenship and treating people fairly will not guarantee the absence of political risks. In those countries where the society contains people who believe the United States is evil and eschew anything American, trying to conform and be fair may not help. Being nice is unlikely to overcome the deep-rooted feelings held against the American way of life. Also, governmental decisions that increase political risks are usually done for self-serving reasons even though the firm and its product may be viewed favorably by the nation's citizens.

Economic Cooperation among Nations

Many of the political problems of marketing in foreign countries can be eliminated if governments affiliate and cooperate economically. All cooperating governments agree to relinquish various aspects of their sovereignty and integrate in ways that benefit everyone in the cooperating countries economically. As a result of this cooperation, business conditions in the participating countries are improved, and international marketers obtain improved environmental stability for conducting business. The international marketer needs to appreciate the various economic integrations of nations around the world because of the opportunities and benefits that can be achieved by doing business within them.

Six common types of economic integration are recognized. In each, the participating governments are willing to relinquish a different amount of sovereignty. The degree to which economic, social, and political cooperation exists among the participating nations ultimately determines the kind of integration. The six recognized forms of integration are listed in Exhibit 8.3.

Exhibit 8.3

Types of Economic Integration

- Preferential trading agreement
- Free trade association
- Customs union
- Common market
- Economic and monetary union
- Political union

A **preferential trading agreement** is the weakest form of integration, which is formed when member nations give preferential access to select products. Agreed-to tariff reductions are granted on these products when shipped between member nations. Each member nation retains its own tariff barriers against products entering from nonmember nations. The international marketer can benefit from this integration by receiving a lower tariff than do sellers from nonmember nations when products are shipped among any of the member states. Examples of a preferential trading agreement include the South Asian Preferential Trade Area (SAPTA) and the agreement between the European Union countries and seventy-nine African, Caribbean, and Pacific (ACP) countries.

A **free trade association** exists when member nations eliminate trade barriers on agreed-upon products. This means that the agreed-upon products can be freely moved across the borders of member nations with no restrictions. Free movement of merchandise means the international marketer can move products from one member country to another without governmental intervention. No restrictions such as tariffs or quotas can be imposed by member governments against firms in other member nations that want to market their products in any member country. Products can be relocated from one country to another or sold across borders as easily as shipping merchandise between Philadelphia, Pennsylvania, and Trenton, New Jersey. Each member government retains its own external trade barriers with nonmember nations. Thus, managers in firms located outside the free trade association must comply with the trade restrictions imposed by each member country in which business is to be conducted. Examples of free trade associations include the North American Free Trade Agreement (NAFTA) and the Central European Free Trade Association (CEFTA).

A **customs union** will have all the characteristics of a free trade association except that member governments agree on a common set of external trade restrictions to be assessed against imports from nonmember nations. That means international marketers can freely move products among member nations. However, when products are imported from a firm located in a nonmember nation, the trade restrictions confronted will be the same from one member nation to another. Thus, for example, the management of the importing firm will not pay higher tariffs to bring products into one member country than into another. To form a customs union, government leaders must relinquish more of a nation's sovereignty than when forming a free trade association. Examples of customs unions include the Southern African Customs Union, the European Union-Turkey Customs Union, and the Liechtenstein-Switzerland Customs Union.

A **common market** is the same as a customs union with the addition of free movement of labor and capital. Free movement of labor and capital facilitates international business more than just free movement of products does, but requires the relinquishing of additional sovereignty by member nations. Employees can be citizens of one member nation and work in another member nation without restraint or prior approval such as a work permit. One of the concerns that governments must overcome is that foreigners will take jobs away from local people, which will increase the nation's unemployment rolls. Through a common market, government leaders seek to unify their economies while remaining politically independent. Government leaders of member nations seek to harmonize aspects of their economies to facilitate freer trade among the members. Business law, agriculture, and transportation are examples of policies that may be harmonized. Economic integration creates an environment that attracts international marketers because of the commonality of business practices that exist. Examples of common markets include the Caribbean Community and Common Market (CARICOM) and the most successful common market, the European Union (EU).

An **economic and monetary union** has the characteristics of a common market with the addition of a common currency. The government of each member nation must relinquish sovereignty over its ability to issue money and agree to use the single currency adopted by economic and monetary union members. The advantage of a common currency to the international marketer is that sales can be made in any of the member nations without the need to consider currency conversion as a part of the transaction. The Eurozone, comprising the sixteen members of the European Union that have adopted the euro as their currency, is the only economic and monetary union at present.

A **political union** has all the characteristics of an economic and monetary union as well as a supranational government. The governments of the individual member nations relinquish most of their sovereignty to a central government that is composed of representatives of the various member nations that make decisions on behalf of the member governments. The supranational government regulates policy regarding overall business practice. The representatives of the supranational government make laws that bind the member nations and have the power to enforce those laws through the courts. Examples of political unions include the United States of America (the fifty states are bound by the federal government) and the United Kingdom (England, Scotland, Wales, and Northern Ireland are integrated under one government).

Economic integration helps remove tariff and nontariff protectionist barriers to trade. Member nations' governments implement conditions favorable to free trade. As a result, business conditions are improved and the international marketer finds doing business in the member nations easier because of the consistency and stability afforded. Economic integration not only improves the business environment for the international marketer but also expands trade, improving the standard of living for people in the member nations (see the discussion about why international marketing occurs in chapter 4).

EXISTING MARKET AGREEMENTS AMONG NATIONS

Numerous market agreements have been formed for economic purposes among nations in various regions of the world. The success of these organizations is mixed; however, all have benefitted members in some way. Exhibit 8.4 lists economic agreements among nations.

The international marketer can benefit from operating in integrations such as those listed in Exhibit 8.4. The benefits of operating in an economic cooperation of nations include the following:

- access to suppliers
- avoidance of import tariffs
- cooperation and standardization of infrastructure among member nations
- easier access to the markets of all member nations
- easier movement of products from one nation to another
- increased commonality of business practices

Because of the benefits to the international marketers and the resulting improvements to the economies of member nations, the incidence of economic cooperation is increasing. As the world shrinks and populations become increasingly cosmopolitan, differences in

Exhibit 8.4

Economic Integrations

Andean Community of Nations (CAN)
Arab Cooperation Council (ACC)[1]
Arab Maghreb Union (AMU)[2]
Asia-Pacific Economic Cooperation (APEC)
Association of Southeast Asian Nations (ASEAN)
Caribbean Community and Common Market (CARICOM)
Central European Free Trade Association (CEFTA)
Common Market for Eastern and Southern Africa[3]
Common Market of the South (Mercosur)
Cooperation Council of the Arab States of the Gulf (CCASG)[4]
East African Community (EAC)
Economic Community of West African States (ECOWAS)
Eurasian Economic Community (EAEC)
Euro-Mediterranean Partnership (EMP)[5]
European Economic Area (EEA)
European Free Trade Association (EFTA)
European Union (EU)
EU-Turkey Customs Union
Greater Arab Free Trade Area (GAFTA)
Latin American Integration Association (LAIA)
North American Free Trade Agreement (NAFTA)
South African Development Community (SADC)
Southern African Customs Union
Union of South American Nations (UNASUR)[6]

[1]ACC has been inactive since the Gulf Crisis.
[2]AMU is inactive, and the latest initiatives in 2005 were stalled by Morocco's refusal to meet.
[3]Expanded in 2008 to include EAC and SADC.
[4]Also known as the Gulf Cooperation Council (GCC).
[5]Also known as the Barcelona Process.
[6]Formed by the merger of the two main trading groups in South America, Common Market of the South (Mercosur) and the Andean Community of Nations (CAN) in 2008. The name was changed from South American Community of Nations (CSN) in 2007.

lifestyle decrease, minimizing sovereignty issues that impede integration. The international marketer should always be alert to improving business conditions and opportunities presented by changes in existing and newly formed economic integrations.

THE EUROPEAN UNION

By far the most successful and famous integration of nations is the **European Union (EU).** Currently composed of twenty-seven nations, in 2009 the EU has a population of approximately 491 million compared to about 307 million for the United States, and a GDP nearly equal to that of the United States at $14.5 billion.[6] Although the per capita GDP of the EU in 2009 was only $32,700 (compared to $46,400 for that of the United States),[7] these numbers represent a significant market potential and, therefore, an attractive market for the international marketer. The EU is a substantial trading bloc and can offer the international marketer exceptional opportunity.

The EU evolved from a number of events occurring after World War II that were intended to prevent war from ever again occurring in Europe. The war damaged the economies of the European nations. To avoid the economic mistakes following World War I, rebuilding the war-torn economies and restoring viable world trade were high priorities. Also, the idea of some form of European federation was considered desirable. A U.S. initiative, the Marshall Plan, was conceived in 1947 to accomplish the reconstruction process. Over an approximately four-year period, about US$12 billion was appropriated and distributed to various European economies. The **Organization for European Economic Cooperation (OEEC)** was organized in 1948 among seventeen Western European countries to administer and allocate the aid authorized under the Marshall Plan. The Marshall Plan monies were offered to all European countries; however, the aid was refused by leaders of the Eastern European countries that fell under the control of the Soviet Union. An "Iron Curtain" formed between Eastern and Western Europe, leading to a cold war that made participation by the Eastern European countries in the Marshall Plan politically inappropriate. The cold war provided further impetus to the idea of a unified Europe, to counter potential Soviet aggression against West Germany. However, efforts to create a European defense community and a European political community met resistance.

The precursor to the EU was the **Benelux Customs Union**, which was formed in 1944 by the Belgian, Dutch, and Luxembourg governments in exile in London. The Benelux Customs Union formed a free trade area for a limited number of products and entered into force in 1947. It is considered to be the first modern-day attempt at economic integration. As a result of the success of the Benelux Customs Union, leaders of Belgium, the Netherlands, and Luxembourg joined with leaders of West Germany, France, and Italy to form the **European Coal and Steel Community (ECSC)** by signing the Treaty of Paris in 1951. The ECSC provided for free movement of coal and steel among the members. The pooling of steel and coal was considered important to preventing another European war.

Meanwhile, the members of the OEEC could not agree about how best to respond to the cold war threat of the Soviet Union and its Eastern European satellite countries. Two factions emerged, each with different objectives. One group, led by France, advocated a unified Europe. This group of nations was supported by the United States because of the potential for a unified military and the standardization of weapons systems. The other group of nations was led by United Kingdom and favored a looser type of worldwide freer trade. The British favored this arrangement because of their affiliation with the countries scattered around the world that comprised the former British Commonwealth of Nations. As the disagreements between these two factions continued, the six members of the ECSC decided to form the **European Economic Community (EEC)** with the ratification and signing of the Treaty of Rome on March 25, 1957. Two years later, in 1959, the other group of nations, who were more concerned with national rights and maintaining their individual sovereignty, formed the **European Free Trade Association (EFTA)** by signing the Stockholm Treaty on January 4, 1960. The charter nations of the EEC and EFTA are listed in Exhibit 8.5.

EFTA increased membership by adding Finland in 1961, Iceland in 1970, and Liechtenstein in 1991. Subsequently, Austria, Denmark, Portugal, Sweden, Finland,

Exhibit 8.5 **Original Members of the European Economic Community (EEC) and the European Free Trade Association (EFTA)**

European Economic Community	European Free Trade Association
Belgium	Austria
France	Denmark
Italy	Norway
Luxembourg	Portugal
Netherlands	Sweden
West Germany	Switzerland
	United Kingdom

and the United Kingdom left EFTA to become members of the EU. Today only Iceland, Liechtenstein, Norway, and Switzerland remain members of EFTA. Iceland, Liechtenstein, and Norway are members of the European Economic Area (see below) and, therefore, enjoy participation in most aspects of the EU single market without joining.

The OEEC was replaced by the **Organization for Economic Cooperation and Development (OECD)** in 1961 when the purpose of the OEEC was fulfilled and all Marshall Plan aid had been dispensed. The OECD included all the countries that had been members of the OEEC plus Canada, Japan, Spain, and the United States. The representatives of the OECD nations wanted harmonization of tax, fiscal, and related policies of member countries consistent with the requisites for freer trade.

The goals of the EEC were divided into two phases. The first phase was economic integration; the second, political integration. Ultimately, the members of the EEC envisioned a political union that would be comparable to a United States of Europe. The first phase included establishing common policies and rules of conduct such as for competition, trade, transportation, and agriculture and was to be completed within ten years. The timing for this goal was too ambitious; it is still not accomplished. The second phase remains a distant vision.

The success of the EEC surpassed that of EFTA. As a result, other European nations sought to join the EEC to benefit their economies. As the EEC membership grew, the organization's name was changed to the **European Community (EC)** and eventually to the European Union (EU) by which it is known today. Membership is expected to continue to grow and eventually include most European countries. On October 3, 1990, the unification of East and West Germany brought the first of the former Iron Curtain countries into the EU. The 2004 enlargement was an ambitious effort to unite Eastern Europe firmly with the West. Admitting the large number of Eastern bloc countries was motivated by the desire to reunite Europe and to prevent Eastern Europe from ever becoming Communist controlled again. On January 1, 2007, Bulgaria and Romania became members, which increased membership to the current twenty-seven countries. Croatia, Macedonia, and Turkey are candidate members.[8] Exhibit 8.6 lists the current members of the EU and the dates of their admission.

Exhibit 8.6 **Members of the European Union and Membership Dates**

Original Members, 1957	Belgium,* France,* Italy,* Luxembourg,* Netherlands,* and West Germany
January 1, 1973	Denmark, Ireland,* and United Kingdom
January 1, 1981	Greece*
January 1, 1986	Portugal* and Spain*
October 3, 1990	Reunification of East and West Germany (Germany*)
January 1, 1995	Austria,* Finland,* and Sweden
May 1, 2004	Cyprus,* Czech Republic, Estonia, Hungary, Latvia, Lithuania, Malta,* Poland, Slovakia,* and Slovenia*
January 1, 2007	Bulgaria and Romania

*Indicates a Eurozone country that has adopted the euro as its sole legal tender.

Three important recent steps for the EU were the approval of the Single European Act in 1986, the Maastricht Treaty in 1992, and the European Economic Area in 1994. The **Single European Act** established procedures for standardizing remaining impediments to free trade and introduced the concept of European political cooperation. The **Maastricht Treaty** modified the Treaty of Rome, established the European Union, and formed the economic and monetary union that resulted in the creation of a common currency (the euro) on January 1, 1999. On January 1, 2002, the euro currency began circulation, and the individual country currencies were phased out in all countries that were then EU members except Denmark, Sweden, and the United Kingdom, which were exempted. Since then the members that use the euro (euro area or zone) have expanded to sixteen countries. Those countries are indicated by an asterisk in Exhibit 8.6. Although not members of the EU, Andorra, Kosovo, Monaco, Montenegro, San Marino, and the Vatican City have adopted the use of the euro as their official currency. Also, a large number of countries have pegged their currencies to the euro. The **European Economic Area** was created to enable EFTA countries to participate in the EU without the necessity of joining. With these three efforts complete, the opportunity is enhanced for the EU to become a true political union.

The economic cooperation afforded by the EU and its predecessors, the EEC and EC, provides an environment that results in at least five advantages to member nations:

- *Changed attitudes toward progress.* As a result of the improved business environment and improved standard of living, people look more favorably at increases in productivity, technology, and modernization.
- *Economies of scale.* The larger market is conducive to business growth. Prior to the integration, small family-owned and -operated businesses were the norm. After integration, the size of businesses tended to enlarge. The expanded market size provided the opportunity to increase sales, resulting in economies of large-scale production and a reduction in the number of small family-owned businesses.

Exhibit 8.7 **European Union License Plates**

Even the format for license plates issued by EU members is standardized. All will eventually have a white or yellow background with black numbers and letters and a blue stripe on the left containing the twelve stars of the EU flag and the country code.

- *Growth of the middle class.* As businesses have expanded and grown, the number of jobs has increased along with salaries. More people have moved into the market economy, which has resulted in reduced spreads in income for labor and a concomitant rise in the number of middle-class people.
- *Improved standard of living.* The welfare of people improves with growing employment, rising salaries, and declining prices. People have more money and can afford to buy more and better products.
- *Reduced prices.* The result of economies of scale is reduced costs that are passed along to consumers in the form of lower prices.

The benefits of economic cooperation, as exemplified by the success of the EU, provide advantages to the international marketer. Entrance into any member country of an economic cooperation of nations gives the international marketer access to the citizens of all member nations. Tariffs are removed for business conducted among member nations. The international marketer finds the movement of products, people, and money to be facilitated. Business practices are standardized, simplifying production and legal considerations. The costs of doing business are reduced because of the common business practices. The international marketer should consider the benefits offered by an economic integration when making the decision to enter foreign markets (see chapter 5).

THE LEGAL ENVIRONMENT

No international judicial body exists to address problems arising among citizens of different countries. Likewise, no international organization seeks out and prosecutes business people who behave unethically or illegally. Although an organization called the World Court does exist, it has no real international power and cannot enforce decisions. Because of sovereignty, each nation has its own legal system that is binding on the international marketers doing business there. Therefore, international marketers must abide by the laws of each country in which they are conducting business. The international marketer must be prepared to encounter laws governing business practices in foreign countries that are different from those existing in the United States.

The legal systems of all countries can be conveniently grouped into three basic categories:

- code law (civil law)
- common law
- Islamic law (Shari'a or sacred law)

In countries where **code law** exists, policies regarding various issues have been specified in advance in the form of written guidelines. The courts follow the intent of these policies or codes in rendering decisions. For example, in Brazil, the builder is responsible for ten years after a project is completed for all construction-related problems, regardless of the reason. For another example, in the EU, the seller is required to replace any mail or parcel shipments that do not reach the buyer regardless of the reason. Some codification of U.S. law has occurred with the Uniform Commercial Code.

Common law predominates in the United States, the United Kingdom, and most countries under the influence of the United States and the former British Commonwealth of Nations. Questions of law are based on precedents set by previous court decisions, and, therefore, courts will try to interpret the present imbroglio in terms of decisions rendered previously in similar situations.

Islamic law is based upon following the provisions of the Quran. The Quran is the sacred book from God directed to the prophet Mohammad. Appropriate conduct is determined by consulting the Quran. Islamic values taken from the Quran are the core of an unwritten law in Islamic countries such as Saudi Arabia, Egypt, Turkey, and Iran.

What are the implications of different forms of law for the international marketer? Contract terms may be interpreted differently depending upon which law is applied. For example, "customary merchandisable quality" has a different meaning in Germany than in the United States. A German requesting beef livers of a "customary merchandisable quality" was shipped a mixture of cow and steer livers by a U.S. supplier. The German complained that the cow livers were not of "customary merchandisable quality" because they were softer than steer livers and had to be sold for a lower price. To the U.S. supplier, "customary merchandisable quality" meant full and unbroken livers from either gender of animals that were approved by the United States Department of Agriculture (USDA). Obviously, should the dispute go to court, the decision would be affected by which country's law would be applied.

Similar confusion is possible where the term *ton* is used. A ton may be considered to be 2,000 pounds by law in most Far Eastern countries and 2,240 pounds in the United States. See chapter 2 for information about the difference between the metric and American ton measures. Likewise, what is implied or not implied in a contract may vary. A U.S. customer ordered oranges from an Israeli supplier to be delivered by ship. Upon arrival, the oranges were all spoiled. The U.S. buyer had failed to stipulate that the oranges should be shipped in a refrigerated container. During shipment the oranges spoiled from the heat in the hold of the ship. The U.S. buyer had assumed that since oranges are perishable, the seller would be obligated to use refrigerated transportation. For another example, trademark protection depends on registration in code law countries and on proof of first use in common law countries. And a strike may be considered an act of God in code law countries because it is unpreventable, but a strike is not an act of God in common law countries because it is considered preventable. Thus, inability to fulfill a contract because of a strike by labor would be viewed differently in a code law country than in a common law country.

The courts generally interpret contract terms on the basis of customary trade practices when the intentions of the buyer and seller are known. The implication for the international marketer is to specify fully, concisely, and accurately all conditions to an agreement in the written contract. The courts must base decisions on what is contained in the contract and cannot determine intent without written direction. Careful preparation of the contract is necessary so that, if a dispute arises where litigation is required, the court will be able to accurately discern intent.

Even when a contract is well written, problems can occur because of the laws in the foreign country. For example, if the decision is made to terminate a relationship with an agent or distributor, many costs can be incurred because of the protection afforded these intermediaries by local law. Ending the relationship may require giving several years advance notice or paying a large termination fee even if the termination is lawful and legitimate.[9] Regardless of the reason for terminating the relationship, the decision and action may be deemed to deprive the intermediary of the ability to earn a livelihood. Because of the subtleties, the manager must be familiar with foreign law and choose channels carefully.

The seller should also include a force majeure clause in the contract. A **force majeure clause** protects the seller from the inability to fulfill a contract because of events that are beyond the seller's control (acts of God). Unexpected events over which the seller has no control cannot be used as an excuse for noncompliance. For example, assume delivery was promised to a buyer in France on July 24. After the product was delivered to the Port of Philadelphia for export, a hurricane damaged the dock, preventing the ship from loading. Repairs had to be made to the dock before products could be loaded on the ship. As a result, the product did not arrive at the buyer's location until August 15. The fact that the delivery was late is a breach of contract. If a force majeure clause were included in the contract, the seller would not be held liable for the late delivery. The seller cannot control the weather and therefore is not culpable.

THE JURISDICTIONAL CLAUSE

More than one country is involved when an international sale occurs. In which nation should the case be tried if litigation is required? When an international dispute arises, the court must decide which country's law should be applied. Suppose an American company is shipping a product purchased from a seller in Italy to a buyer in Canada by means of a Greek steamship company on a ship registered in Liberia and piloted by a Spanish captain with a Mexican crew. The American firm did not receive payment from the Canadian buyer. The American firm wants to go to court to seek restitution. Which country's law should be used during the litigation?

The seller should always include a **jurisdictional clause** in a contract that specifies the law to be applied. Courts will honor the intent of the contracting firms if specified in the contract. In the case of a conflict, the court will determine the jurisdiction for trying the case based on the jurisdiction specified in the contract. If no jurisdictional clause was included in the contract, then the decision is based on where the parties entered into the contract. If this cannot be determined, then the court will determine where the provisions of the contract were performed. The law of this country will be applied during litigation even if the seller's lawyers are unfamiliar with it. To prevent the possibility that law will be used that is unknown or undesirable, the seller should specify the law desired by including a jurisdictional clause in the contract. If the buyer objects to the nation chosen, which will generally be the seller's domestic country, then the law of the buyer's country can be specified. If that country's law is unacceptable to the seller, then a third country's law that is acceptable to both parties should be identified and written into the contract.

The courts are not obligated to uphold a jurisdictional clause, although they normally do. In the past, when the contract has not been completed within the country indicated in the jurisdictional clause, courts have occasionally disregarded the specified country's law and used different rules in determining what law applies. If the law is specified in the contract, the probability is greater that the desired law will be employed.

SETTLING DISPUTES

As a general rule, settling international legal disputes out of court is preferred to suing. Going to court should be avoided if possible for at least four reasons:

- *A court appearance is costly.* Considerable expense is incurred in any litigation. Lawyers must be hired to represent the firm and prepare the case. Management's time must be redirected to assisting the lawyers and away from revenue-producing activities. Travel to court may be required for all people involved. In the case of an adverse decision, financial restitution may be required.
- *Litigation is time consuming.* The case must be prepared, which will involve considerable time prior to the court appearance. Arguing a case can also be a lengthy and drawn-out process.

- *Resolution of the problem may be unfavorable.* The court may be unfamiliar with the country's laws, the other party's lawyers may argue more forcefully and skillfully, and the court may be unsympathetic. Thus, an undesirable decision could be rendered, management could become frustrated with the process, and additional expense and time for appeals could be incurred.
- *Unfavorable publicity may result.* Even though the case may be won, the press in the foreign country may be negative, creating a poor image of the company. Eliminating the immediate problem may cause bigger concerns in the future because of changed consumer attitudes toward the firm and its products. As a result, the potential for a loss of business might occur.

Unless the dispute is significant (involves large sums of money, strategic implications for management, or other such repercussions of importance), management would be advised to seek an out-of-court settlement. Such efforts may conclude more fairly for both parties to the contract, be less time consuming and expensive, and permit favorable long-term customer relationships to be maintained, even if the result is less than what could have been had via a court verdict. The accepted wisdom is to follow a three-step approach to settling international legal disputes:

1. placate
2. arbitrate
3. litigate

The initial effort should be to alleviate the dispute in a mutually agreeable manner. For example, a negotiated reduced payment may be financially superior to costly litigation even if full payment is granted by the court. Normally, the relationship with the buyer can be maintained when friendly gestures are used to resolve the misunderstanding. Placation should be the first resort to resolving any dispute.

If placation proves unsuccessful, the next step should be arbitration. Arbitration will be successful if both parties are willing to accept and be bound by the ruling of the arbitrators. The concept of arbitration is that each party to the dispute selects a representative to present its position. A third, impartial, individual acceptable to each party will then hear the representatives and make a decision. Often, established arbitration boards, such as the American Arbitration Association, with established rules, procedures, and permanent tribunals are employed. If the two companies' representatives to the dispute agree to arbitrate, the ruling of the arbitrators is enforceable in a court of law. A provision for arbitration may be written into the contract. However, questions have been raised about the legality of such agreements when made prior to a dispute.

Litigation should be considered the last resort for settling international business disputes. For the reasons mentioned previously, litigation should be avoided if another option is available. Attorneys must become integrated with the firm's business, knowledgeable of various countries' laws, and capable of acting locally in any country in which the firm has a presence.[10] The best advice is to avoid getting into legal disputes in the first place. Make sure contract provisions are complete, thorough, and inclusive enough to minimize the potential for problems. Try to consider possible dilemmas that could appear and make provisions in the contract to minimize their occurrence. Good planning and careful contract preparation can help minimize the chances of legal disputes.

CHAPTER SUMMARY

The international marketer is a guest in a foreign country and is therefore subject to the policies and desires of the foreign government. To be successful the international marketer must assess the prevailing and anticipated future political climate of any country entered. The form of the foreign government and its stability can affect the political risks of doing business in that country. Policies implemented by foreign governments for national or fiscal purposes can have undesirable consequences for the international marketer. To lessen the risk of political vulnerability, the international marketer must be a good citizen in the foreign country and treat foreigners fairly. Showing management's interest in the well-being of the nation can help minimize the chances of policies being implemented that may be detrimental to the firm.

Nations can improve business conditions for the international marketer through economic cooperation. Harmonization and standardization of government policies affecting business is facilitated through economic integration. The international marketer enjoys numerous benefits from operating in countries forming an economic integration. Of all the existing economic integrations, the European Union has been the most successful.

The EU, currently composed of twenty-seven nations, should continue to increase membership to include most European countries. Although an economic and monetary union presently exists among only sixteen member nations, inclusion of all members is desired. The goal for the EU is to become a political union. The EU offers international marketers a huge market with common business laws and policies. The sovereign influence of each member government on business practice is minimized; thus, the conduct of business among member nations is easier and more efficient.

The international marketer must adhere to the laws of each country in which business is conducted. Differences in laws have implications for the meaning and interpretation of contract terms. The international marketer must be careful in writing the contract so the intent of management is clear should a dispute have to go to court. A force majeure clause inserted into the contract protects the seller from acts of God. A jurisdictional clause should be included in the contract to specify which country's law will be applied to settle a dispute. Litigation should be avoided when possible because of the cost, time, and potentially unfavorable image problems that may occur from going to court. Try to settle any disputes that arise by mutual agreement so relationships with the buyer can be maintained. Arbitration is an alternative that might be pursued if the problem cannot be resolved mutually. Litigation should be considered as the last resort to settling international legal disputes. In situations requiring court involvement, be sure the contract wording is precise. Care and good planning in drafting the contract can help minimize the opportunities for legal disputes to occur.

KEY TERMS

Benelux Customs Union
Code law
Common law
Common market
Customs union
Economic and monetary union
European Coal and Steel Community (ECSC)
European Community (EC)
European Economic Area
European Economic Community (EEC)
European Free Trade Association (EFTA)
European Union (EU)
Exchange controls
Expropriation
Force majeure clause
Free trade association
Import restrictions
Islamic law
Jurisdictional clause
Maastricht Treaty
Organization for Economic Cooperation and Development (OECD)
Organization for European Economic Cooperation (OEEC)
Political union
Preferential trading agreement
Price controls
Single European Act
Tax holiday

REVIEW QUESTIONS

1. Which of the political risks do you believe is the most devastating to the international marketer? Why?
2. What should the international marketer do to become less vulnerable politically?
3. Why is economic cooperation among nations beneficial to the international marketer?
4. List and describe the six types of economic integration that nations may adopt.
5. Trace the historical development of the European Union.
6. On a map of Europe, locate the current twenty-seven member nations of the European Union.
7. Do you believe the European Union will achieve the status of a political union by the year 2025? Why or why not?
8. What is a force majeure clause? Why should a force majeure clause be included in a contract?
9. What is the purpose of a jurisdictional clause?
10. How should the international marketer go about settling international legal disputes?

NOTES

1. "Argentina Imposes New Forex Controls," BBC News, March 25, 2002, http://news.bbc.co.uk/1/hi/business/1893088.stm.

2. Federico Fuentes, "Venezuelan Land and Factory Expropriations as Seen from the Labor Ministry and the Union Federation," Venezuelaanalysis.com, October 13, 2005, http://www.venezuelananalysis.

com/analysis/1412; and Ian James, "Chavez Says Mall to Be Expropriated in Venezuela," Associated Press, December 21, 2008, http://abcnews.go.com/Business/wireStory?id=6506658.

3. Jonathan Lynn, "WTO Approves Import Restrictions for Ecuador," Forbes.com, June 4, 2009, https://www.truthabouttrade.org/index2.php?option=com_content&do_pdf=1&id=14056.

4. Will Grant, "Chavez Boosts Food Price Controls," BBC News, March 4, 2009, http://news.bbc.co.uk/2/hi/7923073.stm.

5. Jeremy Ames, "Macedonia's New Flat Tax," NuWire Investor, February 15, 2007, http://www.nuwireinvestor.com/articles/macedonias-new-flat-tax-51002.aspx. and Aleksandar Stojkov, Marjan Nikolov, Borce Smilevski, "Flat *Tax Policy Assessment In Macedonia*," USAID, Center for Economic Analysis, September, 2008, http://www.cea.org.mk/Documents/CEA%20Final%20fiscal%20report_final.pdf.

6. Central Intelligency Agency, "United States," in *The World Factbook,* http://www.cia.gov/library/publications/the-world-factbook/geos/ee.html.

7. Ibid.

8. European Union, "Delegation of the European Commission to the USA," http://www.eurunion.org/eu/index.php?option=com_content&task=view&id=57&Itemid=51.

9. Andrea Knox, "The European Minefield," *World Trade* (September 1999): 36–39.

10. Michael Brownell, "Global Departments Must Balance Consistency, Autonomy," *Corporate Legal Times* (March 2001): 80–88.

9 Financial Risks and Currency Concerns

Eduardo Matrone is legal representative and CEO for Belatriz Artefatos de Metais Ltda. Belatriz, located in Paranavaí in the state of Paraná in southern Brazil, has experienced rapid growth since opening its business in June 1991. The Brazilian economy is about the fourth fastest growing in the world. The company, a small firm with 100 employees and sales of about one million U.S. dollars, produces high-quality 925-silver-, rhodium-, and 18-carat-gold-plated jewelry sold through wholesalers. Currently, jewelry is being supplied under the brand Belatriz Jewelry to buyers in forty-four countries.

Management stresses the quality of its products. All pieces are produced in nickel-free tombac, a type of brass with a low percentage of zinc. Two copper layers are applied over the tombac, and each piece is finished with three layers of gold, silver, or rhodium applied in an electroplating process. Product lines include casting rings, pendants, earrings, chains, bracelets and anklets, stamping rings, bangles, and rosaries. Jewelry designs include pieces with or without precious, semiprecious, and artificial gemstones. Management has established as its mission the production of high-quality, innovative jewelry. A team of designers is constantly searching for new international jewelry trends and creating innovative and exclusive designs in jewelry pieces.

Buyers pay for purchases via wire transfer. Products are shipped by Sedex in Brazil and FedEx to all other countries. Currently all sales are made by export. Were Matrone to consider selling jewelry in neighboring Argentina or another country from a sales office located in that country, price quotations and payment would be required in the other country's currency. Such a move would involve decisions about what to do with the foreign currencies received. Should income generated by a foreign sales office above anticipated operating expenses be retained in a bank account in that country or immediately converted to Brazilian reals? What kinds of problems will the foreign currencies cause for the accounting department when valuing sales generated by the new sales office? Considering how to handle the foreign currencies would be important to the firm's marketing efforts and bottom line.

Source: Based in part on information from Belatriz Jewelry at http://www.belatriz.com.

CHAPTER OBJECTIVES

After reading this chapter, you should:

- understand the impact of price inflation on marketing transactions;
- be able to convert one country's currency to an equal value of another country's currency;
- know how to protect a transaction from the effects of currency fluctuations;
- know how to protect assets from price inflation or devaluation; and
- know what administered exchange rates are and their effect on international transactions.

THE VALUE OF A COUNTRY'S CURRENCY

Since marketing managers prefer to receive monetary payment for transactions, currency and financial concerns become an integral part of international marketing. Currencies must be converted to facilitate payment. Thus, exchange rates are an important issue that can affect profitability. The **exchange rate** is the amount of a country's currency that can be exchanged for one unit of another country's currency. The exchange rate designates the value of one currency in terms of another, and thus the price at which a currency of a particular country can be bought or sold. For example, if the exchange rate for one U.S. dollar is 1.15352 Canadian dollars, you can receive 1.15352 Canadian dollars for every U.S. dollar exchanged.

The exchange rates of currencies fluctuate up and down relative to each other for reasons such as the supply of and demand for the various currencies, government debt, business conditions, inflation, banking and government trading of currencies, and confidence in the country's currency. Consequently, the worth of one country's currency is constantly changing relative to the value of another country's currency. To maintain financial stability and confidence in a country's currency, a government may elect to **peg** (fix) its currency to another major world currency such as the U.S. dollar, euro, or to a basket of currencies. The country's central bank must hold enough of the currency to which its currency is pegged to guarantee the exchange rate. If that cannot be done, as in the case of countries such as Mexico (1995), Russia (1997), Thailand (1998), and Kazakhstan (1999), the currency becomes overvalued, holding the currency becomes undesirable, and governments are forced to change the exchange rate of their currencies to the true market value.

Since 1985, governments with strong currencies do not peg their currencies but allow the exchange rate to be determined by a float instead. A floating exchange rate reflects the market conditions for the currency, resulting from supply and demand and other fiscal and business conditions occurring within the country. Thus, the exchange rate is changing up or down constantly in response to changes in these conditions. In this way, the worth of any country's currency relative to another is easily established. For example, assume one U.S. dollar is equivalent to two Brazilian reals and one U.S. dollar equals three Lithuanian litai. Then, one Brazilian real will be approximately equal to 1.5 Lithuanian litai. Since each real is worth 50¢ ($1 ÷ 2) and each litas is worth 33.3¢ ($1 ÷ 3); each real is worth 1.5 litai (50¢/33.3¢ = 1.5).

Exhibit 9.1 **Hypothetical Devaluation of the Philippine Peso (PHP)**

Before devaluation		
US$1 = PHP50	or	PHP1 = 2¢
After devaluation		
US$1 = PHP100	or	PHP1 = 1¢

Acute changes in the exchange rate of one country's currency for that of another country result in devaluation or revaluation of the currency. **Devaluation** is the reduction in the value of one currency vis-à-vis other currencies. In other words, the currency is worth less relative to the value of other currencies after devaluation. As a result, more of the devalued currency is required to purchase an equivalent worth of other currencies. Devaluation is frequently employed as a means of helping to correct a nation's balance of payments' deficit. Although the permissible size of devaluation is regulated by the International Monetary Fund, any sovereign government may ultimately devalue its currency by any amount. Devaluation means the government sets the exchange rate at approximately the market rate. The rate is usually changed immediately in an effort to avoid currency speculation and panic. For example, Kazakhstan's central bank recently devalued the country's currency, the tenge, by 18 percent. The move caused Kazakhstan to join the recent currency devaluations of Ukraine (47 percent) and Belarus (21 percent), two other emerging markets in the region. The central banks of all three countries were unable to prop up exchange rates as currency reserves dwindled.[1]

To illustrate how devaluation works, an example is shown in Exhibit 9.1 for a hypothetical devaluation of the Philippine peso (PHP). After devaluation, the Philippine peso is worth less in terms of U.S. dollars than it was prior to devaluation. That is, more Philippine pesos are required to buy one U.S. dollar than were required before devaluation. In this example, the Philippine peso was devalued by 100 percent, because twice as many pesos were needed to equal a dollar after devaluation. To prevent large devaluations, governments may elect a "crawling devaluation" in which the currency is devalued slowly, in small steps. With this method, the government hopes faith in the currency will remain and panic selling of the currency can be avoided. However, the outcome is the same for holders of the currency whether or not the devaluation occurs all at once or slowly over a period of time—a loss of money in terms of other currencies.

How does devaluation improve a country's balance of payments? Two situations occur. First, imports are discouraged by devaluation, and second, exports are encouraged. In our hypothetical example, a Filipino would need to pay twice as much (PHP100 instead of PHP50) for a product imported from the United States priced at $1. The resulting higher prices for imports will encourage purchases to be changed from foreign suppliers to local Filipino suppliers. Also, after devaluation, an American can buy products for half the price from a Filipino supplier. The item that costs the American $1 before devaluation can be bought for 50¢ after devaluation. As a result, Filipino suppliers will find increased demand from foreign buyers. These situations contribute to a reduction in outflows of currency and an increase in the influx of currency that help improve the balance of payments exigency.

Exhibit 9.2 **Euro to U.S. Dollar Exchange Rate for Two Months**

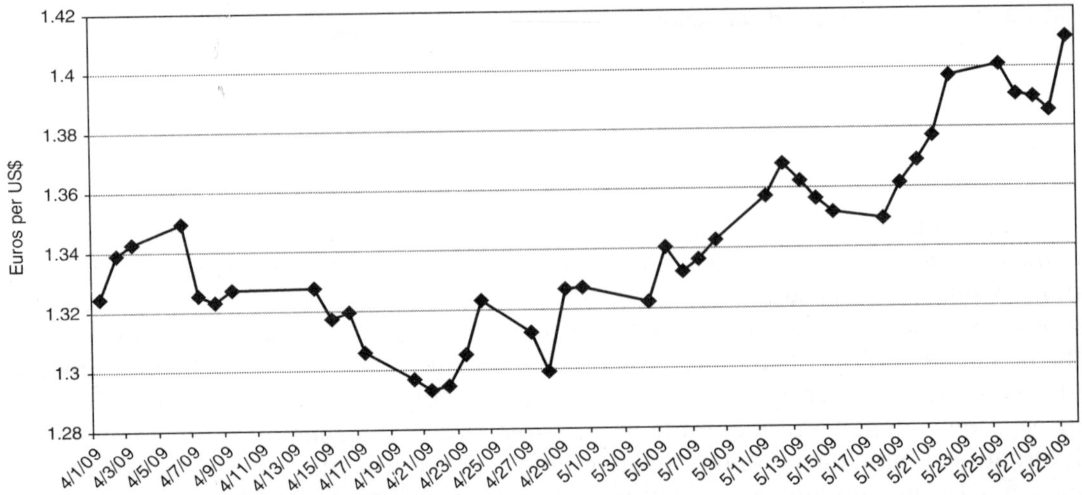

Source: European Central Bank, USD. http://www.ecb.int/stats/exchange/eurofxref/html/eurofxref-graph-usd.en.html.

The opposite of devaluation is revaluation. **Revaluation** is an increase in the value of one currency relative to other currencies. A given amount of the revalued currency will buy more of other currencies than was possible before the revaluation.

If the exchange rate changes slowly, the results can be the same as an immediate devaluation or revaluation. **Price inflation** is the slow loss of value of one currency vis-à-vis other currencies. The hypothetical change in the value of the Philippine peso shown in Exhibit 9.1 could have occurred over a period of months or years. The peso would still be worth one half of its original value. Therefore, price inflation occurring over a long period of time can be just as detrimental to the international marketer as devaluation. In fact, price inflation may be more devastating than devaluation because it occurs so slowly. Unless the exchange rates are carefully monitored, management may not be cognizant of the ever-so-slow loss in value. Price inflation can be thought of as gradual devaluation. Exhibit 9.2 shows the loss in value of the U.S. dollar to the EU euro during the two-month period from April 1, 2009 to May 29, 2009. During this time the dollar lost 0.6 percent of its value although the fluctuation was as great as 0.9 percent between the lowest (May 29, 2009) and highest (April 21, 2009) exchange rates. Exchange rates for any day for most currencies can be easily obtained from banks, publications such as the *Wall Street Journal,* or a variety of Internet financial sites such as the Universal Currency Converter at XE—The World's Favorite Currency Site (http://www.xe.com/ucc/).

EXCHANGE RATE CONVERSIONS

The international marketer will be required to convert one currency to another for reasons such as travel and valuing of transactions. Therefore, understanding how to work with exchange rates and make conversions is essential.

Exchange rates can be expressed in terms of one unit of either of the two currencies in question. For example, the exchange rate for the U.S. dollar and the Australian dollar can be expressed as 1 U.S. dollar equals 1.263 Australian dollars or 1 Australian dollar equals 0.7918 U.S. dollars or 79.18 U.S. cents. When one conversion rate is known, the rate in terms of the other currency can be easily calculated. Accomplish this by dividing the larger number into the smaller. To illustrate, if the conversion rate of 1 U.S. dollar = 1.263 Australian dollars is known, what is the conversion rate in terms of Australian dollars? Simply divide both sides of the equation by 1.263 to determine the number of U.S. dollars per one Australian dollar.

US$1 = AUD1.263, and dividing both sides of the equation by 1.263 gives

$$\frac{US\$1}{1.263} = \frac{AUD1.263}{1.263}$$

The right side of the equation reduces to AUD1, and the left side becomes US$.7918 or 79.18¢. Thus, AUD1 = US$.7918.

A general approach to making conversions is accomplished by using the same ratio technique employed in Chapter 2 for metric conversions. The conversion factor is placed in the denominator. The known quantity (in this case the possessed currency) is placed in the numerator on the appropriate side of the equation, and the unknown (desired currency) is placed in the numerator on the other side of the equation.

$$\frac{X}{US\$1} = \frac{AUD1}{AUD1.263}$$

Cross-multiplying gives AUD1.263(X) = US$1(AUD1). Solve for X by dividing both sides of the equation by AUD1.263.

$$\frac{AUD1.263(X)}{AUD1.263} = \frac{US\$1(AUD1)}{AUD1.263}$$

The left side reduces to X and AUD cancels out in the right side.

$$X = \frac{US\$1}{1.263}$$

$$X = US\$.7918$$

The same technique can be used when the exchange rate is expressed for one Australian dollar. If AUD1 = US$.7918, what is the exchange rate in terms of one US$? Place the exchange rate in the denominator. The known quantity is placed in the numerator on the appropriate side of the equation and the unknown is placed in the numerator on the other side of the equation.

$$\frac{X}{AUD1} = \frac{US\$1}{US\$.7919}$$

Cross-multiplying gives US$.7918(*X*) = AUD1(US$1). Solve for *X* by dividing both sides of the equation by US$.7918.

$$\frac{US\$.7918(X)}{US\$.7918} = \frac{AUD1(US\$1)}{US\$.7918}$$

The left side reduces to *X*, and US$ cancels in the right side.

$$X = \frac{AUD1}{.7918}$$

$$X = AUD1.263$$

The following problems can be calculated to help gain skill, speed, and confidence in converting from the exchange rate expressed in one currency to the exchange rate expressed in the other currency. The unit of currency for selected countries is listed in Exhibit 9.3.

Review Set 1

			Answer:
1.	GB£1 = US$1.6083	US$1 = GB£ ______	.6218
2.	US$1 = JP¥98.2766	JP¥1 = US$ ______	.010175
3.	US$1 = MXN13.4387	MXN1 = US$ ______	.0744
4.	HKD1 = US$.129	US$1 = HKD ______	7.7519

CURRENCY CONVERSIONS

The international marketer may need to convert various amounts of one currency to another currency. For example, a transaction for electric motors priced at US$257,000 is equivalent to what amount of South Korean won (KRW)?

The ratio technique can be used to make this conversion. Simply place the exchange rate in the denominator, the known amount of $257,000 in the numerator over the dollar side of the exchange rate (left side in this case), the unknown amount as an *X* in the numerator over the won side of the exchange rate (right side) and solve for *X*. If the exchange rate is US$1 = KRW1,263.68, then (ignoring the currency names):

$$\frac{257{,}000}{1} = \frac{X}{1{,}263.68}$$

Exhibit 9.3 **Currency Units for Selected Countries**

Country	Currency unit	Country	Currency unit
Argentina	Peso (ARS)	Mexico	Peso (MXN)
Australia	Dollar (AUD)	Netherlands	Euro (EUR €)
Belgium	Euro (EUR €)	New Zealand	Dollar (NZD)
Brazil	Real (BRL)	Norway	Kroner (NOK)
Canada	Dollar (CAD)	Pakistan	Rupee (PKR)
China	Yuan Renminbi (CNY)	Peru	Nuevo Sol (PEN)
Colombia	Peso (COP)	Philippines	Peso (PHP)
Denmark	Krone (DKK)	Portugal	Euro (EUR €)
Ecuador	Sucre (ECS)	Russia	Ruble (RUB)
Finland	Euro (EUR €)	Saudi Arabia	Riyal (SAR)
France	Euro (EUR €)	Singapore	Dollar (SGD)
Germany	Euro (EUR €)	South Africa	Rand (ZAR)
Greece	Euro (EUR €)	South Korea	Won (KRW)
Hong Kong	Dollar (HKD)	Spain	Euro (EUR €)
India	Rupee (INR)	Sweden	Krona (SEK)
Indonesia	Rupiah (IDR)	Switzerland	Franc (CHF)
Iraq	Dinar (IQD)	Taiwan	Dollar (TWD)
Ireland	Euro (EUR €)	Thailand	Baht (THB)
Israel	New Shekel (ILS)	Turkey	Lira (TRY)
Italy	Euro (EUR €)	United Kingdom	Pound (GBP £)
Japan	Yen (JPY ¥)	United States	Dollar (USD $)
Laos	Kip (LAK)	Venezuela	Bolivar (VEB)
Malaysia	Ringgit (MYR)		

Cross-multiplying yields:

$$X = 275{,}000(1{,}263.68)$$
$$X = \text{KRW}347{,}512{,}000$$

Any conversion from one currency to another can be easily made if this ratio method is followed. Changing from a foreign currency to U.S. dollars is accomplished with the same method. For example, how many U.S. dollars are equivalent to 5,300,000 Swedish kronor? If the exchange rate is US\$1 = SEK7.8284, then:

$$\frac{X}{1} = \frac{5{,}300{,}000}{7.8284}$$

Cross-multiplying yields:

$$7.8284X = 5{,}300{,}000$$

Divide both sides of the equation by 7.8284.

$$X = US\$677{,}022.12$$

Whether the exchange rate is expressed in terms of one dollar or one krona does not matter for the purposes of the computation. If in the previous problem the exchange rate was expressed as SEK1 = US$0.12774, that exchange rate is placed in the denominator and the problem would be set up in the same manner.

$$\frac{5{,}300{,}000}{1} = \frac{X}{.12774}$$

Cross-multiplying yields:

$$X = 5{,}300{,}000(.12774)$$
$$X = US\$677{,}022.00$$

The small difference of 12 cents is due to the precision with which the exchange rate was expressed, i.e., the number of decimal places provided.

The following problems can be worked to help gain skill, speed, and confidence with currency-to-currency conversions.

Review Set 2

			Answer:
1. US$15,684 =	________ JP¥	US$1 = JP¥98.2766	JP¥1,541,370.10
2. US$25,396 =	________ SAR	SAR1 = US$.267	SAR$95116.10
3. 56,255 =	________ US$	US$1 = .7207	US$78,056.06

4. How many Indian rupees can be obtained for US$43,776 if the exchange rate is INR1 = US$.02103? INR2,081,597.70
5. 75,645,225 Brazilian real can be exchanged for how many Great Britain pounds if the exchange rate is £1 = BRL3.1562? £23,967,183.00
6. If the exchange rate is HKD1 = COP266.156, what is the amount of Columbian pesos that can be had for 25,000 Hong Kong dollars? COP6,653,900.00

EXCHANGE RATE IMPLICATIONS

What are the implications of exchange rate fluctuation for the international marketer? Whenever the international marketer holds or will receive currency that will lose value relative to a stronger currency (will suffer from price inflation), the marketer will lose money. To illustrate, suppose a contract has been completed to sell corn priced at US$4 million to a buyer in India, and the U.S. seller agrees to accept payment in rupees when the corn is delivered ninety days later. Because the rupee is a weaker currency than the U.S. dollar, if the American seller does not take steps for protection, money will be lost when payment is received.

If the exchange rate at the time the contract was negotiated was US$1 = INR47.6036, the American seller contracted for 190,414,400 rupees.

$$\frac{4{,}000{,}000}{1} = \frac{X}{47.6036}$$

Cross-multiplying gives:

$$X = 4{,}000{,}000(47.6036)$$
$$X = 190{,}414{,}400 \text{ rupees}$$

If the exchange rate at the time the corn arrives and payment in rupees is made deteriorates to US$1 = INR48.5517, and payment is made in rupees, the 190,414,400 rupees can be exchanged for only $3,921,889.40.

$$\frac{X}{1} = \frac{190{,}414{,}400}{48.5517}$$

Cross-multiplying gives:

$$48.5517X = 190{,}414.400 \text{ and}$$
$$X = \$3{,}921{,}889.40$$

The loss is $78,110.60 ($4,000,000 – $3,921,889.60) or a little over 1.95 percent of the selling price.

$$\frac{\$78{,}110.60}{\$4{,}000{,}000} \times 100 = 1.95276\%$$

The sum of $78,110.60 was lost simply because of the change in the exchange rate and inactivity on the part of the American seller.

Money held in a weaker currency in a bank will experience the same fate. If the money is held long enough, price inflation over an extended period of time will have the same effect as devaluation. For example, if the Indian government decided to devalue its currency 15 percent, from US$1 = INR47.6036 to US$1 = INR54.7441, holders of rupees would immediately lose 15 percent of their worth in terms of U.S. dollars or other stronger currencies. If the exchange rate for the Indian currency were to slowly change over a period of two years from US$1 = INR47.6036 to US$1 = INR54.7441 because of price inflation, the consequence would be the same for holders of the Indian currency. The only difference would be that the loss occurred immediately from devaluation and slowly over time from price inflation. Price inflation might be considered more insidious, because management can be unaware of what is happening if it is not monitoring the apparently benign, miniscule day-to-day fluctuations.

The following problems can be calculated to help gain skill, speed, and confidence with understanding the impact exchange rates can have on marketing transactions.

Review Set 3

1. How many dollars will be lost if an American exporter agrees to accept Turkish lira in payment 120 days after the contract is signed? Assume the exchange rate at the time the contract is signed is US$1 = TRY1.3181, and the exchange rate when payment is made is US$1 = TRY1.551. The value of the shipment is US$759,328.

   Answer: US$114,021.59

Solution

When the contract was signed, the American exporter agreed to accept 1,000,870.24 lira in payment.

$$\frac{759{,}328}{1} = \frac{X}{1.3181}$$

Cross-multiplying yields:

$$X = 759{,}328(1.3181)$$
$$X = TRY1{,}000{,}870.24$$

When payment is made 120 days later, the TRY1,000,870.24 received will be converted to $645,306.41 at the exchange rate that prevails then.

$$\frac{X}{1} = \frac{1{,}000{,}870.24}{1.551}$$

Cross-multiplying yields:

$$1.551X = 1{,}000{,}870.24$$
$$X = \$645{,}306.41$$

The loss is US$114,021.59 (759,328 – 645,306.41) or about 15 percent of the value of the shipment. Depending on the profit margin for the transaction, the profit could be substantially reduced or even wiped out by the effects of price inflation.

2. How many dollars will be lost if a foreign buyer in Iraq is delinquent in paying a bill by 15 days? Assume the exchange rate at the time of sale was IQD1 = US$0.0008567, and the exchange rate when payment is received is US$1 = IQD1,194.4662. The price of the purchased merchandise is US$499,950.

   Answer: US$3,149.76

Solution

When the sale was made, the equivalent value was 583,576,510.00 dinars.

$$\frac{X}{1} = \frac{499{,}950}{.0008567}$$

Cross-multiplying gives:

$$.0008567X = 499{,}950$$
$$X = IQD583{,}576{,}510.00$$

When payment is received, the 583,576,510.00 dinars were worth $488,566.78.

$$\frac{X}{1} = \frac{583{,}576{,}510.00}{1{,}194.4662}$$

Cross-multiplying yields:

$$1.194.4662X = 583{,}576{,}510.00$$
$$X = US\$488{,}566.78$$

The loss is US$11,383.22 (499,950.00 – 488,566.78). Almost 2.3 percent of the value of the sale was lost in a two-week period.

3. How much money was gained by converting 40,174 Swiss francs held in a savings account for two years in Switzerland to U.S. dollars? The exchange rate when the francs were deposited was CHF1 = $.81334, and the exchange rate when the francs were converted two years later was CHF1 = $.920516.

   Answer: US$4,305.69

Solution

If the francs were converted at the first exchange rate, $32,675.12 would be obtained. In other words, the equivalent of US$32,675.12 were deposited in Swiss francs.

$$\frac{40{,}174}{1} = \frac{X}{.81334}$$

Cross-multiplying yields:

$$X = 40{,}174(.81334)$$
$$X = \$32{,}675.12$$

If the francs were held and converted at the later exchange rate, $36,980.81 would be obtained.

$$\frac{40{,}174}{X} = \frac{X}{.920516}$$

Cross-multiplying yields:

$$X = 40{,}174(.920516)$$
$$X = \$36{,}980.81$$

By holding the Swiss currency for the additional time, an extra US$4,305.69 (36,980.81 – 32,675.12) could have been gained. In this case, the Swiss franc increased in value relative to the U.S. dollar, and continuing to hold the francs was desirable. The gain is independent of any interest that may have been earned while the francs were on deposit.

A cost will normally be incurred to convert one currency to another. The bankers and financial agents who facilitate the conversion will charge a fee, quote a less favorable exchange rate, or both. The difference between their quoted exchange rate and the market rate is their price or commission for the service. These charges and fees must also be taken into account when currencies are converted to determine the amount that will be obtained from the exchange.

PROTECTING ASSETS FROM PRICE INFLATION OR DEVALUATION

International marketers that receive payment in foreign currencies will need to take the risks of price inflation and devaluation into consideration. Price inflation and devaluation can affect the value of current assets such as cash, receivables, inventories, short- and long-term investments, earnings scheduled for repatriation, and declared or anticipated financial dividends in terms of the home country currency. The longer it takes to turn the asset into cash (the less liquid it is), the more vulnerable it will be to the effects of price inflation and devaluation. Most fixed assets in the country experiencing price inflation or devaluation will retain their value—become worth more in proportion to the loss in value of the currency.

What should be done to protect vulnerable assets from the loss of value when held in countries experiencing price inflation or where the risk of devaluation exists? The basic rule governing the international marketer is to secure and hold strong currency. Never hold weaker currency. When requesting payment, accept only the stronger of the two currencies involved. For example, if an American is making an export sale to a buyer in Argentina and the Argentine peso is weaker than the U.S. dollar (the Argentine peso is suffering from price inflation), the American should request payment in dollars and not pesos. Accepting payment in pesos is risking monetary loss; as the value of the peso declines relative to the dollar, the American will receive fewer dollars for the pesos when exchanged.

Research indicates that willingness to accept weaker foreign currencies in payment is related to sales volume.[2] The larger the size of an individual transaction, the larger the amount of sales to a customer, and the longer the relationship with the customer, the more willing the seller is to accept payment in the buyer's currency. As might be expected, the profit margin of firms in which management is willing to accept payment in the weaker currency tends to be lower than that of firms in which management requires payment in the stronger currency.

Obviously, working entirely in the stronger currency is not always possible. For example, if a sales branch or production facility exists in Argentina, then sales to Argentines will of necessity be in pesos. Asking local Argentine buyers to pay in U.S. dollars, for instance, would be as impractical as your local grocer requesting payment in some foreign currency. Thus, steps must be taken to minimize the risks inherent in price inflation or devaluation. Do business in the stronger of the two currencies whenever possible. When that is not possible, precautions must be taken to protect the firm's financial position.

What precautions can be taken to help protect the firm's financial position? Specific precautions that may be used will fall into one of these two categories:

- minimize current assets
- maximize current liabilities

Any effort consistent with these two rules will reduce the size of potential financial losses due to exchange rate fluctuations.

Assuming the home country currency is stronger than other currencies, activities compatible with these two basic principles may include the following:

- Borrow working capital from sources in the countries having weaker currencies. Doing so will permit repayment with less money denominated in the stronger currency units.
- Convert all idle (not required for working capital) foreign cash (weak currency) into the home country currency (strong currency). Hold as little of the weaker currency as possible. Obviously, working capital will be needed to maintain day-to-day operations in countries with weaker currencies. Transfer what is needed daily so excess stocks of the weak currencies are not held.
- Engage in a currency hedge. A **currency hedge** is an arrangement that reduces the risk of a transaction by acting as a buffer against currency fluctuations.

Exhibit 9.4 **Forward Contract Currency Hedge**

Merchandise Transaction (Customer)	Financial Transaction (Bank)
When contract is negotiated	
Agree to sell for US$1,000 equivalent to PHP50,000 at the spot rate of US$1 = PHP50 with delivery in 180 days.	Agree to sell PHP50,000 for US$909 in 180 days at the 180 days forward rate of US$1 = PHP55.
When contract is fulfilled and payment received (180 days later)	
Receive PHP50,000 equivalent to US$500 at the depreciated rate of US$1 = PHP100 (loss = US$500).	Sell PHP50,000 for US$909 at the agreed to forward rate of US$1 = PHP55 (loss = $91).

At least six kinds of hedges, described here, are available to the international marketer.

— A **currency swap** is the simultaneous purchase and sale of a foreign currency at a fixed exchange rate. Initially, both parties exchange equal amounts of their currencies (swap currencies) at the spot rate. Transactions take place between the two parties using their swapped currencies over the time period agreed for the currency swap. At the maturity of the swap, the principle (original) amount is re-swapped at the predetermined exchange rate, allowing both parties to have their own (original) currencies. This hedge is useful when frequent sales are made in a particular foreign currency, or when seeking financing in a foreign country.

— A **forward contract** is a sale of one currency for another at a fixed rate on a specified future date. Arrangements are made with a financial institution such as a bank to link the date of the currency sale with the date payment will be made. In this way, the exchange rate is secured and future volatility in exchange rates will have no impact. The exchange rate fluctuation risk is shifted onto the banking system. If price inflation or devaluation causes the value of the currency you agreed to sell to deteriorate below the agreed- to exchange rate, the bank is obligated to buy the weaker currency at the agreed- to exchange rate. As a result, money is saved in terms of the stronger currency. The prevailing exchange rate at the time the contract is signed and the hedge sought is referred to as the **spot rate**. The exchange rate that a third party (bank) will agree to pay for the currency at a specified later time is known as the **forward rate**. A forward contract currency hedge, using the hypothetical exchange rates employed in Exhibit 9.1, is illustrated in Exhibit 9.4.

In this hypothetical case, the forward contract saved the seller US$409 ($500 – $91). The $409 would have been lost if the seller had agreed to payment in Philippine pesos and converted them to dollars when payment was received 180 days later. As indicated earlier, 100 percent devaluation is severe and unlikely; however, price inflation extended over a period as short as six months can result in a significant decline in the value of some currencies and have a severe impact on a transaction's profit.

— A **nondeliverable forward contract** is a form of forward contract that can be used for emerging market currencies where a conventional forward market does not exist or is restricted. The transaction does not involve the exchange of currencies and is settled in the seller's currency. At maturity, the difference in value between the specified forward rate and the prevailing spot rate is given to the seller in the seller's currency.

— An **option contract** is an agreement that gives the international marketer the right, but not the obligation, to sell a specified amount of a foreign currency at a specified exchange rate within a specified period of time. Unlike the forward contract, the option does not have to be used. Thus, if the exchange rate should improve, the option is not used, and the currency is exchanged at the favorable rate. However, if the exchange rate deteriorates beyond the specified rate, the option can be used.

— A **spot contract** is an agreement to sell a foreign currency at the spot rate two business days after the spot contract agreement is reached.

— A **window forward contract** is an agreement to sell a foreign currency at the spot rate within an agreed range "window" of days. Window forwards are useful when the actual payment date is uncertain.

- *Increase inventories of items that must be imported into countries with weaker currencies.* Buying now may be desirable because the prices of these products will increase as the values of the weaker currencies decline over time. Of course, the benefits of saving money now must be weighed against the costs—such as damage, pilferage, obsolescence, and storage—of holding additional inventory.
- *Increase payables in the countries with weaker currencies through longer credit terms.* Try to extend the payment date as far into the future as possible so fewer units of the stronger currency will be required to liquidate the debt. When doing this, take care to not become over-leveraged with debt.
- *Reduce receivables in countries with weaker currencies* by accelerated collection, discounting customer notes, and reducing the length of time permitted for paying on credit. Requiring payment at time of sale is most desirable to avoid receiving payment in the future with weaker currencies, which will be worth less in terms of the stronger currency. However, a trade-off does exist between speed of payment and the ability of certain customers to pay. To keep certain accounts as customers, the marketing concept and relationship marketing require taking the customer's financial situation into account. As a general rule, however, receiving payment in weaker currencies is more advantageous now than later so money is not lost when converted to the stronger currency.
- *Repatriate profits, dividends, royalties, fees, and interest as quickly as possible.* Pay all intra-company debts promptly. Holding the weaker currencies as they lose value means fewer units of the harder currency will be obtained when the conversion is made, resulting in lost income.
- *Request payment in the stronger currencies* when exporting to countries with weaker currencies, and reduce payment terms.

- *Transact all financing with sources located in countries with the weaker currencies.* Make payment guarantees in the weaker currencies. When repayment is made in the future, fewer units of the stronger currency will be required, saving money.
- *Pay with the weaker currencies and extend payment terms* when purchases are imported into countries with weaker currencies.

EXCHANGE CONTROLS

The international marketer must be cognizant of countries with exchange restrictions. Various exchange restrictions can interfere with the ability to convert from one currency to another or force exchanges at unfavorable exchange rates. Exchange restrictions are most likely to be encountered in poor and developing nations. The governments of these countries may believe exchange restrictions are necessary to help retain and prevent shortages of foreign exchange.

Administered exchange rates occur when the rates at which currency is bought and sold are artificially set at a rate different from the free market rate. If the government wants to restrict exchanges, the buying rate is set below the free market rate. Thus, when a given amount of the foreign currency is exchanged for another currency, less of that currency is obtained than would be the case at the free market exchange rate. Consequently, the international marketer must charge a higher price than usual so that the desired amount of the other currency can be obtained after an exchange. To charge the normal price would result in receipt of less of the exchanged currency than desired. Charging a higher price to obtain the desired amount of exchanged currency often results in a noncompetitive price, reducing demand, or making sales of the product difficult. Therefore, an administered exchange rate is a form of nontariff barrier (see chapter 5). An example of an administered exchange rate is shown in Exhibit 9.5.

Exhibit 9.5 **Administered Exchange Rates: Taiwan Dollar**

<table>
<tr><th>Buying Rate</th><th>Selling Rate</th></tr>
<tr><td>US$1 = TWD32.2981</td><td>US$1 = TWD35.75</td></tr>
<tr><td colspan="2">The buying rate is the amount of a bank's or money changer's national currency it is willing to exchange for one unit of another currency (the amount of the local currency that can be obtained for one unit of a foreign currency).</td></tr>
<tr><td colspan="2">The selling rate is the amount of a bank's or money changer's national currency it must receive in exchange for one unit of another currency (the amount of the local currency that must be given to obtain one unit of a foreign currency).</td></tr>
</table>

A product you want to sell for US$1 would have to carry a price of TWD32.2981 in Taiwan to be priced competitively. When the TWD32.2981 received for the product is converted back to dollars, the international marketer will have to exchange at a rate of TWD35.75 for the dollar. Thus, TWD32.2981 can be exchanged for only US$0.90 (90 cents). Since one dollar is needed for the product, the administered exchange rate makes the sale impractical. To receive a dollar, the price of the product must be TWD35.75, which causes your product to be overpriced relative to the competition that is selling its product for around TWD32.2981.

Doing business in Taiwan under these conditions is possible only if payment can be demanded in U.S. dollars or if income earned in Taiwan dollars is reinvested in Taiwan and not converted into U.S. dollars. If currency does not need to be taken out of Taiwan and profits can be retained in Taiwan dollars, business can be conducted as usual. If money must be taken out of the country, business becomes impossible unless creative ways such as countertrading are sought (see chapter 16).

Occasionally, an administered exchange rate known as a multiple exchange rate is encountered. A **multiple exchange rate** exists when more than one rate is established at which a country will exchange its currency. That is, fixed or administered rates and floating rates can exist simultaneously. Usually the fixed rates are established for products the government considers critical and wants to restrict or encourage as imports or exports. The various categories of administered rates can be discriminately applied to specific foreign currencies, industries, categories of products, purposes for the currency's use, or even specific firms. For example, at one time Russia established different exchange rates for tourists at banks, for commerce and business transactions, and for central bank transactions. Different administered exchange rates can be set for various situations, such as restricting or discouraging the importing of products government leaders consider nonessential and encouraging the importing of those products considered essential. Black markets may arise for the exchange of money from countries employing exchange restrictions. Like any exchange control, multiple exchange rates can make doing business in the country using them difficult or unprofitable.

CHAPTER SUMMARY

Doing business in a foreign country can leave the international marketer vulnerable to the impact of exchange rate fluctuations when conversions from one currency to another are made. If payment is received in the foreign currency, exchange rates can have an impact on the amount of money received after conversion to another currency. When exchanges are made from countries where the currency is experiencing price inflation or devaluation, financial losses may result.

Consequently, the international marketer needs to know how to convert one currency to another to understand the potential impact of currency conversions on the firm's financial situation. The international marketer also has to know how to protect the firm's assets and transactions from the effects of price inflation and devaluation and how to benefit from currency revaluation. The safest approach is to receive the stronger of the two currencies. When that is not possible, various steps consistent with minimizing current assets and maximizing current liabilities can be employed. A frequently used procedure is a currency hedge.

The international marketer should also be alert for countries in which administered exchange rates are utilized. Administered exchange rates make converting a foreign currency for the market rate amount of another currency impossible. Administered exchange rates can interfere with the ability of the international marketer to do business profitably in the foreign country.

KEY TERMS

Administered exchange rates
Buying rate
Currency hedge
Currency swap
Devaluation
Exchange rate
Forward contract
Forward rate
Multiple exchange rate
Nondeliverable forward contract
Option contract
Peg
Price inflation
Revaluation
Selling rate
Spot contract
Spot rate
Window forward contract

REVIEW QUESTIONS

1. What is price inflation?
2. What is the difference between price inflation and devaluation?
3. Explain what is meant by "exchange rate fluctuation risk."
4. Explain how an amount of Jamaican dollars can be converted to (a) U.S. dollars and (b) euros.
5. What are the implications of price inflation for the international marketer when making an export sale denominated in the currency of a country experiencing price inflation?
6. Discuss the ways an international marketer can protect the firm's assets from the effects of price inflation occurring in the foreign country.
7. What are the exchange rate implications for holding a foreign country's currency in a bank in that country?
8. Explain how a currency hedge works.
9. On a piece of paper, list five strong currencies and five weak currencies and explain why each is considered as strong or weak.
10. Explain how an administered exchange rate affects the international marketer's ability to conduct business.

NOTES

1. Nariman Gizitdinov, "Kazakh Central Bank Devalues Tenge 18%, Ends Support," Bloomberg News Service, February 4, 2009, http://www.bloomberg.com/apps/news?pid=20601087&refer=home&sid=aROyGJTxpQbA.

2. Saeed Samiee and Patrick Anckar, "Currency Choice in Industrial Pricing: A Cross-National Evaluation," *Journal of Marketing* 62 (July 1998): 112–24.

10 Organizing for International Marketing

Video Gaming Technologies, Inc. (VGT), grew 9,720 percent in one three-year period. The company was founded by Jon Yarbrough in 1991, and manufactures and leases Class II gaming machines to American Indian casinos in Oklahoma, South Carolina, and other places in the United States. Class II gaming includes bingo, pull tabs, punch boards, tip jars, instant bingo, and other games of chance similar to bingo.

A private company with headquarters in Smyrna, Tennessee, and facilities in Charlottesville, Virginia, and Tulsa, Oklahoma, VGT leases video terminals to American Indian tribes in about seventy facilities such as Comanche Nation Games, Cherokee Casinos, and Choctaw Gaming Centers. Yarbrough attributes the company's success to technological innovation and in-depth knowledge of gaming markets. Realizing that companies in this industry that do not innovate and offer new products of interest to customers become obsolete, Yarbrough works closely with gaming operators to create exciting games, adds requested features, develops player tracking capabilities, and meets specific needs. Because of this philosophy, VGT was first to the Oklahoma marketplace with LCD touch screens, stepper-reel live draw bingo games, and the revolutionary narrow-width gaming cabinet that lets facilities place two machines in the space traditionally taken by one game. Live-Call Bingo, the top-earning bingo Class II gaming platform for American Indian casinos, is manufactured by VGT. The VGT Treasure Quest Skill Game System combines high-resolution graphics and CD sound effects. A proven revenue generator in both domestic and foreign markets, the system offers nine proprietary VGT games such as Lucky Ducky, Mr. Money Bags, Red Hot Rubies, and Silver Dollar Shootout for customers to choose with each player station.

With revenues of US$152.1 million and only a 30 percent share of the Oklahoma market, future domestic growth is all but assured. Each leased gaming machine can generate in excess of US$50,000 per year for VGT, and as many as 2,000 machines can be leased to one casino. However, Yarbrough expects the greatest growth to come from foreign markets. Efforts are being made to enter China and several South American markets, as these two combined are expected to dwarf the U.S. market.

The future for VGT may be in foreign markets. However, as the company grows, a strain could be placed on the firm's organizational structure. With the firm's rapid growth, the organizational structure could stay in a constant state of flux. Keeping manufacturing, research and development (R&D), customer support, technicians to service machines, and marketing support adequate and efficiently organized could become increasingly challenging if not well managed. Management might need to consider questions such as the following as the firm grows: As foreign operations expand, how will the firm be organized to the best advantage? Can the firm function adequately with an export manager to oversee everything, or should a separate international subsidiary be created? If the business grows as expected, VGT could eventually realize more foreign sales than domestic sources. Management would have to put a lot of thought into what organizational structure will adequately support the anticipated foreign growth.

Sources: Based in part on information from Video Gaming Technologies, Inc., at http://www.vgt.net/; Allen P. Roberts Jr., "The Number 1 Company: Video Gaming Technologies Has Grown 9,720% in Three Years," Inc., November 1, 2005, http://www.inc.com/magazine/20051101/no1.html.

CHAPTER OBJECTIVES

After reading this chapter, you should

- know the organizational structures that may be used to support international marketing;
- understand how organizational structure affects the role of international marketing in the firm; and
- appreciate how management's commitment to international marketing affects the evolution of the role of marketing in the organizational hierarchy.

MARKETING'S PLACE IN THE ORGANIZATIONAL HIERARCHY

How should marketing be organized for international operations? What should be the location of the international marketing effort in the firm's organizational hierarchy? The answers to these questions should be influenced by the degree of the firm's international efforts and the importance management places on international sales. Obviously, the answers vary from firm to firm, and no one answer is universally correct. However, the placement of international marketing can be incorporated into at least five basic organizational orientations or structures. As the firm's international sales increase, management's commitment to international operations will change, precipitating modifications to the organizational structure. Thus, the process is somewhat evolutionary as management's international orientation changes; international sales increase in importance as a component of the firm's business, and commitment to international markets in turn increases.

Exhibit 10.1 **Customer Organizational Structure**

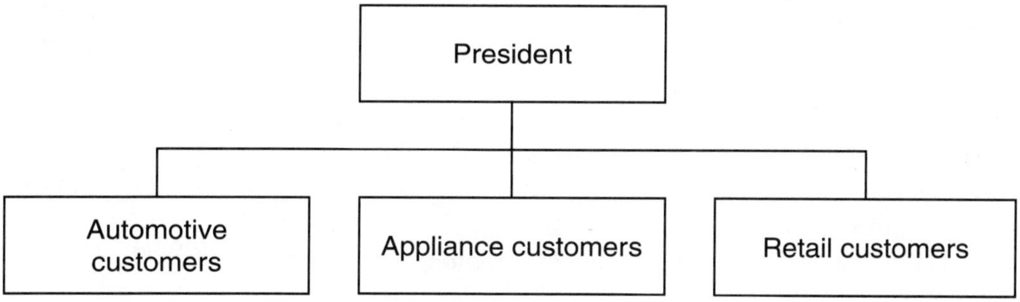

Exhibit 10.2 **Functional Organizational Structure**

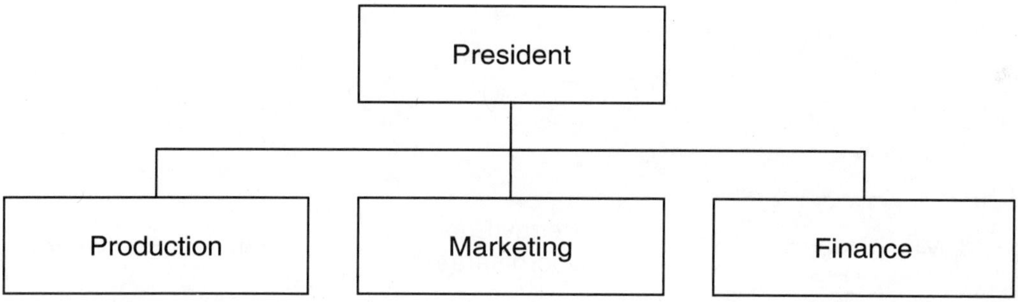

ORGANIZATIONAL ARRANGEMENTS

Management can employ any of the five different organizational arrangements listed below. Simple diagrams illustrate each orientation.

- *Customer.* Various kinds of customers can be grouped together. The various divisions are organized around the various customer categories. For example, if the firm's product is a switch and those switches are sold to a variety of industries and consumer groups, organizing by customer type may be desirable. The customer organizational structure is illustrated in Exhibit 10.1.
- *Function.* Business operations are segmented according to various applicable business disciplines when a functional arrangement is used. Thus, the divisions of the firm are arranged according to the kinds of work (functions) involved in the business. This structure is illustrated in Exhibit 10.2.
- *Location.* A geographic grouping may be desirable when customers in different areas of the market are unique. Climate, culture, and other unique characteristics may necessitate organizing divisions based on customers' geographic region. Exhibit 10.3 illustrates this organizational structure.
- *Product.* The various divisions of the firm are organized around the various products or product lines that are produced and sold. Each product or product

Exhibit 10.3 **Locational Organizational Structure**

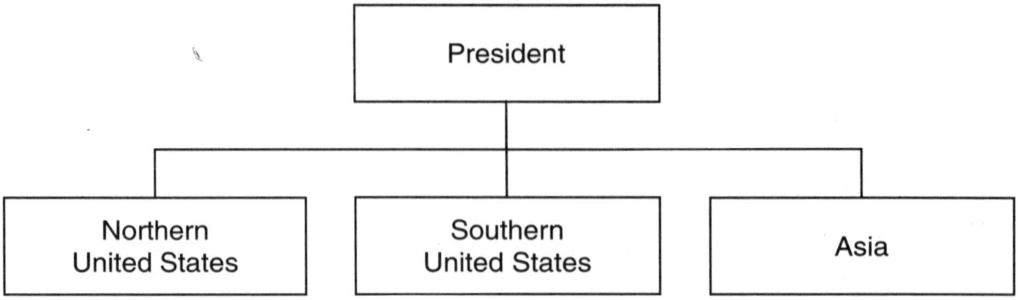

Exhibit 10.4 **Product Organizational Structure**

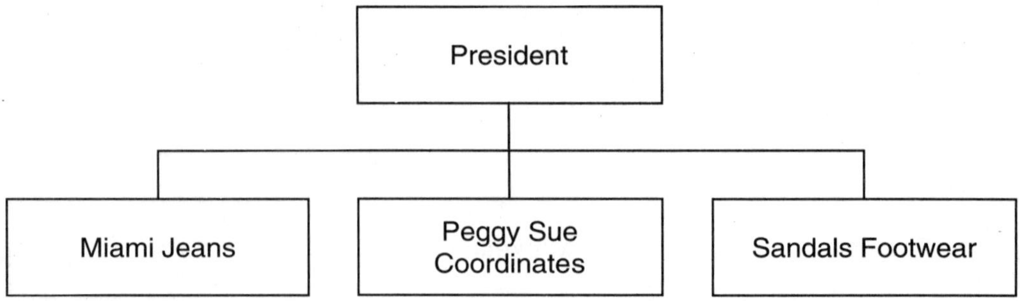

line is its own entity with a unique and distinct corporate identity. Exhibit 10.4 illustrates the product organizational structure.

- *Combination.* Combinations of the first four organizational arrangements are possible. For example, organizing by products and functions within product divisions is one possible method. In larger firms a hybrid or combination arrangement is common.

International Organizational Structures

The involvement of management in international marketing has been shown to be an evolutionary process.[1] Thus, initially, unless the firm was begun as an international business, organizational structure will contain no international marketing involvement. The location and importance of international marketing in the organizational structure will progress as international involvement increases. To illustrate the nature of these changes, a functional organizational arrangement will be employed. Any of the organizational arrangements described previously could be used; however, the functional arrangement permits the marketing activity to be displayed easily. The names used to describe the organizational structures are emblematic of the evolutionary nature of the internationalization process. The names do not have universal application, and the structures are sometimes labeled with different names. Regardless of the terminology used, the structures discussed are representative of the changing nature of the firm's involvement in international marketing as the evolution progresses. Also, the examples used for illustrative purposes must be simplifications of the various structures because every firm will have a unique arrangement that fits its organizational needs. Thus, no firm is likely to have a structure exactly like any of those shown. The structures presented represent basic organizational approaches; depending on the size of the firm and the nature of the firm's business, variations of the structures possessing greater complexity will be found in practice.

BUILT-IN EXPORT DEPARTMENT (NO EXPORT DEPARTMENT)

Initially, all sales are domestic unless the firm was started as an international business. As explained in chapter 5, management's attitudes become favorable to considering international opportunities as a result of either endogenous or exogenous influences. Although this may be an overt decision to seek business in a foreign market, the influence may be simply a fortuitous order received from a foreigner. When a foreign order is received, no mechanism is in place to process it. Therefore, existing personnel who are not really internationally trained must see to the order. Someone in marketing with international exposure from a source such as self-education or completion of a college course in international marketing will be assigned to fill the order. The person selected must be familiar enough with processing an international transaction to do a competent job. In addition to undertaking self-training where knowledge is lacking, this individual will have to seek the help of outsiders such as bankers and freight forwarders to get the job done. This responsibility is simply added on to the employee's normal work requirements. If a good job is done, future international orders will be assigned to this individual. This arrangement forms a **built-in export department** organizational structure because **no export department** formally exists. It is the first phase of the evolutionary process, in which export orders are processed by the domestic marketing staff without a designated support structure.

No real encouragement for exporting is provided in the firm's organizational structure, nor is an exporting function recognized as a separate entity. In other words, an identifiable international component of the firm does not really exist at this time. All international sales are treated the same as domestic sales in terms of the firm's organizational structure. The international efforts of the firm are housed in and considered a part of the firm's domestic marketing activities. Management tends to be ethnocentrically oriented, concentrates on domestic business, and pays little attention to international opportunities or the possibility of growing international sales. International orders are processed as received and considered to be supplemental business. No conscientious and organized planning is done to grow or expand international business. Management may even consider international sales as an undesirable requirement of doing business. These sales are nice to have but not really sought. The built-in export department organizational structure is shown in Exhibit 10.5.

Exhibit 10.5 **Built-in Export Department Organizational Structure**

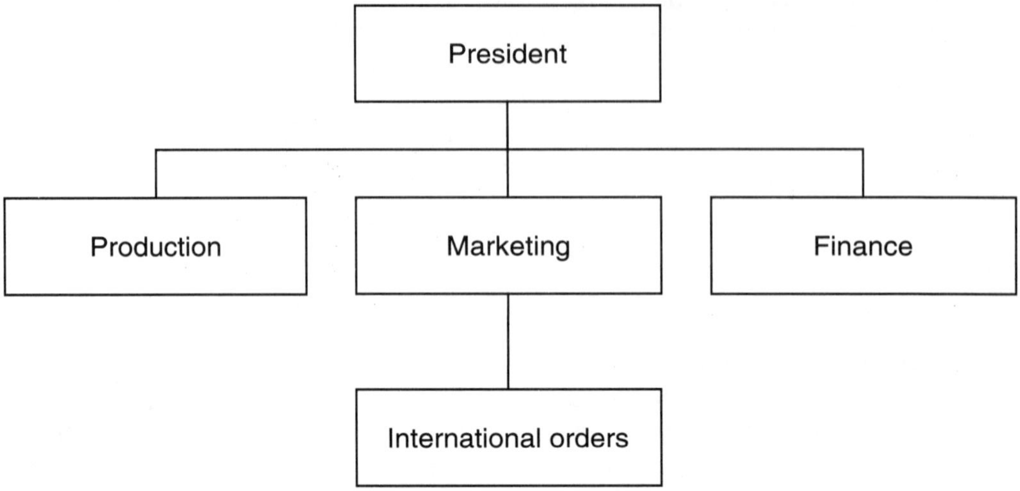

EXPORT DEPARTMENT

As the number of international orders grows, the workload of the individual designated to process them increases. Initially, this individual can facilitate the increased workload by working some additional hours or having some minor responsibilities reassigned to other marketing staff. Eventually, as the number of international sales becomes large enough, this individual cannot handle the international orders in addition to the regular domestic responsibilities even by working overtime. At this point, some major domestic responsibilities must be reassigned so adequate attention can be directed to processing international orders. As international sales increase, more and more domestic responsibilities must be assigned to others until this individual is devoting almost exclusive attention to the international component of the business.

If international business continues to grow, this individual will not be able to process all the international sales alone. Additional employees will have to be assigned to the international function as the workload increases. Also, as international sales increase, management becomes more aware of the impact being made by these sales on the firm's income and the potential that exists internationally. Eventually, when international business reaches some critical level, management begins to consider carefully how to expand foreign sales. Planning for new international business begins, and resources start to be allocated to support the international marketing efforts.

International promotions are started as the first effort to stimulate additional international business. Initially, the promotion efforts may be directed to the U.S. Department of Commerce in the form of trade shows and listings in foreign embassies through the International Buyer Program (IBP) and similar free and inexpensive means. As business increases, promotional efforts are increased and advertisements are placed in trade publications that have foreign readers. Eventually ads are placed in local publications printed and distributed in the various foreign markets and through direct mail pieces or other suitable media.

Exhibit 10.6 **Export Department Organizational Structure**

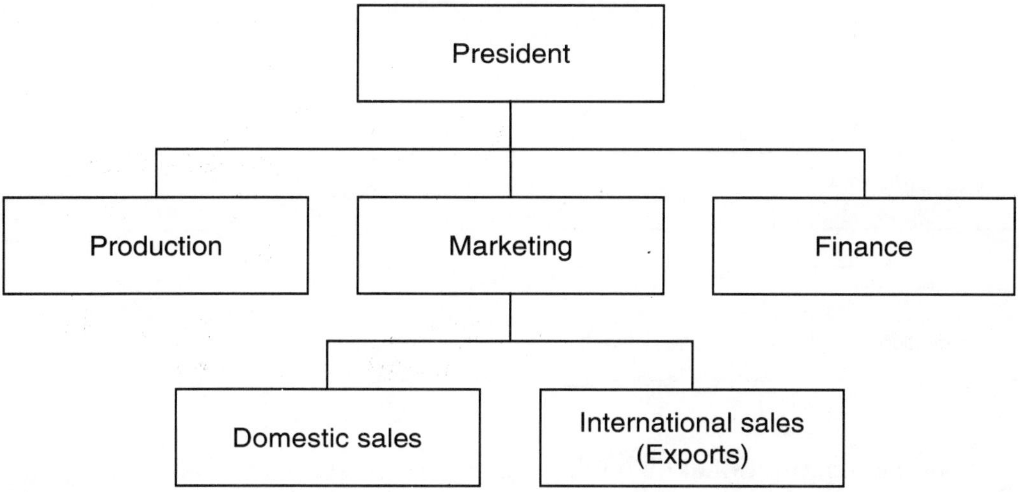

Management is now consciously seeking international sales as a component of the firm's market. Management realizes the potential of international business as a component of the overall business. To adequately direct the firm's international efforts and activities, a manager for foreign operations is required. A formal department must be established with a support staff appropriate for the amount of international business generated. An **export department** organizational structure is formed when management creates a separate marketing function to accommodate export business. Initially, this may consist of one individual or one individual and an assistant. Additional staff will be added as needed as international sales increase. Initially, international sales are derived entirely from exports. As international business increases, joint ventures may be explored. The international marketing component is separate from the domestic marketing effort and located in available facilities. Because the export manager may not have as much status as the domestic marketing manager or as much power in formulating corporate business policy as the domestic marketing manager, the international component may not receive all the resources needed to expand. International sales of up to about 10 to 15 percent of the firm's total sales may be accommodated with this organizational structure. Obviously, as the amount of business resulting from foreign markets grows, top management will pay more attention to export activities and the importance of the export department will increase along with its resources. The export department organizational structure is illustrated in Exhibit 10.6.

INTERNATIONAL DIVISION

As international business continues to grow, the export department form of organizational structure will gradually become inadequate to support the needs of a more involved and diverse international involvement. The international personnel are located

Exhibit 10.7 **International Division Organizational Structure**

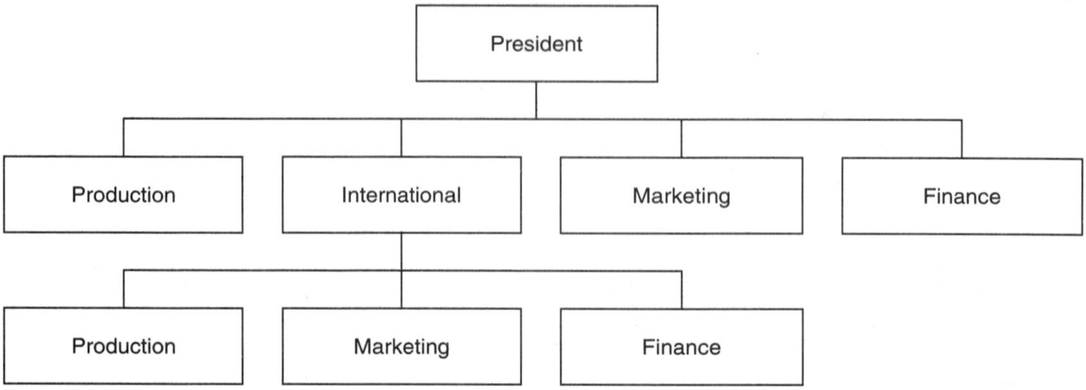

too low in the organizational hierarchy and cannot exert the leadership necessary to support the desired growth with just an export department. This will occur especially as the number of different products sold and foreign markets entered increases, and joint ventures and foreign direct investments are added as market entry methods. A structure designed to facilitate primarily exports will be unable to support the expanded involvement.

As foreign business reaches about 15 to 25 percent of sales and involves other market entry methods besides exporting, the staff required to manage such an international involvement will necessarily expand significantly. The activities that must be supervised become too much for one individual. Specialists in various aspects of the firm's international operations must be added to assure that operations function smoothly and supervision is adequate. The organizational structure will slowly evolve to an international division organizational arrangement. An **international division** organizational structure is distinguished by the existence of an international business function located at a top level in the firm's organizational structure. Support appropriate to a diverse and significant involvement in numerous international markets is provided. The international efforts will be considered as important as any other aspect of the firm's business operations. The international division organizational structure is shown in Exhibit 10.7.

With an international division organizational structure, the firm's international marketing activity is moved to a top level in the organizational hierarchy. This structure is feasible until foreign sales reach approximately of 25 to 40 percent of the firm's business. Market entry by means of joint ventures and foreign direct investments increases at the expense of exports. International operations are a part of the company at the top level even if the international division is located separately from the domestic part of the business. However, management still considers the firm primarily a domestic business with an international presence. The international division usually is located in the same facilities or city as the firm's headquarters. The fact that that location may not be in or near one of the cosmopolitan business centers such as New York City or San Francisco where access to international support is convenient is insignificant.

Exhibit 10.8 **International Headquarters Company Organizational Structure**

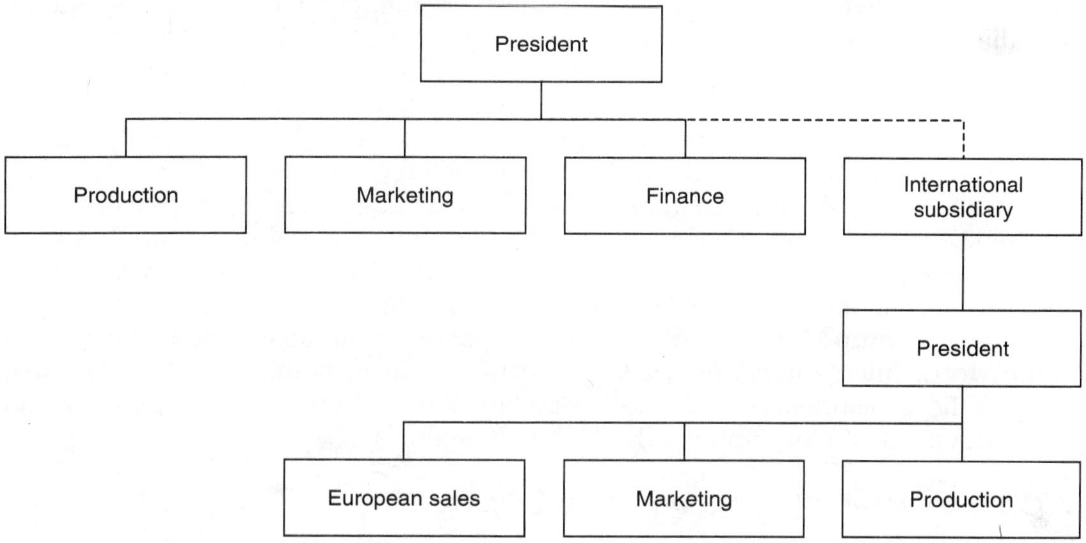

Occasionally, the international function is located away from the firm's headquarters in an internationally oriented city, or even in the foreign country contributing the largest amount of business. When the international division is separated from the firm's headquarters, it does not function independently, however. The international division remains an integrated part of the firm and is considered equivalent to any other division. Physical separation, when utilized, usually occurs as sales become a significant part of the firm's total business and as the organizational structure prepares to evolve into the international headquarters company organizational form. Being on an equal basis with the other functions of the firm, management of the international division can compete more effectively for resources and team support.

INTERNATIONAL HEADQUARTERS COMPANY

As international sales continue to grow, the percentage of the firm's total revenue from foreign sources will eventually exceed revenue from domestic sources. Consequently, separating the international component of the company from the domestic section becomes important. The international component becomes the predominant force of corporate success. Thus, international activities command an increasing share of the firm's resources, making separation appropriate. Eventually, organizing the international component as a separate corporation or subsidiary is necessary. An **international headquarters company** organizational structure results when the international business component is organized as a separate company but maintains affiliation with the domestic parent. International marketing is independent of domestic marketing yet structurally connected for business purposes. The international headquarters company organization structure is portrayed in Exhibit 10.8.

The president of the international subsidiary is also an officer of the parent company. The dashed line in Exhibit 10.8 indicates the international subsidiary operates separately yet is connected to the domestic parent company. The international subsidiary has its own board of directors that interlocks with the board of the parent company. All international operations are controlled and directed by the international subsidiary. The international subsidiary is normally physically separate from the domestic parent and usually in a foreign location. If located in the parent country, the international subsidiary will be in a cosmopolitan center such as New York City. The management of the international subsidiary makes decisions independently of the domestic parent and controls its own destiny. International marketing has been elevated in importance in the organization. An example of an international headquarters company organization is Altria Group, Inc., which until March 2008 was the parent company for Philip Morris USA, Inc., and Philip Morris International, Inc. Although Philip Morris International, Inc., was spun off from Altria, both firms continue to sell many of the same brands of cigarettes. Another example is the IBM Corporation and its subsidiary IBM Corporation UK (United Kingdom).

WORLD COMPANY (TRANSNATIONAL COMPANY)

A world company organizational structure is also known as a **transnational company** organizational structure, and both terms may be encountered when this organizational arrangement is employed. A **world company** organizational structure is distinguished by management that does business in most countries, considers all countries as potential markets, and considers no one country a domestic market. The organizational structure permits all foreign markets to be supported in the most efficient way possible. The world company organizational structure is illustrated in Exhibit 10.9. Since the firm is incorporated in more than one country, the boards of directors are identical.

As international sales increase, business from the country of the domestic parent becomes a smaller percentage of total business. At some point, management considers the company a truly global entity. That is, the world is the firm's market and no one country is more important than another in terms of business opportunity. Decisions to enter and leave markets are made on the basis of profit and not on the basis of country loyalty or national affiliation. Since currency transactions are important as a means of maintaining profits and net worth, moving large amounts of money from a weaker to a stronger currency is considered just part of normal business practice. This contrasts with the orientation of management in a firm in which the international division structure is employed, for example. If management in a firm employing the international division organizational structure were to face price inflation and a weakening of the domestic company's currency, efforts to convert that country's currency to a stronger one would be unlikely. Management would hold a domestic country perspective rather than a global perspective. But, management in a firm with a world company organizational structure would embrace a global perspective and consider such currency conversion necessary and routine. Since loyalty is owed to no country, management will tend to undertake efforts that are in their own best interest regardless of the potential impact on the country. The country's interest is considered only when it benefits the firm.

Exhibit 10.9 **World Company (Transnational Company) Organizational Structure**

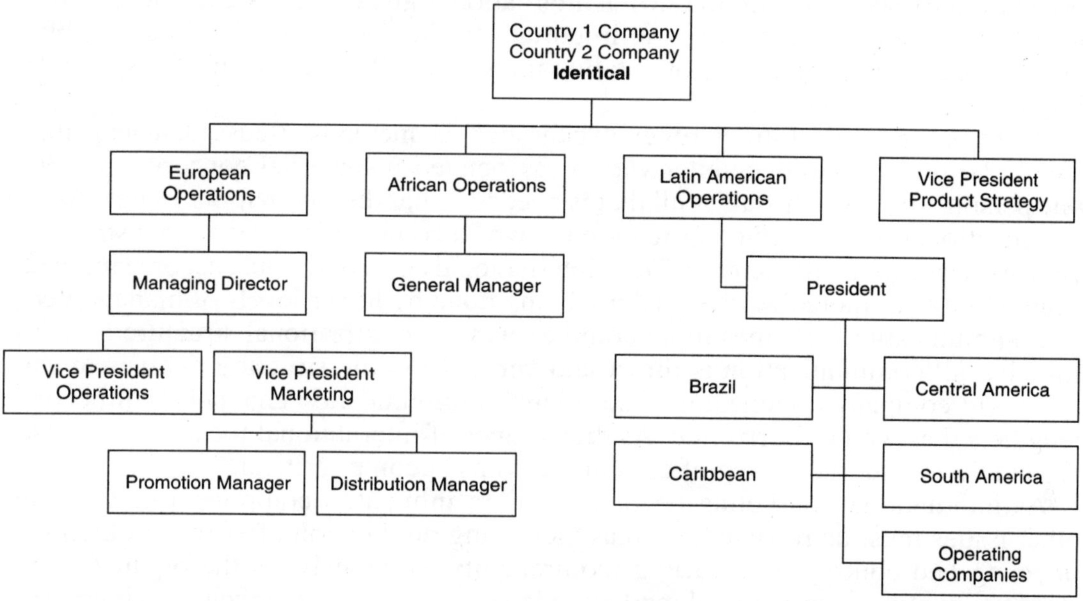

An example of a firm utilizing a world company organization structure is Unilever. Unilever NV (Netherlands) and Unilever PLC (United Kingdom) are the parent companies. With corporate centers in London and Rotterdam, the two companies operate as one. Another example of a firm with a world company organizational structure is Reed Elsevier, which was formed by the merger of Reed International Ltd., a British trade book and magazine publisher, and Elsevier NV, a Dutch science book publisher. Reed Elsevier is composed of two parent companies: Reed Elsevier Group PLC, a United Kingdom–registered company that owns the publishing and information businesses, and Reed Elsevier Finance BV, a Netherlands-registered company that owns the financing business. Royal Dutch Shell PLC is another firm that operates like a world company. In 1907, two holding companies, NV Koninklijke Nederlandsche Petroleum Maatschappij (Royal Dutch Petroleum Company NV), with headquarters located in the Netherlands, and Shell Transportation and Trading Company PLC, with headquarters located in the United Kingdom, began to cooperate and operate as one firm. In 2005, the two firms were unified and incorporated in the United Kingdom as Royal Dutch Shell PLC; however, the firm's headquarters and tax residence are in the Netherlands.

IMPLICATIONS OF CHANGING ORGANIZATIONAL STRUCTURE

As involvement, commitment of resources, and effort in international marketing increase, changes in organizational structure will need to occur to accommodate the growing participation. As the organizational structure changes, an evolution occurs that requires that the international marketing function be elevated in importance.

This is necessary if management is to assure that the correct customer and marketing orientation exists to sustain the firm's international growth. The rationale is similar to the marketing concept that is so important to the success of the domestic business. Maintaining a marketing orientation internationally as the firm grows is just as important as it is domestically.

As the organizational structures evolve through the methods discussed, management should be prepared to encounter various associated managerial concerns. Initially, one person with a small staff is all that is needed to handle international sales. As the organizational structure evolves toward the world company organizational structure, personnel and staff will increase. Thus, international operations must become more decentralized with more decision making being done by lower levels of management.

Communication becomes more complex as the organizational structure evolves. Initially, all communication is direct and vertical. As the structure evolves toward the world company organizational structure, communication channels will become lengthened as well as horizontal. As the number of international locations increases around the world, the timing of communications becomes critical.

As international marketing becomes a more influential component of the firm, other issues must be resolved, such as increasing duplication of effort, problems of planning and control, and staffing requirements. Obviously, as the organizational structure evolves, international marketing is elevated in the organizational hierarchy. As a result, management of the international marketing function can now have more input into and control of international marketing activities. Since decision making for international marketing is done at a higher level in the organization as the firm's organizational structure evolves, planning and controlling of international efforts are facilitated. This can have an invigorating effect on international growth.

Changes in organizational structure are necessary for growth in international business. Increases in international sales necessitate accommodating changes in the organizational structure. Management must stay abreast of the growth in international markets so that the organizational structure will keep pace. The organizational structure must constantly be monitored and revised to prevent it from growing obsolete and unresponsive to the needs of the foreign marketing efforts. Failure to employ an appropriate organizational structure to support international marketing efforts can adversely impact the effectiveness of the firm.

CHAPTER SUMMARY

Initially, management has no foreign sales unless the firm was created as an international business. Since all profits are derived from domestic customers, the firm's organizational structure does not contain an international marketing component. As foreign orders begin to be received, either fortuitously or by being sought, accommodations must be made in the firm's organizational structure. The responsibility may be given to an existing employee who has the ability to process international transactions or is willing to learn how, or by a new hire with the requisite international competency. Regardless of the option, management has taken the first step toward internationalization and is employing a built-in export department organizational structure.

The exact nature of the organizational structure will vary from firm to firm. However, as involvement in international marketing increases, the organizational structure also must evolve. This evolution involves at least five basic organizational structures that accommodate the degree of involvement and international commitment management has chosen. Each change in organizational structure reflects a movement toward a global marketing orientation or world company organizational structure.

The amount of international sales and commitment management makes to international marketing will influence which of the five organizational structures will need to be employed. As the organizational structures evolve, the international marketing effort will be elevated in importance and raised in the organizational hierarchy. A strong commitment to international marketing must be combined with giving priority to the international marketing function. As the level of international marketing in the organizational hierarchy is elevated, marketing decisions will, of necessity, receive increasing priority.

Evolving organizational structures have implications for resources and personnel needs. As the organizational structure evolves toward the world company organizational structure, decentralization results, communications become complicated, and duplication of efforts occurs. Management must constantly reassess the organizational structure and be willing to make changes that will facilitate the planning and controlling of international marketing efforts. What kind of organizational structure management employs at any point in time will be influenced by how oriented management is to marketing internationally and will help determine how well responses can be made to conditions confronted in the foreign market.

KEY TERMS

Built-in export department
Export department
International division
International headquarters company
No export department
Transnational company
World company

REVIEW QUESTIONS

1. Why is the firm's organizational structure so important to the success of international marketing?
2. For an international food products firm, give examples of how that firm might be structured by function, product, customer, location, or a combination of these.
3. Describe the built-in export department organizational structure.
4. Explain how the firm's organizational structure might evolve from the built-in export department organizational structure to the export department organizational structure.
5. Which of the five forms of organizational structure do you think most firms use? Why do you think this is true?
6. In what ways is the international headquarters company organizational structure different from the international division organizational structure?

7. What is unique about the world company organizational structure?
8. Which form of organizational structure would you recommend, and why, for a firm that exports to South America and the Caribbean? For a firm that has joint ventures in the Near East? For a firm that has foreign direct investments in Europe?
9. How does the international commitment and involvement of management affect organizational structure?
10. Explain what implications an evolving organizational structure to support international marketing has for management.

NOTE

1. Jan Johanson and Jan-Erick Vahlne, "The Internationalization Process of the Firm—A Model of Knowledge Development and Increasing Foreign Market Commitments," *Journal of International Business Studies* 8 (1) (Spring–Summer 1977): 23–32.

11 International Distribution Strategy: Marketing Channels

Stoudt's Brewing Company was the first microbrewery established in Pennsylvania. The brewery, located in Adamstown, was started in 1987 by Ed and Carol Stoudt. It has earned worldwide recognition for brewing some of the finest European-style lagers and ales and has won numerous awards at national beer competitions. All of its beers are produced in accordance with the German Purity Law of 1516 using only premium malt barley, fresh hops, true brewer's yeast, and pure Adamstown spring water.

Stoudt's produces four categories of beer: lagers, ales, big beers (about twice the alcohol content of lagers and ales), and seasonal beers. The company's lagers include Pils, a traditional German-style beer made with the acclaimed Czech Republic Saaz hops, and Gold Lager, recognized as one of the finest German-style beers brewed in America. Ales include American Pale Ale and Scarlet Lady Ale, an English-style ale brewed with Marris Otter (considered to be the finest barley for beer production) and Caramel malts. Big beers include Triple, which is brewed with an authentic Belgian yeast strain, Double IPA (India Pale Ale), and Fat Dog Stout, a British-style stout. Seasonal beers include Heifer-in-Wheat brewed in the summer, Oktober Fest available in the fall, Winter Ale sold in the winter, and Karnival Kolsch sold in the spring. All Stoudt's beers are packaged in quart or 12-ounce bottles. A bottling machine was purchased in 2004 for filling 12-ounce bottles. Prior to that time, 12-ounce bottles were filled under contract at out-of-town breweries.

From the brewery and through wholesale distributors and restaurants, Stoudt's beers are distributed to Pennsylvania, neighboring states of New York, New Jersey, Delaware, and Maryland, Washington, D.C., and the more distant states of Ohio, Massachusetts, Michigan, Virginia, Tennessee, Georgia, and California. Sales are coordinated by Eddie Stoudt, sales manager, and Michael Pearlman, sales representative. Also, several of the firm's beers are handled by Tom Buonanno, who once was a sales representative for Stoudt's Brewing Company, and is currently the brand coordinator for Muller, Inc., a beer wholesaler in Philadelphia. Were President Carol Stoudt to consider expanding sales to new domestic markets, it is likely the work for Eddie Stoudt and Michael Pearlman would become too great and another sales rep would have to be hired to support any significant market expansion.

Should Carol Stoudt ever consider expanding sales to foreign markets, one of her concerns would have to be what channel to use. She would certainly need to research the export market and become knowledgeable about various export-assisting intermediaries. If she wanted an arrangement that is similar to that of a wholesale distributor, with which she is familiar, a good choice might be an export management company (EMC). An EMC would perform activities similar to what Buonanno does at Muller, Inc. Additionally, some EMCs would work on commission, reducing the financial risk of developing the international market.

To evaluate the desirability of prospective EMCs, a preliminary investigation of firms in Category 22 (Beverages, Spirits, and Vinegar) in the Directory of Export Management Companies produced by the Federation of International Trade Associations (FITA) might be helpful. Three firms from the directory list appear to be good prospects. GD International Foodservice Marketing, located in nearby Allentown, Pennsylvania, represents fruit juices, protein drinks, and other nonalcoholic beverages, and currently exports to Canada, Mexico, Central America, the Caribbean, and the United Kingdom. JMB Capital Import Export Company, Inc., located in nearby Reisterstown, Maryland, represents juices and wine, and exports to Canada, Mexico, Central and South America, most of Eastern and Western Europe and Asia and the Far East. The third prospect, Robert Wright & Associates, Inc., deals exclusively in wine, is located in San Rafael, California, and exports to Western Europe, Oceania, and Japan. Contacting these companies to get more information about what each might be able to do would be desirable. In the end, however, Carol Stoudt would have to decide whether an EMC would be the right intermediary.

Sources: Based in part on information from the Web sites of Stoudt's Brewing Company, at http://www.stoudtsbeer.com/, and the Federation of International Trade Associations, at http://www.fita.org/emc.html.

CHAPTER OBJECTIVES

After reading this chapter, you should

- know what an international channel of distribution is;
- understand the difference between and desirability of direct and indirect channels;
- explain the factors that influence the international channel decision;
- know the intermediary institutions that may be part of an international channel;
- be able to identify an appropriate international channel; and
- know the causes of and responses to a blocked channel.

INTERNATIONAL CHANNELS

International distribution involves establishing the most efficient, timely, and cost-effective means of delivering the product or service to the customer. The international distribution system differs from the domestic system in one basic way—the various intermediary institutions that may serve as channel members. A variety of intermediary organizations that do not get involved in domestic allocations are available to facilitate only international distribution. These intermediaries are unique to international marketing and provide services specifically designed for international sales.

INTERNATIONAL CHANNEL DEFINED

Internationally, the nature of the channel is similar to that of a domestic channel. An **international channel of distribution** consists of organizations that facilitate the flows of transaction and ownership. In terms of logistics, distribution consists of two distinct flows or processes. One is the flow of title, or ownership, and the other is the flow of the product, or the physical movement and possession of the product. The physical flow of the product can coincide with the flow of title (ownership), but may not. Since the flow of the product can be different from the flow of the title, the two should be viewed separately. The physical movement of the product is associated with shipping and transportation while the nonphysical movement or flow of title is the means by which the transaction is consummated. The organizations that assist with the nonphysical movement or flow of title comprise the channel of distribution. The organizations that support the relocation of the product from the producer to the consumer constitute the shipping or transportation process.

Separating the two movements or flows is necessary because the actual possession or physical movement may not follow the route (channel) of the negotiations that make possession and movement possible. For example, the product may be sold by an international agent who simply represents the product and does not keep inventory or see the product that is sold. The product is subsequently shipped from the producer's warehouse directly to the foreign buyer. Or, consider the sale of a tank of oil located in Newark, New Jersey, by its owner living in Atlanta to a buyer located in London. After the transaction is completed, the oil may remain in its storage tank and not be moved. The separation of the flow of title and the product are illustrated in Exhibit 11.1.

The flows of movement and title are important for the international marketer. However, when discussing the marketing channel, only the organizations and institutions that expedite the contract and sale will be considered. While some intermediaries help with both flows, others confine their assistance to one. The flow of the product—shipping and transportation—will be discussed in chapter 12.

IMPORTANCE OF THE CHANNEL DECISION

The international channel decision is important for at least four reasons.

• Channel decisions tend to be long-term and difficult to change. Arrangements that are made may involve contracts for extended periods of time, which are not easily broken if mistakes have occurred. Also, making changes may be undesirable

Exhibit 11.1 **Distribution Flows**

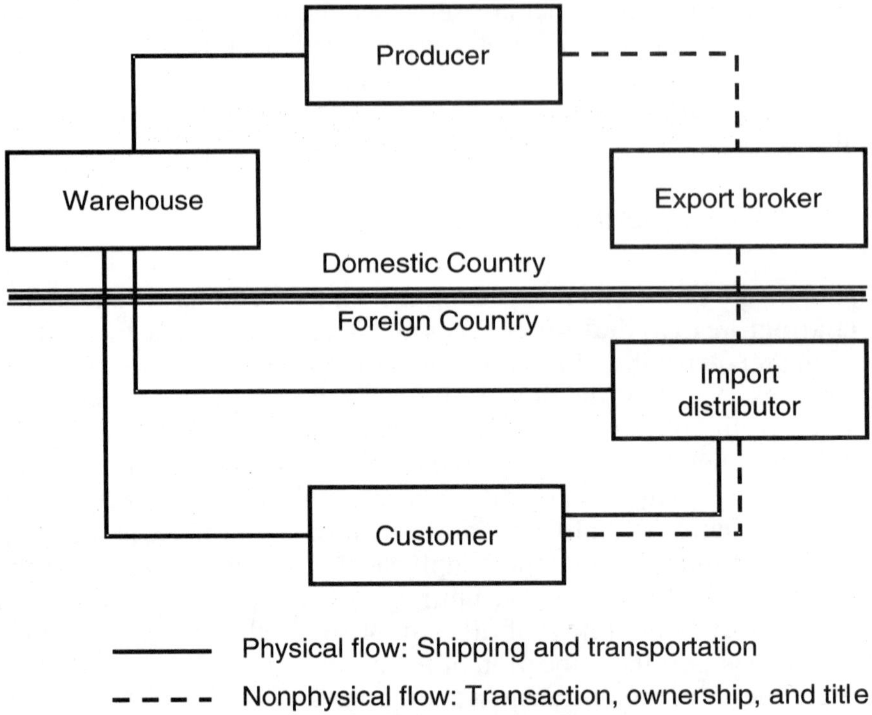

because a country's laws may favor the intermediary. Even if making changes is possible, doing so could result in acquiring an unfavorable reputation in the foreign market that adversely affects the ability to develop relationships with other channel intermediaries.

- Channel decisions will determine how and where the product or service will be made available to the target market. If suboptimum channel decisions are made, sales will be adversely affected, resulting in poorer performance and less success than otherwise would be possible.
- International channel decisions have an impact on the other variables in the marketing mix. How the product or service is distributed can provide opportunities or limitations for the development of the remainder of the marketing mix. The channel selected will influence the price that can be charged and methods of promotion that can be used, for instance.
- The international channel must be coordinated and managed to be effective. The channel selected will influence the amount of time, money, and effort that must be allocated. Channel members are usually self-seeking and make decisions to maximize their own positions. They do not normally make punctilious decisions intending to maximize the manufacturer's or supplier's position. Only to the extent that helping themselves helps the producer or supplier will both benefit.

Developing the international channel is an important process that requires careful consideration and planning. Mistakes can be costly for these reasons.

Exhibit 11.2 **Bags of Potatoes**

The channel decision determines where the product will be sold. Here, only potatoes are offered for sale along the side of the road.

CHANNEL ALTERNATIVES

Two basic marketing channel alternatives exist for the international marketer—a direct channel or an indirect channel. Although the terminology used is the same as for domestic marketing, the concepts are different. In domestic marketing, a direct channel means a single link approach in which intermediaries are not used, and title and ownership flow directly from the producer to the consumer. And, an indirect channel is a multi-link approach in which one or more intermediaries are inserted between the producer and consumer. In international marketing, the length of the channel is not the factor that determines whether a channel is direct or indirect. Rather, the distinction is based on the country of residence of the intermediary or the customer with whom the seller negotiates, and whether or not the seller has direct contact with someone in the foreign market.

In international marketing, if the seller negotiates the sale with an intermediary or customer whose residence is outside the domestic market, the channel is designated a **direct channel**. If the seller negotiates with an intermediary whose residence is in the domestic country, the channel is called an **indirect channel**. Where the negotiations take place is not relevant. For example, a foreign intermediary or buyer could consummate a sale in your office in the domestic country or you could travel to the foreigner's office to finalize the agreement. In both instances, the channel is direct because the buyer is a

Exhibit 11.3 **International Channel Alternatives**

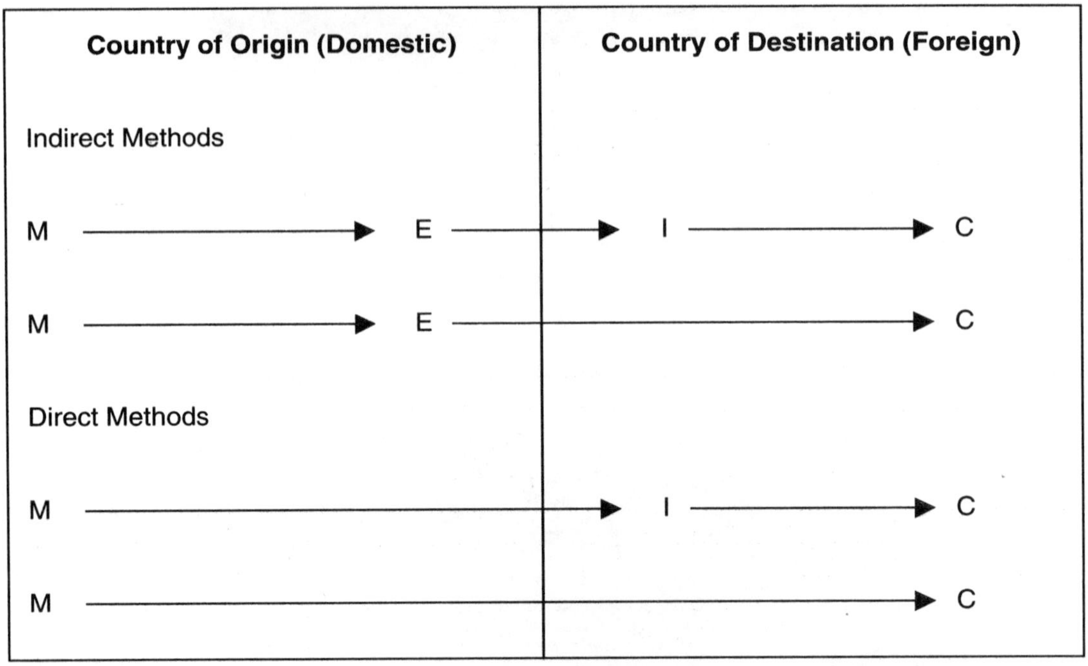

M = Manufacturer I = Importing intermediary E = Exporting intermediary C = Customer

resident of another country. Thus, any arrangement in which negotiations for transfer of title are with a company or person who is domiciled in a foreign country, whether that individual is the final user or not, is a direct channel. And, any arrangement where negotiations are with a domestically domiciled intermediary is an indirect channel. The direct/indirect channel dichotomy is illustrated in Exhibit 11.3.

Two basic alternatives are possible in each channel form. These alternatives are generalizations for a number of specific channel arrangements that have the same or similar basic structure. That is, a variety of options is possible within each of the four basic alternatives depending upon the number and type of intermediaries used. For example, the first direct method (M → I → C) could include more than one intermediary located in the foreign country. A distributor and a retailer might be utilized between the import intermediary and the customer. The only consideration, as previously indicated, is the citizenship of the buyer negotiating for transfer of title. As is apparent and contrary to the definitions of domestic channels, a direct channel can include intermediaries and be multi-link as long as the intermediaries reside in the foreign country. Also, a direct channel can be longer (include more intermediaries) than an indirect channel.

CHANNEL DESIRABILITY

The international marketer must use either a direct or indirect channel. Which channel alternative will be more desirable? That decision will depend on a variety of factors that are of importance to management. Each method offers certain advantages and disadvantages that must also be considered.

Benefits of Indirect Channels

Indirect channels are associated with the following benefits:

- Little knowledge of the foreign market is required. The export intermediary will take care of most of the responsibilities associated with preparing and executing the shipment.
- No long-term commitment needs to be made. Therefore, changes in business conditions can be accommodated more easily.
- Payment is received in the domestic currency, so currency concerns with a foreign buyer are eliminated.
- The attractiveness of the foreign market can be explored to determine how much commitment is desirable.
- The time, money, effort, and personnel devoted to the export process will be minimal. Usually, the resources available in-house are adequate and no special capabilities have to be acquired.
- The transaction is essentially a domestic sale. Thus, the international risk assumed is minimal.

Limitations of Indirect Channels

Indirect channels are associated with the following limitations:

- Control over the marketing program is lost. Thus, the way the product is marketed in the foreign country could damage the firm's reputation or image.
- Export intermediaries may not represent the firm's product as aggressively as management may desire.
- Lack of involvement in the export process results in little improvement in the knowledge of exporting. Without additional knowledge, making a more concerted commitment to the foreign market is more difficult.
- Profit may be lower than desired because the financial incentive that must be paid to export intermediaries can be large.

Benefits of Direct Channels

Direct channels are associated with the following benefits:

- A closer relationship exists with the foreign buyer and market. Thus, knowledge of the needs of the foreign buyer can be improved and accommodated.
- Control over the marketing program is enhanced. Management can increase the likelihood that the foreign marketing program will conform to corporate objectives.
- Management can react more quickly to changes in the foreign market.

- Profits can be increased because the share of revenue paid to export intermediaries can be retained.
- The chances of the firm's product being aggressively represented are enhanced.

Limitations of Direct Channels

Direct channels are associated with the following limitations:

- All aspects of the export process are management's responsibility. Therefore, an in-house capability is required, which normally entails adding staff possessing the necessary expertise.
- Currency matters can become a priority. Also, assuring payment is received in a timely manner becomes important.
- Familiarity with the foreign market must be maintained. Marketing research will be required to provide the required information.
- The attention management must devote to foreign sales increases. The planning process for international activities becomes more complex.
- The commitment to the foreign market must be long term.
- The investment of time, money, and resources will need to increase.

Obviously, indirect channels are ideal for management that is just becoming involved in international marketing or knows little about it. Because of the low risk and the ability to transfer exporting responsibilities to experts, the novice can begin in international marketing without the need for much preparation. However, as knowledge of the foreign market and international marketing skills improve, management may want to investigate the opportunity of direct channels, because improved profit is possible.

ESTABLISHING THE CHANNEL

Creating the channel is not much different internationally than domestically. The process involves these four steps.

1. Determine the objectives for the channel. Specify the goals to be accomplished through the channel.
2. Identify all of the alternatively feasible channels that will facilitate obtaining the channel objectives.
3. Evaluate the appropriateness and desirability of the alternatives based on appropriate selection criteria.
4. Choose the best channel alternative or alternatives.

Although the channel choice decision appears to be the manufacturer's prerogative, the manufacturer cannot compel intermediaries to become members of the channel. Conditions acceptable to both the firm's and intermediary's managements must be negotiated. Opportunities must be made attractive enough to the intermediary to obtain its cooperation. Intermediaries may also request inclusion in the channel and thus initiate the process. Management in the manufacturing firm must evaluate the intermediary to determine whether or not inclusion in the channel is desirable.

Channel decision making is an evolutionary process.[1] Initially, indirect channels are employed because of the lower risk and commitment involved. As management gains international experience and becomes more involved in and committed to international marketing, a desire to switch to direct channels arises because of the potential to improve profits. Unique situations may influence the process. For example, direct channels are preferred if the product is perishable or if the seller requires direct contact with the buyer to provide installation or improve service after the sale.[2] High-control channels are preferred by larger firms, while small firms with sales under US$10 million are more likely to employ low-control channels.[3] Also, when foreign sales are marginal (less than 25 percent of total sales), low-control channels predominate. When foreign sales are high (more than 75 percent of total sales), high-control channels prevail. The domestic channel is occasionally extended into the foreign market when product characteristics are similar, to help gain economies of scale.[4]

FACTORS INFLUENCING THE CHANNEL DECISION

The factors that influence the channel decision are the same internationally and domestically. Although certain considerations are basic to the decision process, uniqueness in each firm may require other aspects to be taken into account, and the importance attached to each factor may vary. Although numerous factors may be listed, management's attitude toward the five salient factors in the process is what influences the decision.[5] The salient attributes are:

- The amount of *control* the manufacturer desires to exert over channel activities. How important is controlling marketing programs? Would this be essential to the image, quality, and reputation of the firm and its products?
- The *effectiveness* of the channel for selling the firm's products. Will intermediaries promote marketing efforts? How aggressive must channel members be? Some intermediaries will represent the firm and its products, and pursue potential customers, more vigorously than others.
- The availability of *information* about the foreign market provided by the channel. How much information is required from intermediaries about buyer behavior and the nature of the market? Sometimes this information is important to conducting business and sometimes it is not.
- The amount of *paperwork and documentation* for which channel members and the producer are responsible. How much of the shipping procedures are to be delegated to channel members? Willingness or unwillingness to assume these responsibilities will influence intermediary selection.
- The amount of *selling cost* associated with the channel. How much money must be spent to gain the cooperation of the intermediaries? Financial concerns are always important, and channel arrangements vary in cost depending upon what intermediaries are required to do and their efficiency.

In addition to the five salient attributes, international marketing managers may also want to consider other factors that are important to their businesses and marketing situation. Two additional factors that are usually worthy of consideration are the following:

- The marketing *functions* intermediaries will perform. What marketing activities will be delegated to channel members? How effective are channel members in performing those activities? The nature of the functions the intermediary will perform will influence the types of intermediaries that will be viable alternatives.
- The *availability* of the various intermediaries. Are the desired intermediaries available and willing to participate? Are the intermediaries that are available acceptable? Preferred channel members may or may not be available or willing to participate.

Management must select the channel after evaluating the alternatives in terms of at least these seven factors. The types of acceptable intermediaries will be identified. The arrangements these channel members may form will help structure the channel. The assessed desirability of individual channel members, from those that are available within the acceptable types, will influence which intermediary will be selected.

INTERMEDIARY INSTITUTIONS

A variety of intermediary organizations and institutions serve to facilitate marketing via direct and indirect methods. The organizations may be associated with the seller or be independent.

Two categories of intermediaries may be represented in both direct and indirect international channels: merchants and agents. A **merchant** buys and takes title to the product, and earns income based on resale ability. An **agent** does not buy or take title to the product, but brings the buyer and seller together to facilitate the sale. The agent earns income by charging a fee or commission for services rendered. The seven types of intermediaries described below fall into one or the other of these two categories.

Although the various merchants and agents involved in international marketing are frequently identified according to precisely defined titles and characteristics, defining them too strictly is risky. In reality, intermediaries are more accurately identified in terms of their relationships with individual sellers. International intermediaries tend to provide a variety of services appropriate to specific situations and, therefore, may deviate from their normal roles. Thus, agents can behave as merchants and vice-versa, depending on the situation, opportunities, and needs of the buyer and seller.

As indicated in Exhibit 11.3, those merchant and agent intermediaries that facilitate direct channels may be located in the domestic firm's country, the foreign country in which the sale is made, or another foreign country. The merchant and agent intermediaries facilitating indirect channels are located only in the domestic firm's country.

The principal types of organizations that facilitate direct and indirect channels may be categorized into seven groups as shown in Exhibit 11.4. Knowing the nature of the various intermediaries is useful to help determine the appropriateness of each as a possible channel member. Therefore, each of the alternative intermediaries will be described briefly.

Exhibit 11.4 **International Channel Organizations and Institutions**

Indirect methods	Direct methods	
Domestic location	**Domestic location**	**Foreign location**
Export merchants	**Parent company entities**	**Import merchants**
Export house	Built-in exporting	Dealer
Export management company	Mail-order house	Distributor
Piggyback marketing	Export department	Import jobber
Trading company		Retailer
Export agents	**Legislative entities**	**Import agents**
Export broker	Export trading company	Foreign factor
Export commission house	Webb-Pomerene Association	Import broker
Resident foreign buying agent (Confirming house)		Managing agent
Export management company		Manufacturer's representative
Manufacturer's export agent		
		Representatives
		Traveling sales rep
		Selling office

Export Merchants

Export merchants buy products from producers or suppliers and resell them to buyers located in foreign countries. Therefore, purchases are usually made only when a guaranteed market for resale has first been arranged. Export merchants normally specialize in particular lines of products, particular countries or geographic market areas, or both. Competing lines of merchandise may be handled, and normally a minimum of service is provided. Products may be sold with the original brand mark or label, or the export merchant may attach its own brand or label. Employing an export merchant is essentially the same as making a sale to a domestic customer, because payment will be received in local currency and the exporting details are usually not of concern to the producer. Unfortunately, control over the export process is limited, and the way the export merchant represents the product in the foreign country could be detrimental to the producer's image or reputation. Following are descriptions of four types of export merchants.

Export House. An **export house,** sometimes referred to as an **export merchant,** is a firm that buys products from a domestic producer and engages in marketing efforts to locate buyers in foreign markets. This intermediary represents itself, has an overseas marketing effort, and oversees the entire export transaction including financing and documentation from the port of export to arrival at the buyer's location.

Export Management Company (EMC). An **export management company** functions as an export department for various producers. By means of a contractual arrangement, this firm buys merchandise from the producers it represents at an agreed price and resells it to foreign customers. An EMC can relieve the domestic producer of some or all of the export responsibilities as needed. Also, export management services can be provided to domestic firms as requested. In these cases, sales are solicited for the producer, and the EMC does not take title. Functioning as an agent, it provides services for a commission or a retainer plus a commission. An EMC will usually specialize in certain product lines and foreign countries or markets.

Piggyback Marketing. **Piggyback marketing** occurs when a domestic firm that markets in foreign countries agrees to distribute the products of another domestic firm. The firm that allows its products to be piggybacked gains access to the foreign markets without incurring the marketing and distribution costs associated with exporting. Complementary products are most easily sold internationally via piggyback. Piggybacking is most likely to occur when a foreign buyer seeks a wide range of products, all of which the domestic seller does not carry. This seller will locate a domestic producer that can supply the products not carried and add them to the shipment.

Trading Company. A **trading company** is a firm that buys products from producers located in many countries and markets them to buyers in a large number of countries. This intermediary is usually quite large in size and handles high sales volumes at small profit margins.

Export Agents

Export agents usually represent a number of noncompeting producers and locate foreign buyers for the products produced by those firms. Export agents may also represent foreign buyers by negotiating purchases for clients. Firms that utilize an export agent are expected to sign an export agency agreement for one or two years with the option to renew when the period expires. An export agent may act as the firm's export department by advertising, locating foreign buyers, arranging sales, giving advice about or arranging insurance, export documentation, and shipping. Payment is normally made to the export agent for services rendered in the form of a commission on sales produced. Export agents can reduce the time, cost, and risk involved in developing foreign markets. They are particularly useful if the resources needed to establish foreign sales offices are lacking. These intermediaries are familiar with differences in customs and business practices in the foreign markets and are specialists in export activities. Unfortunately, export agents may not always represent the firm's product in the manner desired or work as aggressively as preferred. Five types of export agents are described below.

Export Broker. An **export broker** is a firm that locates buyers for sellers and vice versa. This firm charges a fee for its services and is not a party to the actual sales transaction. That is, once the potential buyer and seller have been located and introduced, the export broker's responsibilities are fulfilled. The actual terms and conditions of sale are finalized by the two firms the export broker located.

Export Commission House. An **export commission house** is a firm that functions as a purchasing agent for one or more foreign buyers. A commission is charged for its services.

Resident Foreign Buying Agent (Confirming House). A **resident foreign buying agent** is a firm that serves as the purchasing agent for a foreign company that wants to purchase certain products. This firm searches for the domestic producer of those products that will offer the lowest prices. A buying agent purchases the product for its foreign client and receives a commission for its services.

Export Management Company. See the description under the export merchant heading above.

Manufacturer's Export Agent. A **manufacturer's export agent** acts on behalf of a domestic producer to develop a foreign market for its products. This firm provides a foreign presence for the domestic firm by representing its products to potential customers. A manufacturer's export agent is usually granted exclusive rights to represent the producer's products in a particular foreign country or geographic area, and is usually paid a commission on sales generated.

Parent Company Entities

Parent company entities are organizations that function within the firm for directing exporting activities. The amount of exporting assistance required varies depending upon the exporting experience and sophistication of the firm's management and employees. The firm's own employees handle export sales that have been stimulated by advertisements, telephone, mail, the Internet, and personal contact through trade shows or visits to foreign countries. These arrangements are contained in-house, part of the producer's company, and utilize only export facilitating organizations such as banks, insurance companies, and shippers. Three types of parent company entities are described here.

Built-in Exporting. As explained in chapter 10, the **built-in export department** arrangement requires export sales to be handled by members of the domestic marketing department. No foreign sales effort exists, and sales come primarily from unsolicited orders. Once a relationship has been established with the foreign customer, further orders received from foreign buyers continue to be processed by the marketing staff, usually with the assistance of a freight forwarder or similar shipping firm.

Mail-Order House. A **mail-order house**, sometimes referred to as a catalog retailer, uses catalogs rather than a sales force to generate sales. The catalogs are mailed to potential customers who submit orders for products selected from the catalog. Shipments are mailed or shipped via parcel delivery service from the producer's factory directly to the customer. With the advent of the Internet, e-commerce on producers' Web sites is replacing or supplementing catalogs.

Export Department. As explained in chapter 10, an **export department** arrangement requires the creation of a staff of employees whose job involves locating and processing foreign sales. This staff promotes products to potential buyers and handles exporting procedures either on their own or with the assistance of a shipping facilitator.

Legislative Entities

A **legislative entity** is an export association authorized by the U.S. Congress that provides an export incentive or benefit such as exemption from antitrust laws. The following are two types of legislative entities.

Export Trading Company (ETC). An **export trading company** is created by several firms that sell similar products. This company helps the participating producers be more competitive in foreign markets by improving the availability of export financing and providing exemption from U.S. antitrust laws. Through cooperation, inter-firm rivalry is avoided, and cost savings from endeavors such as the pooling of efforts, realization of economies of scale, and improved negotiating ability are possible. An ETC can serve as a firm's export department or purchase products from the manufacturer for export.

Webb-Pomerene Association. A **Webb-Pomerene Association** is a firm that markets the products of competing manufacturers for the purpose of export sales. The firm is jointly owned by the competing firms, and collectively the participating firms can provide the benefits of a larger firm when competing for international sales. Thus, this firm can enhance the opportunity for generating foreign business for the participating firms. A Webb-Pomerene Association is exempt from U.S. antitrust laws with respect to the collusion of competing firms. Since the purpose of the firm is to assist with export product sales, domestic marketing, imports, and exporting of services are not permitted.

Import Merchants

The **import merchant** category includes foreign buyers at the wholesale and retail levels. These firms are located in the foreign market and purchase products from the domestic manufacturer for resale in the markets in which they operate. Merchants may represent the firm's product in specified geographic areas. Described below are four types of import merchants.

Dealer. A **dealer** is an individual or firm that acts as a principal in the purchase and sale of products. This firm operates from a store, warehouse, or other business establishment, buys and maintains an inventory of the products it represents, and resells those products to the public on a wholesale or retail basis.

Distributor. A **distributor** is a type of wholesaler that sells complementary, nonconflicting products to retailers and other intermediaries, but not directly to the public. This firm may buy directly from a domestic producer and keep inventories for the products purchased. Support and service are usually provided, relieving the domestic producer of these responsibilities.

Import Jobber. An **import jobber** is a type of wholesaler that buys job lots of specific lines of products from producers and other wholesalers. This firm resells directly to retailers and other merchants.

Retailer. A **retailer** is the last link in the marketing channel prior to the final consumer. This firm buys products in quantities that will be needed by end users who shop in its stores. A retailer may be large or small and have one or more locations. Large retailers may buy directly from the domestic producer.

Import Agents

The **import agent** category includes foreign firms that represent the domestic firm's products. The import agent may or may not hold inventory, may sell in the name of the manufacturer, and may function as a foreign sales branch for the firm. Import agents may also represent foreign buyers and negotiate purchases of products their principal requests. Four types of import agent are defined here.

Foreign Factor. A **foreign factor** is a type of agent that sells consigned or delivered merchandise for a commission known as factorage. This firm may buy and sell for the principal either in the name of the principal or on its own. A factor may also get involved with the management, control, and disposal of products to be bought and sold. A factor has the right to place a lien on products it buys and sells on behalf of others.

Import Broker. An **import broker** is a type of agent that works with potential buyers and sellers, and assists them with the negotiation of the terms and conditions of their sales agreement. This firm is paid a fee or commission for services provided. Brokers usually specialize in primary commodities such as grain and fossil fuels. They buy and sell only in the name of their principal, and do not get involved with the management, control, or disposal of the products.

Managing Agent. A **managing agent** oversees the marketing operation of a domestic producer. This firm assures that contracts are fulfilled and all aspects of the export sale are in order. The managing agent manages the export affairs of the producer in the foreign country. The producer contracts with the managing agent for the responsibilities to be provided.

Manufacturer's Representative. A **manufacturer's representative** is a firm that represents a domestic producer in the foreign country by providing services the producer requests to facilitate and assist with finalizing sales. This firm functions as the domestic producer's sales force but does not normally get involved with shipping procedures.

Representatives

Representatives are extensions of the manufacturing firm in a foreign country. They augment the firm's operations and reside in the foreign country. Two types of representatives are discussed in this section.

Traveling Sales Representative. A **traveling sales representative** is a salesperson who travels to the foreign country for the purpose of locating wholesale and retail buyers and purchasing agents who are interested in the manufacturer's products, and to address the questions and concerns of customers. This person functions as a manufacturer's representative and handles complementary lines that do not conflict. A traveling sales representative receives a commission on sales and is under contract for a specified period that may be renewed by mutual agreement.

Selling Office. A **selling office** is a sales office of the producer located in the foreign country. This office maintains a staff of employees who represent the firm's product to potential buyers and respond to inquiries. Selling offices usually are expected to be responsible for a certain region or geographic area within the foreign market.

THE CHANNEL SELECTION DECISION

When management decides to enter the foreign market, it must select an appropriate channel arrangement from the available alternatives. An analysis of the salient factors discussed previously will help formalize the channel selection decision. Management's perceptions of these factors will be influential in the decision-making process whether or not those perceptions are accurate. Therefore, obtaining as much accurate information as possible to permit a thorough assessment of the opportunities and requirements of alternative channel arrangements is essential. Exhibit 11.5 lists the various channel intermediaries and rates them in terms of the five most influential salient attributes.

By consulting Exhibit 11.5 the international marketer can compare the viable alternatives. However, careful interpretation of each attribute is important because of the unique relationships between the supplier and intermediaries that may be possible and the generalized nature of the attribute. For example, the amount of control the seller has over the marketing efforts of an intermediary may vary because control tends to be issue specific.[6] That is, various channel members may control various aspects of the channel. The producer, for instance, may be able to control price while an intermediary may have control over inventory levels.

The ratings for each attribute in Exhibit 11.5 are generalizations and indicate only the normal situation. Although only generalizations, the manager's attitudes regarding

Exhibit 11.5 **Relative Characteristics of Channel Entity Attributes**

Channel entity	Control	Information	Selling cost	Effectiveness	Paperwork
INDIRECT METHODS					
Export merchants					
Export house	N	VL	H	G	N
Export management company	VL	S	M	G	N
Piggyback marketing	VL	VL	M	P	N
Trading company	N	S	H	P	L
Export agents					
Export broker	N	L	M	F	A
Export commission house	N	VL	H	P	M
Resident foreign buying agent (confirming house)	N	VL	H	P	M
Export management company	S	C	M	G	L
Manufacturer's export agent	S	S	L	P	L
DIRECT METHODS					
Parent company entities					
Built-in exporting	VH	L	H	VP	A
Mail-order house	VH	N	L	P	A
Export department	VH	S	H	F	M
Legislative entities					
Export trading company	L	S	M	F	S
Webb-Pomerene Association	S	VL	M	F	S
Import merchants					
Dealer	S	S	M	G	S
Distributor	H	C	L	F	S
Import jobber	L	VL	L	F	S
Retailer	VL	N	H	P	M
Import agents					
Foreign factor	L	S	H	VP	M
Import broker	L	VL	M	P	M
Managing agent	H	S	L	G	S
Manufacturer's Representatives	S	S	L	G	S
Representatives					
Traveling sales representative	VH	S	M	F	A
Selling office	VH	E	H	VG	A

Source: Donald L. Brady and E. Terry Deiderick, "An Evaluation of the Desirability of Alternative Exporting Institutions for Small Business." In *Proceedings Small Business Institute Directors' Association National Conference,* ed. Richard J. Judd (San Francisco: SBIDA, February 10–13, 1982), pp. 62–69.

Key:

Control	Information	Selling cost	Effectiveness	Paperwork
N = None	N = None	L = Low	VP = Very poor	N = None
VL = Very little	VL = Very little	M = Moderate	P = Poor	L = Little
L = Little	L = Little	H = High	F = Fair	S = Some
S = Some	S = Some		G = Good	M = Most
H = High	C = Considerable		VG = Very good	A = All
VH =Very high	E = Extensive			

Exhibit 11.6 **A Partial List of Factors to Assess when Selecting an Individual Channel Intermediary**

Factor	Description
Adequacy of facilities	Equipment and use of technology
Customer base	Number, size, location, and growth rate
How the firm's product will be represented	Support and maintenance
Marketing orientation	Mission, objectives, strategy, and tactics
Market representation	Number and kinds of products sold, markets covered
Past and projected performance	Sales trends and growth rates
Personnel	Organizational structure, management, and support staff
Plans for the future	Expansion, investment, and markets
Promotional strategy	Budget, media, and frequency
The size of the company	The number of salespeople and market coverage

the position the firm should take concerning the listed attributes may influence the channel arrangement selected. For example, if the international marketer desires to exercise considerable control over the activities of the channel members, either parent company entities or representatives are most appropriate. If the international marketer also needs significant foreign market information, then the various types of representatives become the most attractive choices. The representative options are further reduced as additional conditions are stipulated for the remaining attributes. Thus, the manager's preferences regarding these attributes indicate which channel arrangements will be the most appropriate and most likely to help achieve channel objectives.

After intermediary categories have been determined, the international marketer must decide which individual firm in that category will be most appropriate. Analysis and comparison of those firms judged to be appropriate and available candidates are required. The international marketer must determine which firm will be the most appropriate representative of the company's products in the desired market. The marketing functions the intermediary is to perform must be decided, and terms and conditions of arrangements with the intermediary negotiated. To accomplish this, factors such as those listed in Exhibit 11.6 should be assessed by the international marketer for each firm under consideration.

BLOCKED CHANNELS

Even when the most desirable channel is identified, the international marketer may find that particular channel unavailable or unattainable. When the manager is prohibited from using the desired channel, that channel is **blocked**. Blockage can occur for at least six reasons.

- Government intervention may preclude use of some channel members. Legislation creating prohibitions on the use of intermediaries can be politically imposed. Although the desired channel members exist, the government can decline permission to employ the intermediaries.

• The desired channel may be culturally precluded. Customary marketing procedures may prevent the acceptance of particular intermediaries. In other cases, customary practices may require the inclusion of intermediaries that may be viewed as unnecessary by the manufacturer. Obtaining adequate market coverage with the desired channel will not be accepted, because of the additional channel members that have been included historically. Trying to bypass such an intermediary will be viewed unfavorably by society. In Italy, for example, channel efficiency can be reduced due to preference for longer channels.

• The desired channel member or members do not exist. In third world countries in particular, the preferred intermediary may not be available. Even though a mass merchandiser such as a discount house might be identified as the most appropriate outlet, for example, adequate market coverage through discount houses may be impossible in most of India or Brazil.

• The desired channel member or members do not want to participate. Even though the intermediary may exist, a refusal to participate may occur. The intermediary may find the financial and other incentives offered unattractive or simply will not want to represent the product.

• The channel member or members may be representing competitive products. To represent additional products, sometimes other products have to be deleted because of limited storage area. The intermediary may perceive a risk in adding a new and unknown product at the expense of a successful and known product. Also, the intermediary may find exclusive distribution attractive and not be willing to give up the currently represented product.

• Trade associations may close the desired channel. Powerful trade groups may influence their members in an effort to keep out unwanted products. Intermediaries affiliated with the trade group may feel compelled to follow the admonition of the trade association. Trade groups are quite influential in Japan, for example.

When the desired channel cannot be used, an alternative must be sought. Regardless of the reason for blockage, management must evaluate other options and develop another channel strategy. Any of three options may be appropriate:

- Do not enter the market. This means selecting another market segment to serve and satisfy, or avoiding the market altogether. Obviously, this option requires a return to step one in the market entry process, selecting another country or a different target market within the preferred country.
- Select an alternative channel. If another channel arrangement is identified, perhaps the second most desirable channel in the evaluation process, a suboptimum channel, is implemented. Choosing another option may be the simplest and most prudent course to follow. However, the second choice is not the best choice, and therefore should be expected to produce less than optimum results in terms of market coverage, efficiency, and, ultimately, profitability. Of course, settling for slightly less performance than desired may be superior to trying to identify another market segment, or avoiding the market completely and searching for another country. The decision depends on an assessment of all options and a determination of acceptability versus preferability.

- Create the desired channel. In this option, management must build the desired channel network. Setting up and operating the various intermediary organizations that do not exist or cannot be convinced to participate is necessary. Obviously, expense and cultural acceptability are necessary. Also, management may not be skilled in or efficient at establishing and operating the desired channel network.

Regardless of which option management elects, a less adequate channel may result. Since the channel decision has implications for decisions made for the rest of the marketing mix, adjustments may have to be made in price, promotion, and the nature of the product itself to compensate for channel differences. If the alternatively selected channel is substandard, the long-run profitability of the firm is jeopardized. Such a decision, although expedient, may have implications for the future direction of marketing efforts in that market. The channel decision is not to be taken lightly. Because of the legal environment (see chapter 8), dismissing channel members may be difficult and expensive. Making correct channel decisions initially is preferable to making changes later.

INTERNATIONAL RETAILING

The last link in the marketing channel before the consumer is the retailer. Therefore, a strong retail presence is an important component of international marketing strategy for managers of consumer products firms, particularly if a presence in the foreign country exists via a joint venture or foreign direct investment. Integrating retail strategy into the overall international marketing strategy is essential. The international marketer should be prepared for similarities and differences in retail practice in international markets. The differences may create a need for strategy adjustments.

In general, marketing practices of retailers around the world lag behind those of retailers in the United States.[7] Even in the developed countries retailing tends not to be as advanced as in the United States. Marketing tends to be considered a more important part of business operations by U.S. retailers than by retailers in other countries. Foreign retailers, as a group, tend to be less marketing oriented and are frequently more accounting oriented in their philosophy. This means the marketing concept is considered less important and is not embraced or practiced as aggressively as by retailers in the United States. Business decisions by foreign retailers are not made as often with the interests of the consumer in mind and are often made for financial reasons, with attention to costs and profits as the primary motivation. Foreign retailers tend to focus more on their own needs than the customers' needs. Obviously, this is a generalization, and foreign retailers do exist that are extremely customer oriented. As a whole, however, foreign retailers do not market as well or as effectively as U.S. retailers do. This observation becomes more acute in countries where the market economy is not as well developed as in countries with more advanced market economies.

Foreign retailers are more likely to rely on neighborhood residents for their customers, and therefore may not feel the need to market aggressively or focus on the firm's

Exhibit 11.7 **Working from Home**

As the market economy grows, people turn garages and houses into small neighborhood stores. The front yards and living rooms of the two homes in this building have been converted into small retail stores.

overall marketing position and orientation. If a clientele of loyal customers can be developed who live nearby, then the need to stress competitive marketing practices is reduced. Management perceives that all efforts need to focus on these customers each time they visit the store. This reliance on customers living in close proximity to the store is fostered by the fact that foreigners tend to be less mobile than U.S. customers. Retailers, therefore, have a somewhat captive clientele. The drawing power of stores tends to be less and the need to promote perceived to be less necessary.

Retail stores in foreign countries tend to be smaller in terms of square feet of floor space than stores in the United States. Less floor space means fewer products can be offered for sale. Thus, the ability to stock merchandise from competing producers is reduced. As a result, the product mix tends to be narrower, the product line depth tends to be shorter, and customers tend to have fewer options from which to choose. Often only one brand or a few different brands are stocked, causing brand name merchandise to be considered less significant for attracting customers.

Foreign retailers tend to advertise less than U.S. retailers and consider advertising, in general, less important. Because of the reliance on neighborhood customers, window displays and literature are commonly used means of advertising. Sales promotions such as retail markdowns and point-of-purchase displays tend to be more important to foreign retailers than to U.S. retailers.

Exhibit 11.8 **Simple Window Display**

Although retailers consider window displays important, this one is quite plain with clothing simply suspended from hangers.

Differences in retail practice between foreign and U.S. retailers exist in numerous areas. Noteworthy differences include the following. Relative to U.S. retailers, the trend is for foreign retailers to:

- Consider window displays as a more important means of attracting customers. Although window displays tend to be rather plain, such displays are considered an important means of obtaining and retaining customers.
- Engage in franchising less. Stores tend to be independently owned and operated.
- Place less emphasis on price competition. Considering competitors' prices when setting price is not as important. Cents-off coupons are also less important.
- Place less emphasis on store appearance and atmospherics. A more casual or less orderly approach is taken toward store amenities that provide psychic shopping pleasure such as music and color. Window displays tend to be simple and less attractive and may consist of simply hanging products on hangers or laying items on the floor.
- Provide slower service. Salespeople are slower to approach customers and offer assistance.
- Rely more on customers who live within walking distance.
- Stay open only a few evening hours. Convenience and accessibility to customers is less important.

- Use less promotion. Advertising on television and by direct mail is less important.
- Use less scrambled merchandising. Retailers tend to specialize in one product category and seek consistency in product lines.
- Use more cooperatives. Producers will bind together for the economies and benefits available.

All of these differences are indicative of a more casual approach toward the importance of a marketing orientation as a component of strategy. The marketing concept is less likely to be the guiding philosophy of foreign retailers. Structural, cultural, and competitive differences in the areas of store size, customer mobility, and customer shopping habits are likely to be responsible for these differences.

Although considerable differences exist between foreign and U.S. retail practices, notable similarities occur. Both foreign retailers and U.S. retailers consider:

- Loyal customers necessary. Developing store-loyal customers and repeat purchases is necessary for success.
- Purchases from repeat customers important. Developing store-loyal customers is imperative.
- Retail markdowns an essential part of marketing strategy. Merchandise must be offered on sale regularly to attract new customers and retain existing customers.
- Store layout important. The manner in which the interior of the store is physically organized is important in retaining customers.
- The gender of sales assistants unimportant. In certain areas of the world such as the Middle East, male sales associates may be more important for religious reasons. However, elsewhere the effectiveness of salespeople is not considered to be affected by gender.
- The helpfulness of sales assistants to customers important. Salespeople need to be pleasant and accommodating to customers.

Commonalities in retailing structure and shopping habits across markets influence similarities. The importance of customers is the same throughout the world. Without customers, the retailer would be out of business. Therefore, paying attention to customers is universally important. However, the manner in which that attention is shown varies and therefore influences the degree of marketing orientation exhibited by a retailer. When customers are perceived as a more captive audience because of a lack of mobility, for example, understanding why a less customer-oriented perspective is embraced is possible.

As retail practices evolve throughout the world, differences will decrease. Retailing practices throughout the world are becoming more and more like retailing practices in the United States. For example, foreign retailers are adopting and emulating the self-service practices of U.S. retailers. Self-service gas stations were introduced in Japan in 1998. Even before self-service became available, the management of McDonald's Corporation entered into agreements with the managements of two major Japanese oil companies to operate McDonald's restaurants in some of the firms' gas stations.[8] Discount supermarkets that can charge 30 to 50 percent less for groceries than ordinary supermarkets are spreading in Europe.[9] Also, as in the United States, department stores are beginning to confront increasing competition from up-market specialty stores and the increasing availability of nonfood items in grocery stores.[10]

CHAPTER SUMMARY

An important component of efficient international distribution is the marketing channel. The international channel is associated with the efficient movement of title for the product from the producer to the customer. Two basic channel alternatives exist for the international marketer—a direct channel and an indirect channel. A direct channel is formed when negotiations for the sale are made with an intermediary or customer whose residence is outside the domestic country. An indirect channel is formed when negotiations are made with an intermediary whose residence is within the domestic country. Direct channels require management to be involved with business, marketing, and cultural concerns in the foreign country. With indirect channels, the transaction is much like any other domestic sale with a minimum of concern about the foreign market required.

Management's attitude toward the amount of control, information, selling costs, effectiveness, and paperwork and documentation required from the channel influence the channel decision. These five factors along with other relevant concerns, such as the functions management expects intermediaries to perform and the availability of various intermediaries, determine the exact intermediaries and nature of the most appropriate channel.

The international marketer must identify alternatively feasible channels and evaluate the appropriateness and desirability of each, if the best channel arrangement is to be identified. When the desired channel is unavailable or unattainable, the channel is blocked. Blockage prevents the international marketer from using the most appropriate channel. When blockage occurs, management must select another market segment, avoid the market all together, select an alternative channel, or create the desired channel. Creating the desired channel is expensive and may not be culturally acceptable. Selecting an alternative channel or market segment may result in a suboptimum decision, producing long-run implications that are unacceptable for marketing strategy.

Differences between domestic and international retailing practices are common. Internationally, retailers tend to be less marketing oriented than in the United States. However, differences are decreasing as retail practices evolve throughout the world.

KEY TERMS

Agent
Blocked channel
Built-in export department
Dealer
Direct channel
Distributor
Export agent
Export broker
Export commission house
Export department
Export house
Export management company (EMC)
Export merchant
Export trading company (ETC)

(continued)

KEY TERMS *(continued)*

Foreign factor
Import agent
Import broker
Import jobber
Import merchant
Indirect channel
International channel of distribution
Legislative entity
Mail-order house
Managing agent
Manufacturer's export agent
Manufacturer's representative
Merchant
Parent company entities
Piggyback marketing
Representative
Resident foreign buying agent
Retailer
Selling office
Trading company
Traveling sales representative
Webb-Pomerene Association

REVIEW QUESTIONS

1. What is an international channel of distribution?
2. Explain the difference between the flow of title or ownership and the flow of the product or physical movement.
3. Explain why the flows of title and product may be separated.
4. Define and differentiate between a direct and indirect international marketing channel.
5. Why can a direct international channel include more intermediaries than an indirect international channel?
6. List the salient factors influencing the channel selection decision. How does each of these factors influence the decision?
7. Select two of the organization types listed in Exhibit 11.4. Accessing the campus library and the Internet, research each type and explain its nature and characteristics. Give an example of each.
8. What is a blocked channel?
9. What specific conditions cause the desired channel to be blocked?
10. List the options available to the international marketer when the desired channel is blocked. Why would each of these options be desirable? Undesirable?

NOTES

1. Donald L. Brady, "The Influence of the Length of Exporting Involvement on the Method of Distribution Used by Small Manufacturing Firms," in *Proceedings of the Atlantic Marketing Association*, ed. Michael H. Morris and Eugene E. Teeple (Orlando, FL: AMA, October 8–11, 1986), 93–98.

2. Donald L. Brady and E. Terry Deiderick, "An Evaluation of the Desirability of Alternative Exporting Institutions for Small Business," in *Proceedings of the Small Business Institute Directors' Association National Conference,* ed. Richard J. Judd (San Francisco, CA: SBIDA, February 10–13, 1982), 62–69.

3. Frank Bradley, "Does the Firm's Technology and Marketing Profile Affect Foreign Market Entry?" *Journal of International Marketing* 8 (4) (2000): 12–37.

4. Rod McNaughton and Jim Bell, "Channel Switching between Domestic and Foreign Markets," *Journal of International Marketing* 9 (1) (2001): 24–39.

5. Donald L. Brady and William O. Bearden, "The Effect of Managerial Attitudes on Alternative Exporting Methods," *Journal of International Business Studies* 10 (Winter 1979), 79–84.

6. Brady and Deiderick, "An Evaluation of the Desirability of Alternative Exporting Institutions for Small Business."

7. Donald L. Brady, Ian Mills, and Karen D. Mendenhall, "A Binational Analysis of Marketing Programmes Used by Small Retailers in Great Britain and the US," *International Journal of Retailing* 4 (5) (1989): 27–38. Information provided in this source serves as the impetus for the discussion about the similarities and differences between U.S. and foreign retailing presented in this section.

8. Michael A. Lev, "In Japan, McDonald's Means Great Marketing," *Chicago Tribune,* February 25, 1997, http://www.licenseenews.com/news/news161.html.

9. "Food Retailing in Europe: The Germans Are Coming," *The Economist*, August 14, 2008, http://www.economist.com/business/displaystory.cfm?story_id=11920665.

10. "Learn about the Department Store Retailing in Europe," Reuters, February 20, 2009, http://www.reuters.com/article/pressRelease/idUS116399+20-Feb-2009+BW20090220.

12 International Distribution Strategy: The Role of Logistics in Managing the Supply Chain

Gary Slater was appointed president and CEO of UNARCO Material Handling, Inc., headquartered in Springfield, Tennessee, in March, 2005. He had been serving as vice president, sales, at UNARCO since 1999.

UNARCO manufactures and sells a variety of pallet racks to fit any warehouse and distribution center storage requirement. Products range from standard pallet racks to complex drive-in and drive-through module systems for high-density storage situations that utilize the firm's RhinoTrac and RhinoDeck roller conveyor systems.

UNARCO was the first pallet rack manufacturer and is also one of the largest. With over fifty years of production, engineering, and design experience, UNARCO offers more capability in the areas of simple pallet racks, elaborate radio frequency identification (RFID), and electronic order-picking systems than any other firm. Slater believes that UNARCO, which is supported by the widest product assortment in the industry, can make available the best material handling and supply chain tracking capabilities. Slater knows the company has always been customer oriented, and he is proud of the one-on-one customer attention offered.

Were Slater interested in the potential the firm's products might have in foreign countries, exporting would certainly be a possibility. A need for products UNARCO sells surely exists in foreign countries. For example, France's Groupe Carrefour is the largest European retailer and the world's second largest (it has over 15,000 stores and opened its hundredth express market in Spain in 2009); Sweden's Inter Ikea Systems B.V. sells low-priced home furnishings all over the world from warehouses located in Germany, Belgium, the Netherlands, and Sweden; and Germany's C&A clothing giant has 1,037 stores throughout Europe. All of these companies have extensive warehousing operations that could benefit from UNARCO's products.

Going wherever the business is, particularly when UNARCO can provide products that are superior to those of most of the competition, seems like a good idea. However, Slater would need to evaluate thoroughly the feasibility of the export process before proceeding. Questions that he might want answered could include: How would it be done? How complex is the paperwork and documentation required? What changes will have to be made to make exporting a reality?

Sources: Based in part on information from the following Web sites: UNARCO Pallet Rack and Warehouse Storage at http://www.unarcorack.com/; Carrefour Group at http://www.carrefour.com/english/homepage/index.jsp; Ikea Group at http://www.ikea-group.ikea.com/; C&A at http://www.c-and-a.com/; and The Renco Group Inc. at http://www.rencogroup.net/about/operating.html.

CHAPTER OBJECTIVES

After reading this chapter, you should

- be knowledgeable about the stages involved in the export process;
- understand and be able to explain the steps necessary to complete an export transaction;
- be able to identify the risks inherent in foreign trade and understand the threats each poses to the exporter;
- understand how to manage these risks to eliminate or limit their effects;
- understand the role and value of the facilitating organizations the exporter can utilize for assistance with the various export procedures;
- appreciate the export process and the components involved;
- appreciate how the responsibility of the exporter changes with various kinds of international transactions;
- understand the interrelationship of a sound international distribution network and outsourced services providing supply-chain management;
- be aware of the paperwork that must be completed to accompany an export shipment; and
- know the conditions for which a validated export license is required.

BACKGROUND

As was indicated in chapters 5 and 11, exporting, particularly the indirect exporting channel, is the market entry method used most frequently by managers engaging in international marketing for the first time. Exporting is also an important method of doing business for many managers who have been involved internationally for long periods of time. Although exporting is the market entry method that minimizes risk, important risks still exist that must be appreciated and effectively managed to be successful. Therefore, an understanding of the nature of exporting relationships, the kinds of perils involved, and the export process are essential.

The movement of products from the seller to the buyer is a complex industry, one that includes both international and domestic carriers—road, rail, sea, and air. Also included are government departments that regulate transport and other aspects of the industry. As well as the seller and buyer, other organizations that can be involved include packers, chambers of commerce, freight forwarders, logistics operators, customs authorities, the international banking system, and insurance companies. Because this industry is devoted to both domestic and international trade, the scope of activities becomes truly global in perspective.

OUTSOURCING

Before considering the mechanics of international trade, the players and how each understands its relationship with exporters and importers must be understood. An appreciation of how distribution works is also essential.

Usually, one person or the employees of one firm cannot perform every task necessary to consummate an export transaction. Regardless of an employee's specialization, other members of the team have to be trusted to fulfill a variety of procedures that that person is unable to do. This is true for the manufacturer also. The international marketer will rely on producers of raw materials and subcomponents, distributors, and other title and negotiation assisting organizations to achieve corporative objectives. The manufacturer takes responsibility only for core interests such as the design, production, and sale of merchandise at a profit. The same holds true for exporting, and both the seller and buyer will need the assistance of other organizations to enable the cross-border transfer of the product. These intermediaries are specialists at providing appropriate competencies. Logically, then, when management embarks on an export strategy, information specific to a particular aspect of distribution will be required. Therefore, outsourcing is necessary to obtain these capabilities.

LOGISTICS AND SUPPLY CHAINS

The term **logistics** was used originally by the military to describe the total effort applied to moving troops globally. For the past three decades, the term has come to be applied to the commercial movements of products and a new type of organization that has appeared, the **third party logistics operator (3PL)**. The 3PL generally provides a service, which is focused on a company's international or domestic distribution requirements, or both. In modern terminology, the term **supply chain** is applied to describe the coordinated system of organizations, people, activities, information, and resources involved in moving products from supplier to buyer. Supply chains can apply to movements of materials, components, and parts to a manufacturer as well as delivery of finished products to the final customer. Thus, a single manufacturer can be involved in more than one supply chain, delivering into that manufacturer and dispatching to distributors, final customers, or both. From a competitive point of view, management is unlikely to use only one 3PL to service all of its supply chains.

Among the services 3PLs supply are haulage and storage. Haulage enables collection and delivery of the principal's products. Storage provides warehousing for the principal's products until delivery is requested. Storage is particularly important to today's global economy as manufacturers increasingly embrace the principles of just in time (JIT) for production schedules.[1]

To provide the range of expertise required by management, the 3PL will usually have the ability to provide facilities that complement the haulage and storage of inventory, including packing, origination of documentation, inspection, loading and unloading, and customs procedures. The 3PL may also serve as an extended freight forwarder with branches in various global locations. Particularly in this capacity, the 3PL relies heavily upon information technology (IT) skills in tracking and communicating with the other intermediaries involved in the transit of merchandise.

These capabilities ensure exporters and importers will utilize the services of the 3PL or freight forwarder as an outsourced provider of expertise. Customer satisfaction depends on these abilities.

THE MECHANISM OF EXPORTING AND IMPORTING

What changes have to be incurred to make exporting a reality? From management's point of view, entering a foreign market has the potential for increased profits; however, a change in mindset at the corporate level must be demonstrated for that potential to be realized.

As has been pointed out previously (see chapters 1 and 5), a substantial difference exists between marketing a product domestically and doing so internationally. However, the objective remains the same—earn profit while satisfying the buyer. Successful marketing must be achieved in international markets in spite of changed criteria such as language, culture, currency, and law.

Profit is fine, but what risks lie in the pathway to profitability? This concern, along with how to manage those risks, is expansive in the minds of management. Foreign markets will be successful only if the new supply chains are managed as rigorously as the domestic ones. If international markets are to be supplied successfully over a long period of time, changes are absolutely necessary to facilitate the international dimension. The international marketer will need tactical answers that enable decisions to be made quickly, yet also provide knowledge and enable corporate strategy to be changed in the long term. Prevention of discrimination between domestic and foreign customers must be avoided because foreign customers will expect to be treated equally with domestic customers.

What are the risks involved in foreign trade and what information will the international marketer need to manage those risks? To what extent will management be able to oversee new foreign business? What additional costs will be incurred and have to be added to the budget to facilitate international shipments? All of these questions are addressed elsewhere in this book. However, management of the risks associated with transportation and documentation in international trade is also necessary to be successful.

Delivering orders to new, foreign customers will involve managing new concerns. Where should the international marketer look for assistance in assessing and managing the new risks caused by these concerns? As explained in chapter 11, management that lacks exporting expertise needs to utilize an indirect channel and seek the assistance of outside experts. **Freight forwarders** that specialize in the export process and the movement of products internationally will provide valuable help and information.

Locating an appropriate freight forwarder can be facilitated by the local chamber of commerce or researching any of the numerous freight forwarding organizations, directories, or indices such as the National Customs Broker & Forwarders Association of America, Inc. After talking with representatives of the selected organization, the criteria appropriate to management's particular needs can be identified. These discussions will address various aspects of the export process that management can outsource to the freight specialist, including any or all of the following:

- contract of sale
- production
- inspection
- packing for foreign shipment
- preparing the necessary documentation
- delivery of the products to the main carrier
- shipment of the products
- advice to the buyer about shipment details
- depending on the agreed method of payment, contact with the international banking system
- monitoring of the transit of the merchandise to the point at which the products are delivered to the buyer and the seller's responsibility ends
- contact with the buyer to confirm receipt of the merchandise and determine acceptability of the products
- receipt of the buyer's payment
- closing of the job file

Although elements of handling domestic distribution coincide with the export process, a new dispatch section has to be constructed to accommodate exports. The alternative is to outsource to the freight forwarder all the elements associated with the export process. A cost-benefit analysis will be conducted to determine which option is appropriate based on anticipated sales volumes, internal capabilities, and management's desires. When a firm is beginning exporting and sales volumes are low, the freight forwarder is normally the preferred alternative.

If the freight forwarder is used, products can be transferred directly to the freight forwarder's facilities for storage once packaged. The freight forwarder's personnel will ship products at the appropriate time to the customers specified by the producer's dispatcher. Thus, the items listed above from "inspection" through "contact with the buyer to confirm receipt of the merchandise" are delegated to the freight forwarder. Of course, the method of payment (see chapter 14) will determine the degree of the forwarders' involvement with the banking system. As the volume of exports increases, management expects to experience a reduction in overhead because activities previously handled internally would be outsourced to the freight forwarder.

THE RISKS OF EXPORTING

Because the international environment is different than the domestic one, new risks will be encountered in exporting. The risks inherent in the firm's supply chain involving exporting exist in the following five areas:

- The risk that the buyer will refuse to pay—buyer risk.
- The risk that the buyer will not be allowed to pay because of restrictions imposed by the foreign government—country risk.
- The risk of reduced profit margin resulting from currency fluctuation—exchange risk.
- The risk of misunderstanding occurring between the seller and buyer regarding the responsibilities of each in arranging the transit of the goods—knowledge risk.
- The risk of the goods being lost or damaged while in transit from seller to buyer—transit risk.

MANAGING EXPORT RISK

These five risks will be present in all export transactions unless steps are taken for elimination or reduction. Of course, the problems of buyer risk and transit risk are already considered in domestic trade. However, since the shipping methods for export shipments differ from those for domestic shipments, domestic responses are inadequate. The other risks are new and not encountered domestically. The international marketer must thoroughly understand the manifestations of these risks and develop appropriate avoidance responses.

Buyer Risk

The problem of buyer risk relates to whether the buyer will be able to pay for the merchandise. Although the buyer may be able to pay when the transaction is consummated, when the time to pay arrives, the buyer's financial position could have changed. The result could be a cash flow problem and the inability for payment to be made. Of course, the intent of the buyer cannot be known with certainty. Even though the buyer's financial position is strong, payment may never have been intended. Therefore, unless the international marketer knows the buyer well, appropriate checks on the buyer's past record of and reputation for paying for products and services received are essential. A fast and efficient way for the international marketer to obtain this type of information is to go through a credit agency. The banking system can also be used for this purpose. However, while the banking system may be a good source of information for companies in the domestic country, this may not be true for quickly obtaining up-to-date information for companies in other countries. Internationally, other means may be required to assess credit records, such as a credit insurer or a factoring service.

The real risk is when no information can be gained about the buyer's record. In that event, the international marketer must choose carefully the method of payment that will have to be agreed on with the buyer, before supplying the goods. Situations can arise where the buyer will not agree with the international marketer and will insist on another method of payment such as open account, which places all risks on the seller.

Buyer risk can be nonexistent where the buyer and international marketer have a long and good relationship. However, where that does not exist, the international marketer must take extreme care to ensure that payment will be received. Obviously, the management of risk will depend on the value of the order. Even if the buyer is unknown to the international marketer, a low-value order may not constitute a problem for the firm's finances if payment is not forthcoming. For a discussion of payment methods see chapter 14.

Country Risk

Country risk occurs when a country suffers from economic or political instability, or both. Either of these situations may well contribute to a low reserve of hard foreign currencies. When this happens, government officials may place a hold on any foreign payments until reserves become adequate. Such circumstances will affect the buyer's making payment, and the international marketer will have to wait until conditions improve and hard currency is available.

Management will have to establish the likelihood of this risk occurring. If country risk is perceived to be a potential threat, and the international marketer still wants to do business, then the risk will have to be managed. The use of a confirmed, irrevocable documentary credit or insistence on cash with the order can be employed to help manage this risk. The use of either of these methods, obviously, will depend on the readiness of the buyer to accede to the international marketer's wishes. Another alternative is the use of credit insurance. This is a type of insurance that covers the seller against buyer default in payment because of failure of the buyer's business or stoppage of payment by the buyer's government.

Exchange Risk

Exchange risk can be avoided by always insisting on payment in the stronger currency, whether that is the buyer's or the seller's. Otherwise, techniques such as a hedge (presented in chapter 9) could be employed to reduce exchange risk. Management should assess this factor when the enquiry for the product is first received. If the buyer's currency is blocked or nonconvertible (is not traded on the Forex market and cannot be exchanged for any other currency; the Uzbekistan som, for example, is nonconvertible), the two parties will have to agree on which hard currency will be used. Even though the currencies involved may be hard and convertible, the value of each can fluctuate. This problem can be accentuated if the international marketer has to give the buyer time to pay.

Thus, if the international marketer provides a quotation to the buyer in the buyer's currency with the agreement that payment be made, for example, 90 days after receipt of the merchandise, the exchange rate may change during the intervening 90 days. As explained in chapter 9, such changes will either leave the buyer's currency strong or weak against the seller's, and the final payment will provide the seller with either a profit or a loss. Management will have to monitor the long-term trend of the exchange rate for the two currencies to assess future conditions. And then, short-term fluctuations can be contrary to long-term trends, making exchange risk difficult to assess. Exchange risk is often disregarded or not considered; management may feel that the risk of exchange rate fluctuation loss does not justify the cost of protection, or the risk is simply not recognized. For a discussion of exchange risks see chapter 9.

Management of exchange risk may be accomplished best through the international banking system's foreign exchange facilities, where bankers will enter into a currency hedge contract to buy or sell a foreign currency at a date in the future at a specific exchange rate. Bankers will charge a commission on currency hedge contracts, and therefore, that cost will have to be included in the seller's price quotation. Additionally, the cost of nominal interest on the value of the order where credit is given to the buyer will also have to be factored into the price quote.

Knowledge Risk

Language differences that cause a lack of complete understanding between the international marketer and buyer contribute to knowledge risk in international trade. For example, one of the parties involved may not fully comprehend what responsibilities are required to arrange for the transportation of the merchandise to take place. Inexperience in exporting can contribute to a knowledge problem. To minimize the knowledge risk, shipping specialists such as freight forwarders can be used.

Transit Risk

Transit risk describes the possibility of the merchandise being lost or damaged while being transported from the international marketer to the buyer. In the event the merchandise is lost, from a legal point of view, the seller is in breach of contract. The products will have to be replaced, at a cost to the international marketer. The cost of replacement may possibly be recoverable from the party that caused the loss. A similar situation occurs when the merchandise is damaged. Thus, making arrangements for the potentiality of loss or damage to be covered through insurance makes sense.

Effective management of buyer, country, exchange, and transit risks is possible through the use of various supporting organizations. Although using such assisting entities can help manage these risks, the party involved in the loss may not always be able to recover 100 percent of the value lost. For example, credit insurers will settle only about 85 to 90 percent of the value. Using foreign exchange facilities to hedge currency fluctuations will not guarantee an exchange rate that is exactly equivalent to the market exchange rate on the day the hedge is exercised. And, transit insurers will usually retain a deductible from the settlement amount.

The secret in the management of risk is to understand the risk and the factors that are affecting the transaction. Although the buyer is unknown, the international marketer may decide to make the sale on open account, based on a low value of the order and the opportunity to gain favor with the buyer for future business. However, nothing is always as it seems, and doing a credit check of all customers and suppliers every six months makes good sense. Even if provisions have been made to minimize exporting risk, the buyer will still perceive any mistake made by an assisting organization to be the seller's. So, the buyer will place the blame squarely on the international marketer, who could suffer the loss of further orders.

LOGISTICS AND MARKET ENTRY METHOD

The method of market entry will influence the distribution or logistics for the international marketer. The needs are quite different for managers who export occasionally and those who are involved in foreign direct investments and have a significant presence in the foreign country. The occasional exporter may be concerned with little more than packaging and transportation methods if indirect channels are used. Those already involved in foreign direct investments will need to consider a coordination of logistical activities from exporting through distribution.

For management directly involved with the foreign market through direct exporting, joint ventures, and foreign direct investments, familiarity with the export process is essential. Whether the finished product is shipped to intermediaries or sales offices located in the foreign country for resale, or components and parts are moved to foreign locations for further processing before being sold, the international marketer needs to coordinate shipping and other logistical activities.

THE EXPORT PROCESS

The export process or **export mechanics** entails the logistical steps or procedures involved in exporting products from one country and importing them into another country. Knowledge of the activities, documentation, and assistance of facilitating organizations is vital to successfully organizing and arranging export transactions, providing for contingencies, and receiving payment. To assure nothing is overlooked and all exigencies are considered, management must fully understand the requirements to consummate export transactions. Prerequisites are knowledge of the procedures involved and documents required to bring an export sale to completion. The stages of the exporting process are shown in Exhibit 12.1 and described in the list below:

Exhibit 12.1 **Stages of the Export Process**

Solicit Sales → Negotiation → Prepare order → Ship → Conclusion

1. The first stage of the process entails seeking foreign business. Management must prepare adequately, and consider everything required to satisfy a potential buyer's needs, including locating a potential buyer and stimulating interest.
2. The second stage is concerned with concluding a contract acceptable to both the buyer and seller. Negotiation of terms may be required before the contract is consummated.
3. The third stage involves preparing the order for shipment. Involved are contacting organizations that will help with facilitating the shipment, preparing the product for shipment, and making export arrangements.
4. The fourth stage is the shipping process. Moving the product from the point of production to the location designated by the buyer must be accomplished.
5. The last stage comprises activities that occur after the product arrives at its destination. Concluding the sale, making the product available to the buyer, and acknowledgments are involved.

The precise steps involved in each stage are shown in Exhibit 12.2. All the possible contingencies are depicted. Some steps in the process may be omitted depending on the nature of the exporting arrangement and the conditions appropriate to the buyer and seller. All of the steps should be considered, however, to guarantee all procedures are done correctly and nothing is overlooked.

Exhibit 12.2 **Steps in the Export Process**

Solicit Sales

Make export decision → Locate potential buyer → Prepare quote

Negotiation

Submit offer → Negotiate terms → Sign contract → Arrange financing

Prepare Order

Make product → Prepare for shipment → Prepare export documents

Ship

Ship product to port → Place on carrier → Ship product to destination

Conclusion

Process documents → Receive product → Clear customs → Correspondence

SOLICIT SALES

The exporting process begins with the decision to engage in foreign business. As was explained in chapter 5, management decides to export a portion of production to another country for a variety of reasons such as excess capacity, declining domestic sales, or the perceived opportunity for expanding sales and profits. Whatever the reason, a stimulus must exist that motivates management to investigate the potential for international marketing and make the decision to export.

Once the exporting decision is made, the next step is to locate potential buyers. Again as explained in chapter 5, the decision may be precipitated by situations such as a fortuitous order, responding to a foreigner's inquiring about buying the firm's product, or a conscious effort by management to locate customers such as through the World Traders Data Reports available from the U.S. Department of Commerce. Identifying the country or countries to enter and developing an exporting strategy are involved, as well as deciding on promotional appeals and how to best reach the target market with those communications. To procure foreign sales, potential customers first have to be made aware of the product and its ability to meet their needs and solve their problems.

Successful marketing efforts to locate and inform potential customers will result in inquiries for information from foreigners that will help them assess the desirability of the firm's product. The foreigner will require all the facts about the product and conditions relevant to the sale. Facts such as packaging, service, quality, price, shipping terms, and delivery times will be requested. This means the seller must prepare an offer with the conditions of sale for the product of interest to the foreigner.

It is important to remember that the foreigner has not yet placed an order. The potential customer has simply expressed an interest in the firm's product. If the product is available from inventory in sufficient quantity, financial information from accounting will permit cost determination and immediate delivery is possible. However, if the product must be custom made or inventories are not sufficient to accommodate the order, the product must be produced. The materials, parts, and components needed to produce the product will have to be purchased. Purchasing these additional materials will be desirable only if the foreigner decides to buy the product. Therefore, suppliers must be contacted to determine the availability and price for required materials. The prospective delivery date that can be promised to the buyer will depend on when materials are shipped and received, production schedules, the time involved for production, and the time required for shipment. Confirming an option to buy the needed materials will assure their availability if the foreigner decides to buy the product. The option can be cancelled if the foreigner declines the offer.

To prepare an offer for the prospective buyer, details of the proposed sale must be determined. Therefore, shipping information regarding the proposed order must be communicated to a carrier. This can be done directly by the seller or by using an intermediary such as a freight forwarder. The carrier needs to know the weight of the shipment, the number and type of containers or packages involved, the dimensions of the containers, contents, destination, and approximate shipping dates. This information will help the carrier determine the shipping costs for the potential order. Also, an option for the required space should be obtained to assure timely delivery if the order is received.

Usually the most cost-effective shipping method is by water. If time is critical, shipment by water may be impractical because a ship travels at a slow speed, which increases shipping time. Also, if the seller's and buyer's locations are land connected, transport by water may be infeasible or less desirable. **Liner companies** operate cargo ships that sail on regular schedules to and from specified seaports by means of established sea routes. Cargo available at the port of export at the designated date for sailing will be included in the shipment. Alternative shipping is available from **tramp vessels** that have no fixed ports of call or designated sailing schedules. The manifest for such a ship is prepared from cargo that has been contracted to be shipped at a particular time and to a particular destination. For example, as cargo destined for northern Europe becomes available in relatively contiguous ports on the East Coast of the United States—such as New York City, Philadelphia, Baltimore, and Charleston—a manifest is created.

Determining all expenses so the appropriate price can be ascertained is an important aspect of preparing the offer. Along with material costs, manufacturing costs, packaging costs, and shipping costs, the manager needs to consider a variety of other expenses. Financing or payment procedures may involve the services of a commercial bank. Payment methods will be discussed in chapter 14. The costs vary with such factors as currency, credit risk, and instrument of payment. If a letter of credit is employed, for example, the bank will help prepare the paperwork and make arrangements with the foreigner's bank. The cost for banking services can range from about 4 percent to 10 percent of the value of the shipment. Other costs, if such services are utilized, can include the following: insurance (up to about 20 percent of value), paperwork for the Export-Import Bank of the United States, and lawyers (about 1 percent), Foreign Credit Insurance Association (FCIA) insurance (from 1 to about 3 percent), export management company fee (1 to about 4 percent), and special charges for such items as a consular invoice (from a few dollars to 3 percent), contract translation, and quality tests from independent testing laboratories. All costs need to be identified so that the correct price can be quoted.

NEGOTIATION

From the information gathered in the preparation stage, the international marketer will determine the price and delivery and financing terms. Once these have been established, an offer is drafted and submitted to the foreign prospective buyer. The offer is made in a piece of correspondence that specifies precisely and clearly the proposed selling terms. The offer specifies exactly what the seller will do for the buyer for this particular transaction.

After receipt of the offer, the foreigner will compare the offer with others received and with what is considered acceptable based on experience and expectations. After this assessment, three courses of action can occur. First, if the terms and conditions are acceptable as proposed, the foreigner can respond affirmatively. Second, if the terms and conditions are unacceptable, the foreigner can reject them and buy from another supplier. Third, if some of the terms and conditions are acceptable while others are not, the foreigner can make a counteroffer with preferred terms and conditions to replace those that are unacceptable. Management may accept the counteroffer, reject it, or counter the counter. Depending on how much the sale is needed, management can continue the negotiation process until the parties reach agreement or submit a final offer, or terminate negotiations.

If mutually agreeable terms and conditions are determined, a contract is prepared. The seller prepares the contract by placing the "conditions of the sale" in writing. Care must be taken in writing the contract because only the details specified are part of the agreement. Once the contract is signed, both parties are bound by the written terms and conditions unless each agrees to changes. If the buyer wants a copy of the contract in the foreign language, the translation must be accurate so that the meaning of the various provisions remains unchanged. In some countries, placing a copy of the contract with a validator such as a consul or notary is required or desirable. When doing business in countries with a reputation for unscrupulous business practices, validating a contract may be advisable to help prevent forgery. Today's technology can make changes to a contract difficult to detect; if the foreigner tries to change the contract, the true and legal version can be determined by consulting the validator's copy. Preparing the translated version of the contract is usually the seller's responsibility.

Before the contract is signed, the international marketer must consult the Export Administration Regulations available from the U.S. Government Printing Office or Export.gov to ascertain that no export restrictions exist for the product or shipments to the buyer's country. Export.gov is managed collaboratively by the U.S. Department of Commerce's, International Trade Administration along with nineteen Federal Agencies that offer export assistance programs and services. A license from the federal government is required to export any product from the United States. Most products are not sensitive products or sold to sensitive countries and may be shipped under a **general license.** This is also known as open exporting because the only requirement is to list the ten-digit number code for the product obtained from Schedule B, on the Shipper's Export Declaration both of which are available from the U.S. Department of Commerce.

The nature of the product and the country of destination determine whether a general license is appropriate. Restricted commodities and countries require a formal application for permission to export known as a **validated license**. A validated license is known as closed exporting because government permission is required before the product can be shipped. In most cases where the value of the shipment exceeds US$5,000, the buyer or a representative of the foreign government must prepare and submit forms to accompany the validated license application.

Products for which a validated license is required include weapons, high-tech products that might have military implications for the United States and its allies, items in short supply in the United States, as well as products that may be considered strategic in nature. Regardless of the country to which such products are to be sent, a validated license is required. Regardless of the product being exported, a validated license is required for countries with which the United States does not have diplomatic relations or where tensions exist. These countries are classified into categories depending upon their relationships with the United States. Exporting is essentially banned to embargoed countries with unfriendly governments and countries designated as supporting terrorist activities such as Cuba, Iran, North Korea, Sudan, and Syria. This list of countries is available from the U.S. Department of Commerce, Bureau of Industry and Security. No export license is needed to export from the United States to Canada, however. The important point to remember is that the authorities expect the exporter to be aware of whether or not the product requires a validated export license. The exporter has the responsibility to ascertain the specific situation.

The importing regulations of specific countries need to be thoroughly scrutinized. Management must be certain no restrictions or quotas exist. Electrical codes and food content requirements of the importing country, for example, may prohibit exporting the product in its existing form. Modifications may be required for the product before it will meet the foreign country's import requirements.

After the contract is signed, the international marketer notifies the bank or financial institution to facilitate payment when a letter of credit or documentary collection is involved (see chapter 14 for a discussion of payment methods). The banker will assist by making appropriate contacts with foreign corresponding banks, assuring required exporting documents are transmitted, and arranging for payment at the appropriate terms and time.

PREPARE ORDER

The signed contract means the buyer is obligated to purchase, and therefore, management can begin to fulfill the agreement. The first concern is securing the product ordered. If the product is in stock in sufficient quantity, the shipment can be prepared. If the product is not in stock or is a custom-made item, it may be bought from a supplier or manufacturer. If the product is to be manufactured, suppliers contacted during the preparation of the offer must be notified to ship the required materials, components, or parts. Options opened during the preparation stage will be exercised. Other facilitators that were contacted during the offer preparation, such as the carrier, the insurance agent, and the freight forwarder, will be alerted that the contract was secured, and their services will be required as previously arranged. The carrier needs to know the date the shipment will arrive at the port so a manifest for shipping can be prepared.

Management needs to comply with the buyer's specifications and have the product ready for dispatch at a date that will meet the shipping time requirements of the agreed-upon delivery date. Increasingly, buyers and the buyers' banks are insisting on the goods being inspected before packing and shipment. This inspection is conducted by an inspection agency, usually at the buyer's expense, and is to ensure the buyer's specifications have been met. This is an important part of the contract because the inspecting agent will issue a "Clean Report of Findings" only if the specifications in the contract of sale have been met. Failure to obtain this document will usually mean no payment being made, because the seller is in breach of contract.

After manufacturing is complete, the product must be adequately prepared for shipment. Normally, the product cannot be shipped in the types of packages used for domestic shipment. The product may be stored outside of a building at the port for a long time with no protective covering before being loaded into the conveyance vehicle. Also, if the mode of conveyance is a ship, exposure to ocean water, which can be corrosive because of its salt content, is possible. Normally, additional handling is required for export shipments, which increases the probability of damage and breakage. Therefore, tightly secured packages and containers are recommended.

For bulky or oddly shaped products, wooden container boxes may need to be constructed. Packages should be waterproofed or the product sealed inside a plastic covering. Intermediaries can be employed to prepare packaging of the product for shipment, thus relieving the international marketer of that responsibility. Containers for export must be appropriately marked prior to shipment. This may include weight, the number of each box (container), the total number of boxes in the shipment, port markings, an indication of the center of gravity, forklifting locations, and slinging locations. A picture of an umbrella indicates the package is to be kept dry, and a picture of a wine glass indicates the package is fragile. Any writing on the package should be in the buyer's language as well as in English. Pictures and the foreign language are used because foreign stevedoring companies employ workers who cannot read English words. Therefore, standardized international communications are required. The international symbol meaning "no" (a red circle with a diagonal line through it) is often indicated with pictures. For example, a hook inside the circle with a diagonal line across the hook means no sharp hooks should be used to move the package from one location to another.

Containerization

Containerized freight is routinely used to ship appropriately sized products. **Containerized freight** is a system of transport using metal box containers, also known as isotainers, which can easily be loaded on and off truck trailer wheels, railroad cars, and ships. Isotainers are available in five standard sizes (20 feet, 40 feet, 45 feet, 48 feet, and 53 feet in length) and are 8 feet wide and 8.5 feet high. The container capacity of ports and ships is measured in twenty-foot equivalent units (TEUs). The most common container size is 40 feet in length and is designated as two TEU or one forty-foot equivalent unit (FEU), terms that are used interchangeably in the industry. High cube containers (9.5 feet high) and half-height containers (4.25 feet high) for heavy loads are also used.

Approximately 90 percent of all cargo transported internationally is shipped by containerization.[2] The top five container shipping companies, which account for about 41 percent of global capacity, are shown in Exhibit 12.3.

Advantages of containerization are that the container can be carefully packed at the factory, verified for customs, locked, trucked to the port, lifted from the wheel base, conveniently stacked in the ship or plane, attached to another wheel base in the foreign country, and trucked or barged to the buyer's location. Handling of the product is minimized in this way, and damage is less likely. A product in another package is always subject to customs inspection in which customs officials must open the package and examine the contents. Sometimes customs officials do not repack properly, which increases the opportunity for damage. Also, once the package is opened, pilferage

Exhibit 12.3 **Largest Container Shipping Companies**

Company	Number of ships*	TEU capacity
A.P. Möller-Maersk	540	2,028,048
Mediterranean Shipping Company	437	1,545,972
CMA CGM Group	362	963,803
Evergreen Line	175	623,744
COSCO Container Lines Americas	149	496,428

*The number of ships owned and chartered by the company.

Source: "AXS-Alphaliner Top 100: Operated fleets as per 03 April 2009," http://www.lgt.polyu.edu.hk/hkdata/International/News/Maritime/2009/Top%20100%20Ranking%20090430.pdf.

may occur. Non-containerized packages are handled frequently when loaded and off-loaded, increasing damage potential. Products shipped in a container are handled only once, while being placed in the container. Inadequate storage of non-containerized packages in a ship or plane by stevedores is possible, while storage in the container can be done correctly at the factory, reducing the chance for damage. Once loaded into an isotainer, the product is moved to the terminal, airport, or dock head where the isotainer is subsequently loaded on a plane or ship for further shipment. After arriving at the foreign country, the isotainer is off-loaded, and the contents are inspected by customs officials and transported to the final destination.

Specialized Ships

A variety of specialized ships exist for transporting oceangoing cargo such as those designated **lighter aboard ship (LASH)**. LASH ships open in the back at the waterline so that small flat-bottomed barges called lighters can be floated in and stored on elevated racks. Some LASH ships have cranes aboard for the purpose of loading and unloading lighters over the ship's stern. LASH ships can be loaded and unloaded without port or dock facilities. The open- or closed-top lighters can be towed by tugboat to the LASH ship for convenient on-loading. Therefore, LASH is useful in shallow ports where ships that draw too much water to be moored at shore must moor in deeper water offshore. Without lighters, cargo must be ferried to the ship and reloaded onto the larger vessel. Loading lighters into the ship eliminates the transferring process. When handling is reduced, costs and damage potential are reduced. Also, lighters pushed by tugboat are used extensively to move cargo on the well-developed inland waterways and river navigation system in Europe. Obviously, hooking a number of lighters to a tugboat at the port of destination and continuing inland by water can reduce handling and shipping costs.

Other specialized ocean shipping includes roll-on/roll-off ships (Ro-Ro) that are designed to carry freight vehicles or cars without passengers that can be driven on and off the ship. Ore/Bulk/Oil ships (OBO) are designed to carry either liquid or dry cargo such as crude oil and coal. These vessels are also known as product/ore/bulk/oil ships (PROBO) or combination carriers. A ship that carries a cargo of only a liquid petroleum product is known as a tanker or oiler. Ships that carry passengers and cargo are referred to as combo ships or combi ships.

Export Documents

The next step in preparing the order is to complete the required export documents. A number of documents that are not required in domestic trade are required for international sales. The number of intermediaries involved in an international transaction, such as the international carrier (shipping line or airline), customs offices, international bankers, insurers, packing companies, and regulatory authorities is normally greater than encountered in domestic trade. All of these intermediaries rely upon documentation in order to complete their responsibilities. The problem for the seller and buyer is that inaccurate documentation will invariably slow the delivery process. Thus, throughout the transit, documentation that is precise will be required. The exporter might not be aware of all the documentation required so the outsourcing of such responsibilities to appropriate facilitating organizations will be imperative. Since documentation associated with an international transaction can be related to certain facilitating organizations as well as the seller and buyer, each will want particular documents pertinent to the specific activity being performed.

The following are the essential documents for an export shipment:

- commercial invoice
- contract
- contract of carriage such as a bill of lading or air waybill
- insurance
- packing slip
- postal forms if shipped by mail
- Shipper's Export Declaration
- specialized documents as needed

Commercial Invoice. The **commercial invoice** is originated by the seller, provides details of the practical aspects of the merchandise sold, and describes essential facts about the shipment. The commercial invoice is similar to the billing invoice that businesses use, with two exceptions. First, the shipping terms such as Incoterms (see chapter 14) that are used relate to the selling price and must be specified. Second, the country where the shipment originated must be identified. A commercial invoice can include the following:

- name of the carrier
- names and addresses of the seller and buyer
- net and gross weights of the order
- number and type of packing containers
- ocean or air freight charges
- per unit price and total price
- port marks and numbers (pier, berth, and so forth)
- ports of export and import
- quantity and description of the merchandise
- shipping terms (terms of sale)
- statement of origin of the merchandise
- terminal charges (handling, wharfage, lighterage, and so forth).

The invoice is the most important document because it includes all the information about the merchandise. That information will be needed to satisfy customs officials at both origin and destination. From the seller's point of view, the invoice is an accounting document and, once issued and entered into the ledger, becomes a debt due from the buyer at a specified date. Without an invoice, the buyer will not pay, bankers will not honor a documentary credit, and customs authorities will not allow the progress of the order.

Contract. The contract is a legal document that stipulates the agreement between the seller and the buyer and specifies the terms and conditions by which each agrees to be bound relating to the sale. The contract spells out for the seller what amounts of what products will be delivered to the buyer when and for what price. Included will be stipulations about the nature of the product, details about composition, performance, and warranties. The shipping terms and conditions will be indicated, the locations where the product will be exported and imported, the means of conveyance, and the delivery schedule specified. The means by which the buyer must pay will be outlined, and the buyer's obligations will be enumerated. All important aspects of the sale should be included in the contract so that legal recourse can be pursued if any disagreements or misunderstandings should arise related to the sale. The contract stipulates the duties and responsibilities of the seller and buyer with regard to the business arrangement to which each has committed.

Contract of Carriage. Before loading, the carrier will examine the merchandise and packaging for observable damage, shortages, overages, inaccuracies in markings or weights, and other discrepancies. If everything is correct and conforms to the shipping documents, the carrier may mark the contract of carriage "Clean On Board" (see page 223). If discrepancies or damage are observed, those problems are noted on the contract of carriage. The contract of carriage is then considered "Foul," and is marked accordingly. A foul contract of carriage can complicate completion of the contract and delay payment. If no notation or discrepancies are written, the contract of carriage is considered to be clean.

The contract of carriage is usually prepared by the carrier or the freight forwarder and is evidence of

- a contract between the seller or buyer (depending on the shipping terms such as Incoterms being used) and the carrier; and
- receipt of the goods by the carrier.

The contracts of carriage for the four main modes of transport—road, rail, sea, and air—differ from one another in terms of formats. For road, rail, and air carriage, the contracts of carriage are all known as consignment notes regardless of their name. However, carriage by sea is covered by an **ocean bill of lading** (B/L).

The difference is primarily due to sea carriage having been the earliest method of international transport. Because, even today, carriage by sea is the slowest method of transport, provisions must be made to permit buyers to resell the merchandise while it is still in transit. This happens particularly where bulk commodities are involved. Also, because the ocean B/L represents the goods at full value, the carrier has a duty of care to deliver the goods at the destination port in exactly the same condition as received at origin. The carrier will release the goods at destination only on presentation of one of the originals constituting the set of bills of lading.

As a result, the ocean B/L has a third property in addition to the two identified above—a document of title. If merchandise that is in sea transit is to be resold, then the original seller must endorse the originals of the B/L to the second buyer (new owner), to enable that owner to gain release of the products at the destination.

There is normally no need to sell goods when in transit on the other modes of transport, because of their relative speed. Consequently, the contracts of carriage for road, rail, and air are not documents of title and, therefore, are not negotiable in the same way as the ocean B/L. For short ocean trips where the need to transfer title to another buyer is unlikely, a sea waybill is increasingly being used instead of an ocean B/L. The sea waybill is not a document of title but is simpler for the seller to use. The sea waybill is also useful for shipments to established customers whose creditworthiness is not in doubt.

If the product is shipped by truck, as from the United States to Canada or from Germany to Poland, a consignment note called a truck bill of lading is prepared. The Convention des Marchandises Routiers (CRM) specifies conditions for international road carriage and is the form of truck bill of lading used for shipments among some twenty-three European countries. If the product is shipped by air, a consignment note known as an **air waybill** is prepared. A rail waybill is the consignment note prepared for a rail shipment. The use of electric consignment notes known as digital waybills (also called e-waybills) is increasing as a way to reduce costs. If the product is shipped via a liner company, an ocean bill of lading or a sea waybill may be prepared depending upon whether or not title to the cargo may need to be transferred during shipment.

At the time of loading or shortly thereafter, the original bill of lading and usually three copies are stamped "On Board" or "Shipped" and signed by representatives of the liner company. Remaining copies are stamped "Copy, Not Negotiable" and distributed to the parties involved with the shipment for their records. When ownership of the shipment changes hands as indicated by the shipping term used in the contract, the negotiable copies become the property of the buyer. Each of the signed originals is a negotiable document unless marked "Not Negotiable."

The buyer must submit the original ocean bill of lading in clean and negotiable form to the carrier before the merchandise is released. If the bill of lading is "foul" or "claused," the shipper can sign a letter of indemnity to the carrier to get a clean version. Although the original copies of the ocean bill of lading are negotiable, they are normally issued to the order of the seller. Therefore, the seller's endorsement is required for negotiation. Once that endorsement is obtained, the buyer can resell the merchandise even though it is still in transit to the original destination simply by endorsing and signing the B/L to the new buyer. A non-negotiable version of the ocean bill of lading, which does not convey title, will usually be used when the buyer has prepaid for the merchandise.

Insurance. Insurance may be required for exporting, depending upon the shipping terms (such as Incoterms) employed. For instance, the shipping terms may not require the seller to secure insurance; however, doing so is highly recommended. In other cases, the shipping terms employed will shift the responsibility for securing insurance for overseas shipment to the foreign buyer (see chapter 14 for a discussion of shipping terms).

"All risk insurance," with war, strike, riot, and civil-commotion riders, is best. The seller can purchase insurance or have the freight forwarder, if utilized, prepare a policy. Infrequent exporters may find purchasing an insurance policy appropriate.

An insurance policy covers a specific shipment; therefore, each shipment requires an individually written policy to cover only that shipment. Frequent exporters may find obtaining an insurance certificate more convenient. A certificate is a policy that covers all shipments of a particular type during a specified time period. A form of blanket insurance, the certificate reduces the paperwork by eliminating the need to have individual policies issued each time a shipment is exported. The need for the seller to secure an insurance policy depends on the terms of shipment and when the title is transferred.

Packing Slip. The packing slip, also called a packing list, is the same as is used for domestic shipments. The **packing slip** is prepared by the seller and specifies which goods, identified in the invoice, are packed in which case. Without the packing list, customs officials at the destination are unlikely to release the goods and insurers may not want to settle any claim arising from loss or damage to the goods during the transit. The price is not included.

Postal Forms. If the product is exported via U.S. mail, U.S. Postal Service forms must be completed. Copies of these forms are attached to the package prior to shipping.

Shipper's Export Declaration. For shipments from the United States, a **Shipper's Export Declaration** is required if the value of the total sales for any one product contained in a shipment is over US$2,500.00 (except if the shipment is going to Canada) or if it is being shipped via a validated license, regardless of the value. U.S. Department of Commerce Form 7525-V must be used for this declaration. This form is the source of trade information and statistics reported by the government. Since October 1, 2008, electronic filing of the Shipper's Export Declaration, through the Automated Export System (AES) operated by the U.S. Census Bureau is required. The AES makes reporting easier, faster, and less expensive.

Specialized Documents. When appropriate and necessary, the exporter will prepare and submit certain other government forms. Examples include a certificate of origin, a phytosanitary certificate, and a consular invoice. A **certificate of origin** is used to indicate the country of origin of the product, of previously manufactured parts or components that become part of the product, or of both. Some governments require a certificate of origin notarized by the chamber of commerce. For example, Israel requires this document to assure products contain no Arab content. A **phytosanitary certificate** from the U.S. Department of Agriculture may be required to assure products were inspected or treated and certified free of disease. For example, proof that blue rot is not present may be required when exporting lumber. A **consular invoice** (legalization) may be required by the foreign country's consulate located in the country of export. A consular invoice may be required if consulate personnel must approve the shipment. Most major trading nations do not require consularization; however, this is a common practice in Middle Eastern, Latin American, African, and small Asian countries.

Any forms or documents that are required by the buyer or government of the importing country must be prepared by the seller. For example, the buyer may request an independent laboratory report certifying the results of a Shore "A" hardness test for a rubber product to assure the hardness of the rubber meets specifications. A **Canada customs invoice** may be required for verification of the value, quantity, and nature of shipments from the United States to Canada, and a **NAFTA certificate of origin** is required for shipments to Canada or Mexico. Failure to provide any form with the precision in detail required by the importing government officials will normally cause delay in the import clearance of the products, and, possibly, unexpected charges for storage of the goods before release by customs officials.

Depending on the agreed-upon method of payment, such as a letter of credit or bill of exchange (see chapter 14 for a discussion of payment methods), financial documents may also be involved. Reference to pamphlet URC522, published by the International Chamber of Commerce ICC, reveals that when bankers are involved, their only interest is with collections and not with the merchandise. The bankers are providing a conditional guarantee of payment to the seller. Therefore, their main concern is ensuring that the buyer accepts the payments term before shipping and title documents are transferred (documents against acceptance) or that the buyer pays in full before the shipping and title documents are transferred (documents against payment).

SHIP

The seller can begin the movement of the product before all the documents needed for export are taken to the bank and presented for processing. First is delivery of the merchandise to the port of export. Truck or rail inland freight charges will be incurred unless the product is delivered by company vehicle. Products shipped by ocean that are oversized or of an insufficient quantity to fill an entire container (called an LCL–less than container load) go to the liner company's container freight station (CFS) located near the port. There the shipment will be consolidated with other shipments going to the same port of import to help fill a container and save space. Less than truckload (LTL) shipments also go to the CFS.

When the carrier at the port receives the merchandise, a dock receipt, or warehouse receipt, is issued to show that the product has been transferred to its possession. As explained previously, the merchandise is examined for observable damage, shortages, overages, or other inaccuracies in quantity and description. The bill of lading is then properly marked "Foul" or "Clean Received." The cargo will be stored at the port until the appropriate shipping time. If the merchandise is delivered early to the port and must be stored for any length of time, a storage fee is charged. Additional expenses will be incurred to load the cargo onto the ship or plane.

After the vessel arrives at the port, loading begins and is usually completed within twenty-four hours. Tramp ships may take somewhat longer to load. Remember, merchandise being prepared for loading and during loading will be subject to the weather. Storage in a holding area for on-loading can be out of doors in a fenced-in area. Special equipment speeds the loading of containerized ships. Containers are stored in the ship's hold and to a height as high as seven containers above the deck line.

Once loaded, the ship sets sail for or the plane flies to its destination. Since turbulence can occur (the rocking of the ship or air pockets), proper packaging is emphasized. Improperly packaged products sometimes break through the package due to shifting of the cargo and may get lost or stolen, which results in complications for delivery.

Depending on the situation, shipments are sometimes transshipped by the carrier. This occurs when the cargo is switched to another vessel at an intermediate port while en route to the port of import. Transshipping may be required because the original ship does not dock at the desired port or the cargo has to be transferred to another liner company to complete the journey.

CONCLUSION

While the shipment is en route, the export documents are presented to the bank for processing when payment is to be made by letter of credit or documentary collection. When a letter of credit is used, documents must be presented within twenty-one days after the ship sails, unless an earlier time has been specified. The documents should be presented as swiftly as possible so processing can be completed and the documents forwarded rapidly to the buyer. This permits the buyer to quickly claim the product and avoid paying storage charges. If shipping by sea, the documents will normally be processed before the shipment arrives at the port of import. If shipping by air, the merchandise could arrive before the documents are processed.

The buyer or the buyer's bank, according to the terms arranged, makes payment. The buyer presents the documents, verifies ownership, and takes receipt of the product. Upon clearing customs, the product can be shipped inland to the buyer's location. The buyer may have already resold the merchandise; thus, the cargo would be shipped from the port to the new buyer's location. If the buyer plans to resell the product, marketing can begin immediately after the contract is signed. Once a new buyer is obtained, shipping can be redirected to the new buyer's location if desired.

After the transaction is complete, both parties should exchange correspondence, acknowledging that commitments have been fulfilled. The seller thanks the buyer for the business and explores the possibilities for continuing the business relationship. The buyer thanks the seller, acknowledges the product is not damaged, and expresses appreciation for fulfilling the contract. Such letters are not required but are a matter of common courtesy and good business practice.

PAPERWORK REVIEWED

The following paperwork may be involved in an export transaction:

- ocean B/L or other appropriate consignment note such as an air waybill
- Canada customs invoice
- certificate of origin or NAFTA certificate of origin
- commercial invoice
- consular invoice

- contract
- dock receipt or warehouse receipt
- financial document such as a letter of credit
- insurance policy or certificate
- packing list
- postal forms
- Shipper's Export Declaration
- validated license

A **carnet** is another form that may be encountered. A carnet is prepared when a sample of a product is imported by salespeople or for inspection at the request of a potential foreign buyer. The international marketer can avoid paying import duties on the product if the sample is re-exported from the foreign country. If the foreigner buys the sample or the sample is not re-exported (free sample), the importer or foreigner must pay any tariff imposed by the foreign country's government.

If the product is shipped by sea from the United States, the exporter must file an Export Movement Summary Sheet each quarter with the U.S. Customs Service, reporting all shipments during the quarter. This form serves as the statement from which a harbor maintenance fee (one-eighth of 1 percent of the Free Alongside Ship [FAS] value of the shipments) is assessed. The fee is payable by the end of the month following the close of the quarter.

CHAPTER SUMMARY

For the international marketer involved in direct channels of distribution, knowledge of the exporting process is mandatory. The logistics of exporting make it impractical for management to have staff in-house to oversee all aspects of the process. Also, the supply chain involves numerous risks. Normally, at least some aspects of the process will need to be outsourced to facilitating organizations that are specialists in those export functions. Since these firms can do these processes more efficiently than the exporter, costs can be reduced. The risk inherent in exporting needs to be effectively managed and reduced if possible.

The exporting process, called export mechanics, involves the steps and procedures required in exporting a product from one country and importing it into another country. To complete a successful export transaction, the international marketer must first prepare adequately. This requires locating potential buyers and making them aware of the firm's product or service. Once a foreigner becomes interested, an offer must be prepared that includes the terms and conditions under which the sale is proposed to be made. Both parties can negotiate terms, if desired, until conditions agreeable to both are determined; then a contract is signed and financing arranged.

After the contract is signed, the international marketer must prepare the order for shipment. Adequate packaging and preparation of numerous forms and documents is necessary. The required documentation can be prepared by the international marketer or by a facilitating organization such as a freight forwarder that specializes in this activity. Once the shipment is prepared and documentation complete, the product is transported to the port of export and loaded on the appropriate conveyance method. The documents are delivered to the bank for processing once the shipment is in transit. The carrier delivers the cargo to the port of import where the foreign buyer takes possession after clearing customs. Payment is made according to the agreed-to financial conditions, and both parties should send correspondence indicating their compliance with the terms and conditions of the contract. The international marketer will communicate with the foreign buyer and explore the possibilities for future business.

KEY TERMS

Air waybill
Canada customs invoice
Carnet
Certificate of origin
Commercial invoice
Consular invoice
Containerized freight
Export mechanics
Freight forwarder
General license
Lighter aboard ship (LASH)
Liner companies
NAFTA certificate of origin
Ocean bill of lading
Packing slip
Phytosanitary certificate
Shipper's Export Declaration
Third party logistics operator (3PL)
Tramp vessels
Validated license

REVIEW QUESTIONS

1. How are logistics and supply chains related to the export process?
2. Explain the five risks of exporting and what the international marketer can do to manage or minimize these risks.
3. Why must an international marketer be familiar with the export mechanics?
4. What steps are involved in preparing an offer for an international shipment?
5. Differentiate between a validated and general export license.
6. An important export document is the bill of lading. What makes this document so important?
7. What is the Shipper's Export Declaration?
8. Go to the library and write down the title, author(s), publisher, and publication date of three books that provide directions about how to export.
9. Go to the U.S. Department of Commerce Web site and record the services and assistance provided to exporters by this government agency.
10. Use a search engine to locate the name of the state office that assists exporters in your state. What services does this office provide?

ACKNOWLEDGMENTS

A special thank-you is extended to Professor David Snell for helpful suggestions, contributions, and revisions to this chapter. Professor Snell managed his own international trade business for twenty years and has experience buying and selling products internationally, preparing export documentation, and arranging shipping procedures.

Professor Snell is subject leader in international business and teaches international trade operations in the BA (Honors) degree curriculum at Regents Business School, Regents College, London.

NOTES

1. Robert J. Vokurka, Rhonda R. Lummus, and Dennis Krunwiede, "Improving Manufacturing Flexibility: The Enduring Value of JIT and TQM," *Advanced Management Journal* 72 (1) (Winter 2007): 14–22.

2. U.S. Government Accountability Office, "Cargo Container Inspections: Preliminary Observations on the Status of Efforts to Improve the Automated Targeting System," Statement for the Record by Richard M. Stana, Director, Homeland Security and Justice Issues, March 30, 2006, http://www.gao.gov/new.items/d06591t.pdf.

13 International Product Strategy

Until recently, General Motors Corporation, a U.S. firm, sold the Cadillac, Corvette, Chevrolet, Hummer, Opel, Vauxhall, and Saab brands in Europe. As part of a Chapter 11 reorganization, a new company, General Motors (GM), acquired operations from the old General Motors Corporation on July 10, 2009. Following the reorganization, GM's management stopped production of Saturn on October 1, 2009, after Penske Automotive Group's offer to buy the Saturn brand was withdrawn. Management sold Saab to Spyker Cars, N.V., a Dutch firm, on January 26, 2010. In February, 2010, when negotiations with Sichuan Tengzhong Heavy Industrial Machinery Company, Ltd., for the sale of Hummer collapsed because the Chinese government would not give approval, management decided to begin winding down operations with the intent of eventually stopping production.

Now Opel is GM's primary brand sold in Europe, and Vauxhall is the primary brand sold in the United Kingdom. Since 2005, Chevrolet cars for Europe have been produced by GM Daewoo Auto & Technology Company, Ltd., in South Korea. GM's brands are either standardized across markets or, as in the case of Opel and Vauxhall, individualized for specific markets.

Adam Opel AG (Opel) is an automobile maker in Germany. The company, founded in 1863, first made household products and was a leader in European sewing machine sales. In 1899, the company started building automobiles. GM acquired Opel in 1929. Opel is fourth in sales in Europe behind Groupe Renault, Volkswagen AG, and Ford Motor Company.

In the United Kingdom, the Opel is not sold; Vauxhall is the GM brand on the market. Alex Wilson and Company, a firm that built pumps and marine engines, was founded in 1857 and later renamed Vauxhall Iron Works. Automobiles were first built in 1903, and in 1907, the name was changed to Vauxhall Motors, Ltd. GM bought Vauxhall in 1925. From Vauxhall's plant in Luton, England, cars with American-influenced styling were produced and sold in the United Kingdom through the 1980s. A second assembly plant was built in Ellesmere Port, England, in 1960. The Luton plant was closed in 2000.

Initially, the Opel and Vauxhall cars were completely different designs. Both Opel and Vauxhall dealerships competed for sales in the United Kingdom. In 1981, the

Vauxhall and Opel dealerships in the United Kingdom were merged, after which the sale of Opel cars began to be abandoned there. The last Opel car to be officially sold in the United Kingdom was withdrawn in 1988. The management at the headquarters of GM Europe, in Rüsselsheim, Germany, began to standardize model names for Opel and Vauxhall models in the early 1990s. For example, from 1991, the Opel Kadett and the Vauxhall Astra were both given the name Astra, and the Vauxhall Cavalier and Opel Vectra both became Vectra in 1995. Since 1994, body styles for the two brands have been standardized. The logo displayed on the grilles and boots (trunks) of the cars were the only differences. In every other respect the cars were identical. Opels are made at Opel plants located in Bochum, Eisenach, and Kaiserslauten, Germany; in Belgium, Spain, and Poland; and in Vauxhall's Ellesmere Port plant.

The Ellesmere Port plant produces left-hand-drive models and Holdens for export. Holden is a GM brand sold primarily in Australia and New Zealand. In 1852, J.A. Holden & Company was established as a saddlery business in Australia. Automobiles were first produced in 1913, and GM purchased the firm in 1931. Following two name changes, the firm became known as GM Holden, Ltd., in 2005. Holdens produced in Australia are based on Daewoo designs. However, the Opel designs and names are used for the Holden brand cars manufactured in New Zealand and exported to South Africa and Thailand.

Because the Vauxhall and Opel models sold in Europe are essentially the same, consideration has been given to replacing the Vauxhall name in the United Kingdom with Opel to harmonize brand strategy across Europe. The management of Vauxhall is resisting for two reasons: Fleet buyers insist on the Vauxhall brand and brand recognition. The British population is known to be nationalistic and a sense of pride is felt toward the local brand. British people trust the Vauxhall name, as it is associated with quality, performance, and reliability. Thus, management feels that retaining the Vauxhall name definitely will be an advantage for maintaining the firm's image and customers.

The management of GM decided to produce Opel designs in the United States for the 2007 Saturns. For example, the midsize Aura was designed after the Opel Vectra and the Vue had the same design as the Opel Antara GTC. The automobiles being designed in Rüsselsheim are intended to accommodate multiple brands.

Sources: Based in part on information from Jason Stein and Harald Hamprecht, "Opel, Saturn Could Share Flagship; GM's German Division to Add Vehicle by 2009," autoweek.com, January 23, 2006, http://www.autoweek.com/apps/pbcs.dll/article?AID=/20060124/FREE/60123011/1041; GM, "Top Ten Models: Registrations in Europe by Model 2008," http://www.gmeurope.com/company/market_performance_top_ten_models.html; Aaron Gray-Block, "Confidence in Saab the Key to Profits: Spyker CEO," Reuters, January 29, 2010, http://www.reuters.com/article/idUSTRE60S5I120100129; Nick Bunkley, "G.M. to Close Hummer After Sale Fails," *The New York Times*, February 24, 2010, http://www.nytimes.com/2010/02/25/business/25hummer.html; "Saturn Has Been Discontinued, Only 12,000 Cars Remain," Real Car Tips, October 8, 2009, http://www.realcartips.com/news/0081-saturn-discontinued.shtml; General Motors—GM Europe—Brands—Opel, http://www.gm.com/europe/brands/opel/; and General Motors—GM Europe—Brands—Vauxhall, http://www.gm.com/europe/brands/vauxhall/.

CHAPTER OBJECTIVES

After reading this chapter, you should

- know the components of a product;
- know the three-product modification decision alternatives management must consider in a foreign market;
- appreciate the complexity of developing an international product strategy;
- understand the kinds of difficulties that affect the development of an international product strategy;
- be aware that products may need to be modified for the foreign market for a number of reasons;
- understand the financial assessments that influence the decision to standardize or modify product strategy internationally;
- understand methods involved in developing an international product strategy; and
- know why management should be alert for brand pirating, counterfeit products, and parallel imports.

THE PRODUCT REVIEWED

What is a product? The **product** is everything the customer receives in the exchange process. It is more than just the tangible item the customer buys from the seller or the store. From this perspective, the product can be thought of as an offering—everything available for sale that will satisfy the customer's need. Thus, the offering constitutes the physical product as well as all the intangibles that the customer receives. Most commonly, the product is visualized as consisting of the four broad categories of brand, package, physical characteristics, and services.

- The **brand** is a word, name, design, or symbol that identifies the physical item visually, verbally, or in both ways. The brand helps differentiate the product from competitors' products. The brand provides recognition, status, and uniqueness for the product. Not all products are branded; however, when a brand is employed, an intangible quality is added. Included are considerations such as appearance, color, size, recognition, meaning, and shape.
- The **package** is the container or wrapper in which the physical item is kept. The package serves to protect the product from damage or tampering, provides handling convenience, provides promotional appeal and information, and in certain instances such as for milk, keeps the product in its functional form. In some instances, the package is discarded after the product is purchased and before use. In other instances, the package is retained because it is an integral part of the physical product. Examples of the latter are facial tissues, cologne, toothpaste, and aerated shaving cream. Included are considerations such as size, composition, sturdiness, shape, thickness, color, information, design, and appearance.
- **Physical characteristics** are the properties and attributes that identify and distinguish the tangible item. The features and qualities that make the product unique and

capable of performing a particular function are the physical characteristics. Included are considerations such as color, shape, texture, composition material, size, appearance, and weight.

• **Services** comprise the remainder of the product and consist of everything else that is added to provide the customer with maximum value or satisfaction. Services are tangible and intangible efforts and attributes that embellish the product and make acquisition and use easier or more enjoyable. Included are considerations such as warranties, delivery, instructions, seller image, selling atmospherics, installation, repairs, and seller accommodations. Services can be provided during and after the sale.

The product is everything offered for sale and everything the customer purchases. Product strategy is an important component of the international marketing program because management needs to develop the correct assortment of tangible and intangible attributes that appeal to potential consumers. The desired attributes will be established by endowing the product with the appropriate physical characteristics, package, brand, and services that satisfy the needs of the target group of customers. Determining what the customer wants may involve some marketing research and customer analysis. Remember, the foreigner may not look to satisfy a particular need in exactly the same way as the domestic consumer does.

INTERNATIONAL PRODUCT STRATEGY

Should the international marketer try to offer the same product sold in the domestic market, or should the product be changed? In other words, is standardization or modification of the product more desirable? **Standardization** offers at least three benefits and in certain instances is preferable:

- a proven track record
- image and recognition
- reduced costs

An advantage of standardization is the product's proven track record. Management is familiar with the existing product and has improved and fine-tuned features and quality to satisfy customer needs. Changing the product introduces newness and uncertainties regarding functionality, quality, and suitability. Will the modified product be accepted as well as was the standardized product? Modification may necessitate other changes to the marketing strategy, introducing additional newness and risk for the international marketer.

Image and product recognition also benefit from standardization. If the product is the same in every market, customers will be able to identify it easily. A worldwide recognition and reputation can be created for the product. Customers will be able to identify the manufacturer of the product and be assured of receiving the expected quality. With assurances that the product is the same as the one with which the buyer is familiar, confidence in the purchase will be increased.

If the same product is sold in the foreign market as in the domestic, production economies may be realized. Longer production runs normally result in lower costs. If the product is modified, production runs will be shorter than for a standardized

Exhibit 13.1 **McDonald's**

Whether or not you can read the words on the sign, the golden arches identify this establishment as a McDonald's restaurant.

product and require retooling and adjustments to the production line or process. Varying product features or packaging may create handling and storage anomalies. Additional inventories will be required for each modified product. Modified products may necessitate changes in advertising and distribution. Concerns such as these can contribute to an increase in the cost of doing business and adversely affect the price.

Management may utilize any of three approaches to standardize products:[1]

- Global common denominator—identifying a relatively homogeneous global market segment in terms of traits and needs and producing a single product that will appeal to people in that group wherever located.
- Premium prototype—developing a product that meets the needs of the most demanding segment of the foreign market and marketing that product unchanged in other markets.
- Product extension—selling the domestic version of the product in the foreign market.

However, standardization may not be feasible or desirable in particular situations. The culture, laws, and other environmental conditions confronted in the foreign market may necessitate modification of the product in one form or another.

Exhibit 13.2 **The Product Standardization-Modification Continuum**

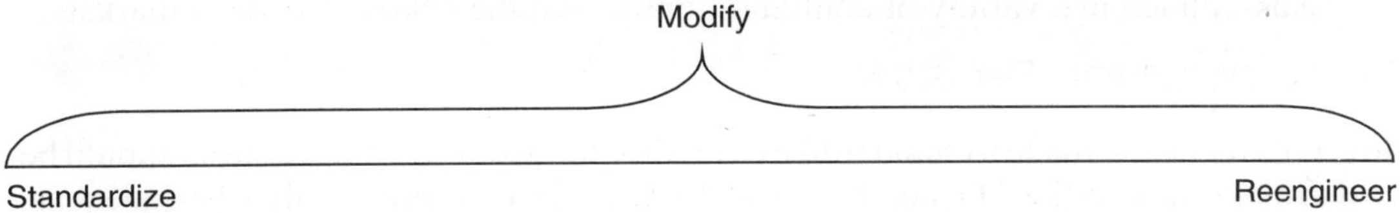

THE DEGREE OF MODIFICATION

The decision to standardize or modify the product can comprise a range of alternatives. The possibilities in fact form a continuum of degrees of standardization or modification that is possible. At one extreme of the continuum is the decision to not modify, to offer the standardized product. At the other extreme is the decision to redesign and reengineer the product—essentially creating a new and different offering. Between those two extremes lie larger or smaller degrees of modification. Thus, the extent of the modification can be essentially insignificant and of little consequence to production and marketing, or significant and of substantial consequence. The range of modification is shown in Exhibit 13.2.

Modifications are made to individualize the product to the tastes, preferences, and specific needs of the target group in the foreign market. Such modifications can be minor (left side of the continuum), such as a color change, or significant (right side of the continuum), such as a change in composition, shape, and appearance. Modifications can therefore include a myriad of adjustments. Such changes and adjustments are usually of one or more of the following types:

- **Brand modifications**—changes in the brand mark or brand name.
- **Feature modifications**—changes that enhance the characteristics of the product so that the number of real or fancied user benefits is increased.
- **Package modifications**—changes made in the nature, shape, and appearance of the package.
- **Quality modifications**—changes that improve reliability, durability, and improve product performance.
- **Service modifications**—changes in the add-ons that accompany the physical product.
- **Style modifications**—changes in the product's appearance. The product functions the same as previously and only looks different.

Where foreign market conditions require significant modifications, two approaches that allow substantial changes to the product yet permit many of the benefits of standardization to be realized may be pursued:[2]

- A core-product approach—developing a standardized core product that is capable of accommodating a variety of individualized parts, components, and attachments to meet the specific needs of each individual market.

- A modular approach—developing a range of standard product components that can be assembled in a variety of configurations to suit the needs of various markets.

THE MODIFICATION DECISION

How is the decision made to standardize or modify the product? What criteria should be used to make the decision? Generally, standardization is appropriate only when adequate demand exists for the standardized product. Because of the benefits, standardization should be preferred when possible and modification made only when necessary. This generalization implies that three product modification decision alternatives exist.

- Modification is inappropriate. In this situation the international marketer is ill advised to modify the product in any manner. The foreign buyer prefers the product to remain unchanged from the domestic product. In those instances in which the product has status or brand recognition, the foreigner wants to purchase the same product for the image or performance provided. If changes were made, the product would be less attractive to the customer. Examples of this decision alternative include French wine and Levi jeans. French wines are from the premier wine-growing region of the world and recognized for their superior quality. Levi jeans have a reputation and status image. Changing either would be detrimental to the perception and image customers have of the product.
- Modification is required. In this situation, referred to as elementary or mandatory adjustments, the standardized product would be unacceptable and could not be sold. Changes would be required before the foreign buyer would even consider the product. Customization is essential in those instances where the product is nonconforming or culturally unacceptable. For example, hamburgers cannot be sold in India because the cow is sacred and beef is not eaten; so another meat has to be substituted. Electrical appliances must be rewired in countries where the electrical systems are different from that found in the domestic country. Products designed to operate on 120 volts will not work in England, where a 220-volt system is in place. Also, electrical outlets differ in shape, requiring reconfigured plugs. For instance, the receptacles in England require a three-pronged plug (arranged in the form of a triangle), and those in Germany require a plug with two round prongs. Failure to make modifications will result in a lack of sales, potential loss of reputation, and possible lawsuits because damage may occur while using the incorrectly constructed product.
- Modification is possible but not required. In this situation, the foreigner will find the standardized product or modified product acceptable, and adjustments are discretionary. Since either a standardized or modified product will be adequate, why would a decision to modify be made? A financial analysis is required before the product standardization or modification decision can be made.[3] The decision should be strictly profit oriented. Although standardization may be possible, doing so may not be economically desirable. If more profit is possible from marketing a modified version of the product, then the standardized product should not be offered. However, if more profit will result from marketing the standardized product, the decision should be not to modify.

Exhibit 13.3 **The Financial Decision to Standardize or Modify a Product for the International Market**

Where: Q = Units sold
P = Price per unit
TR = Total revenue
TC = Total cost
Ω = Profit
s = Standardized product
m = Modified product

And:

For the Standardized Product	For the Modified Product
(Qs)(Ps) = TRs	(Qm)(Pm) = TRm
TRs – TCs = Ωs	TRm – TCm = Ωm

Then: If Ωs > Ωm, then market the standardized product.
If Ωs < Ωm, then market the modified product.

If the product is modified in a manner that meets the needs of the consumer more readily, then economic principles dictate that demand will increase. As a result, more units will be sold, with the most likely outcome being an increase in revenue (this depends on the price elasticity of demand and how much price may rise or decline). However, selling more units will also entail greater expense. If revenues increase sufficiently to offset additional costs and make profits larger than by selling the standardized product, the decision to modify is made. Offering the standardized version is the correct decision, even though volume may be smaller, when profits are greater than they would be if selling the modified product. The economics of the decision are represented in Exhibit 13.3.

In terms of the family of per-unit cost curves, the decision to standardize or modify is illustrated in Exhibits 13.4, 13.5, and 13.6. If management has long-run profit maximization as its pricing objective and conditions exist as depicted in Exhibit 13.4 for a standardized product, then Qs units will be produced and sold in the foreign market. Qs units will be produced because that is the quantity with which MRs = MCs and profits will be maximized. Of course, maximizing long-run profits must be assumed to be management's pricing objective. If management has other pricing objectives such as sales volume or image, this economic explanation will be inadequate. Each unit will be priced at Ps, and total revenue will be the area in the rectangle O,Qs,b,Ps. The average total cost per unit will be at ATCs, where the average total cost curve corresponds to quantity Qs. Total cost will be the area in the rectangle O,Qs,d,ATCs. Total profit for the standardized product will be equal to total revenue minus total cost, or the shaded area in the rectangle ATCs,d,b,Ps.

The same rationale can be used to determine the profit realized from marketing a modified product in the foreign market as depicted in Exhibit 13.5. The explanation is the same as for the standardized product except the location of the curves changes as does the total profit. To maximize profits, management will operate where

Exhibit 13.4 **An Economic Assessment of the Decision to Standardize a Product for the International Market**

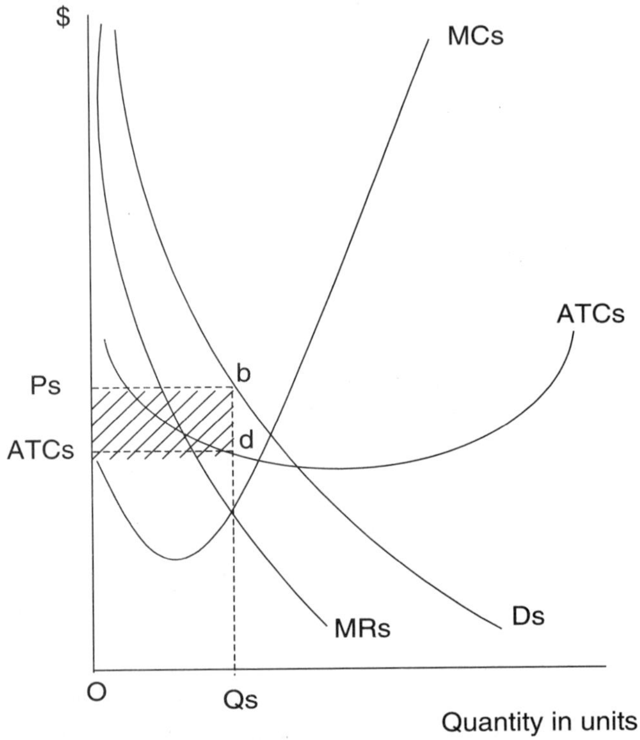

Where: Ds = Demand curve for the standardized product
Ps = Price of the standardized product
Qs = Quantity demanded of the standardized product
MRs = Marginal revenue for the standardized product
MCs = Marginal cost of the standardized product
ATCs = Average total cost of the standardized product

MRm = MCm and produce and offer for sale Qm units. The price per unit will be Pm and total revenue will be the area in the rectangle O,Qm,a,PM. The average total cost per unit will be equal to ATCm, and total cost will be the area in the rectangle O,Qm,c,ATCm. Total profit for the modified product will be equal to total revenue minus total cost, or the shaded area in the rectangle ATCm,c,a,Pm.

If Exhibits 13.4 and 13.5 are superimposed as is done in Exhibit 13.6, then the relationships between the decisions to standardize or to modify can be easily seen. Notice that the demand curve shifts to the right for the modified product, because the modified product meets customers' needs more adequately than the standardized product. Also, notice that the quantity demanded increases from Qs to Qm because the modified product is preferable. To maximize profits, management will operate where MRs = MCs or MRm = MCm and produce and sell either Qs or Qm units, depending on which produces the greatest amount of profit. In this example, the profit generated by the modified product is clearly larger, as represented by the shaded area ATCm,c,a,Pm.

Exhibit 13.5 **An Economic Assessment of the Decision to Modify a Product for the International Market**

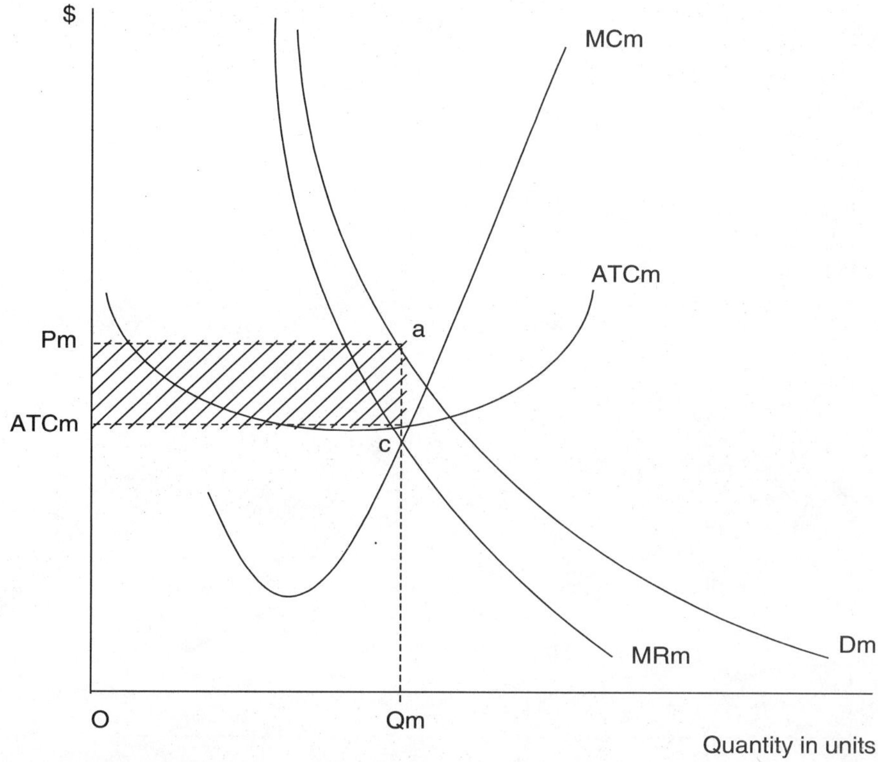

Where: Dm = Demand curve for the modified product
Pm = Price of the modified product
Qm = Quantity demanded of the modified product
MRm = Marginal revenue for the modified product
MCm = Marginal cost of the modified product
ATCm = Average total cost of the modified product

Of course, the price per unit will be Pm. This price is slightly higher than the price for the standardized product because the modified product meets consumers' needs more accurately. Therefore, consumers are willing to pay a higher price.

If the profit for the modified product (ATCm,c,a,Pm) is greater than the profit for the standardized product (ATCs,d,b,Ps), then the correct decision is to market the modified product. If the situation were reversed and the profit for the modified product (ATCm,c,a,Pm) was less than the profit for the standardized product (ATCs,d,b,Ps), then the correct decision would be to market the standardized product even though sales volume would be less. As shown in Exhibit 13.6, the area ATCm,c,a,Pm is larger than the area ATCs,d,b,Ps. Therefore, the international marketer will offer the modified product even though the price of the modified product is higher than the standardized product.

If management has pricing objectives other than profit maximization, such as

Exhibit 13.6 **An Economic Assessment of the Decision to Standardize or Modify a Product for the International Market**

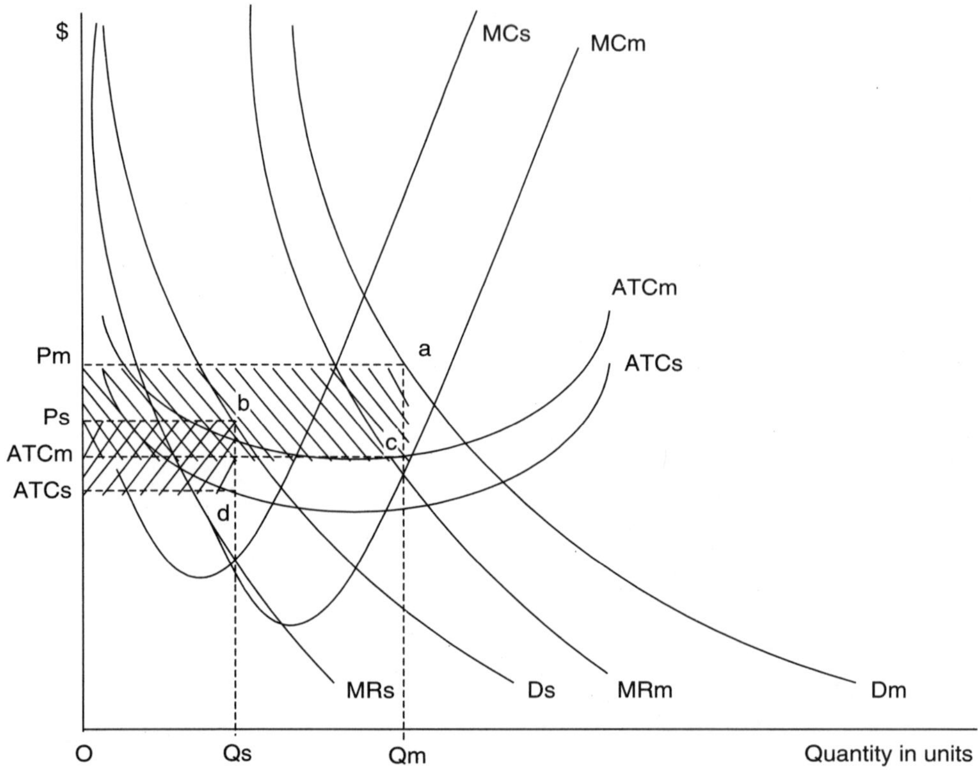

Where:
- Ds = Demand curve for the standardized product
- Ps = Price of the standardized product
- Qs = Quantity demanded of the standardized product
- MRs = Marginal revenue for the standardized product
- MCs = Marginal cost of the standardized product
- ATCs = Average total cost of the standardized product
- Dm = Demand curve for the modified product
- Pm = Price of the modified product
- Qm = Quantity demanded of the modified product
- MRm = Marginal revenue for the modified product
- MCm = Marginal cost of the modified product
- ATCm = Average total cost of the modified product

maintaining an image or building reputation, then some profit may have to be relinquished to help accomplish these objectives. If status and image are important, management may elect to offer the standardized product, even though less total profit will be earned. If the reputation of the product is more important, that will influence the decision. For example, if the firm's brand is top of the line and associated with luxury, offering a low-priced product could damage the firm's reputation and reduce sales of the firm's other products. Modifying the product under these conditions would be detrimental. Therefore, although profit should be an important component of the decision, management may not always make long-run profit maximization the most influential criterion in the standardization-versus-modification decision-making process.

PLANNING PRODUCT STRATEGY

Reasons for modifying a product are numerous. Needed changes may be obvious from evaluating and analyzing product use patterns, cultural patterns, economic conditions, language, legal requirements and product codes, purchase habits, and a variety of other environmental factors. In other cases, the need for modifications is not so obvious, and sophisticated marketing research studies are required to identify and understand the subtle nature of the differences. Richard Robinson has suggested the types of product changes that may be required because of differences in the foreign and domestic marketing environments.[4] Examples of those desirable modifications are presented in Exhibit 13.7.

In most cases, each environmental factor encountered requires only minor changes or adjustments to bring the product in line with the customers' needs. Management must identify the factor that affects the use of the product and then decide the appropriate modification to make the product marketable to the customer. If that modification can be designed and integrated into the firm's production operations, a financial analysis must be conducted to determine the impact on profits. If the modification is required and economical, marketing of the modified product can proceed. If the modification is required but not economical, the market should be bypassed in favor of another alternative. If the modification is not required and not economical, then the standardized product should be marketed as explained previously.

Exhibit 13.7 **Environmental Factors Causing Product Modification for the International Market**

Environmental factor	Product modification
Lower levels of literacy	Simplify product and use picture instructions
Differences in climate	Adapt product to climate
Lower per capita income	Reduce quality and remove features
Lack of technical competency	Simplify product
Heavy use of the product	Limit warranty and improve durability
Lack of maintenance	Increase operating tolerances
Unavailability of service	Improve product reliability and use fewer parts
Different power supply	Rewire and resize
Different standards	Recalibrate and resize
High labor costs	Automation or manualization of product
Lack of availability of materials	Change product structure
Special conditions	Redesign or reinvent product

Source: Richard D. Robinson, *International Business Management* (New York: Dryden Press, 1978).

Exhibit 13.8 **Morfat**

Morfat is a respected brand of cake mix in Greece. However, the brand would probably not be as well received if the cake mixes were exported to English speaking countries, especially those that have an abundance of health conscious consumers.

BRAND STRATEGY

Care must be taken to assure the brand does not have or convey any undesirable meaning or interpretation. Literally translating the brand name into another language can produce undesirable results. A classic example involves the translation testing of a brand name selected for a new soap powder into fifty major languages. The brand name means "dainty" in English and most European languages. In Gaelic the name means "song," in Flemish, "aloof," in Iran, "dimwitted," in one African language, "horse," in Korean, "crazy of mind," and in all Slavic languages, the name was considered obscene and offensive.[5]

Products have been introduced with a seemingly innocuous brand name only for management to discover later an unintended meaning. The management at Sunbeam Products, Inc., introduced a hair curling iron in Germany with the brand name Mist Stick. The word *mist* in German means "excrement." Thus the product was unfortunately named a "manure wand." Cue toothpaste was marketed in France by the management of Colgate-Palmolive Company. The brand name Cue is pronounced similarly to the French word *cul*, meaning the posterior of one's anatomy. Thus the toothpaste was inadvertently called "ass." The management at American Motors Corporation sold a car called a Matador in Puerto Rico, where the word means "killer."

Exhibit 13.9 **Mr. Clean**

Mr. Clean is Mr. Proper in most of Europe.

Ford Motor Company management sold the Pinto car in Brazil, where *pinto* is a slang word for a small penis. Brazilian men did not want to be associated with a car having a brand name that implied they had a small "dick." The Chevrolet Nova was unpopular in Spanish-speaking countries because "Nova" sounds too much like the Spanish "*no va*" (pronounced no wa), meaning "does not go." The Coca-Cola Company's Fresca met resistance in Mexico, where *fresca* is a slang word for "lesbian." The Pet Milk brand, currently owned by J.M. Smucker Company, did not sell well in French-speaking countries where *pet* means, among other things, "to fart."

Brand marks can also create problems. Arab customers interpret a six-pointed star as indicating pro-Israeli sentiments. A red circle used as a brand mark is unpopular in some parts of Asia, because it is similar to the one on the Japanese flag. Because Muslim culture requires Muslim women to cover their faces, the woman's face in the Starbucks Corporation brand mark was removed when the Saudi Arabian market was entered.

Brand policy may be individualized or standardized depending how a product is used or perceived. In the United States, a line of cosmetics produced by Procter & Gamble Company is given the brand name Oil of Olay. The name in the United Kingdom is Oil of Ulay, and in Germany, Italy, Austria, and the Netherlands the name is Oil of Olaz. Palmolive dishwashing liquid, manufactured by the Colgate-Palmolive Company, is named Palmolive washing-up liquid in the United Kingdom. Mr. Clean liquid cleaner, a product of the Procter & Gamble Company, is given a name appropriate to the country. For example, Mr. Clean is branded as Mr. Proper in most European countries, Mastro Lindo in Italy, Don Limpio in Spain, Mr. Propre in France, and Maestro Limpio in Mexico. The management at Eastman Kodak Company and Exxon Mobil Corporation has carefully selected the firm's brand after extensively researching the brand name to deliberately find a word that was pronounceable everywhere, yet had no specific meaning anywhere. Kodak and Exxon are brands that have been successfully standardized and are used throughout the world in all markets.

When a brand is not objectionable, a global brand policy (one used in all markets) may be considered. A one-brand strategy enhances product recognition, provides cost savings, and creates global synergies.[6] However, country-specific brands may be beneficial to help individualize products to better meet the needs of the target market.

PACKAGE STRATEGY

Occasionally, the package will have to be modified to better meet the desires of the foreign buyer. The two-liter soft drink bottle is inappropriate in countries where refrigerators are small and have no compartments or space to accommodate the large bottle. Management at Quaker Oats Company uses vacuum-sealed tins to hold oatmeal in hot and humid countries. In countries in which large segments of the population are illiterate, pictures are often placed on the package to depict contents. Gerber Corporation prominently displayed a big picture of a smiling baby on the labels of all baby food jars, with a product description on the label. In one African nation, illiterate buyers misconstrued the picture as indicating the contents and avoided buying the product. In the United Kingdom, aspirin tablets are individually sealed in tin foil and packaged in sheets of about six tablets each in cardboard boxes rather than loosely packed in glass or plastic containers as in the United States. In Quebec, the French-speaking province of Canada, all packages must be printed, by law, in French as well as English.

Packages may have to be reshaped or redesigned to accommodate the product or fit the needs of the foreign customer. One peanut butter manufacturer found that its product had to be placed in metal containers in one foreign market because the container would serve a secondary purpose of holding water after the peanut butter was fully consumed. In some countries, reusable beverage bottles having attached ceramic stoppers with rubber seals can still be found. Three sizes of coffee cup are available in Starbucks Corporation restaurants in the United Kingdom, while a fourth, smaller, size is also sold in Japan. Because of the cost of producing smaller-sized bottles, the management of the Coca-Cola Company opted for small cans in the United Kingdom. The triangular package of Toblerone chocolate, a product of Kraft Foods Schweiz AG, is standardized in every market; however, the labels are customized. For example, in Switzerland, the labels are printed in German, French, and Italian—the languages spoken there. In the United Kingdom, English is inserted instead of Italian.

Package appearance can help get the buyer's attention if it has visual and promotional appeal. Containers for products sold in foreign countries are not always visually appealing. The box for Close-Up toothpaste in Brazil was once solid dark blue with

Exhibit 13.10 **Bulgarian Milk**

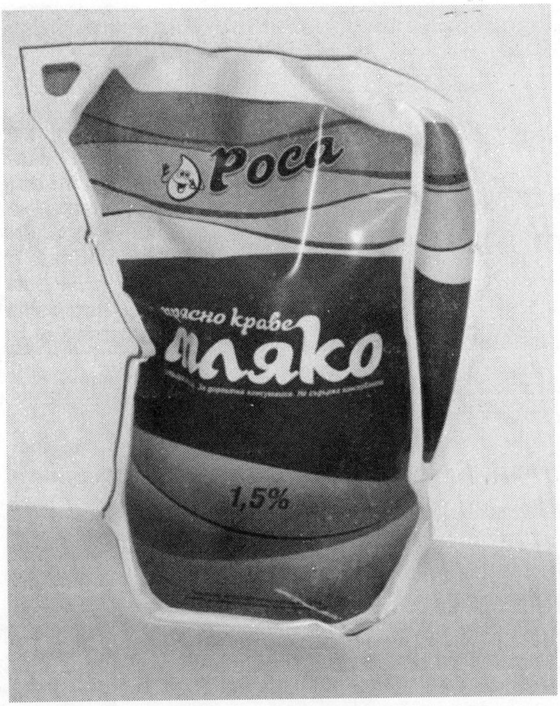

Fresh milk in Bulgaria is available in plastic pouches or plastic containers similar to this one with a handle for easy pouring but no closure.

white letters. The package was rather plain and drab with no real eye appeal. The tube containing the toothpaste also lacked visual appeal, being white with blue lettering and the brand name in large block letters.

The package must be designed to accommodate the product. Therefore, if the product is reconfigured, the package is likely to need modification also. The package has to be designed with the target market in mind.

PHYSICAL CHARACTERISTICS STRATEGY

Because of uniqueness in the foreign market, changes in the physical characteristics of the product may be appropriate. Changing product shape and content may be appropriate to accommodate cultural preferences. In the United Kingdom, for example, consumers prefer to buy Jell-O (known as "jelly" there) in solid, rubbery cubes that melt in hot water rather than in the powder form available in the United States. Thus, changing the form of the product from a powder to a solid cube would be desirable for that market. Also in the United Kingdom, milk chocolate is commonly made with vegetable fat. Since taste preferences are different, recipe modifications are sometimes necessary.

Color and fragrance preferences can vary as well. Comparisons of Palmolive soap sold in the United Kingdom, Brazil, and the United States, for example, reveal dif-

Exhibit 13.11 **Examples of Cereal Boxes from Other Countries**

In some cases, breakfast cereals from Hungary, Greece, and other countries are quite different in physical appearance and taste than those available in the United States.

ferences. The Brazilian and U.S. bars are similar in color, while the British bar is a yellowish-olive green. The U.S. bar has a perfume fragrance while the Brazilian and British bars, although having slightly different aromas, are less perfumed and smell more soapy. Changing the aroma of products is desirable to satisfy the fragrance preferences of the foreign customers.

Colors may have special meanings, making their use either desirable or undesirable. For example, the green is popular in many Muslim countries, so a product with a green color would be attractive. However, green can be associated with an unfaithful wife in China and should be carefully assessed for use in that country. Blue is considered a masculine color in most cultures; however, in the United Kingdom and France red is a more appropriate masculine color. Pink is regarded as a feminine color in the United States; however, yellow is considered to be the most feminine color in most of the remainder of the world.

Taste preferences of the foreign buyer must be considered in the modification decision for food products. The management at Campbell Soup Company changed the flavor of some of its soups to fit European market preferences. Campbell's management also found condensed soups unpopular in the United Kingdom when first introduced. The British saw a smaller quantity in the package and assumed they were getting less for their money. Sales improved after water was added to make the soup volume equal to that of competitive products. Nestlé S.A.'s management reformulated

Nescafé coffee to local taste preferences. Kosher chicken was introduced in KFC Corporation restaurants in Israel and halal beef is used exclusively in McDonald's restaurants in the Middle East. To accommodate the taste preferences of the Japanese, the management of Groupe Danone modified the yogurt sold there to be milder and contain less sugar and acid in the fruit flavors. And, McDonald's Corporation management added noodles to the menu in China and Japan, and curry sauce and bread to the menu in India.

Various preferences also come into play with other products. For example, the management at Philip Morris Companies, Inc., found that the Virginia-type tobacco of U.S. cigarette blends was unpopular in Canada. The cigarettes had to be reblended to the taste preferences of Canadians. In India, the tanning products of L'Oréal Group are not sold because light skin, which is associated with wealth and upper class, is a desirable characteristic. To appeal to this desire, a new line of "White Perfect" cosmetics for lightening the skin was introduced after certain cosmetic formulations were modified.

If the standardized product is inappropriate, the international marketer must endow the product with the physical characteristics the foreign consumer prefers. Research may be required to determine the appropriate characteristics.

SERVICES STRATEGY

Since services augment the product, the international marketer must determine what services the foreign buyer really wants and needs. If service centers are not readily available, warranties may have to be modified so that warranty periods are shorter or fewer components are warranted. At a minimum, instructions will need to be translated into the foreign language. Accurate translation will be necessary. Delivery, credit, and other services frequently provided may have to be altered. Because extra services increase the cost of the product, they will have to be carefully designed to keep the selling price competitive within the economic conditions, and thus, make the product more affordable. Local conditions must be assessed before an appropriate service policy is determined. For example, a washing machine producer discovered that sales could not be made in the Latin American markets without the extension of credit.

MANAGING PRODUCT STRATEGY

Many factors must be considered to develop an appropriate product strategy. These factors relate to cultural conditions, economic conditions, legal concerns, and competitive conditions. Management must make a thorough and meticulous analysis of those factors that affect product desirability and acceptability before making the decision to standardize or modify the product. After completing this process, if the decision is to modify, the correct adjustments must be assessed. The appropriate changes in the physical characteristics must be determined. Whether a package, a brand, or any services should be offered must also be decided. In countries with low per capita incomes like China, cigarettes, for example, can be purchased individually without a package. Not all products need to have a brand name, nor do services provided in the domestic country necessarily have to be included as part of the product in the foreign country. Remember, give the customer what the customer wants.

Although the desire is to standardize the entire product when economically feasible, that is not always possible. The international marketer should be prepared to change whatever parts of the product are required. For instance, the physical characteristics, package, and services may be appropriate to standardize; however, the brand may have to be changed to prevent an undesirable meaning. Thus, one or more of the components of the product may have to be adjusted, resulting in a modified product.

Product line strategy may also need adjusting. The width and depth of the product line may have to be different than in the domestic country. Usually, the product line depth will be shorter, with fewer versions of the product offered. This is particularly true in LDCs and when the product is first introduced. For example, if boxes of breakfast cereal are available in five different weights domestically, only two or three may be needed in the foreign market initially. Product line width may also be narrower. For example, in the domestic country, three lines of lawnmowers may be offered—riding mowers, gas push mowers, and electric push mowers. In the foreign market only one line—gas push mowers—may be appropriate.

LEGAL PRODUCT STRATEGY ISSUES

Other product considerations of a broad nature that can have legal implications are also important to the international marketer when developing product strategy. Three of these are the potential problems of brand pirating, product counterfeiting, and parallel imports.

BRAND PIRATING

The product brand is a valuable asset to the firm and provides recognition, enhanced image, and quality to customers. Management can spend considerable time, money, and effort to develop a brand in the foreign market. Registering brand names and marks is necessary to protect the value the brand adds to the product and firm. The granting of ownership to brands and trademarks is a sovereign prerogative of every nation-state. Therefore, laws differ widely from country to country regarding what can be protected, the limits of the protection, and the period of time over which the protection extends.

Treaties do exist among numerous countries. Examples are the Paris Convention and the Madrid Convention, whereby brand protection is extended to foreign firms; however, differences in interpretation can still be an issue. For example, in common law countries, the first user of a brand will be considered the owner. Thus, registration may be prevented because another firm is already using the desired brand. Similarly, in some countries, registration of a brand name is permitted before the brand is used. Therefore, a desired name may have been speculatively filed previously, preventing its use.

Perhaps even more disconcerting is the problem of foreign firms illegally using the firm's brand. This practice, known as **brand piracy**, is usually employed when the product is extremely expensive or a status symbol in short supply. Brand piracy

Exhibit 13.12 **D&G Belts**

These D&G belts are on a bargain rack and priced at the equivalent of about US$3.50. Are these real Dolce and Gabbana belts?

happens when a similar product made by another manufacturer is branded with the firm's reputable brand. Although the other firm's product may be inferior in terms of quality, the buyer has difficulty determining this. Because of the identical-looking brand name or mark, the buyer may be unaware that the legitimate product is not being purchased. These products are copies in every respect, although their appearance and brand image cannot be discerned visually from those of the real item. Obviously, the firm's reputation can be damaged when consumers of these copies become disillusioned with their performance and communicate derogatory word-of-mouth advertising. Also, brand piracy diverts sales away from the firm that owns the brand, reducing income.

COUNTERFEIT PRODUCTS

Counterfeiting occurs when a product is sold that has an identical or similar appearance to that of the real product. For example, the package is the same color and has a similar design to the original. The appearance of the product may not be exactly the same as the original, but is close enough to confuse the buyer. The brand may or may not be pirated. For example, having D&B imprinted on a handbag does not necessarily mean it was manufactured by Dooney and Bourke, and the Louis Vuitton name on a handbag does not necessarily make it a Louis Vuitton Malletier product. A

T-shirt showing the image of Bugs Bunny and bearing a Mickey and Company label is definitely counterfeit even if both the image and label are identical to the actual ones. Why? Bugs Bunny is a Warner Brothers character and is not affiliated with the Walt Disney Company, which owns the Mickey and Company brand. However, the product looks legitimate and the unsuspecting buyer, not knowing these facts, ends up with a fake product.

The consumer is duped into buying the counterfeit, thinking the original product is being purchased. Because of the similarity of the counterfeit to the legitimate product, the consumer has difficulty telling the difference, particularly when the purchase is made hastily. Modern technology allows counterfeiters to copy products closely. Although appearances may be identical, quality is usually lacking. For instance, a fabric with fewer threads per inch or a cheap electrical mechanism can be hidden from the consumer.

Between 3 and 6 percent of all world merchandise trade is estimated to be counterfeit.[7] Counterfeiting is estimated to cost the U.S. economy between US$200 billion and US$250 billion per year.[8] Although certain kinds of products are more frequently counterfeited (high-priced products with status brands), any product made can be counterfeited. Since the products appear identical, preventing counterfeiting is difficult.

PARALLEL IMPORTS

Parallel importing refers to the process of exporting a brand name product from a country where the product sells at a relatively low price to a country where the product sells for a relatively high price. Once the product is in the relatively high-price country, it can be sold at a somewhat lower price than the same brand being sold there at a higher price. The parallel importer is able to underprice competitors, because its costs are lower as a result of purchasing in the relatively low-price country.

Parallel imports, also known as gray products, are sold in the relatively high-price country without the manufacturer's knowledge or permission. As a result, the manufacturer is deprived of revenue equal to the difference in the price for which the product would be sold in the relatively high-price country and the price for which the product is purchased in the relatively low-price country.

A product's price will vary from country to country for numerous reasons, such as differences in production and marketing costs, demand, brand image, and competition. Assume a manufacturer exports a product to two countries, and prices at P_1 in the first country and P_2 in the second country. If P_2 is higher than P_1, then a parallel importer can purchase the product in the first country at the lower price and export it to the second country. The parallel importer will usually price the product somewhere between P_1 and P_2 at, let's say, P_3. The difference between P_3 and P_1 represents the parallel importer's profit. The difference between P_2 and P_1 represents the income lost by the manufacturer.

The laws regulating parallel imports differ from country to country. For example, parallel importation is permitted in Hong Kong and prohibited in the United States. Neither the Berne Convention for literary and artistic works nor the Paris Convention for industrial property explicitly prohibits the practice. The concept of exhaustion, a basic principle of intellectual property law (brands, trademarks, copyrights, and patents), is generally applied throughout the world to address parallel import claims. According to the **concept of international exhaustion,** a trademark owner has no further control over the distribution of a product once it is placed on the market by or with the trademark owner's consent. Thus, unless expressly forbidden, parallel importing is legal. For example, the assurance of free movement of products among member states of the European Union, provided by the Treaty of Rome, causes parallel importing to be governed by the concept of exhaustion.

The concept of exhaustion does not apply to all situations. In the 2003 Glaxo Group, Ltd., case, the UK court upheld the European Court of Justice ruling that a parallel importer cannot repackage pharmaceutical products even if the brand mark is unaffected.[9] However, in the Boehringer Ingelheim Ltd. case, repackaging of pharmaceutical products with subsequent sale under a generic brand name (debranding) was ruled not to be passing off (trademark infringement that confuses consumers), because pharmacists and customers were not deceived by the repackaging.[10]

Parallel importing should not be confused with brand piracy or counterfeiting. Parallel imports are the brand owner's original products and not inexpensive copies. This is true even if the product is repackaged and the new package appearance or language is different, for the market in which the parallel import is being sold, than the package designed by the manufacturer. The parallel importer is simply selling the manufacturer's product, only in another geographic jurisdiction.

CHAPTER SUMMARY

International product strategy involves making decisions about the product's physical characteristics, package, brand, and services. Standardization is preferred because of the benefits of lower cost, universal recognition, and management's familiarity and experience with the product. When the standardized product is inappropriate, modification is required. Modification can be made in any of the four components of the product and can range from minor changes to complete reengineering. Therefore, the modification decision will fall into one of three options:

- Modification is inappropriate because the standardized product is preferred.
- Modification is required because the standardized product is unacceptable.
- Modification is possible but not required.

When modification is possible but not required, the decision is based upon a financial assessment. Although modifying the product will increase demand and possibly revenue, depending on the price elasticity of demand, modification will also increase costs. The product should be standardized when the expected profit obtainable from standardizing is larger than that obtainable from modification. The product should be modified only when the expected profit obtainable from modifying the product is larger than what is obtainable from offering the standardized product.

A product may need to be modified for numerous reasons, such as differences in cultural conditions, economic conditions, legal concerns, and competitive conditions. Physical characteristics may have to be modified for concerns such as color, aroma, tastes, and preferences. Concerns that influence the need to modify the package include the desired visual and promotional appeals, shape, content, and type of package. The primary reasons the brand will need to be changed are offensive or inappropriate appearances and meanings. Services may have to be adjusted because of how the product is used and the ability or inability of the seller to provide them because of the nature of the marketplace.

Product strategy needs to be effectively managed and tailored to the needs of the foreign buyer. The width and depth of the product line may also require adjustments. Preventing parallel imports, brand pirating, and product counterfeiting are concerns that the international marketer may also have.

KEY TERMS

Brand
Brand modifications
Brand piracy
Concept of international exhaustion
Counterfeiting
Feature modifications
Modifications
Package
Package modifications
Parallel imports
Physical characteristics
Product
Quality modifications
Service modifications
Services
Standardization
Style modifications

REVIEW QUESTIONS

1. What is a product?
2. Why is the decision to offer a standardized or modified product an important part of international product strategy?
3. What is a modified product? How can a product be modified for the foreign market?
4. When would selling a standardized product be appropriate?
5. When would selling a modified product be required?
6. How is the decision made to modify or not modify the product when the market will accept either the standardized product or a modified product?
7. Draw a graph like the one pictured in Exhibit 13.6 for a situation in which selling a standardized product would be preferred to selling a modified product.
8. Select a product and suggest and support what changes might be appropriate when the consumer is illiterate. What changes are appropriate when the consumer has a low per capita (disposable) income?
9. Talk with a foreign student and identify a product that is different in that student's home country from what is available in the United States. Ask the foreign student why the product was modified.
10. Why is brand pirating a concern for the international marketer?

NOTES

1. Peter G.P. Walters and Brian Toyne, "Product Modification and Standardization in International Markets: Strategic Options and Facilitating Policies," *Columbia Journal of World Business* 14 (4) (Winter 1989): 37–44.

2. Ibid.

3. Donald L. Brady and W. Cary Heath, "Product Modification for International Markets: An Economic Theory," in *Proceedings of the Atlantic Marketing Association,* ed. Steven G. Green (New Orleans, LA: AMA, October 2–5, 1985), 107–111.

4. Richard D. Robinson, *International Business Management* (New York: Dryden Press, 1978).

5. David A. Ricks, *Blunders in International Business*, 4th ed. (Malden, MA: Blackwell, 2006), 36.

6. David Aaker and Erich Joachimsthaler, "The Lure of Global Branding," *Harvard Business Review* 77 (6) (November–December 1999): 137–44.

7. Nejdet Delener, "International Counterfeit Marketing: Success Without Risk," *Review of Business* 21 (1/2) (Spring 2000): 16–20.

8. Amanda D. Wilson, "Commerce Department Enlists Consumers in the Fight against Fakes," *International Trade Update,* May 2007, U.S. Department of Commerce, http://www.trade.gov/press/publications/newsletters/ita_0507/stopfakes_0507.asp.

9. *Glaxo Group Ltd v. Dowelhurst Ltd,* IN THE HIGH COURT OF JUSTICE, CHANCERY DIVISION, PATENTS COURT, Before: The Hon. Mr. Justice Laddie, HC 1999 No. 02054.

10. *Boehringer Ingelheim KG & Another v. Swingward Ltd & Others,* IN THE HIGH COURT OF JUSTICE, CHANCERY DIVISION, Before: The Hon. Mr. Justice Laddie, HC 1999 No. 00017.

14 International Price Strategy

Marlboro has been the best-selling brand of cigarettes in the world since 1972. Philip Morris USA, Inc. (PMUSA) and Philip Morris International, Inc. (PMI) were wholly owned subsidiaries of Philip Morris Companies, owner of the Marlboro brand, until 2003 when stockholders approved a name change to Altria Group, Inc. (AGI). In March 2008, PMI was spun off as a separate company to AGI shareholders. Today AGI is the parent company for five separate subsidiaries.

- John Middleton Company
- Philip Morris Capital Corporation
- Philip Morris USA, Inc.
- Ste. Michelle Wine Estates, Ltd.
- U.S. Smokeless Tobacco Company, LLC

The sales of PMI are larger than those of any other firm in the international market. In 2009, PMI held a 15.4 percent share of the cigarette market outside of the United States. Seven of the top fifteen selling brands belong to PMI. Internationally sales of the Marlboro brand in 2009 were 302 billion cigarettes, more than the sales of the three next-largest competitors combined.

AGI began in 1847 when Philip Morris, Esq., a tobacconist, opened a shop on Bond Street in London. Morris began making cigarettes in 1854, and following several ownership changes after his death, the company became a U.S. corporation in 1919. In 1954, Philip Morris (Australia) was established as the firm's first subsidiary outside the United States. Since then, international marketing continued to expand as production facilities and licensing agreements were acquired. In 1987, the international division of the company was incorporated as PMI. International expansion continued, and in 2001, the international headquarters was relocated to Lausanne, Switzerland. In 2008, 50.7 percent of all cigarettes sold in the United States were Marlboros. PMI sells to more than 160 countries from the firm's fifty-nine factories. Sales increases have been the largest in countries that includes Egypt, France, Mexico, the Philippines, Russia, Thailand, Turkey, and Ukraine.

The management of PMI continues with efforts to solidify the firm's long-term leadership in China, Indonesia, Japan, and Russia, the world's largest cigarette markets excluding the United States. For example, in 1999, Marlboro production facilities were established in the Leningrad region, and in 2005, the second-largest Indonesian cigarette producer, PT Hanjaya Mandala Sampoerna, was acquired. Also in 2005, an equity joint venture between the China National Import and Export Group Corporation, a wholly owned subsidiary of the China National Tobacco Corporation and PMI, was formed for the licensed production of Marlboro cigarettes. Management continues to invest in opportunities to expand the production and sale of the Marlboro brand. Examples of these opportunities are:

- a production and sales licensing agreement with Spain's Tabacalera SA—which subsequently merged with Seita SA (Société Nationale d'Exploitation Industrielle des Tabacs et Allumettes) of France to form Altadis SA;
- an agreement with Jordan's International Tobacco and Cigarettes Company, Ltd., to produce Marlboros; and
- an agreement with Al Robban Trading Company to distribute them.

But what about the pricing of Marlboro cigarettes in the company's various markets? The prices of a product sold at retail will vary from market to market and even from store to store within any market. The table here lists the reported selling price of a pack of Marlboro cigarettes for eighteen randomly selected countries.[1] The prices in the local currencies have been converted to U.S. dollars for comparison purposes.

Country	Price (US$)	Country	Price (US$)
Australia	3.46	Japan	2.34
Brazil	.85	Nigeria	.86
Bulgaria	1.13	Norway	6.48
Costa Rica	.75	Philippines	.67
Denmark	4.00	Thailand	.69
Germany	2.81	Turkey	.89
Greece	2.05	Vietnam	.57
India	1.24	United Kingdom	6.25
Israel	3.22	United States	3.60

As can be seen, the selling price of a pack of Marlboro cigarettes varies widely. Differences in factors such as taxes, production and distribution costs, competition, and economic conditions in each country will influence costs, and consequently, the selling prices for cigarettes. Therefore, to determine pricing policy, the management of PMI must consistently monitor market conditions in all countries where Marlboro is sold.

Sources: Based in part on information from AGI at http://www.altria.com/; Philip Morris International, http://www.pmi.com; Elizabeth LeBras, "Western Tobacco Hits Jackpot With Patriotism," *Moscow Times*, November 14, 2000, http://lists.essential.org/pipermail/intl-tobacco/2000q4/000334.html; Rendi A. Witular, "Philip Morris to Challenge Local Cigarette Giants," *The Jakarta Post*, March 22, 2005, http://lists.essential.org/pipermail/intl-tobacco/2005q1/001200.html; "A 'Great Leap Forward'?" *Tobacco Journal International*, March 3, 2006, http://www.tobaccojournal.com/A__Great_leap_forward.47600.0.html; World Health Organization Tobacco Free Initiative, "Tobacco Industry Monitoring Report," October–December 2002, p. 78, www.who.int/tobacco/media/en/tob-ind-monitoring02.pdf; and www.sampoerna.com/default.asp?language=english&page=aboutsampoerna/history.

CHAPTER OBJECTIVES

After reading this chapter, you should

- know what factors influence the international pricing decision;
- know what price escalation is and why the expenses of marketing may increase internationally;
- understand how to respond to price escalation;
- understand how to price intracompany sales;
- be knowledgeable about international shipping terms and how stipulated terms affect price;
- understand the international payment methods and the risks involved with each; and
- be familiar with sources of financing available to foreign buyers to help finance purchases.

PRICE REVIEWED

What price should the international marketer charge for the product? Pricing internationally should include the same criteria and assessments as those that influence domestic price. The primary differences are the additional costs that can be involved and variations in economic conditions from country to country. Expenses such as shipping fees, tariffs, and taxes will vary from market to market and will affect costs. Per capita income also varies from market to market, affecting the ability to buy. Therefore, price will normally be individualized for each country in which the product is offered for sale.

The price established should be the value customers place on the product or service. Basically, the price should be determined by the customers and be what they are willing to pay. If the price is set too high, revenue will be affected adversely by lower sales, causing profits to be smaller than expected. If the price is set too low, profits can also be lower than what is possible because the profit margin per unit will be reduced. Of course, the price elasticity of demand, production capacity, and costs will have an impact. However, in either event, an incorrectly set price will most likely have undesirable profit consequences.

Price-setting procedures are influenced by management's pricing objectives. Management may establish profit objectives, sales objectives, or image objectives as the basis for pricing policy. The latter two cause economic explanations of price setting to be inadequate. Therefore, three factors need to be taken into consideration that will influence the price decision:

- cost
- competition
- demand

Price needs to be high enough to cover the costs of doing business plus provide an adequate profit. However, if costs are the only factor considered, the result may be a price that is too high or too low. Setting price equal to the domestic price can have the same effect.[2] If costs are high, price will be higher than what the customer is willing to pay. If costs are low, price will be lower than what the customer is willing to pay. The too-high price simply results in lost sales. The too-low price may result in the international marketer being accused of dumping. In the strictest sense, **dumping** means selling below cost so that unwanted inventory is disposed of or to gain market share in a foreign country. Dumping has also been rationalized by various government officials to mean manufacturing a product in a low-cost area and selling in a high-cost area at a lower price than local suppliers. Even though a profitable price is set, that price undercuts local competition by an amount sufficient to be considered inappropriate by the foreign sellers and government. Many foreign countries have stringent antidumping laws that penalize the management of companies for selling at a price that is perceived to be too low. To prevent dumping or pricing too high, management should determine the price customers are willing to pay and then adjust costs accordingly.

The price not only needs to cover costs and provide a profit but also must be competitive. Therefore, the prices competitors are charging for comparable products must be taken into consideration. If the product has no unique distinction and could easily be replaced by a competitor's product, price becomes an important determinant for the customer. Consumers will pay more only when the product possesses greater perceived value than is available from the competition.

Price setting should also take into account supply and demand. The availability of the product, when compared to usage rate, can influence price. If the quantity of the product buyers want to purchase exceeds the quantity available, the price may be set higher than normal. Making the price higher than usual effectively rations the available product and helps reduce demand. If the quantity of the product available exceeds the quantity buyers want to purchase, a lower than normal price is required. Lowering the price will help stimulate demand and reduce excess inventories.

Price determination should include an assessment of all three of these price-setting considerations. Basing the decision solely on one or even two of these considerations is likely to produce an inappropriate price. Although managers are cognizant that correct pricing is important to success in the international market, many choose to ignore or minimize price as part of an effective international marketing strategy.[3]

Exhibit 14.1 **Sale**

The sign announces a seasonal price reduction (sale) from 20 to 50 percent off the regular prices.

This phenomenon occurs because managers do not know how to determine price for international markets or obtain adequate information about foreign competition. Pricing concerns such as exchange rate fluctuation, inflation rates, purchasing power indices, and governmental pricing regulations tend not to be adequately investigated when international price setting is being done.[4]

Pricing decisions should also take into account the psychological impact of the price, the need to adjust price to clear inventories or stimulate purchases, payment terms and procedures, and profit margins. Price changes and incentives are essential to an effective pricing strategy. For example, discounts for quantity purchases or for stimulating the sale of seasonal items in the off season may be required. Markdowns (sales) and other kinds cf price adjustments may need to be implemented from time to time for economic and a variety of other business reasons.

Price Escalation

The price the international marketer must charge in the foreign market may have to be higher than the price in the domestic market because of increased costs incurred in the marketing process. When this occurs, the international marketer encounters price escalation. **Price escalation** refers to raising price because of the added expenses of doing business internationally. These added expenses are not encountered domestically and are beyond the international marketer's control. Extra costs such as transportation, tariffs, and taxes must be incurred as a matter of doing business internationally. As a result, price must be raised to cover the expenses of these additional international activities and still provide an adequate profit.

The following are a few of the commonly encountered causes of price escalation.

Administered exchange rates (see chapter 9) can contribute to higher costs of doing business. Unfavorable exchange rates necessitate a higher price so that an adequate amount of the domestic currency can be obtained when the foreign currency is converted.

Higher intermediary margins that are frequently encountered increase the cost of distribution. Because intermediaries are smaller than in the United States and handle smaller volumes of merchandise, margins granted must be larger so that adequate incomes can be earned.

Higher warehousing and shipping costs may be encountered. In markets such as in LDCs, and countries like Romania, Italy, and Japan where retailers are small and numerous, smaller shipments are required, which increases warehousing and distribution costs. Larger numbers of retailers and extra intermediaries increase the number of shipments required, raising transportation costs.

Longer channels of distribution can be encountered. In countries such as Japan and Spain where channel arrangements have long been established, attempting changes would be culturally unacceptable. Longer channels mean additional, and perhaps unnecessary, intermediaries are involved. The result is additional expenses that raise the cost of distribution. For example, in countries where small grocery stores predominate, distribution costs will be higher than in the United States. Grocers requesting small quantities of a variety of canned vegetables may necessitate the inclusion of an additional intermediary in the channel to individually hand pack the assortment of vegetables requested by each of these small grocery store owners. The Large-Scale Retail Store Law of 1973, amended in 1978, made establishing large, economically efficient retail stores in local Japanese communities difficult. Laws such as this that protect small business cause increased distribution expenses.[5]

Product modification may increase the costs of production and packaging. Customizing the product to the specific needs of the foreign buyer may require retooling or special handling that increase production costs.

Shipping costs may or may not be paid by the buyer, depending upon the shipping terms arranged. See chapter 12 for a discussion of how shipping terms affect the seller's and buyer's responsibility for paying for shipping. When the seller is required to pay the shipping costs, those costs are added to the cost of doing business and will be reflected in the price quoted to the foreign buyer. When the foreign buyer pays the shipping costs, that amount will be considered, by the buyer, to be part of the amount paid for the product. Therefore, regardless of who pays the shipping costs, this expense raises the final cost to the foreign buyer. In addition to carriage charges, shipping costs can include customs fees and handling fees such as storage at port, wharfage, and lighterage. Even though water-borne transportation is the least expensive mode, the distances involved can result in higher transportation costs than those incurred for domestic shipments.

Tariffs may be incurred when exporting or importing the product. See chapter 5 for a discussion of tariffs. Although the buyer normally pays import duties, as with shipping costs, this expense raises the amount ultimately paid by the buyer.

Taxes are an unavoidable part of business regardless of location. Internationally, the marketer can encounter various turnover taxes. **Turnover taxes** are assessed each time the product changes hands while moving through the channel of distribution. Each intermediary involved in moving the product is taxed. These taxes are normally passed on to the buyer in the form of higher prices. Two categories of turnover taxes can be encountered—cumulative and noncumulative.

NONCUMULATIVE TURNOVER TAX

A **noncumulative turnover tax** is assessed on the value each channel member adds to the product. Therefore, this tax is often referred to as a **tax on value added (TVA)** or a **value-added tax (VAT)**. A VAT is a consumption tax that businesses pass on to the final customer. The tax is assessed as a percentage of the selling price to each intermediary. The tax is collected from each intermediary based on the amount due minus what has been paid previously by preceding channel members. The VAT is a commonly employed tax in European countries. An example of a noncumulative turnover tax is shown in Exhibit 14.2 for a hypothetical situation where each channel member assesses a 40 percent markup and the tax is 15 percent.

Exhibit 14.2 **Noncumulative Turnover Tax**

Danish Kroner	VAT (15%)	
34.00		Production costs
6.00		Marketing costs
16.00		40 percent markup on cost (profit to producer)
56.00		Selling price to wholesaler
	8.40	(56.00 × .15)
22.40		40 percent markup on cost (profit to wholesaler)
78.40		Selling price to retailer
	3.36	(78.00 × .15) – 8.40 already paid
31.36		40 percent markup on cost (profit to retailer)
109.76		Selling price to the customer
	4.71	(109.76 × .15) – 11.76 already paid
	16.47	Total tax

CUMULATIVE TURNOVER TAX

A **cumulative turnover tax** is assessed to the total selling price each time the product moves from one reseller to another. Any taxes paid previously by another channel member cannot be used to reduce the amount of tax due as is done with a noncumulative turnover tax. Aruba and South Africa are two countries that use a cumulative turnover

Exhibit 14.3 **Cumulative Turnover Tax**

Danish Kroner	Tax (7%)	
34.00		Production costs
6.00		Marketing costs
16.00		40 percent markup on cost (profit to producer)
56.00		Selling price to wholesaler
	3.92	(56.00 × .07) Tax paid by the producer
22.40		40 percent markup on cost (profit to wholesaler)
78.40		Selling price to retailer
	5.49	(78.00 × .07) Tax paid by the wholesaler
31.36		40 percent markup on cost (profit to retailer)
109.76		Selling price to the customer
	7.69	(109.76 × .07) Tax paid by the retailer
	17.10	Total tax

tax. A cumulative turnover tax is considered to be a regressive tax since taxes paid previously are added in to the selling price each time. This causes the previously paid tax to be taxed again in subsequent transactions. Because of the regressive nature of this kind of tax, the tax rate is usually a lower percentage than for a noncumulative turnover tax. An example of a cumulative turnover tax is shown in Exhibit 14.3 for a hypothetical situation where each channel member assesses a 40 percent markup and the tax is 7 percent.

All turnover taxes are annoying, however, because the amount of tax the buyer pays is usually not shown in the selling price. The consumer does not know how much of the purchase price represents tax unless the seller discloses the amount. This contrasts with the sales tax used in the United States which is added to the selling price at the time of purchase. Since the sales tax is shown at the time of purchase, the buyer knows exactly how much the tax is. However, when turnover taxes are involved, government officials can tax products more heavily without customers being aware of exactly how much tax is being paid. In European countries, the VAT is around 12 percent. In China the VAT is 15 percent.

RESPONSES TO PRICE ESCALATION

Any additional costs of doing business internationally, regardless of the reason, increase total expenses. Unless other expenses within the control of the international marketer can be reduced in proportion, price escalation will occur and higher prices or lower margins will result. When price escalation is encountered, the international marketer needs to investigate ways of controlling or reducing total costs to help keep the price more competitive. Since some price-escalating costs cannot be controlled, management must be creative and look for changes that will not adversely affect the firm's competitive position and ability to satisfy customers. What can be done to reduce costs depends on the situation and may include changes and adjustments such as the following:

Reclassify the product into another tariff category to lower import duties. Minor modifications to the product may permit a reassignment to a lower tariff rate classification. For example, if importing an assembled automobile is accompanied by a high tariff, simply importing the vehicle in parts and assembling them in the foreign country may allow reclassification into a lower tariff category, saving unnecessary expenses.

Use agents instead of merchants in the marketing channel to reduce turnover taxes. Agents represent buyers or sellers or both and facilitate the sale by bringing buyers and sellers together. In this way, less turnover tax is incurred because the product does not change hands as often.

Use less expensive transportation modes. Water or rail, for example, can be used as the volume being shipped reaches a critical level. By shipping a product unassembled, package space can usually be saved, reducing shipping costs. For instance, shipping a table with the legs unattached will reduce the amount of space required for shipping. The legs can be reassembled after the table reaches the destination.

Use shorter channels to lower distribution costs and turnover taxes. Where culturally appropriate, eliminating intermediaries may be feasible. Remember, eliminating the intermediary does not eliminate the functions the intermediary performed. Those functions must be moved up or down the channel to another channel member. This alternative is appropriate only when those channel members that assume the intermediary's functions can perform them as efficiently or more efficiently and less expensively.

If price escalation cannot be controlled, costs may become so excessive that the price that must be charged will not be competitive. When this happens, the international marketer will either be at a price disadvantage or be unable to compete. When exporting is involved, another market entry method may be required to remain in that market. Producing the product in the foreign country by means of a joint venture or foreign direct investment may be the only viable option to allow the international marketer to remain competitive.

Exhibit 14.4 illustrates the potential impact of price escalation on the price the foreigner must pay as compared to a domestic transaction for an identical product. Since the figures are hypothetical and the number of intermediaries may vary, the magnitude of the price escalation indicated in the example is not constant and would be different for other situations. For the figures shown in Exhibit 14.4, if the sale were directly to the buyer, the domestic transaction would be priced at $26.20 ($20.00 + $5.00 + $1.20 [6 percent sales tax]), and the foreign transaction would be priced at $46.25 (let us say the same price as if the sale were to the importer). The amount of the price escalation for a direct sale in this illustration is still $20.30 (77 percent), an amount that cannot be considered insignificant. If a wholesaler and retailer are added, price escalation in this example increases to 147 percent.

INTRACOMPANY TRANSFER PRICING

Another important aspect of international price setting for some firms is intracompany transfer pricing. **Intracompany transfer pricing** refers to the price management

Exhibit 14.4 **Impact of Price Escalation on Selling Price**

	Domestic sale	Foreign sale
Producer's price (Ex-Works)	$20.00	$20.00
Truck transportation to wholesaler		5.00
Truck transportation to port		5.00
Ocean transportation and insurance		8.00
Arrival cost		33.00
Import tariff (25 percent of arrival value)		8.25
Inland transportation		5.00
Price to importer		46.25
Importer's markup (20 percent)		9.25
Importer's VAT		6.66
Price to wholesaler	25.00	62.16
Wholesaler's markup (20 percent)	5.00	12.43
Wholesaler's VAT		2.29
Price to retailer	30.00	76.88
Retailer's markup (20 percent)	6.00	15.38
Retailer's VAT		2.12
Sales tax (6 percent)	2.16	
Price to buyer	38.16	94.38
Percent of price escalation		147

charges itself for sales from one segment to another segment within the company. As was indicated in chapter 4, a significant proportion of international trade is conducted by means other than exporting where joint ventures and foreign investments are located in foreign countries. A foreign subsidiary or branch of the international firm may use materials transferred from departments or divisions of a company located remotely or possibly in another country. These transfers are actually internal sales and can include tangible items such as finished products, raw materials, components or parts, and unfinished products; intangible items such as trademarks, copyrights and patents; services such as research and development (R&D), managerial, consulting, and marketing assistance; and the use of property such as buildings and equipment.

For example, suppose a part is shipped from a plant in the United States to the firm's Mexican subsidiary for installation into a product. After assembly, the product is sold from the Mexican location. What price should be charged to the Mexican subsidiary for the component? Depending on the foreign country's tax structure, charging a low price near or below cost might seem desirable for tax purposes. If the foreign country has a lower tax rate than the United States, earning the maximum of profit there and minimizing profit in the United States would result in lower overall taxes paid and larger profits realized.

Unfortunately for management, the Internal Revenue Service directs how intra-company transfer pricing may be done. In the United States, intracompany transfer pricing procedures must adhere to the provisions of Section 482 of the Internal Revenue Code. The Organization for European Cooperation and Development (OECD), of which the United States is a member, also has provisions pertaining to intracompany transfer pricing specified in the OECD Transfer Pricing Guidelines. **Section 482** provides that pricing procedures may not be structured in any way that results in evading the payment of appropriate U.S. taxes. Any pricing technique must be defensible for tax purposes. Government officials are permitted to review the firm's books and reassign revenues and costs when the pricing method is considered to be inappropriate. Revenues and costs can be reassigned according to what the government officials feel is correct and accurate, and then are used to determine the firm's actual tax amount. Any additional taxes deemed appropriate plus requisite penalties, which can amount to as much as 40 percent of the understated tax, must be paid. Therefore, management must be careful to determine the intracompany transfer price accurately, within the provisions of Section 482, and provide an adequate defense of the procedure used.

What are the pricing provisions of Section 482 and the OECD Transfer Pricing Guidelines? Basically, the requirements are to charge an **"arms-length" price**. Over time the definition of "arms length" has changed and differed between the two guidelines. Because of the ambiguity, revisions to the guidelines occurred several times since 1968 in an effort to define the term more precisely. The changes to the U.S regulations in 1994 and the OECD guidelines in 1995 have resulted in significant standardization between the two concerning how "arms length" should be defined.

In the United States, "arms length" means management is expected to realize from the price set the results that would have been realized if unrelated buyers and sellers would have engaged in the same transaction under the same circumstances.[6] Three factors enter into the pricing decision.[7]

- The best method rule. Management must use the method that provides the most reliable measure given the facts and circumstances.
- Comparability analysis. Because identical transactions between unrelated buyers and sellers are rare, a method of pricing consistent with comparable transactions is employed. Product quality and function, contract terms, risks, economic conditions, and the property or service are influential.
- Arms-length range. If more than one reliable arms-length result is available, a range of prices appropriate to the results is established. Any method used must fall within this range.

Acceptable methods for deciding the intracompany transfer price include the following:[8]

- Comparable uncontrolled price method (CUP) is equal to the price charged in a comparable uncontrolled transaction and is applicable to tangible property.
- Resale price method (RPM) is found by subtracting the appropriate gross profit, derived from comparable uncontrolled transactions, from an actual price and is applicable to tangible property.

- Cost plus method is applicable to tangible property and is derived by adding the appropriate gross profit markup to the controlled cost of producing the property.
- Comparable profit method (CPM) may be used for tangible or intangible property and is the level of profit buyers and sellers in a similar business transaction under similar circumstances would realize.
- Profit-split method assesses if the relative value of the contributions of the profit or loss resulting from the sale is allocated fairly and is applicable to tangible and intangible property.
- Comparable uncontrolled transaction method (CUT), which is essentially the same as the CUP method but applicable to intangible products.
- Unspecified methods not listed above are allowed as long as they conform to the best method rule, comparability, and the arms-length range, are defensible, selected in good faith, and documentation is maintained.

The understanding of arms length and the acceptable price-setting methods in the OECD guidelines are essentially the same as in Section 482 and represent a fair and equitable approach to pricing products and services sold between related business entities.

Because of the arms-length provisions of Section 482, management is prevented from manipulating sales and making so-called paper transactions from low-tax countries like Puerto Rico known as **tax havens**. For example, Liechtenstein charges no corporate income tax. Management could evade taxes by opening an office in Liechtenstein to receive orders while still shipping the product from a location in the United States. Prior to the sale, a paper transfer of the product to the mail drop office in Liechtenstein would be made at or below cost, causing all or most of the revenue to be earned in Liechtenstein and a loss or small income earned in the United States. As a result, U.S. taxes would be minimized and profits maximized in the tax haven. Of course, government officials would conclude that this arrangement was set up for the sole purpose of evading paying U.S. income tax. Income and costs would be reassigned and additional taxes and penalties collected.

Creative methods of pricing intracompany transfers are acceptable as long as the technique can be legally defended. To be correct, management should assure that any method used satisfies the definition of "arms length," and that any deviations can be justified.

SHIPPING TERMS AND PRICE QUOTES

Quoting the price for an export shipment is also an important aspect of setting the retail price of a product. Various trade terms, or shipping terms, employed for international shipments have a direct impact on costs borne by the seller. The terms of shipment specified by the exporter determine what costs are included in the shipping price quotation, that is, for what expenses the buyer and seller are each responsible, and who owns the title to the merchandise while in transit. The terms of sale can be specified in one of three ways:[9]

- Insert a statement into the contract stating that the terms shall be governed by the laws of the exporter's home country.
- Insert into the contract the explicit understanding of the meaning of the export terms to the exporter.
- Adopt one of the standard sets of trade terms available, which define the roles and responsibilities of the buyer and seller in export shipments.

When the third option is selected, the terms specified by the International Chamber of Commerce, known as Incoterms, are frequently employed. **Incoterms** (an acronym for International Commercial Terms) are a set of internationally accepted commercial terms, defining the roles and responsibilities of the buyer and seller in export shipments. Incoterms were first published in 1936 as the International Rules for the Interpretation of Trade Terms and have been revised six times, most recently in 2000. International marketers who want to use Incoterms to govern shipments only need to specify in the contract that the provisions of "Incoterms 2000 govern." The other frequently used standard set of shipping terms is **Intraterms** (an acronym for International Trade Terms) which translate the meaning of shipping terms to understandable language.

The purpose of including trade terms in the contract is to define the method of delivery of the merchandise sold and to help determine the purchase price along with the incidental charges included therein.[10] Stating the intended meaning of the export terms employed in the contract is recommended, thus preventing any misunderstanding by the buyer.

The thirteen Incoterms for international shipments are shown in Exhibit 14.5. The exact meaning and conditions pertinent to each term depend on which of the three previously mentioned alternatives for quoting shipping terms is employed. The responsibilities of each party to the contract will depend then on what source of terms is specified in the contract. For example, the term FOB can have a different meaning in the laws of the buyer's country than in the laws of the seller's country. In general, however, if Incoterms are employed, where the title changes hands can easily be determined so each party will be aware of its financial obligations. Other details of the shipment, such as who is responsible for arranging the shipping and the various risks inherent in the transaction, need not be spelled out specifically in the contract as long as reference to Incoterms 2000 is included.

The Incoterms can be divided into four groups based on the first letter of the abbreviation. The group E terms apply to situations in which the buyer takes possession of the product at the seller's location. The terms in group F apply to situations in which the seller must deliver the product to a carrier designated by the buyer, and the buyer must pay for the carriage. Group C terms apply to situations in which the seller designates and pays for the carriage. The terms comprising group D apply to situations in which the seller is responsible for the product until it arrives at the specified destination. The list begins with Ex-Works, whereby the seller has the least responsibility and the buyer the most. Moving down the list in Exhibit 14.5, each subsequent term provides for increased responsibility for the seller and decreased responsibility for the buyer. When Delivered Duty Paid is reached, the seller has the

Exhibit 14.5 **International Commercial Terms for Shipping (Incoterms)**

Shipping term	Abbreviation	Use
Ex-Works (named place)	EXW	Any
Free Carrier (named place)	FCA	Any
Free Alongside Ship (named port of shipment)	FAS	Sea
Free on Board (named port of shipment)	FOB	Sea
Cost and Freight (named port of destination)	CFR	Sea
Cost Insurance and Freight (named port of destination)	CIF	Sea
Carriage Paid To (named place of destination)	CPT	Any
Carriage and Insurance Paid To (named place of destination)	CIP	Any
Delivered at Frontier (named place)	DAF	Any
Delivered Ex-Ship (named port of destination)	DES	Sea
Delivered Ex-Quay (named port of destination)	DEQ	Sea
Delivered Duty Unpaid (named place of destination)	DDU	Any
Delivered Duty Paid (named place of destination)	DDP	Any

Any = Used for any mode of transportation.
Sea = Used for ocean and inland waterway transportation only.

most responsibility and the buyer the least. Each term must be followed by the appropriate named location, place, port, or destination.

If Incoterms are not used, terms such as Ex-Factory (EXF), Ex-Warehouse (EXWH), and FOB (Seller's Warehouse) may be employed in place of Ex-Works (EXW) when the product is sold at the seller's location. When any of these terms are employed, the buyer buys the product at the seller's location and is responsible for moving the merchandise. EXF and EXWH may be considered more precise terms when the product is stored or located in a different location from where it is produced. EXF, EXWH, EXW, and FOB (Seller's Warehouse) have essentially the same meaning if the warehouse is located at the factory. For these terms, title changes hands when the buyer pays and takes possession at the seller's location. However, if the warehouse is at a remote location, then the seller assumes the cost and risk of moving the product to the warehouse and the buyer takes possession at the warehouse. The buyer takes all other shipping risks, bears the cost of carriage, insurance, and responsibility for export and import documentation. If requested, the seller, at the buyer's expense, may assist with inland shipping and preparation of export documentation. Free on Rail (FOR) and Free on Truck (FOT) are terms that may be used when inland freight is part of the shipment to the port of export. FOR means the seller assumes the responsibility and expense of loading the product on a rail car at the factory or railhead. The same responsibility is assumed for FOT if the product is loaded on a truck instead of a rail car. Free Carrier (FCA) is comparable to FOR and FOT since the seller is responsible for seeing that the product is loaded on a conveyance at the factory and the title does not transfer to the buyer until loading is complete.

FOB is a versatile shipping term since any location can be specified. For example, the following are a few of the ways FOB can be used:

- FOB (Freight terminal)—the seller assumes responsibility until the product is loaded on the carrier at a remote freight terminal. Title changes at the terminal.
- FOB (Baltimore)—the seller assumes responsibility until the product is loaded on the ship at the port of Baltimore, Maryland. Title changes after the product is on the ship.
- FOB (Pier 54, New York City)—the seller assumes responsibility until the product is loaded on the ship at Pier 54. Title changes once the product is on-loaded. FAS (Pier 54, New York City) is comparable since the seller is responsible for the product until located alongside the ship that will carry the merchandise. The only difference is that the title transfers to the buyer once the product is beside the ship prior to loading, and the buyer assumes the cost of loading.
- FOB (JFK Airport, New York City)—the seller is responsible for the product until loaded into the airplane at JFK Airport. Title changes at the airport.
- FOB (Named Vessel, New York City)—the seller assumes responsibility until the product is loaded on the designated ship. Title changes after the product is loaded on the ship.
- FOB (Named Vessel, Rotterdam)—the seller is responsible for the product until arrival at Rotterdam, the Netherlands. Title changes after arrival at Rotterdam.
- FOB (Paris)—the seller assumes responsibility until the product arrives at a freight terminal in Paris, France. Title changes at the foreign terminal.

Obviously, the expenses the seller will incur will be different in each of these examples. The price quoted the buyer has to reflect the amount of risk and cost the seller will incur.

CFR (Hong Kong) means the seller must arrange and pay the cost of shipping (freight) to Hong Kong. Title changes after the product is loaded on the conveyance mode at the port of export.

CIF (Hong Kong) is identical to CFR (Hong Kong) with the exception that the cost and responsibility for securing shipping insurance belongs to the seller.

CIP (Budapest) can be used when the destination is inland and not a port. In all other respects the term is the same as CIF except the seller pays the additional inland transportation (from the port of Istanbul, for example) until the product reaches the destination designated by the buyer in Budapest.

DDP (Rome) can be used when the shipment goes to the buyer's location. The seller is responsible for shipping and insurance to the buyer's location. Title changes when the buyer receives delivery and before the product is off-loaded. The seller must arrange for inland transportation in the foreign country.

When shipments are made entirely by truck or rail, the quote may be delivered at frontier (DAF). For a shipment from a subsidiary in Germany to a buyer in Paris, France, the quote DAF (Saabrücken, Germany) may be used. This means the seller is responsible for the product until the border crossing of Saabrücken is reached. At that point, the title changes and the shipment becomes the responsibility of the buyer.

Exhibit 14.6 **Where Title Is Transferred from the Seller to the Buyer**

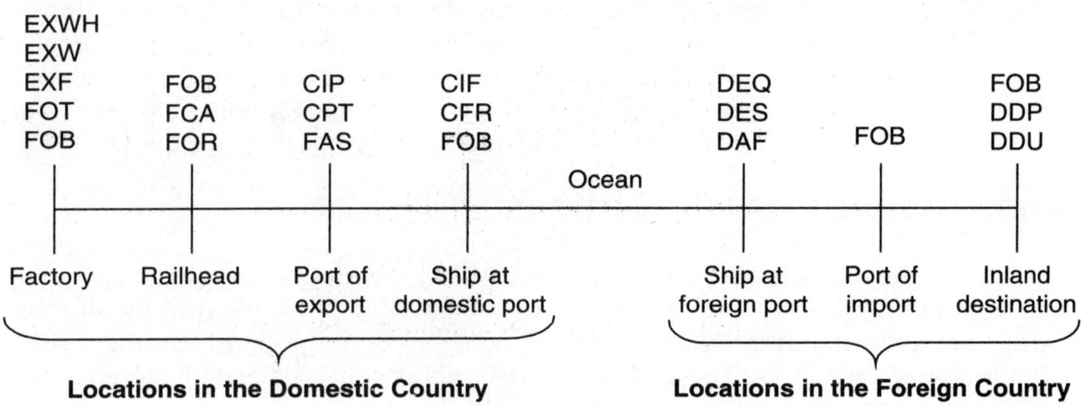

Where title changes for various shipping terms may be depicted as shown in Exhibit 14.6. Locations in the shipping process are shown below the line, and the appropriate shipping terms that correspond to title transfer at those locations are shown above the line.

What are the implications of the shipping term selection process for the international marketer? The shipping terms used will affect the seller's shipping responsibilities and thus the shipping risk and costs incurred. Ultimately the shipping terms will influence the price quoted the foreign customer. Compare EXW with DDP (Paris, France) for example. A product sold EXW becomes the buyer's responsibility at the seller's location. As a result, the seller incurs no expenses for activities such as loading, documentation preparation, transportation to the domestic sea or airport, port charges, ocean or air freight, import duties and taxes, and inland transportation to the buyer. If anything goes wrong with the shipment after the product leaves the factory, rectifying the problem is the responsibility of the buyer. A product sold DDP (Paris, France) does not become the buyer's responsibility until received in Paris. As a result, the seller incurs all the previously mentioned expenses except the inland transportation from Paris to the buyer's location. If anything goes wrong during shipment, rectifying the problem is the responsibility of the seller until the buyer takes possession in Paris. Since the seller incurs additional costs to ship DDP (Paris, France), a higher price must be charged. The lowest possible price could be charged for the EXW sale because the seller incurs no additional expense beyond production.

Consider FOB (New York City) and FAS (New York City). The seller is responsible for all expenses required to get the product on the pier ready for loading with the FAS (New York City) sale, while all expenses required to get the product onto the ship are incurred with the FOB (New York City) sale. Since the expenses associated with FOB (New York City) are greater than for FAS (New York City), a higher price would need to be quoted for the FOB (New York City) sale. Also, if anything happens to the product during loading, the seller owns the merchandise and would have to file insurance claims for the FOB (New York City) sale. While for the FAS (New York City) sale, the buyer owns the merchandise and would have to file insurance claims.

The shipping terms would need to be taken into consideration as part of the cost assessment phase of the export process during offer preparation and negotiations if involved, as discussed in chapter 12 (see Exhibit 12.2). Both the buyer and seller desire the most favorable shipping terms; however, whatever terms are ultimately agreed upon, the seller must take the risks of ownership and shipping along with all associated costs into consideration to determine the appropriate price quote.

INTERNATIONAL PAYMENT METHODS

Another consideration for the international marketer is the manner in which payment is to be made for the product. The payment method must be agreed to by all those involved and written into the contract. Payment can be requested from the foreign buyer in one of four ways. These payment methods and the associated degree of risk for the buyer and seller are shown in Exhibit 14.7.

Exhibit 14.7 **International Payment Methods**

Seller		Buyer
Least risky	Cash in advance	Most risky
↕	Letter of credit	↕
	Bill of exchange (draft)	
Most risky	Open account (credit)	Least risky

CASH IN ADVANCE

Cash in advance is a payment method in which the seller receives payment in full before the product is manufactured and shipped. Cash in advance, also known as prepayment, is used infrequently but is absolutely necessary in countries with blocked (nonconvertible) currencies and unsafe banking systems. Cash in advance is also a desirable method of payment when the seller does not know the buyer's creditworthiness or the seller needs payment up front because of a lack of cash or credit to finance the transaction on extended terms. Cash in advance is the least risky for the seller since payment is assured before the product is shipped. On the other hand, cash in advance is most risky for the buyer, because after payment is made, the buyer has no guarantee the shipment will be made or delivered when requested. Thus, the buyer may lose an amount equal to the purchase price and also receive no product. For these reasons, the buyer may resist paying cash in advance.

LETTER OF CREDIT

A **letter of credit** is a document issued by a bank, which substitutes the bank's credit for that of the buyer and guarantees payment. If properly executed, the letter of credit is almost as safe as cash in advance for the seller. Careful consideration must be

Exhibit 14.8 **Letter of Credit Process**

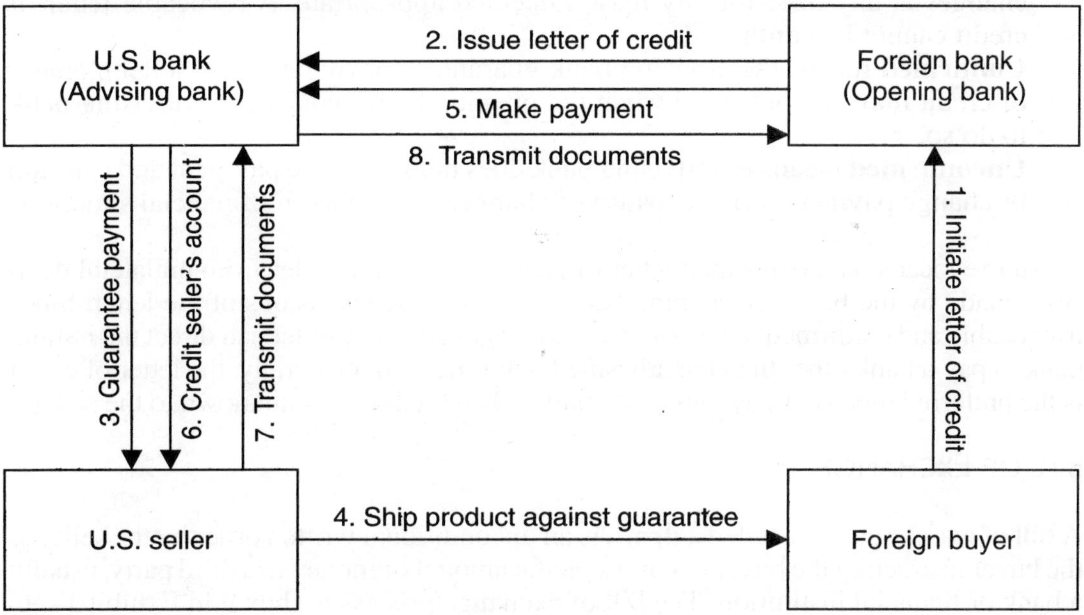

given to verifying the foreign bank involved, as a letter of credit could be drawn on a nonexistent bank. For that reason, the letter of credit is slightly more risky for the seller than cash in advance. For the buyer, a letter of credit is less risky than cash in advance because payment is not made until the shipping documents indicating the cargo is en route are received by the buyer's bank.

When the buyer and seller agree on a letter of credit as the payment method, the buyer will request that its bank initiate the letter. After the bank officials are satisfied that the buyer has sufficient funds or credit, the bank, known as the opening or originating bank, writes the letter of credit. The letter is transmitted by the Society for Worldwide Interbank Financial Telecommunication (SWIFT) or by telex or mail to the seller's bank, known as the advising bank. The advising bank sends the letter to the seller. The seller then proceeds with filling the order according to the provisions of the letter of credit. After the shipment is on its way, the seller forwards the required documents to the advising bank. The advising bank forwards the documents to the buyer after payment is made by the opening bank. The funds are then credited to the seller's account. The process is depicted in Exhibit 14.8.

Make sure the provisions of the letter of credit correspond with the terms of the contract. Regardless of what is written in the contract, the banks consider the letter of credit as the final word on the sale. Various types of letters of credit exist. The best and safest is an irrevocable and confirmed letter of credit:

- **Irrevocable** means changes to the provisions of the letter of credit are only allowed to be made with prior approval of the seller, opening bank, and advising bank.

- **Revocable** means the opening bank can invalidate the letter of credit or make changes at any time for any reason deemed appropriate. A revocable letter of credit cannot be confirmed.
- **Confirmed** means the advising bank guarantees payment to the seller. A letter of credit may be confirmed when the opening bank requests the advising bank to do so.
- **Unconfirmed** means the advising bank does not guarantee payment and can stop or change payment terms because of changes in the buyer's financial situation.

An irrevocable and confirmed letter of credit protects the seller from unilateral decisions made by the buyer or opening bank to change the provisions of the letter. Since irrevocable and confirmed letters of credit are negotiable, the seller can direct the issuing bank to pay a bank other than the advising bank if desired. Generally, the letter of credit is the preferred means of payment, especially when the buyer is unknown to the seller.

BILL OF EXCHANGE

A **bill of exchange,** also called a **draft,** is an unconditional written order by the seller to the buyer instructing the buyer to pay a specific amount of money to a third party, usually a bank or financial institution. The bill of exchange process is shown in Exhibit 14.9.

The seller ships the product, then presents the draft and shipping documents to its bank. The bank forwards the draft, with shipping documents attached, to a foreign bank in the buyer's country with which it has a financial relationship. This may be a correspondent bank or a foreign branch of the seller's bank if the bank is international in operations. The correspondent bank contacts the buyer or the buyer's bank, presents the draft, and requests payment as specified in the draft. When the buyer pays the

Exhibit 14.9 **Bill of Exchange Process**

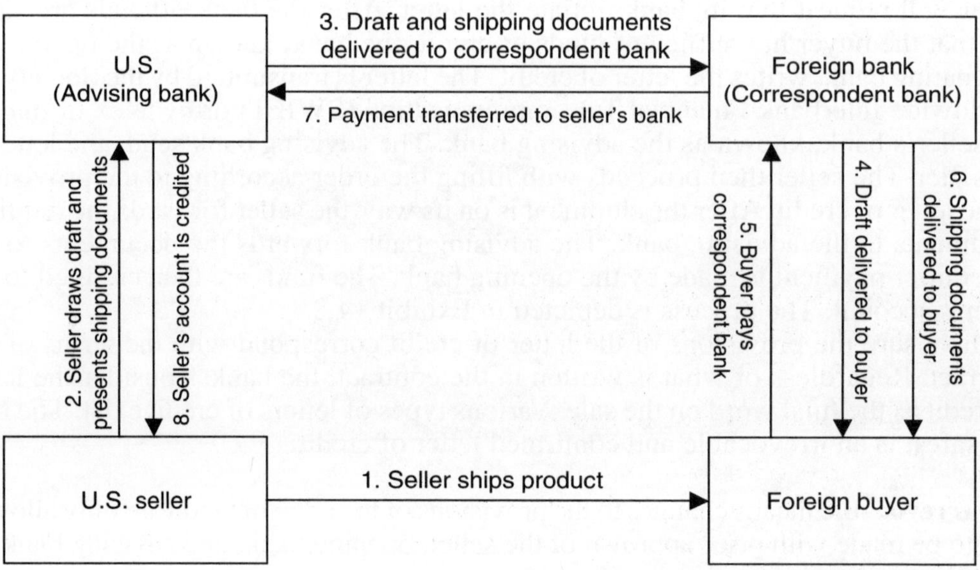

correspondent bank, the shipping documents are delivered to the buyer. Payment is transferred to the seller's bank and credited to the seller's account.

Various kinds of drafts exist. The kind of draft employed depends upon when payment has to be made by the buyer. The following commonly employed drafts are listed from the least risky to the most risky for the seller (from most risky to least risky for the buyer):

- A **sight draft** must be paid immediately upon presentation to the buyer.
- An **arrival draft** must be paid when the product arrives at the foreign port or the buyer's location, depending on what shipping terms are used.
- A **dated draft** must be paid on or before the day, month, and year prescribed.
- A **time draft** must be paid before a prescribed number of days have passed after the draft is presented to the buyer.

Although ocean shipping can be slow, the amount of time passing between the buyer being presented with the draft and the product arriving is generally less than the intervening time for either a dated or a time draft. Conceivably, a time draft could be payable before a dated draft, depending on the time allowed and the date selected. For example, for a draft presented on July 1 requesting payment after thirty days would require the buyer to pay more quickly than a dated draft requesting payment by August 15. Normally, however, time drafts permit a longer period of time than do dated drafts, as long as six months (180 days), before payment is due.

A bill of exchange is more risky than a letter of credit for the seller because the buyer may decide not to pay. The consolation for the seller, however, is that if payment is not made, the buyer does not receive the shipping documents and title to the product. Although the seller retains ownership, the shipment is stranded at the foreign port. Therefore, the seller must locate another buyer or pay to have the product shipped back to the factory. If the product is a standard item, resale may be ultimately accomplished. However, if it is a customized product, the seller could have difficulty finding another buyer and faces the possibility of a financial loss on that shipment. That is why cash in advance or a letter of credit is usually preferred for custom-made products unless the buyer is well known to the international marketer.

OPEN ACCOUNT

Open account or **credit** means the product is shipped with the buyer promising to pay at some future time. Open account is unsecured credit that relies on the buyer's anticipated ability to pay and is not supported by a note or other written evidence of indebtedness. The risk for the seller is the greatest for credit sales because the buyer receives the product and could delay or not make payment. Thus, the seller could lose the income from the sale and the product as well. From the buyer's perspective, open account is attractive because payment does not have to be made until the product is sold and the money secured. Consignment sales are a form of open account since payment is made only if the product sells. Generally, credit should be extended only to buyers with whom the seller is well acquainted and has had an extended business relationship, and whose financial credibility has been documented.

PAYMENT SOURCES

Various sources exist that a foreign buyer can utilize to help finance purchases. If the foreign buyer is unable to pay cash and the seller unwilling or unable to extend credit, these sources of funds provide an alternative to facilitate the sale.

EDGE ACT BANKS

Edge Act banks are authorized under section 25A (known as the Edge Act) of the Federal Reserve Act. These banks are subsidiaries of U.S. banks formed solely for foreign purposes. Edge Act banks are permitted to make short-term and long-term loans to foreigners that can be used to finance international purchases.

OVERSEAS DEVELOPMENT BANKS

Overseas development banks are U.S. governmental organizations that have been established to support the export expansion programs of U.S. firms. The two major organizations are the Export-Import Bank of the United States and the Agency for International Development.

Export-Import Bank of the United States

The **Export-Import Bank of the United States (Ex-Im Bank)** assists foreigners to buy U.S.-made products in three ways:

- Ex-Im Bank personnel make direct loans to foreigners for the sole purpose of purchasing U.S.-made products.
- Ex-Im Bank personnel guarantee loans and provide insurance to domestic banks that lend money to foreigners to buy U.S.-made products. In this way, the domestic banks have less risk when making loans, because if the foreigner cannot repay the loan, the Ex-Im Bank assures repayment.
- Ex-Im Bank personnel provide discounted loans to U.S. commercial banks to help support lending to foreigners who want to purchase U.S.-made products.

Agency for International Development

The **United States Agency for International Development (USAID)** was formed by the Foreign Assistance Act of 1961. USAID supports exporting by providing loans to friendly LDC governments for the purpose of buying U.S.-made products that will assist with infrastructure development.

MULTINATIONAL BANKS

Multinational banks are intergovernmental organizations that provide banking services to a variety of buyers. The primary multinational bank is the World Bank. Other regional multinational banks have been established to assist with the economic development and growth of the countries in the concerned areas of the world.

World Bank Group

The World Bank Group was formed, along with the International Monetary Fund that regulates and coordinates overall financial relations, at the Bretton Woods Conference in 1944 when the world financial structure was reorganized after World War II. The **World Bank Group** is composed of three institutions that are intended to make loans to buyers in third world countries for the purpose of developing infrastructure:

- The **International Bank for Reconstruction and Development (IBRD)** is the central institution of the group and makes loans to those governments that can qualify under conventional terms.
- The **International Development Association (IDA)** makes loans to balance-of-payments-plagued nations that otherwise would not qualify for loans under conventional terms from the IBRD.
- The **International Finance Corporation (IFC)** helps promote the growth of the private sector by making loans to businesses and other nongovernment buyers.

Regional Development Banks

Cooperating nations in a geographic area of the world can form **regional development banks** to facilitate the economic growth of the region. For example, the European Investment Bank was formed to facilitate the economic development and integration of the European Union. A list of regional development banks is shown in Exhibit 14.10.

Exhibit 14.10

Regional Development Banks

African Development Bank (AfDB)
Asian Development Bank (AsDB)
Caribbean Development Bank (CDB)
Central American Bank for Economic Integration (CABEI)
European Bank for Reconstruction and Development (ERBD)
European Investment Bank (EIB)
Inter-American Development Bank Group (IADB)
Islamic Development Bank (IDB)
Nordic Investment Bank (NIB)

Subregional Banks

Subregional banks serve a more limited area than regional banks. Among these are banks such as Corporacion Andina de Fomento (CAF), East African Development Bank (EADB), and the West African Development Bank (WADB), also known as Banque Ouest Africaine de Développement (BOAD). The WADB, for example, was created to serve the French- and Portuguese-speaking countries of Africa. The bank makes long- and medium-term loans to the members' governments and to private businesses pursuing projects that will help improve the region. Lines of credit are also offered to small- and medium-sized firms engaged in business activities deemed economically stimulating to the region.

EURODOLLARS

Eurodollars are U.S. dollar-denominated deposits held in foreign banks or branches of American banks. After World War II, large amounts of U.S. dollars began to be held by foreigners as the result of events such as distribution of aid under the Marshall Plan, the growth of U.S. business abroad, and the increase in products imported into the United States. During the cold war, the Soviets, fearing that dollars they deposited in U.S. banks might be frozen, sought alternatives for their holdings. As a result, some British and French banks began to accept deposits denominated in U.S. dollars. Although this policy began in Europe—hence the name Eurodollar—the practice has spread worldwide. Eurodollar deposits are not subject to the rules and regulations of the U.S. Federal Reserve Board and their associated costs. Therefore, banks accepting Eurodollar deposits can operate on narrower margins than U.S. banks. The banks accepting Eurodollars deposit these dollars in U.S. banks, and can subsequently make loans based on those amounts. Thus, U.S.-dollar loans are available to foreign corporations and other business entities by transferring a portion of the deposits held in the United States.

Along with local commercial banks in the buyer's country, these additional organizations represent potential sources of funds to help make purchases possible. The seller can assist the buyer in locating an appropriate funding source from among these kinds of organizations. Looking to these alternative sources for financing can facilitate the sale when the buyer lacks sufficient reserves and bank credit or is unable to obtain a loan from traditional sources. If the nature of the proposed sale is appropriate and the buyer can qualify for funds from one or more of these alternative sources, the sale can be accomplished at the quoted price without delay.

CHAPTER SUMMARY

Price setting needs to take into account cost, competition, and demand considerations and be interpreted as the monetary value the customer attaches to the product or service. Setting price too high or too low will adversely affect sales and profits, and if too low, could result in accusations of dumping.

A variety of price-escalating factors can be encountered internationally that affect the price. Price escalation is caused by increases in the cost of international marketing, which are beyond the control of the international marketer. Factors such as additional shipping costs, tariffs, turnover taxes, higher intermediary and distribution costs, and administered exchange rates contribute to price escalation. Since these costs cannot be avoided, the international marketer needs to make adjustments that will help minimize the amount of the price escalation. If adjustments cannot be made and the price escalation is severe enough, exports can become too costly to be priced competitively in the foreign market.

How management sells products, components, or parts to itself can affect costs, and ultimately, the final price. Intracompany transfer pricing must be taken into consideration for such transactions. Although intracompany prices may be cost justified, no procedure can be implemented that evades paying a fair income tax. Section 482 of the U.S. Internal Revenue Code holds that an appropriate pricing technique should be at an "arms length." If the IRS concludes that the pricing method used was inappropriate, income and costs can be reassigned according to what IRS officials consider appropriate and additional taxes collected.

The shipping terms employed can also have an impact on price. Shipping terms specify whether the seller or buyer is responsible for the various costs of shipping and when title to the product is transferred. In turn, this affects each party's shipping risks and distribution costs, which ultimately influences the price. Although Incoterms are frequently used, any terms written into the contract are acceptable.

The method used to pay for the shipment also influences the risk of not being paid. The seller wants to use safe and secure payment methods to minimize financial risk. Although cash in advance is the safest way to receive payment, this method is normally employed only in insecure parts of the world because of the risk the buyer incurs from the possibility of not receiving the product. Therefore, the letter of credit is a popular payment method that is widely used.

A variety of funding sources is available to help the buyer pay for the product. These organizations facilitate purchases by lending money and securing and guaranteeing payment. The Ex-Im Bank and USAID are two U.S. government organizations that assist foreign buyers to purchase products from U.S. firms.

KEY TERMS

Arms-length price
Arrival draft
Bill of exchange
Cash in advance
Confirmed
Credit
Cumulative turnover tax
Dated draft
Draft
Dumping
Edge Act banks
Eurodollars
Export-Import Bank of the United States (Ex-Im Bank)
Incoterms
International Bank for Reconstruction and Development (IBRD)
International Development Association (IDA)
International Finance Corporation (IFC)
Intracompany transfer pricing
Intraterms
Irrevocable
Letter of credit
Multinational banks
Noncumulative turnover tax
Open account
Overseas development banks
Price escalation
Regional development banks
Revocable
Section 482
Sight draft
Subregional banks
Tax haven
Tax on value added
Time draft
Turnover taxes
Unconfirmed
United States Agency for International Development (USAID)
Value-added tax
World Bank Group

REVIEW QUESTIONS

1. What factors need to be taken into consideration when setting price? Why?
2. What is dumping? Why is dumping an issue for local foreign competitors?
3. What is price escalation? Give an example.
4. What is a value-added tax? How does a value-added tax influence price?
5. What can the international marketer do to minimize the influence of price escalation?
6. What is intracompany transfer pricing? How should intracompany prices be set?
7. How do shipping terms affect price?
8. Explain how the shipping terms FOB (Baltimore, MD) and CIF (Tokyo, Japan) influence price. What is the difference between these two terms regarding the seller's and buyer's responsibilities and shipping-related costs?
9. Differentiate among and explain the various international payment methods. Which of the payment methods is preferred and why?
10. How is a time draft different from a dated draft?

NOTES

1. Judith MacKade and Michael Eriksen, *The Tobacco Atlas,* "Table B, The Business of Tobacco," World Health Organization, (United Nations, 2004), 102–109, http://who.int/tobacco/statistics/tobacco_atlas/en/.

2. Matthew B. Myers, "The Pricing of Export Products: Why Aren't Managers Satisfied With the Results?" *Journal of World Business* 32 (Fall 1997): 277–87.

3. Ibid.

4. Ibid.

5. Jim Powell, "Protectionist Paradise," Center for Trade Policy Studies, Cato Institute, 1997, http://www.freetrade.org/pubs/freetrade/chap7.html.

6. "Transfer Pricing, History, State of the Art, Perspectives,"Ad Hoc Group of Experts on International Cooperation in Tax Matters, United Nations Secretariat, September 10–14, 2001, http://unpan1.un.org/intradoc/groups/public/documents/un/unpan004399.pdf.

7. Ibid.

8. Ibid.

9. Leo D'Arcy, Carole Murray, and Barbara Cleave, *Schmitthoff's Export Trade: The Law and Practice of International Trade,* 10th ed. (London: Sweet & Maxwell, 2000), 8.

10. Ibid.

15 International Promotion Strategy

Benetton Group, S.p.A., is a global up-market clothing company based in Treviso, Italy. After successfully marketing sweaters knitted by his sister, Luciano Benetton started the firm in 1965 with the opening of a store in Belluno, Italy. A year later, a second store was opened, in Paris, and Luciano's two brothers and sister joined him in the business. Today, Benetton products are sold in approximately 6,200 retail stores in 120 countries around the world. Benetton's clothing (women's wear, menswear, children's wear, and underwear) is marketed in four product lines: Casual (United Colors of Benetton), fashion (Sisley), leisure wear (Playlife), and street wear (Killer Loop). Toiletries, perfumes, watches, housewares, and baby products are also sold.

Benetton is well known for the nontraditional and controversial nature of its advertising during the 1980s and 1990s for the United Colors of Benetton line of products. Until 1982, the firm's advertising contained traditional pictures of young professional models wearing Benetton clothing. The ads' designs emphasized the product through images of young, attractive, and happy boys and girls. In 1972, the small Italian publicity agency used by Benetton was replaced by the Eldorado Agency in Paris, where ad campaigns concentrated on posters and billboards. Luciano Benetton became friends with Oliviero Toscani, a photographer for Eldorado, who worked for the Benetton account. A decision was made in 1982 to change the nature of Benetton's advertising. Images of important world issues raised awareness and created added value for the brand. The first ads Toscani photographed in 1984 employed a multiracial theme. They depicted groups of black and white children or adults wearing Benetton clothing with the logo "All the world's colors" and the company's name. In 1985, the visuals were changed from groups to couples. For example, one poster showed two little black boys kissing each other. In their hair and painted on their cheeks, one boy had little U.S. flags and the other had little USSR flags. The ad was imprinted with the words "United Colors of Benetton."

Initially, the ads were mild in terms of content and acceptable to most people. However, this began to change in the 1990s. In 1990 the theme became confrontation between black and white. By 1991 the themes became even more controversial. For example, posters showed a priest kissing a nun on the lips, and a newborn child with umbilical cord attached, covered in blood. According to Luciano Benetton, the priest and nun picture was a joke showing that the habit does not make the priest or the nun. The ad was banned in Italy after protests from the Vatican but won the Eurobest Award in Great Britain. The newborn child picture produced controversy throughout Europe and was eventually withdrawn from publication in Italy, France, and the United Kingdom. According to Benetton, the intent was to show the beauty of new life. Other posters in 1991 showed the contradictory nature of duality such as war/peace, flirtation/sex, and beauty/pollution. Although the subjects had an ethical dimension, the message was ambivalent and posed no moral position.

Throughout the 1990s, the ads had no relationship to the company or its products. Benetton was probably the first company to produce such ads. Its themes amounted to social crusades against issues such as apartheid, the HIV epidemic, capital punishment, and homophobia. Just a few of the controversial ads depicted:

- an African soldier holding a Kalashnikov and a human leg bone
- black and white horses copulating
- three identical human hearts, each inscribed with the word, "white," "black," "yellow"
- a black woman breastfeeding a white baby
- an angelic-looking white child embracing a black child whose hair was shaped into devil's horns
- two dogs copulating
- David Kirby dying of AIDS, surrounded by his family
- a black child kissing a white child, both of whom were sitting on their potties,
- the bloodied shirt of a dead Croat soldier
- fifty-six pictures of alternating masculine and feminine genitals of people of different races and ages, some of whom appear to be children*
- close-ups of various body parts tattooed in purple with "HIV positive"
- a nude of Luciano Benetton

Critics claimed the ads had no purpose other than shock. Luciano Benetton said he had no regrets about the controversial advertising. Instead, he claimed the ads had a deep effect on public opinion and helped probe emotions and stimulate thinking and debate. He believes the common theme was the battle against prejudice.

Certainly, the ads did get people talking about Benetton and increased its name recognition. However, the nature of the ads provoked negative opinions about Benetton for many customers. French billstickers actually refused to post many of

*In countries such as Belgium, Denmark, Spain, France, Greece, Italy, the Netherlands, Portugal, and Sweden, showing children totally naked (including sexual organs) in ads is permissible.

the ads because they regarded them as "reality advertising" or pure sensationalism. German government authorities banned ads that depicted child labor, human bodies with "HIV positive" tattoos, and a bird stuck in an oil slick because they considered these ads to be exploiting suffering. As a result of the advertising, the management of Sears, Roebuck and Company withdrew from a US$100 million contract with Benetton. The question remains, "Is negative publicity better than no publicity?" Apparently, Luciano Benetton believes it is.

Sources: Based in part on information from "About Benetton—Our Campaigns," http://press.benettongroup.com/ben_en/about/campaigns/history/; and "Press Area," http://press.benettongroup.com/ben_en/; and "Benetton News and Facts History," http://www.fashionunited.co.uk/News/Columns/Benetton_news_and_facts_history_200809286207/.

CHAPTER OBJECTIVES

After reading this chapter, you should

- know the components of promotion;
- understand the need to assure promotion is not offensive;
- know the decision areas that comprise an international advertising strategy;
- appreciate the risks inherent in developing an effective international advertising strategy;
- know what advertising agency alternatives are available;
- understand the problems of using expatriate salespeople; and
- realize the need to assess the appropriateness of sales promotion, public relations, and direct marketing efforts for the foreign market.

PROMOTION REVIEWED

What is promotion? Promotion is a term used to encompass all methods the marketer uses to communicate with the target group of customers. The intent of promotion is to persuade, inform, and remind present and potential buyers of the features, benefits, value, and satisfaction that can be derived from the firm's marketing efforts. Promotion tells customers about the virtues of product, price, and physical distribution—the remainder of the marketing mix. Promotion is most commonly conceived as consisting of the five broad categories of advertising, direct marketing, personal selling, public relations, and sales promotion:

- **Advertising** consists of all paid forms of impersonal communication from an identified sponsor. Advertising is considered to be mass communications because messages are generally intended to reach large numbers of potential consumers. Advertising is implemented through media such as radio, television, magazines, newspapers, billboards, and the Internet.

- **Direct marketing** is communicating directly with targeted consumers by methods other than mass media or face-to-face contact. The communication is sent to customers whose personal information suggests a particular product may be of interest to them. Databases about customers are created and maintained to help identify profiles so that specific messages can be tailored. Examples of direct marketing include postal mail, telemarketing, electronic mail, and other addressable media.
- **Personal selling** involves direct face-to-face communication by sales representatives to potential buyers. Individualized communications consisting of detailed discussions and questioning are possible with personal selling.
- **Public relations** are activities intended to positively influence the attitudes of potential customers and the general public about the firm, its products, and the people working inside the firm. Examples of public relations efforts include news releases, toll-free telephone numbers, informational brochures, community relations, and support of social causes.
- **Sales promotion** consists of a variety of seller-initiated activities, with the intention of making advertising and personal selling more effective. Sales promotions support and unify other promotional efforts and include activities such as point-of-purchase displays, samples, contests, dealer incentives, demonstrations, sponsorships, and rebates.

Promotion represents everything the seller does to influence potential customers and convince them of the desirability of the firm's marketing program. Promotion strategy is an important component of the international marketing program because management needs to make target customers aware of the firm's marketing efforts. This is the only way potential customers can accurately assess the suitability and appropriateness of the firm's product and marketing program compared to those of the competition. Developing an appropriate promotional program requires a familiarity with and understanding of the foreign culture and the communication needs of the target market. Keeping potential customers informed is critical to a successful international marketing strategy.

International Promotion Strategy

Should international promotion be standardized or modified (customized) from country to country? As with the product, standardization offers numerous benefits associated with image, cost savings, media overlap, and worldwide recognition. Customization results in individualization that may be more conducive to the foreign environment.

Since the United States is a world leader in promotional techniques, much of the promotion around the world is patterned after the U.S. approach. The development of trends in international promotion follows the trends established in the United States. The high costs of customization, give management the incentive to standardize as much of the promotional program as possible. Therefore, promotion is the component of the international marketing mix that normally reflects the greatest amount of similarity from market to market. Generally, standardization should be sought and customization avoided unless absolutely necessary.

The decision to modify should be based not on geography but on the motivational patterns of the target market. Promotion should be customized only if consumers in different countries purchase similar products for entirely different reasons or the standardized communication is unacceptable in its existing form. If the need for a product differs or if culturally acceptable communications differ from country to country, then promotions must be specialized to accommodate the differences. Regardless of whether advertising is standardized or customized, the benefits and costs of the decision must be assessed.[1]

ADVERTISING STRATEGY

Because of the similarity in advertising techniques and media around the world, and the benefits of standardization, marketers usually are able to maintain uniformity in international advertising philosophies, objectives, and themes. Thus, the McDonald's Corporation's "I'm lovin' it" advertising theme and advertising clown mascot, Ronald McDonald, have been used almost universally. Beyond these basic considerations, ads may need market-specific tweaking because of various differences that may be encountered in language, acceptability of content, and appeal technique. For example, the management at Exxon Mobil Corporation had to remove the tiger from the "put a tiger in your tank" ads in Thailand, where the tiger is feared and not admired as a strong, powerful animal as in most other countries. Also, although the management at McDonald's Corporation changed Ronald McDonald's name to Donald McDonald in Japan, he has been portrayed as a sexy long-haired woman attired in a yellow dress with a red-and-white-striped blouse.[2] The international marketer needs to carefully assess the appropriateness of every ad before release.

To develop an effective advertising strategy, decisions must be made in at least seven areas.

- Objective—what the advertisement is intended to accomplish
- Budget—amount of money to be spent on advertising
- Message—content, wording, and appeal format
- Media—what instrument should be used to convey the message
- Legality—regulations and limitations
- Timing—when and how often an advertisement is placed
- Effectiveness—results of the advertisement

Objective

The first concern is what the international marketer wants to accomplish through the advertisement. Objectives can vary but must be specific. The more specific the objective, the easier it is to determine the effectiveness of the ad. Objectives generally fall into categories such as announcing information the customer needs to know (for example, sale dates or price), increasing customer traffic, reminding customers of the product's desirability, improving the image of the firm or product, and persuading customers to buy. For example, the objective of advertising in India, where McDonald's eateries are portrayed as family restaurants, is different than in the United States or the United Kingdom, where the firm is represented as a fast-food restaurant chain. Clearly delineated objectives are necessary to make informed decisions about the content of ads and the most appropriate medium or media to use.

Budget

The amount of money needed for advertising support and for a specific ad must be determined. The amount of money available will influence the media used and the timing of ads. An adequate amount of money must be budgeted to permit the desired objective to be accomplished. Budgets are determined in a variety of ways and may be based on a percent of sales (past, present, or anticipated future sales), competitors' advertising expenditures, incremental increases or decreases from previous expenditures, how much management believes it can afford after other expenses are met, and the objective to be accomplished. The most difficult method is setting a budget based on objectives, because the amount and nature of advertising required to achieve the objective may be difficult to determine. Also, whether accomplishing the objective justifies the expense must be determined. However, setting the budget based on objectives is likely to be the most effective method for achieving the most benefits per dollar of expenditure.

Message

The message refers to the content of the advertisement. What is said, how it is said, believability, method of presentation, layout, copy or script, location, appearance, font and point size, and appeal are all considerations affecting the message. The exact message needs to accommodate differences that may be encountered in the three areas of (1) language, (2) acceptability of content, and (3) appeal techniques.

Language

Differences in language necessitate message translations. Translations may be inaccurate; idioms in particular are difficult to translate accurately. Translations may be correct; however, the words used may have additional unintended meanings or may be misunderstood. Occasionally, translation will be unnecessary and English words or phrases can be retained in the ad. When English words are retained, the purpose is usually to enhance the product's image. As a generalization, however, translation is preferred because foreigners tend to view ads containing English words unfavorably.[3]

• An **idiom** is a group of words that together have a different meaning than the dictionary definitions of the individual words, and therefore, idioms cannot be translated literally from one language to another. Because of the unusual meaning

Exhibit 15.1 **Zorbas Ad**

A billboard advertisement for an alcoholic drink.

of the words, the intended meaning is impossible to convey correctly from a literal translation. For example, "break a leg" is an idiom used to wish someone good luck and "when pigs fly" is used to express a belief that something will never happen. If these two idioms were literally translated into another language, the intended meaning would be lost and the words would convey an incorrect connotation.

In Taiwan, the literally translated 1963 PepsiCo, Inc., slogan, "Come alive! You're in the Pepsi generation," unfortunately came out as "Pepsi will bring your ancestors back from the dead." Literal translations can be dangerous because of the unintentional meanings that may result. In these situations the international marketer needs to find a different combination of words that have a similar meaning in the foreign language. For example, the following Persian proverb would have to be reworded in English to convey the same meaning: "Walls have mice; mice have ears." The comparable English might be "Walls have ears." Other Persian proverbs that might not literally translate include "When angry, never make a decision," "Happiness is felt only after you work hard," and "Those who don't know and don't know that they don't know will remain ignorant forever."

• *Misunderstanding* results from a poor choice or arrangement of words that are otherwise correctly translated. The words convey an unintended meaning. For example, management at AB Electrolux, the Swedish firm that manufactures Electrolux vacuum cleaners, approved an ad for the U.S. market that read, "Nothing sucks like an Electrolux." The ad was intended to elucidate the exceptional suction that the cleaner possessed; the translators were unaware of the negative connotation of the word *sucks*. In 2004, a billboard advertisement intended to convey that Tecate beer was available in bottles in addition to cans was introduced by Labatt USA. The ad showed a chilled bottle of Tecate with the words, "Finally, a Cold Latina." The ad drew the ire of the Hispanic community because of the perception that the wording propagated a negative stereotype of Hispanic women as being promiscuous and overly sexual.[4] Although the ad had nothing to do with Hispanic women, the actual meaning turned out to be quite different than intended. When the management of Orange SA launched operations in the United Kingdom in 1994 with the slogan "The future's bright . . . the future's Orange," the turmoil in Northern Ireland was not adequately considered. The term *orange* is associated in Northern Ireland with the Orange Order, a Protestant religious and political organization with strong anti-Catholic policies that is loyal to the British crown. With the fighting that was going on between the Troubles (the Irish Republican Army) and the Orange, the implication to the Irish Catholic population was that the future is bright, the future is Protestant loyalists.[5]

• ***Translation errors*** occur when the wrong word or words are selected, causing the message to convey an entirely different meaning than originally intended. A myriad of examples of errors in translation exists. The following are examples of translation errors. The successful "Got Milk?" advertisement was created by Goodby Silverstein & Partners Advertising Agency for the California Milk Processor Board. The "Got Milk" slogan was eventually licensed to the National Milk Processor Board in 1998 and translated into Spanish. Unfortunately, the translation was done incorrectly, resulting in an ad asking Latino consumers, "Are You Lactating?"[6] A Braniff International Airways slogan, "Fly in leather," publicizing the airplane's seat upholstery, was incorrectly translated into Spanish. Instead of using the word *cuero* for leather, the word *piel*, which usually refers to skin, was selected. Thus, the ad translated as "Fly in your skin" or "Fly naked." Perdue Farms, Inc. erred when Frank Perdue's proclamation that "It takes a strong man to make a tender chicken" was translated into Spanish as "It takes an aroused man to make a chicken affectionate." When translating its slogan "finger-lickin' good" into Chinese, employees at the KFC Corporation accidentally chose words that meant "eat your fingers off." Employees at the Coca-Cola Company translated the Coca-Cola name into Chinese symbols that, when spoken, sound like Coca-Cola. However, depending on the dialect, the translated symbols meant "Bite the wax tadpole" or "Female horse stuffed with wax"; hardly the connotation desired. The mistake was not discovered until thousands of signs had been printed. The name was quickly changed to other Chinese characters that were phonetically similar and translated as "Happiness in the mouth." At Parker Pen Company, an ad containing the claim that the pen "Won't leak in your pocket and embarrass you" was incorrectly translated into Spanish in Mexico. The word "embarazar" picked for "embarrass" actually means "impregnate," so the translated ad read as "It won't leak in your pocket and make you pregnant."

Care must be exercised to assure translated messages read as intended in the foreign language. Having people who speak the foreign language involved in the translation process will help assure translations are accurate. Either of the two techniques discussed previously for translating questionnaires (see chapter 6), back translation and parallel translation, may also be employed to identify translation problems.

• ***Unintended meanings*** occur when words are translated correctly but a word may have more than one meaning and the recipient of the advertising attaches the wrong meaning. For example, the word *bass* can mean a type of fish, a low-pitched voice, or an instrument such as a bass drum or bass horn. Likewise, the word *project* can mean a plan, an undertaking, a complex of inexpensive apartments, or to stick out or throw forward. If the wrong meaning is attached, the intent of the advertisement will be misunderstood. In advertisements for the Parker Pen Company to be distributed in Latin America, the word *bola* was to be used to describe a ballpoint pen. *Bola* means "ball" in some Latin American countries; however, in one country, the meaning is "revolution," in another "a lie," and in another an obscenity. Fortunately for management, the differences in meaning were found before the ad was circulated.[7] Management at Hunt-Wesson, Inc., introduced the Big John brand in Quebec, the French-speaking province of Canada, under the name "Gros Jos." Although "Gros Jos" is a slang expression for "large breasts," ads were not adversely affected. In Spanish-speaking countries, low-tar cigarettes were advertised using the word *brea* for tar. While *brea* translates as "tar," the precise kind of tar is that used in paving streets. Therefore, to the Spanish reader, the ad encouraged people to smoke "low-asphalt" cigarettes.[8] The Dodge Dart was advertised in Spain with the catch phrase "Dodge is power." When translated, a word conveying the wrong meaning for power was used. The translated phrase insinuated that the driver was lacking, but seeking, sexual vigor. Sales were unexpectedly low because most Spanish males did not want to drive a car that impugned the driver as sexually inadequate.

Care must be taken to select the correct word also since some foreign languages are more precise in their grammar than English. For example, Greek has four words for the English word *if.* One word means "if" and what follows is true. Another word means "if" and what follows is false. If what follows could be true or false, a third word is used. Finally, a fourth word is employed when the speaker does not know whether what follows is true or false. Obviously, using the incorrect version of the word *if* could convey the wrong intent.

As with the other three problems with language, careful and meticulous translations are required. Possessing cultural knowledge, both factual and cognitive, and an appreciation of the foreign language is required to avoid these mistakes. Backward and parallel translation procedures can be employed to lessen the chances of erring.

Content Acceptability

Another area in which problems can be encountered is the content of the advertisement. Content is concerned with the layout, appearance, message, and related aspects of ad preparation. Problems can be encountered because of cultural differences, inappropriate content, and brand or product names.

• *Cultural differences* can cause an approach or theme employed in an ad to be inappropriate or unacceptable. The approach used violates acceptable cultural norms or fails to consider the differences in cultural preferences or procedures. An advertisement shown in Middle Eastern countries depicted a man talking on the telephone with his feet propped up on a desk. Although acceptable in most countries, showing the bottom of one's foot is considered an insult in countries such as Turkey and Iran. Another example of a failure to adequately consider the foreign culture occurred in an ad for a laundry detergent that contained three pictures intended to show cleaning ability. From left to right, the first picture showed soiled clothing, the second picture showed the box of laundry detergent, and the third picture showed a pile of clean clothes. In Middle Eastern countries people read from right to left rather than left to right. Thus, the advertisement was viewed in reverse of its intended meaning.[9] A newspaper ad for BiNoca talcum powder showing an apparently nude woman covered with talcum powder appeared in India. All of the critical areas of the woman's body were adequately covered; however, because of the difference in culture, the use of the female form in that manner was considered indecent and offensive.[10] Another example of cultural misunderstanding occurred in Peru. A laundry detergent containing stain-removing enzymes was introduced with an advertisement showing cartoon character enzymes with large mouths eating dirt off clothing. Peruvian women believed clothing had to be boiled to kill germs and make them as clean as possible. Unfortunately, boiling destroyed the enzymes, causing the product not to clean as promised.[11]

• *Inappropriate content* occurs when the advertisement has no meaning to the customer or conveys content that is unsuitable. For example, a television advertisement for a cosmetics firm was aired in Japan showing a statue of Nero, the Roman emperor, coming to life as a pretty woman wearing the firm's lipstick walked by. Unfortunately, the ad was not effective because Japanese women had no idea who Nero was. Nero was not a person the Japanese studied in school; therefore, most people were unaware of his historical significance.[12] The management of another firm included inappropriate content in an ad for a refrigerator in a Middle Eastern country. The ad showed an open refrigerator well stocked with a variety of foods. One of the foods was a large ham. Because Muslims do not eat pork, the ad was considered insensitive and unappealing.[13]

• *Inappropriate names* can convey the wrong meaning or idea. Apparently innocuous brand names can be offensive or inappropriate. For example, the management at Japan's second-largest tourist agency began receiving requests for unusual sex tours upon entering English-speaking countries. Advertisements boldly displayed the firm's name, "Kinki Nippon Tourist Company." In 2005, the management at the Hershey Company received negative press when a candy bar named "Cajeta Elegancita" was introduced to the U.S. Hispanic community. Although *cajeta* means candy in Mexico, in Argentina the word is also a derogatory slang term for the female vulva.[14] Advertisements for Pavian, a fruity drink sold by Bacardi & Company Limited, were not well received in Germany. The word *Pavian* means "baboon" in the German language.

Avoiding unacceptable content will require that the international marketer possess factual cultural knowledge about the foreign country. Having citizens of the foreign country review the advertisement is also desirable. People familiar with the foreign culture can help identify inappropriate and unacceptable content.

Appeal Technique

Technique is concerned with the way the advertisement is structured. The appeal employed must be acceptable. The plea approach and mechanics used in an advertisement should appeal to the customer and not be offensive or incorrect. Appeal techniques include decisions about the use of colors and the appropriateness of the approach and symbols employed.

- *Colors* can imply psychological and special meanings or are otherwise desirable or undesirable.[15] For example, dark red is a popular color in Hong Kong and might give advertisements visual appeal. However, dark red is the color of mourning in the Ivory Coast and is best avoided in ads. As noted in chapter 13, in the United States the color pink is associated with women; however, yellow is considered the most feminine color in most of the world. Green is frequently associated with cosmetics among the Dutch, French, and Swedes and would therefore be a desirable color to use in cosmetics ads in those countries.

- *Inappropriate appeals* refer to ad content that is objectionable or unacceptable. In Saudi Arabia, shopping is more of a social affair than in the United States and is frequently done by groups of people. An advertisement depicting a woman shopping alone would not be the best appeal. The management of the Coca-Cola Company was forced to stop airing a TV commercial in Australia for Coke Zero titled "Breakup as It Should Be." The country's Advertising Standards Bureau said the ad was inappropriate viewing for children and must be modified or discontinued. The ad was considered as degrading to women, promoting casual sex for men, and suggesting women should be available for sex whenever men want it.[16] In the parts of the Middle East where women's bodies must be covered, an advertisement showing a woman in a bikini would be inappropriate.

- *Symbols* are concerned with nonverbal cues and body language. An otherwise appropriate appeal can become an embarrassment because wrong symbols are employed. For example, the "OK" sign commonly flashed in the United States can mean zero, money, or a vulgarity, depending on the country. Ads containing people pointing a finger may be viewed as depicting rude behavior. Head nodding may not necessarily mean "yes" as in many countries. In Bulgaria, nodding the head up and down signifies "no" and shaking it from side to side means "yes." Nodding also may simply mean interest or that what was communicated was understood.

The best way to assure appeals are appropriate is for the international marketer to possess factual cultural knowledge about the foreign market. Knowing what appeals to a society and what does not will help avoid structuring an ad unacceptably. Using people from the foreign country to review the advertisement will also help identify potential problems.

Exhibit 15.2 **Loreal Ad**

The side of this building has been turned into a giant advertisement.

Media

The type of advertisement that will effectively carry the intended message to the customer must be determined. The media available can include radio, television, billboards, newspapers, magazines, public address systems, movies, direct mail, and electronic media. The appropriate medium or media will be influenced by availability, cost, the customers' media habits, and the effectiveness of the medium for presenting the message.

Availability

The availability of the various media can fluctuate from country to country. In some countries, restrictions are placed on certain kinds of television and radio advertising. For example, TV advertising and sponsorship of programs directed toward children below the age of twelve are prohibited in Sweden. In the United Kingdom, restrictions are placed on ads that might result in harm to children physically, mentally, or morally. Ads designed to exploit the natural credulity and sense of loyalty of children are also prohibited. German requirements are similar. In Greece, TV advertisements for toys are prohibited between 7:00 A.M. and 10:00 P.M., and a ban exists on all advertisements for war toys. In Germany and Denmark, advertising bans apply to certain kinds of toys. In France ads for mobile phones to children under twelve are prohibited. Advertising to children under twelve must meet a code of responsiblity in Canada except Quebec where all advertising is prohibited to children under thirteen.

Consider how availability would be affected in Ghana, where fifty-two languages and hundreds of dialects are spoken. The market would have to be segmented into as many as fifty-two groups, many of which are too small to be reached effectively. Doing so would also adversely affect cost. In other cases, insufficient media may make reaching all potential customers difficult. When the availability of desired media is restricted, alternative media are required. Where space is limited, circular billboards may be used, for example. Advertising between features in movie theaters may be more cost effective where media are heavily taxed. Where television and radio advertising are restricted, print media will be substituted, and the most effective and available media sought.

Cost

The costs of the different media vary. For an individual ad, television advertising is more expensive than newspaper advertising. However, more customers potentially can be reached by a single television ad than can be reached by a single newspaper ad. The TV ad can reach a national market, while the newspaper ad may be confined to a regional or local market. Thus, the cost of the TV advertisement is spread over more potential customers, making the cost per exposure (person seeing or hearing the ad) possibly lower than for the newspaper ad. Therefore, advertisers often talk about the cost per 1,000 potential customers exposed.

The amount of money budgeted for advertising must also be taken into consideration when making media choice decisions. In some countries, such as Austria, the government taxes advertising. In 2000, a new federal advertising tax of 5 percent of the cost of the advertising was assessed to advertising disseminated in Austria.

Although the agency commission is normally 15 percent as in the United States, prices are negotiable in many countries. Therefore, price can vary from country to country based on bargaining ability. In the final analysis, the media selected must be cost effective.

Customers' Media Habits

An assessment of what media the target group of customers expose themselves to must be made. Advertisements should be placed in the various media where customers will encounter them. If customers watch television a lot, then placing ads on TV makes sense. Placing ads in other media is a good use of resources if that is where the customers would likely become aware of them. For example, the management of McDonald's Corporation decided to pay hip-hop artists to write the Big Mac into the lyrics of their songs. Rappers are paid up to US$5.00 every time the words *Big Mac* are aired in a song on commercial radio or television.[17]

- *Suitability.* Depending on the product and the situation, some media are more fitting than others for expressing the desired appeal. For example, a product for which color is not important, such as a black automobile tire, can be effectively pictured in a newspaper where the print is black. The use of more colorful media would be unnecessary. Unless motion is essential to accomplishing the advertising objective, a TV advertisement is unlikely to portray the product effectively and would be undesirable. In a highly illiterate country, radio is more effective than a magazine. When literacy rates are low, verbal communications are more effective. Since ads must be self-explanatory, pictures and spoken messages are desirable.

• *Agency Selection.* Management must decide whether advertising should be done internally or an outside advertising agency employed. In general, unless the firm is large and has qualified staff, an ad agency is recommended. The personnel at an ad agency are experienced specialists and are less likely to make advertising mistakes. The international marketer has four alternative agency arrangements from which to choose.

- Use a coordinating agency that contracts with independent agencies in each country. Coordination is improved with the local agency, although the ability of the personnel in the coordinating agency to facilitate with each independent agency may vary. Since local agencies in each country are used, advertising mistakes are less likely to occur. Since advertising agencies exist in nearly every commercially significant country, a professional local presence in almost any country is possible.
- Employ a large international agency, which is likely to have branches in several foreign countries. Coordination will be improved, and agency personnel are more likely to be familiar with foreign conditions. The chances always exist that the agency will not have a presence in all the countries the international marketer has entered. However, with personnel in the foreign country, advertising mistakes are less likely to occur.
- Employ a local agency in each country. This option is more likely to result in appropriate ads that are acceptable to the foreign markets. However, the international marketer must interact with the personnel from the various agencies and from a distance, which can adversely affect coordination. Communication is complicated; the foreign agency personnel are less likely to be familiar with management's philosophy, and costs are likely to be higher.
- Use a domestic agency. Personnel at the domestic agency are likely to be familiar with management's philosophy of doing business and advertising preferences, particularly if the agency is used for domestic advertising. Familiarity of personnel in the domestic agency with conditions in the foreign market is more problematic. Personnel in the local agency may need assistance from support firms in the foreign market to assure ads are appropriate.

Legality

Many foreign governments regulate advertising more than is done in the United States. Care must be taken to assure no laws are being violated. Austria has, perhaps, the most restrictive advertising laws. For example, TV ads are allowed only between programs and may not be inserted in a program except for the broadcasting of sporting and similarly structured events. Advertising-free days exist. TV advertising may not exceed an average of 5 percent of the length of programs (3 minutes per hour) and 172 minutes per day for radio. Obtaining legal representation may be advisable before using any ad to assure laws are not violated.

Timing

Timing has two dimensions: Spacing and frequency. **Spacing** is concerned with the sequencing of ads during an advertising campaign. Decisions are made concerning which days of the week the ad is used or in which media the ad is placed.

For instance, should ads be placed each day of the week or every other day only or once a week? **Frequency** refers to how often an ad appears on any given day or in any given medium. For example, is increasing the number of ads each succeeding day preferable to placing an equal number of ads each day during the campaign? Decisions of this nature need to take into account ad recall and the decay rate of advertising. Ads need to be aired only often enough to maintain consumers' awareness. Additional ads waste money, and fewer ads may result in the consumers' failure to purchase the product.

Effectiveness

The "Louie the Lizard" advertisement for Budweiser beer was humorous and entertaining, but how effective was it? Effectiveness involves determining the value or worth of an advertisement. Did the ad achieve the desired objective? Every ad campaign should include some assessment of effectiveness. Although the ultimate goal of advertising is increased sales, effectiveness cannot be measured by how sales change. Other components of the controllable and noncontrollable international marketing environment can affect sales. Thus, measures to assess specific objectives are required. For example, if the objective is to increase store traffic, traffic before and after the ad is placed can be measured and compared. If traffic increased, the ad was effective. Increased traffic should contribute to increased sales. Commonly used measures of effectiveness include ad recall, assessment of the quality of the ad, and the effect of the ad on consumers' attitudes.

DIRECT MARKETING STRATEGY

Direct marketing is often used to build relationships with established customers. Databases can be built and special incentives and information generated and sent directly to people via postal mail or e-mail. Mailing lists of people who meet certain characteristics of the consumers of the firm's product can be purchased. Direct marketing is the preferred choice of large retailers such as Tesco PLC and J Sainsbury PLC. Direct marketing techniques that work domestically may not be suitable in the foreign market. Access to customers may be hindered because of conditions that exist in the foreign market. For example, if only a small percentage of the population owns computers, communicating by e-mail is restricted. Also, a lack of detail about the population may complicate purchases of mailing labels.

PERSONAL SELLING STRATEGY

When selecting members of the sales force, local people from the foreign country are recommended. Locals are more likely to be familiar with the culture and the acceptable procedures that pertain to personal business interaction. Expatriates from the parent company located domestically may be appropriate for certain foreign customers, occasionally for smaller firms, and when qualified intermediaries are not available. An **expatriate** (expat for short) is a person living in a different country than where raised or legally residing. Expatriates need to become familiar with business procedures and acceptable behavior in the foreign country to assure success. A more broad-based cosmopolitan individual will be sought when an expatriate is used. An expatriate also needs competency in the foreign language. Additionally, competent and qualified local people will be more acceptable to foreign buyers, and thus save money.

The criteria sought in foreign salespeople are the same as those for domestic salespeople. If foreigners are hired, they may require additional training. Often this involves transferring the foreigner to the United States, where selling skills are honed and the philosophy of the firm is instilled. After an appropriate training period, the sales rep is returned to the foreign market and assigned a territory. Occasionally, foreigners who have acquired U.S. citizenship or children of immigrants who speak the foreign language and are familiar with the foreign culture are hired as salespeople.

When expatriates are used, care must be exercised in the selection process. Since the sales rep will be living abroad and be alone in a new environment, emotional stability and maturity are necessary. If the individual has a family, the children will attend school with locals or travel to American schools when available. Interaction with foreigners is required, and the accustomed way of life changed. Being somewhat isolated in a foreign country can become depressing and upsetting. Women can also find their independence and flexibility affected, particularly in Middle Eastern countries such as Saudi Arabia, where women are segregated in social settings and not permitted to drive automobiles. Only secure people of strong character will enjoy living in a culture dissimilar to their own.

The expatriate salesperson should learn as much factual cultural knowledge as possible before going abroad. Orientation classes are provided in many firms to accomplish this. For example, in Germany, discussing business during lunch is inappropriate. Therefore, the lunch cannot be used for sales purposes in the same manner as in the United States. Also, when calling on prospects and customers in Germany, the last name and not the first should be used. Addressing people by their first name is reserved for close friends, unlike in the United States where the desire is to be on a first-name basis immediately after being introduced. Hard-sell techniques are considered impolite in Japan. Therefore, more persuasive selling procedures will need to be avoided there. Conflict avoidance is appropriate in most Asian countries. These and other facts affecting a sales rep's behavior should be learned to prevent embarrassment and inappropriate behavior that could jeopardize the sale.

As foreign sales grow, the size of the sales force tends to increase and adjustments in sales force structure will be needed. For geographically structured firms, this will result in smaller sales territories or increased divisions of labor as sales reps specialize by customer or product line. For product-structured firms, territories will have to be subdivided to keep individual sales work levels within reasonable limits.[18]

As a generalization, personal forms of promotion receive more attention internationally than impersonal forms. In the United States, the trend is reversed. Therefore, advertising tends to be relatively more important in the United States, while personal selling tends to be relatively more important internationally.

PUBLIC RELATIONS STRATEGY

Public relations efforts should not be ignored in international markets. News releases and free press should be used to inform the public about activities undertaken by the firm that may help make people view the company and its products more favorably. Newsworthy activities and events must be communicated to the public. Other public relations activities such as toll-free telephone numbers and informational sheets can also be used successfully.

SALES PROMOTION STRATEGY

Sales promotions that are successful in one country may be unsuccessful in another foreign country. Game cards are popular in the United States. The consumer collects game pieces or follows instructions on cards distributed at the point of sale. Successful customers win merchandise or money. The management of Esso Nederland B.V. considered a game that was successful in the United States to be too sophisticated for the Dutch. A moon race game was substituted, in which moons were rubbed off a playing card. This game was considered more appropriate for the Dutch. In Great Britain, the management of Royal Dutch Shell PLC offered consumers "Promotion Commotion" vouchers each time they purchased petrol at Shell stations. The vouchers could be collected and exchanged for a variety of merchandise.

Trade shows are another popular form of sales promotion used internationally. In general, a greater use of trade shows occurs internationally than in the United States. Trade shows permit buyers to interact with a large number of sellers in a single location. International trade shows are usually held in large cities and are industry specific. Every year, thousands of trade shows are scheduled in cities worldwide with more than a hundred considered to be major shows. These global trade fairs tend to be held in major cities in the United States, Europe, and Asia.

CHAPTER SUMMARY

International promotion strategy entails decisions about advertising, personal selling, sales promotion, public relations, and direct marketing. Promotion is that part of marketing strategy that exhibits the greatest amount of standardization from country to country. Decisions to customize promotion should be based on consumers' motivational patterns and not on geography.

International marketers strive to standardize advertising philosophies, objectives, and themes when possible. Adjustments must be made to accommodate cultural and language differences. An effective international advertising strategy requires attention to advertising objectives, budget, message, media, legality, timing, and effectiveness. The content of the advertisement is critical and can result in problems if not carefully developed. Problems can result from language differences (translation errors), content errors, and mistakes in appeal. The appropriate media selection is influenced by availability of the various media, media cost, effectiveness for presenting the product, and the customers' media habits. Message-related problems can be avoided best by the international marketer's having good factual and cognitive cultural knowledge. Consulting with people from the foreign market and doing backward and parallel translations will also help. Since advertising regulations exist in many countries, the legality of messages needs to be assessed. When ads are placed, their frequency and spacing are also of concern. Some measure of the effectiveness of advertising is needed to help assess how successfully advertising objectives have been achieved.

When advertising is not done in-house, an advertising agency must be employed. The agency arrangement selected will be influenced by considerations such as cost, coordination required, and familiarity with the foreign market.

Personal selling is best done by locals in the foreign country because of their familiarity with the culture and knowledge of acceptable business procedures and conditions. When expatriates are used, appropriate training, cultural education, and screening for emotional maturity are required.

Sales promotions, public relations, and direct marketing are also used internationally. Techniques need to be examined for compatibility and appropriateness with the foreign culture. Effective communications with target customers is just as important in the foreign market as in the domestic market.

KEY TERMS

Advertising
Direct marketing
Expatriate
Frequency
Idiom
Personal selling
Promotion
Public relations
Sales promotion
Spacing
Translation errors

REVIEW QUESTIONS

1. What is promotion? How is developing an international promotional strategy different than developing one domestically?
2. List and explain the seven components of an effective international advertising strategy.
3. Go to the library and locate an ad in a foreign magazine for a product with which you are familiar. What is similar and what is different in that ad compared to the U.S. ad for the same product?
4. In what ways can a different language in the foreign market adversely affect an advertisement?
5. How can errors in translation be avoided in international advertisements? Think back to chapter 6 and the discussion concerning questionnaire construction.
6. How can the self-reference criterion (SRC) (see chapter 7) adversely affect content acceptability of international advertisements?
7. List and explain the criteria that influence the media selection process.
8. What advertising agency alternatives are available to the international marketer? When would each alternative be appropriate?

9. What problems should management guard against when utilizing expatriate salespeople?
10. A contest based on the Parker Brothers Monopoly game was used recently by the McDonald's Corporation in the United States. Suggest reasons why the same sales promotion may not be appropriate for the firm's sixteen restaurants in Croatia.

NOTES

1. Greg Harris, "Factors Influencing the International Advertising Practices of Multinational Companies," *Management Decision* 34 (6) (1996): 5–11.

2. "No Clowning: Ronald Becomes a McHottie!" WorldNetDaily, September 24, 2005, http://www.wnd.com/?pageId=32508.

3. Marinel Gerritsen, "English in Dutch Commercials: Not Understood and Not Appreciated," *Journal of Advertising Research* 40 (3) (July/August 2000): 17–35.

4. Rebecca Taylor, "Billboard Offends Latino Community," Fox 11AZ.com, Tucson, AZ, May 12, 2004, http://www.fox11az.com/news/local/stories/kmsb_local_billboard_051104.1b29f9e75.html.

5. Tex Texin, "Marketing Translation Mistakes," http://www.i18nguy.com/translations.html.

6. Juan Tornoe, "Lost in Translation: When Bad Hispanic Advertising Happens to Good Companies," LatPro Network, November 12, 2007, http://network.latpro.com/profiles/blogs/lost-in-translation-when-bad.

7. David A. Ricks, *Blunders in International Business,* 4th ed. (Malden, MA: Blackwell, 2006), 91.

8. Ibid., 94.

9. Ibid., 60–61.

10. Ibid., 67.

11. Ibid., 71.

12. Ibid., 51.

13. Ibid., 69.

14. Tornoe, "Lost in Translation."

15. Thomas J. Madden, "Managing Images in Different Cultures: A Cross-National Study of Color Meanings and Preferences," *Journal of International Marketing* 8 (4) (2000): 90–107.

16. Kelvin Healey, "Coke Pulls TV Ad Where Women Seen as Sexual Toys for Men," *Herald Sun,* May 4, 2009, http://www.news.com.au/heraldsun/story/0,21985,25424338-662,00.html.

17. "'Return of the Mac'—Coming Soon," BBC News, March 29, 2005, http://news.bbc.co.uk/2/hi/business/4389751.stm.

18. Jeffrey E. Lewin and Wesley J. Johnston, "International Salesforce Management: A Relationship Perspective," *Journal of Business and Industrial Marketing* 12 (3/4) (1997): 32–48.

16 Countertrade

Countertrade is a marketing technique that has been used by governments to obtain needed products for years. For example, in the 1950s and 1960s the U.S. government used barter to sell agricultural products acquired through the Department of Agriculture's price support programs. Business firms can also engage in countertrade with other businesses and government purchasing agencies. Anytime the demand for products exceeds a nation's ability to obtain hard currency to pay, removing monetary payments via countertrade becomes a viable alternative. After all, barter was the original way of doing business before money existed. That is, when one farmer who grew only wheat also wanted to eat beans, that farmer would have to locate a bean farmer who wanted wheat. The two farmers would decide what amounts of the two foods would be of comparable worth to trade and then swap those amounts.

One of the best-known countertrades involves Pepsi-Cola and Stolichnaya vodka. Pepsi-Cola is a brand name owned by PepsiCo, Inc., a U.S. company that was founded in 1965 through the merger of Pepsi-Cola Company and Frito-Lay, Inc. Subsequently, PepsiCo acquired Tropicana Products, Inc., Quaker Oats Company, and the Gatorade Company. It is recognized as the world leader in convenient foods and beverages, with sales in nearly 200 countries and territories.

The preparation for this historic countertrade deal dates back to 1959. Farsighted management, contemplating the possibility of eventual Pepsi sales in the Soviet Union, arranged to exhibit Pepsi at the American National Exhibition in Moscow. Pictures were made and publicized of Soviet Premier Nikita Khrushchev drinking Pepsi when he and U.S. Vice President Richard Nixon visited the exhibit.

In 1972, a countertrade agreement was made between PepsiCo and Soyuzplodoimport Federal State Enterprise, the state-run trade organization and middleman that distributed and owned the trademark rights to Stolichnaya vodka. The management at PepsiCo agreed to ship Pepsi syrup to Soyuzplodoimport, to be bottled and sold under the Pepsi-Cola brand name, in exchange for an equivalent value of Stolichnaya vodka and exclusive rights to market Stolichnaya in the United States. This countertrade agreement made Pepsi-Cola the first foreign product sold in the Soviet Union. Subsequent agreements were signed with representatives of the Soviet Union in 1988, when the first Pepsi advertisement was run on Soviet TV, and again in 1990. Stolichnaya was the fifth-most-popular brand of vodka in the United States in 2006, with sales of about US$375 million.

Sources: Based in part on information from PepsiCo, "Company: Our History," http://www.pepsico.com/Company/Our-History.html#block_2008; Frank Gray, "Countertrade Still Thrives," fDimagazine.com, December 8, 2003, http://www.fdimagazine.com/news/fullstory.php/aid/458/Countertrade_still_thrives.html; Jason Bush, "Vodka Wars Spill into the U.S.," *Business Week*, April 7, 2006, http://www.businessweek.com/globalbiz/content/apr2006/gb20060407_359060.htm?chan=globalbiz_europe_companies; PepsiCo, "Company," http://www.pepsico.com/Company.html; William F. Buckley Jr., "Pepsi at the Summit," *National Review*, June 24, 1988, http://www.highbeam.com/library/doc0.asp?DOCID=1G1:6794725&ctrlInfo=Round20%3AMode20a%3ADocFree%3AResult&ao=; Astrid Wendlandt, "Struggle for Cristall Vodka," Friends and Partners, http://www.friends-partners.org/oldfriends/spbweb/times/221-222/struggle.html; and Maria Ermakova, "Stoli Owner SPI Rejects Pesce Bid, Wants Distribution Partner," Bloomberg.com, August 11, 2008, http://www.bloomberg.com/apps/news?pid=newsarchive&sid=aWP_aMElayjk.

CHAPTER OBJECTIVES

After reading this chapter, you should

- know what countertrade is;
- understand why countertrade is a way of doing business internationally;
- know the advantages and risks of using countertrade;
- know the forms of countertrade that may be used in international markets; and
- appreciate how to manage countertrade transactions.

COUNTERTRADE IN PERSPECTIVE

Countertrade is a term used to describe the exchange of products or services for other products or services. That is, payment is made in products, services, or both instead of cash. Countertrade is a means by which international trade may be accomplished in nations that are experiencing balance of payments problems, that suffer from severe inflation, have weak or blocked (nonconvertible) currencies, and have insufficient amounts of foreign exchange. Countertrade becomes increasingly attractive during periods of worldwide tight money and high interest rates. Managers who engage in international marketing outside Western Europe, Canada, and Japan may encounter requests to countertrade.

Countertrade is in reality barter trade and is the only way trade can be accomplished when money is not available to facilitate conventional trade. Although barter trade has always existed and was practiced prior to the modern-day monetary economy, countertrade became a widespread way for doing business with Russia and the Eastern bloc nations after World War II. The Russians sought countertrade because of a shortage of hard currency to pay for imports. Additionally, when global conditions of high unemployment, inflation, and recession occur, government leaders may attempt to force trading partners to accept trade on their own terms to help abrogate imbalances that occur. When this happens, countertrade can also become a fashionable way, and sometimes the only way, of doing business internationally.

Countertrade emerged as an acceptable way of doing business in the late 1970s. During the 1980s, countertrade continued to expand as trade with Russia and the Eastern European countries expanded in spite of the weak currencies in those countries. The use of countertrade declined during the 1990s with the fall of the Berlin Wall and the emerging of market economies in the Eastern European countries. The declining value of the U.S. dollar and subsequent strengthening of weaker currencies during this time were also contributing factors. However, at the end of the twentieth century and into the 2000s, countertrade rebounded as a result of the weakening currencies in some Asian and Latin American countries.[1] With these countries encountering difficulties paying for imports, the need to countertrade grew. While countertrade has declined in those parts of the world that previously have made extensive use of the technique, utilization is strengthening for financing government procurement in developing countries.[2] Countertrade will continue to thrive wherever hard currency is scarce and the need exists to obtain essential products.

Although no statistics are collected on countertrade transactions, experts estimate that the value of countertrade transactions has remained fairly constant at 20 to 25 percent of worldwide trade.[3] That means that the value of worldwide countertrade activity is somewhere around US$500 billion; more than the dollar value of all the exports from the United States. Approximately 130 countries throughout the world, mostly third-world countries, require countertrade in one form or another.[4]

Because of the amount of countertrade business occurring internationally, international marketers who avoid countertrading forgo the potential of expanding markets and gaining additional business. A tremendous missed opportunity may result. Because of the nontraditional character and potential risks involved, countertrade may not be appropriate or beneficial for every business. Management needs to carefully assess the pros and cons of each situation before making the decision to countertrade. However, even though the international marketer may not be seeking countertrade, management may be confronted with requests for countertrade. For example, if the firm is a subcontractor and the management of the prime contractor decides to enter into a countertrade, management may be requested by the prime contractor's management to take partial payment in countertraded merchandise. And, for some firms, such as Monsanto Company, which participates in countertrade transactions in excess of US$200 million each year, countertrade is a significant way of doing business.[5]

REASONS FOR USING COUNTERTRADE

The reasons for using countertrade are not much different than those for cash transactions. The underlying reason for engaging in any business transaction, whether cash or countertrade, is to increase sales and profits. Countertrade is a way for the international marketer to expand the firm's market through increased exports. Entrance into new export markets that are unavailable with conventional cash transactions is possible via countertrade. Through countertrade, additional business is possible that, otherwise, would be bypassed.

Seeking exports by countertrade can be a means of gaining that little edge over the less aggressive or more hesitant competition. If these markets are entered first, benefits such as image, name recognition, and reputation accrue that later-arriving competitors often find difficult to overcome.

Using countertrade can also help sustain business during economic slowdowns. When sales are flat, countertrade can be used to help provide a lift in orders, reduce inventories, and keep workers employed. Also, countertrade will be required if entrance is desired in those countries that make countertrade a requisite for doing business. Without countertrade, these markets would be inaccessible, resulting in the forgoing of the potential sales each would provide.

The following are reasons why the international marketer may encounter requests from potential buyers to use countertrade in certain countries:

- Employment can be maintained. Products that are exchanged in the countertrade must be produced. This permits workers to remain employed who might otherwise have to be laid off or terminated because of a lack of sales created by currency problems with the central bank in a potential customer's country.
- Government leaders are attempting to prevent or eliminate balance of payment deficits.
- Governments are too poor to pay for imports. Sources of money do not exist because of the government's poor credit rating or inability to borrow or to receive drawing rights from the International Monetary Fund.
- Insufficient foreign exchange is available in the country's banking system to pay for imports. Either the seller gets in a queue and completes the sale at some time in the future when foreign exchange becomes available, or the seller engages in countertrade if the sale is desired immediately.
- Trade can be continued when nonconvertible or blocked currencies would obstruct trade under conventional terms.

ADVANTAGES OF COUNTERTRADE

Countertrading has certain advantages. Although most of these advantages accrue to the buyer, the primary advantage to the seller is the ability to complete the sale. The seller can keep workers employed, increase sales, and potentially profit from the sale or use of the products received in the countertrade. Other advantages of countertrade for the seller include the following:

- Cash is released for other uses. Since cash need not change hands, this money can be used in other ways.
- Excess production and inventory can be reduced. Products with excessive inventory are prime candidates to be offered for countertrade. In this way, an inventory that is losing value can be converted to a receivable on the financial statement.

- Markets can be entered without the need for development. That is, arranging a distribution network is unnecessary. The firm receiving the product in countertrade accomplishes the distribution process through established channels or undertakes the selling and distribution functions.
- New markets can be entered that cannot be cultivated through conventional financing. Countertrade may be the only method that permits market entry where nonconvertible and blocked currencies exist.
- The real transaction price can be disguised. If the products involved in the countertrade are not assigned cash value or are valued at or below cost rather than at list price, taxes might be reduced. Import tariffs will be lower, for example. Also, if the product received in the countertrade is used as an input in the production process, the cost of the manufactured product can be reduced.

PERILS OF COUNTERTRADE

Countertrade presents considerable peril for the international marketer. The fact that countertrade is a nontraditional means of conducting business, along with management's lack of familiarity with the process, can cause apprehension. The danger of using countertrade should not be underestimated and must be adequately considered when contemplating a countertrade transaction. The following are potential hazards of countertrade.

First, if the product received in the countertrade is delivered by the foreign firm over an extended time, the international marketer has no guarantee of receiving complete compensation. Promised products may not be shipped, and shipments could be delayed. Even substitute products could be sent when future conditions prohibit shipping of the agreed product. The countertrade partner's business conditions could change in a way that adversely affects the original agreement. Also, the value of products received over time could decline and cause the income received as the products are resold to be appreciably lower than anticipated.

Second, in the case of a buyback (capital equipment is shipped in countertrade for output from that equipment; see page 305) involving technological products, the international marketer may be equipping the foreigner to be a competitor in the domestic market.

A third hazard is that negotiating and completing a countertrade agreement is more complicated and complex than it is for straight cash-for-products transactions. Sales agreements can be more complicated. Additional contracts may be required when products are "switched," and costs may increase because of additional legal considerations. Also, disposing of received products can create additional problems and costs.

Fourth, products received from a countertrade partner may be difficult to resell. Products received may be poor in quality by U.S. standards. Inferior products may have to be sold at a discount from their normal market value and can adversely affect anticipated profits. Also, the items offered for countertrade are frequently products that the foreign firm has difficulty selling. No need exists to countertrade products that can be easily sold on the world market. Consequently, products offered for countertrade may be oversupplied. Therefore, the management in the U.S. firm may find little or no demand for the products received in the countertrade.

The fifth danger of countertrade is that products received from a countertrade partner may be unrelated to the firm's business. Therefore, the marketing structure of the firm may not be conducive to the reselling process. The products will not fit well with the firm's distribution network. For example, screwdrivers received in countertrade by a firm in the clothing business could hardly be sold through conventional channels and retail outlets.

Finally, products received from a countertrade partner that are used internally may disrupt established supply channels. Vendors can become disgruntled when business is disrupted and they learn that some of their business has been diverted to a foreign firm. Long-standing supplier relationships that took years to develop could be jeopardized.

The countertrade opportunity, along with potential perils, must be assessed prior to entering into any agreement. The return compared to the exposure must be acceptable. Although the perils may exceed the benefits in numbers, the benefits may be greater when weights are attached. The terms and conditions under which the countertrade is conducted can make all the difference. For example, when inferior quality or over-stocked products are offered, negotiating an increase in the quantity received can offset the estimated loss in income. One-and-a-half-million dollars worth of products may have to be received and resold at a lower price to recoup the million-dollar value of the products that were exchanged in the countertrade.

Forms of Countertrade

While each possible countertrade alternative differs in arrangement and complexity, all involve methods of compensation other than cash. Unfortunately, unanimity of nomenclature is lacking; a variety of terms is used to define the various countertrade techniques. Here, the basic countertrade procedures will be identified with commonly encountered names.

The basic forms of countertrade presently in use can be conveniently classified into two categories, depending upon whether or not cash is exchanged in the transaction. In all forms of countertrade the international marketer receives compensation either directly from the buyer, indirectly from a third party, or indirectly by using the product received within the firm. Exhibit 16.1 shows the most common countertrade alternatives.

In those forms of countertrade in which money is involved, the purpose is simply to facilitate the transaction. The money provides the countertrade partners security if either party reneges. If the countertrade should encounter problems, no one loses

Exhibit 16.1 **Forms of Countertrade**

Money is not exchanged	**Money is exchanged**
Barter arrangements	*Clearing arrangements*
Bilateral barter (classical barter)	Counterpurchase (parallel barter)
Triangular barter	Precompensation
	Blocked currency
Compensation arrangements	
Buyback	

property without the possibility of receiving financial compensation. This reduces the risk associated with shipping the product and receiving nothing in return. When money is involved, the currency acts only as a lubricant or precipitator for the transaction. When the countertrade is complete, the money returns to the original owner and no one gains or loses in terms of cash received or paid.

BILATERAL BARTER COUNTERTRADE

A **bilateral barter,** also known as an offset, is countertrade in the classical sense. Bilateral barter countertrade occurs when the management in two firms agrees to exchange products or services. No money is involved, and the amount of products or services that are exchanged is determined by an exchange ratio that is set by negotiations. The trading value of each product or service is set in terms of the other product or service. For example, assume the two products being countertraded are pens and screwdrivers and both participants agree that a pen is worth US$1.00 on the market and a screwdriver is worth US$2.00. Then, for whatever dollar value involved in the barter, two pens would have to be exchanged for every screwdriver to assure the participants receive equal worth. The management of the U.S. firm obtains money by selling the product or service received, or by using the product or service in the business. Bilateral barter is the simplest form of countertrade and is illustrated in Exhibit 16.2.

Exhibit 16.2 **Bilateral Barter Countertrade**

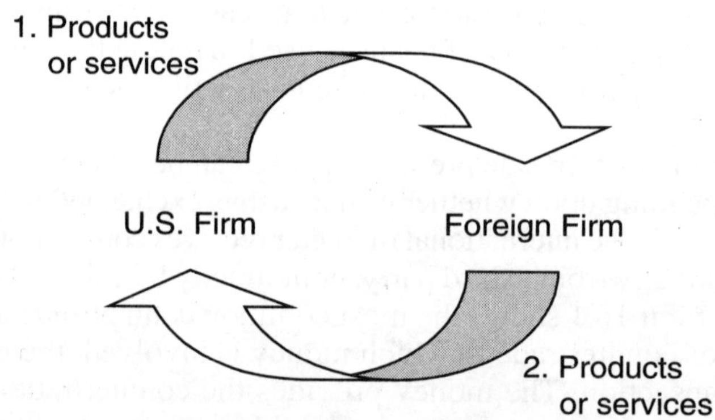

TRIANGULAR BARTER COUNTERTRADE

Triangular barter countertrade is similar to bilateral barter countertrade except three firms are involved. If the management of the U.S. firm does not want the products or services offered by the management of the foreign firm, a third participant is required. The management of this firm will accept these products or services in exchange for some other product or service the management of the U.S. firm needs. In this way, products or services are relocated to another buyer that needs them in exchange for products or services that are acceptable for the management of the U.S. firm. Sometimes, the third firm may be willing to pay the U.S. firm money for the value of the products received from the foreign firm instead of paying with its products or services.

Exhibit 16.3 **Triangular Barter Countertrade**

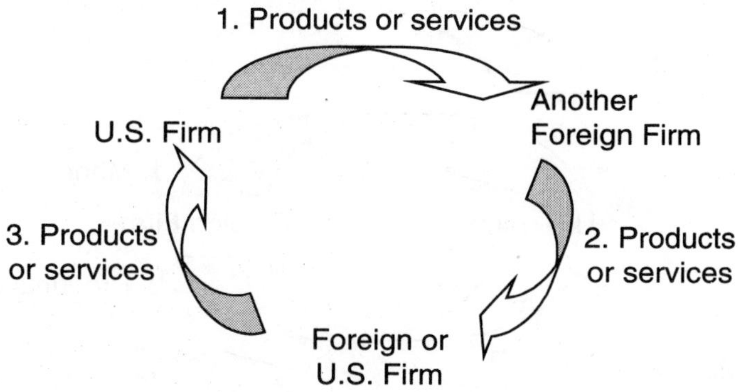

Although locating three parties willing to participate in a countertrade is more difficult than agreements between two parties, this may be necessary to accomplish the contract. Barter with more than three parties participating is also possible. Triangular barter countertrade is illustrated in Exhibit 16.3.

BUYBACK COUNTERTRADE

The management in the U.S. firm sells products or services (usually capital equipment, expertise, or technology) to a foreign buyer. The foreign buyer repays over an agreed time with an equivalent value of products manufactured with the purchased equipment or from the production process the expertise or technology helped establish or improve. **Buyback** countertrade is illustrated in Exhibit 16.4.

Exhibit 16.4 **Buyback Countertrade**

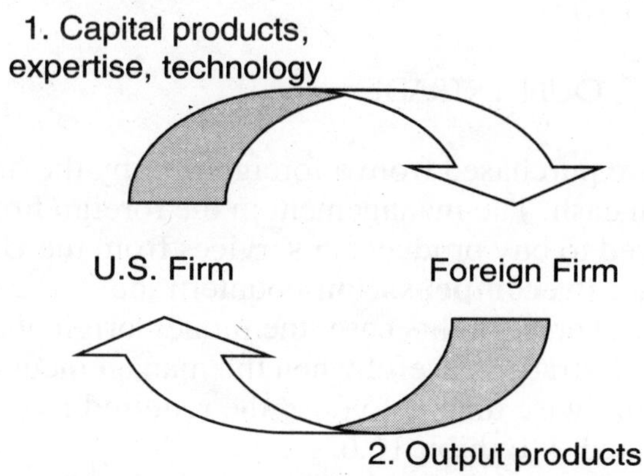

COUNTERPURCHASE COUNTERTRADE

The U.S. seller is required to purchase a given percentage (maybe as much as 100 percent) of the contract value in other products or services from the foreign buyer. The purchases are made in cash and may be separated in time. Each transaction involves money and is,

Exhibit 16.5 **Counterpurchase Countertrade**

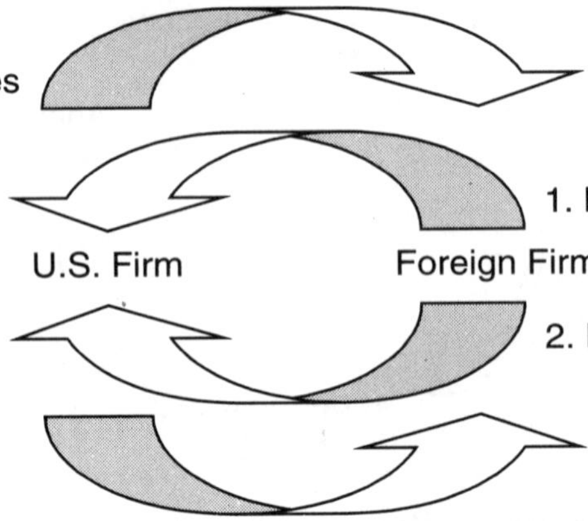

in essence, a separate business transaction, although the two are tied together in a contract. Therefore, the management in each firm is both a buyer and seller at some point.

Counterpurchase countertrade provides more security and less risk than barter arrangements since payments are made in cash. For the management of the U.S. firm, the agreement is more secure. Should the management of the foreign firm be unable to deliver the counterpurchased products or services, the management of the U.S. firm can retain the money received for the products shipped during the first phase of the countertrade. The second phase of the counterpurchase countertrade requires the money received from the first phase be used to pay for the products shipped from the foreign firm. When the counterpurchase countertrade is complete, the money has been repaid to the foreign firm where it originated. Thus, the money serves as a facilitation mechanism to accomplish the countertrade. Counterpurchase countertrade is illustrated in Exhibit 16.5.

PRECOMPENSATION COUNTERTRADE

Products or services are purchased from a foreign firm by the management of a U.S. firm and payment is in cash. The management in the foreign firm agrees to use all or part of the cash received to buy products or services from the U.S. firm immediately or at some future time. **Precompensation** countertrade is the same as counterpurchase countertrade in reverse. In this case, the money originates with the U.S. firm. Precompensation countertrade is useful when the management of the foreign firm is underfinanced or is otherwise unable to raise the required money. Precompensation countertrade is illustrated in Exhibit 16.6.

BLOCKED CURRENCY COUNTERTRADE

The management of the U.S. firm sells products or services to a foreign firm and receives the foreigner's currency. Because of currency restrictions or the nonconvertibility of the currency, the foreign currency cannot be repatriated and must remain in

Exhibit 16.6 **Precompensation Countertrade**

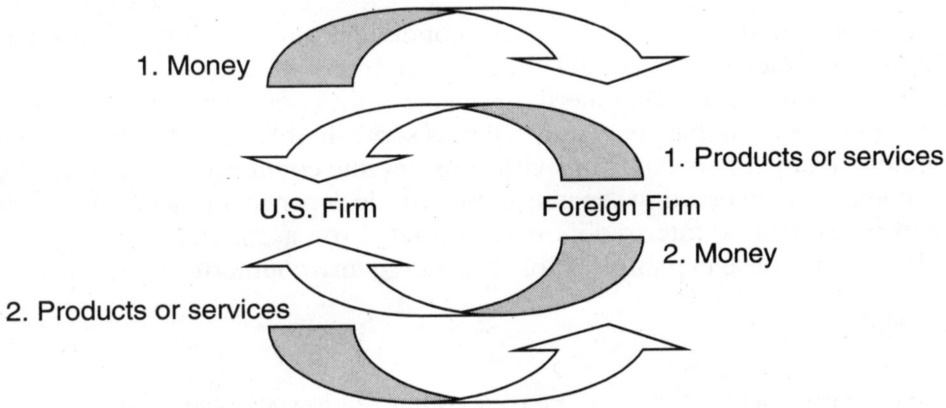

Exhibit 16.7 **Blocked Currency Countertrade**

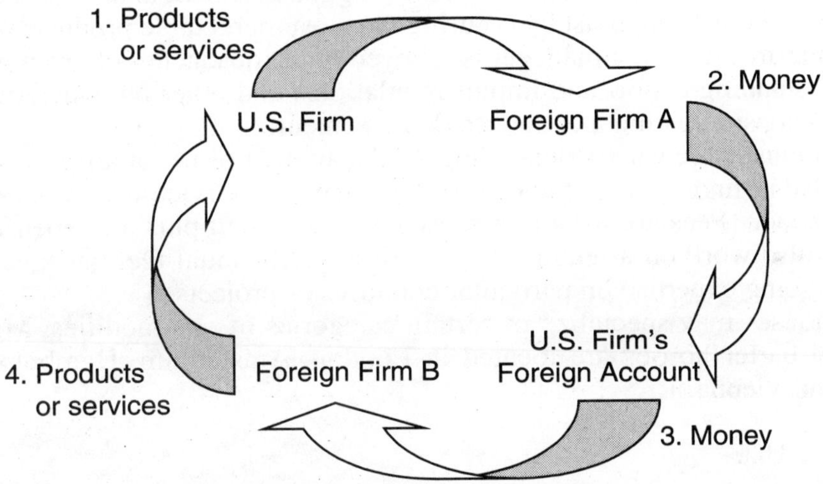

the foreign country. Therefore, the management of the U.S. firm buys other products or services from another firm in that country with the nonconvertible foreign currency. The purchased products or services are then exported to the U.S. firm. **Blocked currency** countertrade is illustrated in Exhibit 16.7.

FACILITATING COUNTERTRADE

The international marketer can engage in countertrade in one of three ways.

1. Create a countertrade department within the firm.
2. Employ a barter house.
3. Employ a trading house, switch house, or bank.

COUNTERTRADE DEPARTMENT

A countertrade department is not usually economical unless sufficient countertrade business is available, and personnel skilled in countertrade exist in-house or can be hired. With lesser amounts of countertrade business, the countertrade staff is frequently part of the purchasing department and can thus serve double duty. Normally, only the management in larger firms or firms with considerable countertrade business find the risk and complexity of creating separate countertrade departments acceptable. Smaller firms and infrequent countertraders usually find using a countertrade expert more desirable than in-house capabilities for facilitating any countertrade business.

BARTER HOUSE

A **barter house** provides the services of a countertrade specialist who puts together countertrade contracts and is involved from negotiations to disposal of the countertraded products or services. Although a barter house may act as a principal and buy for resale, the usual arrangement is as an agent representing management in the transaction.

A barter specialist can assist by securing the most marketable products or services on the best terms. Also, the manager is relieved of the headaches of arranging a contract, understanding export and import regulations, and other bureaucratic red tape involved in consummating a countertrade agreement.

The specialist's fee varies, depending on the amount of negotiating involved and the difficulty in finding a customer for the product or service that was received in the countertrade. Fees are usually assessed as a per diem plus all expenses. Barter specialists also work on a retainer basis. For a fixed annual fee, the specialist will provide ongoing expertise on particular countries or projects.

Barter houses may specialize in certain categories of commodities. Most of the specialized barter houses are located in London, Amsterdam, Hamburg, Zurich, Munich, and Vienna.

SWITCH HOUSE

Switch houses or intermerchants help management to dispose of countertraded products. A variety of services are provided that include locating buyers, arranging transportation, obtaining insurance, securing warehousing, and assisting with financing. Commissions can be as high as 50 percent of the value of the product or service received in the countertrade, depending on the services provided and the difficulty in selling the merchandise. Frequently, the switch house takes a commission as the difference between what the customer pays for the products or services and what the seller is willing to accept. For example, assume the management of a U.S. firm that receives products or services in countertrade is willing to accept cash at 70 percent of the value of the merchandise. If a customer can be found that is willing to pay cash at 75 percent of value, the switch house earns a 5 percent commission.

As evidenced by this example, countertraded products or services may have to be discounted to attract a buyer. The international marketer must, therefore, estimate the price at which the merchandise can be sold and build an adequate buffer into the price of the products or services being countertraded. Thus, the value of received products or services may have to be sufficiently greater than the value of shipped products or services to compensate for the discounting required to secure a buyer.

To minimize the chances of financial loss because of the need to discount prices of countertraded merchandise, products and services that can be easily sold or used within the firm should be identified. Generally, technological products should be avoided, particularly from developing countries, because of the frequent lack of capability of firms to produce sophisticated, quality products. Raw materials and foodstuffs are considered to be the easiest to resell, and therefore, the most desirable countertraded merchandise to receive. Because raw materials and foodstuffs are relatively easier to resell, commissions charged by countertrade specialists tend to be lower for these products. The international marketer should seek these products when obtainable.

COUNTERTRADE ASSISTANCE

As just discussed, countertrade specialists can assist with developing countertrade arrangements. These specialists can also help locate buyers for countertraded merchandise after the fact. Suppose a contract was negotiated for products that are not really wanted. A countertrade specialist can be contacted after the sale to help locate another buyer before the merchandise is shipped or during shipment. Products that are en route to the U.S. seller can be diverted to another buyer identified by a barter house or switch house prior to arrival. The specialist will prepare new contracts and transship the merchandise. Helping the seller obtain money or other products or services in this manner for the merchandise received in the countertrade is called **switching.** Switching is illustrated in Exhibit 16.8.

The U.S. government considers countertrade to be contrary to free trade, however, it provides information and assistance about countertrade through the Financial Services and Countertrade Division, Office of Finance, of the U.S. Department of Commerce's International Trade Administration. Although the U.S. government generally discourages such transactions, in 1982, the Export Trading Company Act was passed, which enables U.S. banks to provide financing to support countertrade. The Export Trading Company Act repealed the provisions of the 1933 Glass-Steagall Act, which forbade U.S. banks to engage in countertrade. **Bank credit countertrade** that is now legal has helped make countertrade purchases easier for foreigners that previously were unable to participate without the assurances given by a bank. When a barter arrangement was unacceptable and neither party was willing to provide the cash for a counterpurchase countertrade or precompensation countertrade, the sale did not occur. When this happened, the foreign buyer looked elsewhere for a countertrade partner, and U.S. firms lost business to foreign competitors. In bank credit countertrade, the U.S. bank lends money to the foreign buyer to facilitate the transaction. From this point the transaction is a classical counterpurchase countertrade in terms of the exchanges of cash and products. When the countertrade is complete, the foreign firm repays the money received via the counterpurchase to the bank. Bank credit countertrade is illustrated in Exhibit 16.9.

Exhibit 16.8 **Switching**

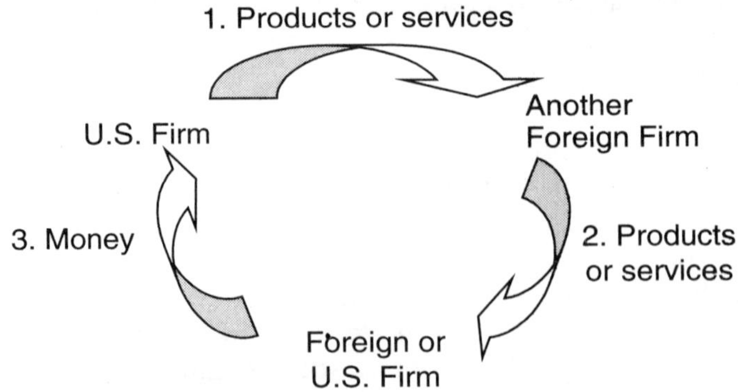

Exhibit 16.9 **Bank Credit Countertrade**

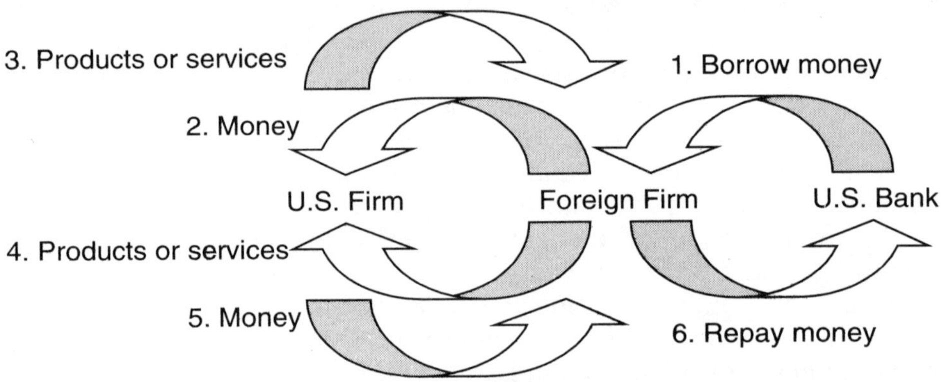

MANAGING COUNTERTRADE

Countertrade is an innovative approach to doing business internationally. According to information provided by representatives of the American Countertrade Association, counterpurchase is the most frequently employed form of countertrade.[6] The results of one study indicated that more than half of the merchandise received in a countertrade is used in-house by the U.S. seller rather than being resold. The study also found that the main reason management engaged in countertrade was to satisfy requirements of the foreign buyer.[7] Subsequently, the international marketer is not using countertrade to its full potential as an integral part of international marketing strategy. To be employed effectively, management needs to develop a countertrade strategy.

COUNTERTRADE STRATEGY

Countertrade strategy concerns the position management takes in planning and utilizing countertrade in international sales. Four strategies have been suggested that the international manager may embrace.[8]

Defensive

Management avoids countertrade arrangements. Although management disavows countertrade, participation in barters may occur under certain circumstances. In these instances, an intermediary that takes title to the products is used, making the transaction appear to be a conventional export and import rather than an exchange. This is done only when a cash transaction is impossible to obtain and the business is deemed important enough.

Passive

Management considers countertrade as an undesirable but necessary tool. The use of countertrade is at a minimal level and on an ad-hoc basis. Management is not really interested in countertrade, but realizes the importance of doing so to obtain business. Management will engage in countertrade only if the foreign buyer makes the request. Management will not initiate countertrade or offer countertrade as a sales incentive.

Reactive

Management uses countertrade as a competitive tool when it believes the sale cannot be completed otherwise. Management is comfortable engaging in countertrade agreements. Countertrade use is part of marketing strategy for existing accounts; however, management will not use countertrade as a tool to expand business. This is the most commonly used countertrade strategy.

Proactive

Management views countertrade as a marketing tool and aggressively seeks business involving countertrades. Countertrade is considered as an opportunity to expand business, rather than as an inconvenience. Countertrade is an advantage to doing business and not a hindrance.

Management embracing a proactive countertrade strategy will participate in creative forms of countertrade as well as the more ordinary agreements. Examples of conventional countertrades would be the managements of two Malaysian firms, Padiberas, Bhd. and Federal Flour, Bhd. that worked together to exchange palm oil for rice and maize with National Cereal Oils and Foodstuffs Import and Export Corporation, a Chinese firm. The management at Ford Motor Company exchanged automobiles in a countertrade for sheepskins that were made into seat covers and sold through the firm's European dealer network. The management at PepsiCo, Inc., sold Pepsi products to the former Soviet Union for twenty naval vessels. Money was obtained for the vessels by selling them for scrap metal.

Examples of more creative countertrades include a blocked currency countertrade in which a country's nonconvertible currency was used to hire a local movie studio to produce a movie that was exported to the United States. Payment for the products shipped in the countertrade was received through ticket sales to people who viewed the movie. The management of DaimlerChrysler AG exchanged automobiles in countertrade for grain in Argentina. At Monsanto Company, saccharin was exchanged in a countertrade with a Chinese company for frozen mackerel. The management of the Boeing Company exchanged commercial jets in a countertrade with the Algerian government for liquid natural gas. The gas was resold to a Boston utility company. One firm receiving Jamaican bat manure in countertrade exchanged the manure for mayonnaise that was subsequently exchanged for cruise line accommodations that were sold for cash.

RISKS IN COUNTERTRADE

Obviously, certain risks are incurred in any countertrade. The more creative a countertrade arrangement is, the more risks the international marketer is likely to encounter. Management must plan for and effectively manage countertrade risks. The following are the kinds of risks that are inherent in any countertrade transaction.[9]

Currency Risks

Two concerns affect convertibility of currencies. The first is soft or nonconvertible currency, and the second is exchange rate fluctuations. Nonconvertibility can be covered by obtaining political risk insurance or by obtaining guarantees from the foreign government that conversion will be allowed. Adverse exchange rate fluctuations can be avoided by hedging, requiring payment in U.S. dollars or in another currency that is stronger than the foreign currency.

Disposing of Merchandise Received in Countertrade

Disposing of countertraded products or services may be difficult and is often the greatest risk. This is particularly true when the products are unfamiliar and do not fit in the firm's distribution system. For example, how does the management of a firm in the clothing industry dispose of lubricating oils or garden tools that will not fit into existing marketing channels? The international marketer should try to find merchandise that fits the firm's channels or can be used in-house. If unfamiliar products must be taken, utilize the services of a countertrade specialist who can help locate potential buyers or arrange swaps.

Interference between the Countertrade Contract and the Resale Contract

Failure of the countertrade to be completed on time could result in the resale partner being injured because of inability to produce or perform on other contracts. The resale partner could sue for damages. The two contracts should be separated so that failed performance under one contract would not affect the other. This would be more difficult to do in code law countries where the entire transaction tends to be viewed holistically. In common law countries this is more feasible, and thus a good reason for including a jurisdictional clause in the contract.

Nonperformance

Nonperformance occurs when merchandise received in a countertrade is not shipped, delivery is late, partial delivery is received, and products received are either damaged, defective, or out of specification. The risk can range from financial loss to legal loss because of noncompliance with contract terms. To minimize this risk, make reasonable contracts that management is sure the countertrade partner can fulfill. The use of experienced countertrade specialists can help assure the countertrade partner is reputable and can produce the promised products. Also, insurance can be obtained to cover noncompliance. If nondelivery is considered a possibility, assurances must be sought. For example, a standby letter of credit, performance bonds, and cash deposited in an escrow account are options.

Pricing Risks

When products are received from a countertrade over a long period of time, the value of the product may decline gradually because of depreciation. Contracting to receive the products at a fixed price could result in losses or inability to sell because of a noncompetitive price. Also, if a low quality product is received, the value received may not correspond to the price attached. The resale price will have to be reduced to reflect the lower quality. Finally, the shipping terms used to value the countertrade must also be taken into consideration. For instance, buying on an FOB basis and selling on a CIF basis (see chapter 14) will result in additional cost being incurred. A logical approach to reduce this risk is to base price on the world market price. When lower quality products are received, the quantity involved must be increased to compensate. Understanding shipping terms will help avoid that aspect of pricing risk.

Product Resale Liability

Products received in countertrade can be inferior in quality or perform poorly. This is particularly true for high-tech products and products received from third-world countries. These products may not meet standards normally expected for the product or can cause damage. Buyers of these products will hold the management of the firm redistributing the merchandise received in the countertrade liable for any harm or loss. Avoid engaging in countertrade for products where quality may be lacking. If such products must be accepted, use a countertrade specialist who will take responsibility, obtain appropriate liability insurance if not too expensive, ask the countertrade partner to indemnify the firm if sued, or provide appropriate guarantees. Also, make no guarantees to the buyer or attempt to contract the liability from the sales agreement with the buyer.

Obviously, entering into a countertrade should be a deliberate undertaking. All care should be exercised to assure various contingencies that may occur are addressed in the agreement. Never agree to a countertrade arrangement without being completely cognizant of all conditions. A careless approach can result in encountering risks such as those just discussed. Exercising discretion and taking adequate precautions can help reduce risks associated with countertrade. Properly done, countertrade can give management a competitive edge on more hesitant and less willing competitors.

CHAPTER SUMMARY

The more involved management becomes in international marketing, the more likely countertrade will be encountered as a method of doing business. Countertrade occurs when a buyer pays for a purchase with products or services of comparable value. Countertrade is a form of barter that is likely to be encountered by international marketers doing business outside Western Europe, Canada, and Japan.

Buyers in countries that are short of hard currency often seek countertrade transactions. When cash is unavailable to pay for purchases, the only option a foreign buyer has is paying with merchandise.

Countertrade offers numerous advantages, including accessing foreign markets that would be unable to be entered otherwise. Since no cash is involved, that money is available for other uses. Also, the value of a countertrade can be somewhat arbitrarily set since no money is involved. By valuing products in terms of other products, cost and tax advantages might be realized.

The perils of countertrade are considerable. Not understanding countertrade can result in receiving poor quality products and products that are difficult for management to resell through existing channels. Contracts are more complicated than for traditional international sales, and products received in a countertrade used internally may disrupt established supply channels. To minimize countertrade risks, countertrade specialists such as a barter house or switch house can be employed.

Various forms of countertrade arrangements exist. The simplest forms are standard barter arrangements in which no cash is involved. More sophisticated arrangements that involve money are frequently encountered. These techniques utilize money to protect the buyer and seller from nonperformance. The money simply facilitates the transaction, and upon completion is returned to the countertrade partner from which it originated. The money is simply a form of insurance. Counterpurchase is the most commonly employed form of countertrade in which money is involved. Since the passage of the Export Trading Company Act of 1982, U.S. banks have been permitted to assist international marketers develop countertrade agreements. The banks can lend money to foreign buyers who need cash to arrange a counterpurchase. Bank credit countertrade has made entering into countertrade more feasible for many U.S. businesses. Switching is useful for disposing of unwanted products when the merchandise received in a countertrade is unfamiliar. Prior to being imported, products are transshipped to another buyer, which can use the products.

The international marketer may embrace a defensive, passive, reactive, or proactive strategy toward countertrade. The perceived importance of countertrade as a means of conducting international marketing will affect the strategy selected. Regardless of which strategy is adopted, management must plan effectively to avoid the risks inherent in countertrade.

KEY TERMS

Bank credit countertrade
Barter house
Bilateral barter
Blocked currency
Buyback
Counterpurchase
Countertrade
Precompensation
Switch house
Switching
Triangular barter

REVIEW QUESTIONS

1. What is countertrade?
2. Why is the international marketer likely to encounter requests to countertrade from foreign buyers?
3. What advantages accrue to the international marketer when using countertrade?
4. Discuss the risks inherent in countertrade. Which of these risks do you believe is the greatest and why?
5. Explain the difference between the two broad alternatives of countertrade available to the international marketer.
6. How does bilateral barter differ from counterpurchase?
7. Explain how blocked currency countertrade works.
8. What are the roles of the barter house and switch house in countertrade?
9. Explain how bank credit countertrade works.
10. The international marketer may embrace any of four different countertrade strategies. Name all four and explain each.

NOTES

1. Frank Gray, "Countertrade Still Thrives," *fDi Magazine,* December–January 2004.

2. David Hew, director's statement, Asia Pacific Countertrade Association, 2004, http://www.apca.net/index.asp.

3. W. Tim G. Richardson, "Countertrade," July 11, 2005, http://www.witiger.com/internationalbusiness/countertrade.htm.

4. David Hew, "What is Offset Countertrade and Structured Finance?," Asian Pacific Countertrade Association, 2004, http://www.apca.net/articles/getarticles.asp?id=1.

5. Dan West, "Countertrade—An Innovative Approach to Marketing," *BarterNews* 36 (1996), http://www.barternews.com/approach_marketing.htm.

6. Prema Nakra, "Countertrade and International Marketing: Take a Proactive Approach!" International Business Training, December 27, 2005, http://www.i-b-t.net/anm/templates/trade_article.asp?articleid=206&zoneid=3.

7. Laura B. Forker, *Countertrade: Purchasing's Perceptions and Involvement* (Tempe, AZ: Center for Advanced Purchasing Studies, 1991).

8. C.G. Alex and Barbara Bowers, "The American Way to Countertrade," *BarterNews* 17 (1988), http://www.barternews.com/american_way.htm.

9. Neil K. Rutter, "Managing Risks in Countertrade Transactions, Part 1," *BarterNews* 37 (1996), http://www.barternews.com/managing_risks.htm.

17 International Marketing Strategy

In November 2008, InBev, SA, became the world's largest brewer by acquiring Anheuser-Busch Companies, Inc. (ABC). The new company, named Anheuser-Busch InBev, is headquartered in Leuven, Belgium. After the acquisition, ABC, located in St. Louis, Missouri, became a wholly-owned subsidiary of Anheuser-Busch InBev, and has been designated as the company's North American headquarters. With the addition of ABC, Anheuser-Busch InBev sells four of the ten top-selling beers in the world and holds the number one or two position in over twenty key markets.

ABC consists of eight business units including Anheuser-Busch, International, Inc. (ABI). Beer for the U.S. market is produced by ABC, and beer for foreign markets is produced by ABI. ABC is the largest brewing company in the United States with a 48.8 percent share of beer sales by volume. ABC and ABI produce the two best-selling beer brands in the world, Budweiser and Bud Light, with sales of 47.38 million and 36.98 million barrels, respectively, in 2008.

ABI operates seventeen breweries: fifteen in China, one in India, and one in the United Kingdom. Budweiser is also brewed under licenses and equity joint ventures via direct supervision of Anheuser-Busch brewmasters in Argentina, Canada, Ireland, Italy, Japan, Panama, Russia, South Korea, and Spain. The marketing objective of management at ABI is to make Budweiser the leading international premium beer brand. To accomplish this objective, four fundamental marketing strategies are employed:

- maintaining Budweiser's signature taste, which is lighter than that of European beers because of the addition of rice and beech wood chips during the brewing process, and a somewhat higher carbonation
- developing and implementing sales tools to propel distribution and service at retail
- delivering innovative marketing to build Budweiser's global image
- maintaining a global network of local sales and marketing professionals to manage the firm's operations in key international markets

Management believes in the "one world-one beer" philosophy and is intent on product standardization to maintain the same taste and quality wherever Budweiser is brewed.

However, management faces one significant obstacle to a marketing strategy of product standardization—the brand name. Budweiser is also the brand name of a beer brewed in the Czech Republic. ABC's founders, Eberhard Anheuser and Adolphus Busch, chose the name Budweiser from a city on a map because they thought the name sounded German, was easy for Americans to pronounce, and would appeal to German immigrants. Unfortunately, the town picked was České Budějovice in Bohemia, Czech Republic. The problem arises because the German name for the town is Budweis, and any beer originating from the town would be referred to as Budweiser. Thus, Budweiser refers to the style of beer first brewed in České Budějovice much as Pilsner refers to the style of beer first brewed in Plzeň (Pilsen in German) in the Czech Republic.

Although the Budweiser style of beer has been brewed in České Budějovice since the thirteenth century, the Czech brewer Budějovický Budvar, n.p. (BB), has been in existence and selling its Budweiser only since 1895. Since Budweiser was first brewed by ABC in 1876, nineteen years earlier, its management claims ownership of the brand name, which was registered at that time as a trademark in the United States.

Disagreement over the trademark ownership began in the late nineteenth century when both brewers began to expand their markets to foreign countries. The managements of both firms entered into a tacit agreement in 1911 to share markets, with BB to not sell north of the Panama Canal and ABC to not to sell in Europe. However, as ABC began to grow rapidly through market expansion, and the fall of the Soviet Union opened the Central and Eastern European markets, the agreement was disregarded. The dispute erupted into a legal battle in markets of interest to both firms. Rulings differed, with neither firm gaining rights to the name in all markets. ABC was granted rights in most of the world, while BB was successful in fewer instances; however, the battle continues in many European countries. Where BB won, ABC was forced to change to names such as Bud and Anheuser-Busch B; and where ABC won, BB is marketed with names such as Budvar, Budweiser Budvar, and Czechvar. In the United Kingdom, the courts ruled that both firms may use the name Budweiser. In 2007, a financial agreement was reached between the managements of both firms that grants ABC the right to market BB in the United States and several other countries.

As long as the brand dispute exists, the management of ABC will be unable to standardize Budweiser across all markets, creating problems for obtaining the "one beer" objective. BB, which is owed by the Czech government, is thought to be considering privatization. If that should happen, ABC's management would definitely want to consider takeover of BB as part of its marketing strategy. The problem could be easily solved if ABC were able to own BB.

Sources: Based in part on information from Anheuser-Busch, "Company—Historical Timeline," http://www.anheuser-busch.com/History.html; Anheuser-Busch InBev, "Annual Report 2008," http://ab-inbev.com/go/media/annual_report_2008; "InBev Completes $52 Billion Acquisition of Anheuser-Busch," *Chicago Tribune*, November 19, 2008, http://archives.chicagotribune.com/2008/nov/19/business/chi-wed-brf2-inbev-nov19; and Mark Jarvis, "Which Bud's for You?" Brandchannel, January 5, 2004, http://www.brandchannel.com/features_effect.asp?pf_id=191.

CHAPTER OBJECTIVES

After reading this chapter, you should

- understand the marketing management process;
- appreciate the steps involved in the international marketing management process;
- know how to accomplish the international planning process;
- understand the responsibilities and activities involved in developing an international marketing strategy;
- understand how market entry strategy affects international marketing planning;
- know how to develop an export strategy;
- appreciate the role ethics play in marketing strategy and plans; and
- understand how a free trade zone can complement international marketing strategy.

UNDERSTANDING THE MARKETING MANAGEMENT PROCESS

To be as successful as possible, the marketing manager must approach the management task in an orderly and systematic manner. What must be done to assure the marketing management process is effective? What constitutes a good marketing management process? The marketing management process involves five components and is consistent with the basic functions of all management. The marketing manager must plan, assemble resources, implement, administer, and control. The components of the management process are depicted in Exhibit 17.1.

Exhibit 17.1 **The Marketing Management Process**

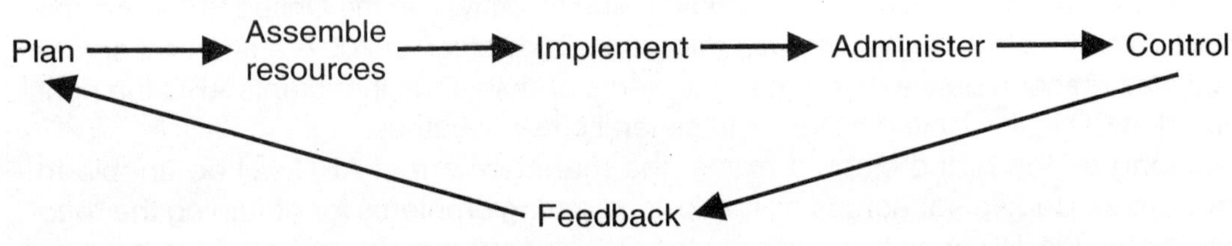

PLAN

All marketers need to engage in planning to achieve an effective marketing strategy. Although this planning can vary in degree of sophistication and thoroughness from firm to firm, effective planning is essential. Management may use computers, statistical analyses, and simulations or simply analyze opportunities, threats, and alternatives in a more unpretentious, yet consummate, manner. Regardless of the procedure or techniques employed, the best course of action must be identified. Planning involves analyzing the marketing environment; identifying circumstances, possibilities, contingencies, and exigencies; specifying alternative feasible courses of action; evaluating the desirability of each course of action for achieving objectives; and selecting the most desirable and appropriate course of action. Without extensive, thorough, and complete planning, international marketing strategy will likely be suboptimal.

ASSEMBLE RESOURCES

To put the planning into action, the marketing manager must bring together the resources required for support. This includes activities such as staffing needs, obtaining equipment and physical plant, and arranging financing. Locating, organizing, and preparing the support needed to supplement implementation is involved. Providing the means necessary to sustain planning will help minimize implementation problems.

IMPLEMENT

A good plan can fail because of poor implementation. Therefore, correctly executing the plan is essential to good marketing management. Management must proceed in a timely and orderly manner, and manage everything effectively to assure the plan is operationalized as devised and intended. Progress toward meeting objectives must be planned and measured carefully. Developing an environment that is conducive to instituting and supporting the components of the plan will help assure success.

ADMINISTER

Effective supervision and motivation are essential for the most successful implementation of the plan. Once implemented and operational, direction and oversight are required. The marketing manager must do what is necessary to assure the resources are being used as efficiently as possible. Without effective direction, inefficiencies occur that can cause suboptimum results.

CONTROL

No planning will be ideal unless supported by an effective set of controls. The actual performance of the implemented plan must be compared with the anticipated performance consistent with achieving objectives. Unacceptable differences indicate a problem with the plan or its implementation. Based on a variance analysis, deviations considered excessive are thoroughly evaluated, and the reasons for nonconformity determined. Favorable deviations may indicate the plan was not aggressive enough, or something was overlooked. Unfavorable deviations may indicate the plan was too aggressive, unexpected contingencies occurred because of changes in the marketing environment, or the implementation was lacking. In any event, adjustments will be required either in implementation to bring actual performance in line with the plan, or in revisions to the plan to more accurately reflect the real marketing environment. The results of the controlling process provide feedback for revising or adjusting the plan.

FEEDBACK

In reality, the marketing management process is an ongoing effort. Since the components are interrelated, the controlling process provides essential feedback that completes the loop and begins the planning process anew. Control must conform to the plan and be coordinated. Implementation and performance adjustments are done within the overall plan, or the plan is adjusted based on the controlling process. Good coordination between controlling and planning requires adequate feedback.

PURPOSE

Having an effective and successful marketing management process involves many decisions, which collectively are intended to provide satisfaction to the target market. That is, a strategy is established so that more satisfaction is provided than available from the competition. Limitations exist on what can be done for the customer since strategy decisions are constrained by budgets. However, within budget limitations, the intent is to solve the customer's problem better than the competition, thus providing more satisfaction than any other competitor. In addition to providing satisfaction, the marketing manager also wants to build a relationship with the customer that links the two. In this way, each benefits the other and future business is assured. A good marketing management process is long-term oriented and assures that all responsibilities are undertaken at the correct time and in the correct order.

THE INTERNATIONAL MARKETING MANAGEMENT PROCESS

The international marketing management process involves the same considerations as does a domestic process. The only difference is that the process is applied to the foreign situation. Consider the components depicted in Exhibit 17.1 as each applies to international marketing.

INTERNATIONAL PLANNING PROCESS

International planning is an important function that needs adequate attention, perhaps more than does planning for domestic marketing because of the additional, uncontrollable, international environment. Also, planning gives direction to the remainder of the international marketing management process. Exhibit 17.2 shows the procedures involved in international planning, and how planning for the international market fits into the firm's overall planning process.

The planning process begins with an evaluation of the marketing environment. A SWOT (strengths, weaknesses, opportunities, and threats) evaluation or similar assessment can be made. The business situation, both past and anticipated, is analyzed, so the organization's existing and potential conditions can be assessed. This allows management to determine the condition of the firm's internal circumstances and the business climate in which the firm operates.

From the information gathered in the environmental evaluation, management will

Exhibit 17.2 **Planning for International Marketing**

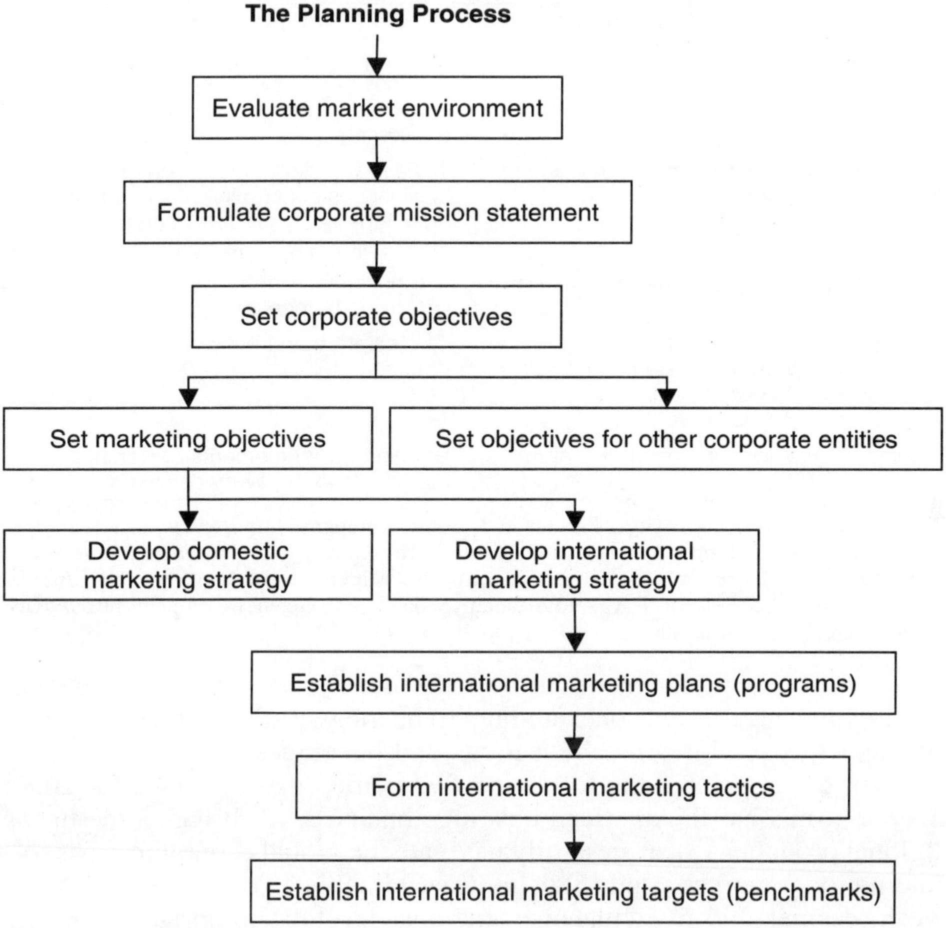

decide what the firm's purpose or mission should be. The mission will be articulated in a concise and brief declaration known as a **mission statement** that specifies management's vision for the firm. The mission statement specifies how the firm will be positioned to compete in the target market. See Exhibit 17.3 for examples of corporate mission statements.

After the mission has been decided, objectives consistent with that mission are set. **Objectives** at the corporate level are broad statements of what the management of the organization wants to accomplish. Objectives specify the direction the firm must take to accomplish the mission. The corporate objectives serve as the basis for the objectives set by managers who direct the various parts of the firm such as production and marketing. The objectives established for these other corporate entities must help achieve the corporate objectives. Thus, objectives form a hierarchy. Also, objectives become more specific at lower levels of the hierarchy. Thus, the objectives set for the firm's marketing efforts must be consistent with achieving corporate objectives and include increased specific details. Of course, the marketing objectives must be

Exhibit 17.3 **Corporate Mission Statements for Selected Companies**

Corporation	Description	Mission Statement
The Procter & Gamble Company	A U.S. firm that provides products for the home, personal care, and good health.	We will provide branded products and services of superior quality and value that improve the lives of the world's consumers. . . .
Mannesmannröhren-Werke GmbH	A German steel tube and pipe manufacturer.	To have world-renowned competence in all issues concerning steel tube and pipe, top-quality products and services, and—ultimately—satisfied customers.
Merck & Company, Inc.	A U.S. pharmaceutical firm.	Our business is preserving and improving human life.
Inter Ikea Systems B.V.	A Swedish firm that franchises stores that sell low-cost home furnishing products.	To create a better everyday life for many people.
Hershey Company	A U.S. candy manufacturer.	Bringing sweet moments of Hershey happiness to the every day word.

Sources: The respective firms' Web sites: Procter & Gamble Company, http://www.pg.com/en_US/company/purpose_people/index.shtml; Mannesmannröhren-Werke GmbH, http://www.mrw.de/english/frames_1-unternehmen.html; Merck & Company, Inc., http://www.merck.com/about/our-values/home.html?WT.svl=mainnav; Inter Ikea Systems B.V., http://franchisor.ikea.com/; Hershey Company, http://www.thehersheycompany.com/about/profile.asp.

measurable to permit accomplishments to be assessed. For example, the management at PepsiCo, Inc., has the mission statement to be the world's premier consumer products company focused on convenient foods and beverages. To fulfill the mission, management has stipulated the following five marketing objectives for 2009: (1) Revitalize the firm's North American beverage business, (2) broaden the firm's portfolio of global products, (3) successfully navigate the global economic crisis, (4) expand in international markets, and (5) achieve sustainable growth.[1]

To achieve the desired objectives, management must develop appropriate marketing strategies. **Marketing strategy** refers to a nonspecific long-term plan of action that provides the procedures to be followed to accomplish marketing objectives. The marketing strategy serves as a guide for efficiently allocating resources in order to differentiate the firm and obtain a competitive advantage. For example, at PepsiCo, marketing strategy is consistent with marketing objectives. Components of marketing strategy include:

- Keep the beverage portfolio relevant to consumers of all ages.
- Increase acquisitions and partnerships and coordinate research and development across the company into one innovation team.
- Institute a "Productivity for Growth" program designed to generate more than US$1.2 billion in pretax savings over the next three years and consolidate the distribution system by acquiring control of bottlers to cut costs.
- Increase foreign capital investments and develop products that appeal to local tastes.
- Maintain high standards for product quality, safety, and integrity while reducing the firm's environmental impact through water, energy, and packaging incentives.[2]

The marketing strategy devised for the international market will be different from the one developed for the domestic market. Although coordination is necessary between domestic and international marketing strategies, the uniqueness of the conditions confronted necessitates individuality. Therefore, the **international marketing strategy** is a guide for marketing efforts to effectively cultivate the foreign market. For example, international marketing strategy at PepsiCo is to remain globally active with sustainable growth of the markets outside North America. Such endeavors include partnering with JSC Lebedyansky (Russia's leading juice company), acquiring firms, and expanding a partnership with Unilever. To assure international growth is maintained at an acceptable level, a diverse and culturally inclusive group of employees with world-class talent will be recruited.[3]

Once the international marketing strategy is developed, the international marketer will establish international marketing plans or programs. **International marketing plans** are the policies and programs implemented to align marketing activities with the international marketing strategy to achieve international marketing objectives. Conditions in the international market will need to be clearly understood to prepare effective international marketing programs. International marketing plans involve the identification of the target market, determination of the proper balance among the components of the marketing mix designed to satisfy that group of customers, and the specifying of budgets to implement marketing activities. The international marketing plans specify the marketing procedures that will be implemented. The course of action stipulated covers the marketing program in general, but does not identify how specific activities are to be accomplished. For instance, the plan may specify the magazine advertising efforts necessary to reach the target market, but will not specify the content of the ads, the particular magazines to be used, or the frequency of exposure. In other words, the international marketing plan provides the essentials of a general—not specific—marketing effort required to appeal to the target market. For example, at Frito-Lay North America, the snack food division of PepsiCo, Inc., the mission statement is to be the world's favorite snack and always be within arm's reach. To accomplish this, management's international marketing strategy included purchasing leading regional potato chip manufacturers. Recent acquisitions include Walkers Shortbread, Ltd., in the United Kingdom, the Simba Group, Ltd., in South Africa, and Sabritas S. de R.L. de C.V. in Mexico. International marketing plans include changing the local brands into one global brand—Frito-Lay.[4]

After appropriate plans are established, the international marketer will formulate international marketing tactics that are appropriate for the plan. **International marketing tactics** are the specific techniques required to implement the international marketing plan. These are the methods by which the target customer will be reached and satisfied. The uniqueness of the foreign market and conditions like the culture will influence the details of every decision. To carry out the advertising plans, decisions will be made about the orientation of the ad, the copy, the appearance, the size, where the ad will appear, and so forth. Choices will be made to take advantage of the unique market conditions that exist in the foreign market.

Consider management's actions, at Frito-Lay North America, to change local brands such as Walkers, Simba, and Sabritas to one global brand. The tactics used

Exhibit 17.4 **Star Barbecue Chips**

Star Foods, a Romanian snack food producer, was purchased by PepsiCo in 2004. Following management's international marketing tactics, the package was changed to include the red banner and yellow sun signifying a Frito-Lay product.

will bring the change gradually. First, the Frito-Lay logo was redesigned to enhance brand perception globally. A red banner signifying "celebration" with a yellow sun symbolizing "universality" was chosen. Then, as the first step in the brand overhaul, the new brand image was introduced in the United Kingdom, retaining the local Walkers brand name on the red banner. Similar changes are planned for Simba in South Africa and Sabritas in Mexico. Ultimately, the local brand names will be phased out and replaced with Frito-Lay to complete the brand globalization process.[5]

Finally, **international marketing targets** will be established. These are the benchmarks by which attainment of the international marketing objectives will be judged. If the international marketing plans and tactics are successful, the performance levels specified by the targets will be reached. What management expects ideal performance to be for all aspects of the international marketing strategy will be quantified. Targets for factors such as sales, profits, expenses, and the number of various types of outlets carrying the product will be established for overall performance, geographic areas, and other criteria the international marketing manager deems appropriate. The international marketing targets also serve as guidelines for the international marketing control process.

Exhibit 17.5 **Assembling Resources for International Marketing**

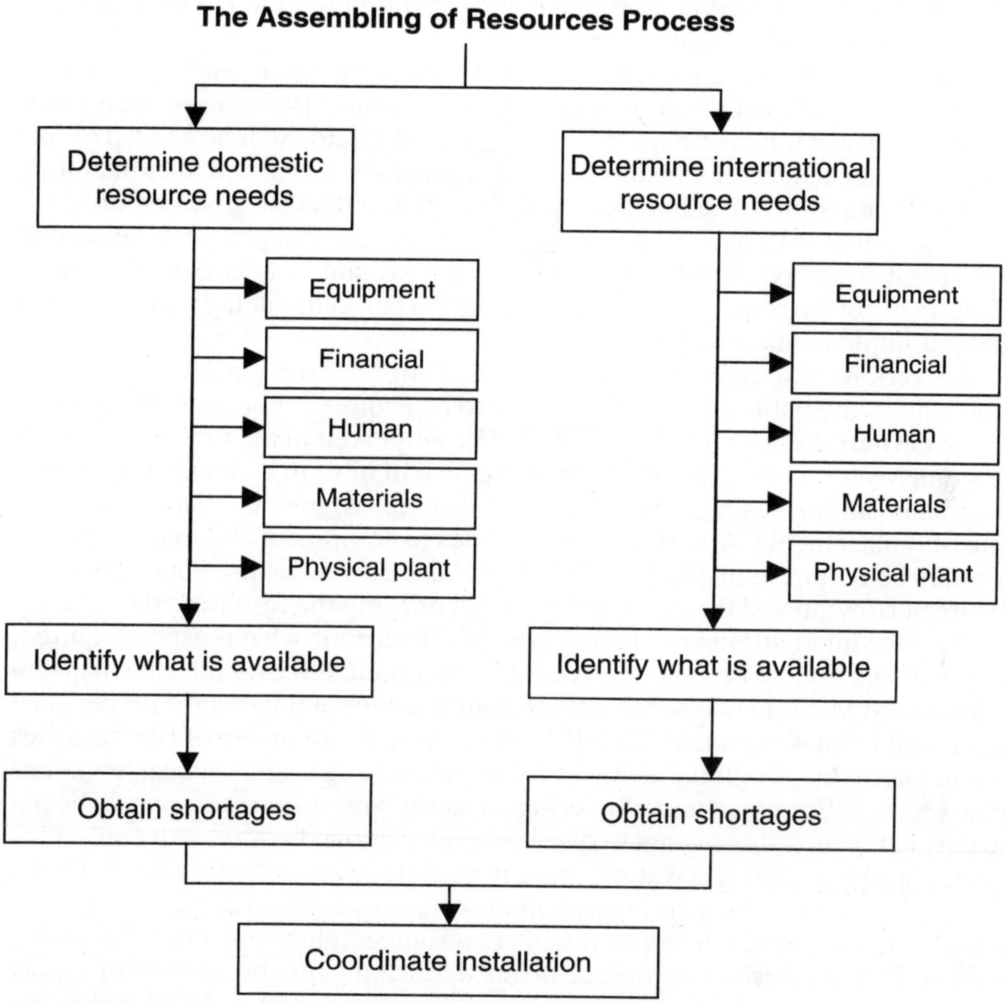

INTERNATIONAL ASSEMBLING OF RESOURCES PROCESS

After the planning process is complete, the international marketer will assemble the resources required to implement the international marketing strategy. The responsibilities involved in assembling resources to support the international marketing effort are illustrated in Exhibit 17.5.

The assembling of resources process may require locating the availability of resources in both the domestic country and the foreign market. For example, a part could be built in one of the firm's domestic locations and an intracompany transfer made to a manufacturing or assembly facility abroad. Thus, resources to support the international effort would need to be organized and put in place domestically. At the minimum, the time of some domestic company personnel will need to be allocated to oversee the international endeavor. Therefore, the international marketer's job in assembling resources can be double faceted, with attention required to be directed to domestic needs and international needs.

The international marketing manager will determine the amounts and types of various resources required to support the planned undertaking. Human resource needs will be assessed. What kinds of personnel with particular skills will be needed? What financial exigencies will be encountered? What machinery, tools, and manufacturing equipment will be required? What factory and work area facilities will be utilized? What raw materials, components, and parts will be needed to support the project? A myriad of details must be determined in each of the possible categories of resource needs. Failure to get the required resources in position can cause delays and problems with efficient implementation of the plan.

After the various resource needs are identified, the international marketer will determine what is available and what will have to be acquired. For example, personnel with the desired skills and abilities may not be employed in the firm. If this is the case, new employees possessing the desired talents will have to be located and hired. Even if capable employees already exist in the firm, reassignments may necessitate the hiring of replacements. Additions and upgrades to equipment and manufacturing facilities may be required, in addition to the purchase of new items. Financial needs may require borrowing and the use of reserves. Identifying the resources that already exist will help the international marketing manager determine what must be acquired. Items not available need to be located, ordered, or recruited. For example, the management at Advanced Micro Devices, Inc., a U.S. manufacturer of microchips for personal computers, will be making a US$2.5 billion upgrade and expansion of two factories in Dresden, Germany. As global demand for microchips is rising, management has decided to increase European manufacturing capacity. This requires resources be put in place during the next three years to overhaul and refit one factory with equipment to accommodate larger silicone wafers, expand capacity in a second factory, and build a new "clean room" where final preparation of wafers will take place.[6]

Finally, the arrival and installation of necessary resources must be assured. The timing of arrival of the various resources must be planned. Locating reliable sources of supply that can deliver the desired quality and quantity on time is important. Late or misdirected arrivals will disrupt the plan. Assuring the resources arrive on time and are secured is paramount. Also, if resources must be in place in the domestic country to support the international operations, coordination of resource deployment or installation with foreign needs will be necessary. Resources may be acquired from foreign sources or domestic sources for subsequent delivery to the foreign market. Getting everything in place at the right time in both locations will require organization and synchronization.

International Implementing Process

Even though the strategy, plans, and tactics developed may be ideal, improper implementation will result in poor performance. The international marketer must assure everything is executed as efficiently as possible. The procedures required to accomplish proper implementation are depicted in Exhibit 17.6.

Exhibit 17.6 **Implementing for International Marketing**

The Implementing Process

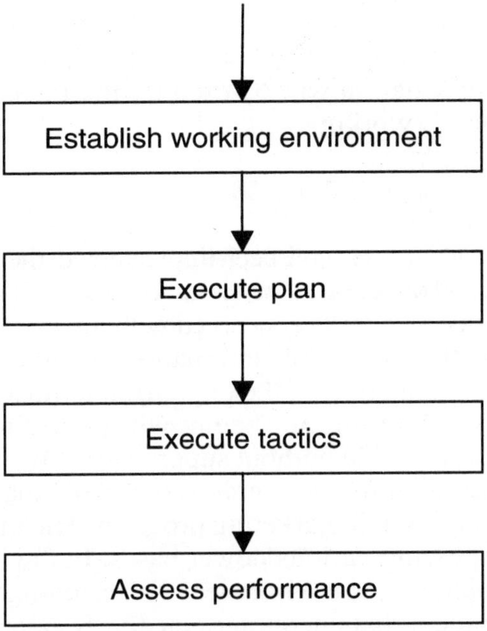

Appropriate implementation begins by establishing a favorable working environment. Preparation is necessary to arrange the correct working conditions and create appropriate attitudes among line and support employees. The international marketer must set up a working atmosphere conducive to the plan. Because of cultural and legal differences existing in the foreign market, the international working environment may be somewhat different than what exists domestically. The working environment is the foundation upon which the marketing program is built.

Once the correct working situation is established, the plan may be executed. The specifics of the marketing program are set in motion as conceived. Superlative oversight of those in supervisory positions is critical. Adherence to the precepts of the plan must be timely and orderly. The game plan must be followed as intended. For example, the events occurring in China are creating great opportunities for the management at General Electric Company. China's need for clean energy technologies such as coal gasification is expanding. The country's economy modernization and expansion plans include an estimated fifty new airports expected to be built by 2013.[7] Even though the firm's global revenues decreased by 5 percent between 2008 and 2009, revenues from sales to China increased 16 percent.[8] GE's management must continue implementing the plans required to keep its products in demand in the Chinese market if the growth being experienced is to persist. To assure the marketing program is properly implemented, the tactical details are executed. Each aspect of the plan requires the execution of various procedures to assure proper implementation. The tactics employed must be appropriate for the foreign market conditions.

After the tactical details are arranged, and the marketing program is operational, the international marketing manager will assess performance. What is actually happening is measured. What are the results of the marketing program as implemented? The results are calculated for the specific quantified targets or benchmarks established during the planning process for the pertinent criteria that will be used to assess achievement of objectives. This information will be used during the controlling process to determine how well the plan is working.

INTERNATIONAL ADMINISTERING PROCESS

Once the marketing program and tactics have been implemented, the international marketer must provide administration and direction to the endeavor to assure the plan is followed and executed. Exhibit 17.7 indicates the tasks concerned with international administration.

Administering involves all efforts of the international marketing manager that are directed toward organizing and managing the ongoing activities of the firm's international marketing endeavors. Administration begins with providing oversight. Nothing will operate as effectively as possible without supervision. Oversight is a continuous and ongoing process, which monitors and guides the performance and activities of those involved with the international marketing program. The international marketer assures compliance by employing various power bases. In the international market, supervision requires maintaining a job environment that encourages employee achievement and a buying environment that encourages customer satisfaction.

Exhibit 17.7 **Administering for International Marketing**

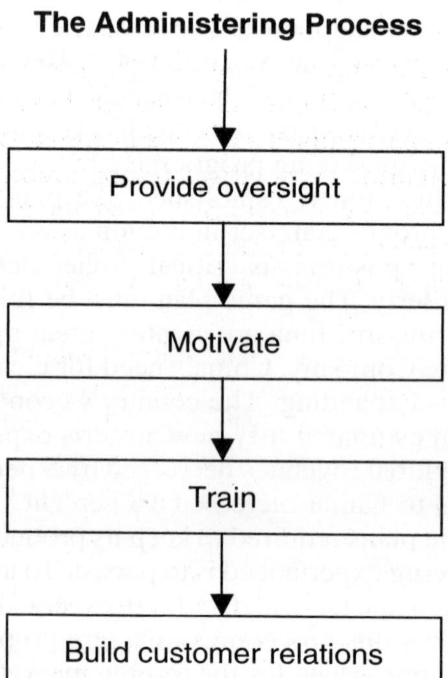

Appropriate administration also involves motivation. Not only must the international marketing manager assure the plan is constantly followed, but the manager must also see that employees eagerly conform. What motivates the international employee or consumer may be different from what motivates the domestic employee or consumer. Therefore, motivation involves determining the reasons that induce people to act and providing the proper incentives to move them to the desired action. Since people do not always respond as intended to motivational incentives, motivation also involves conflict management. Motivation is influencing others to willingly engage in behaviors that will accomplish the needs of the international marketer—adherence to the international marketing program. For instance, Oberto Sausage Company, a U.S. producer of over 400 meat snacks, is known primarily for beef jerky. The company's products are distributed through Frito-Lay's distribution channels. The firm's chairman, Art Oberto, knows the importance of good administration. Part of his equation for success is happy employees and customers. Part of the equation to motivate employees includes annual Christmas parties, company picnics, and a company-owned motor home that employees may borrow for personal use.[9]

Training is an integral part of supervision. Employees will not perform at an optimum level when critical knowledge is lacking. The supervisory process will identify where employees are not performing as anticipated. If performance is inappropriate because skills are lacking, training is indicated. The international marketer will provide direction and arrange instruction to teach employees correct procedures as stipulated in the marketing program. Training is necessary to help assure the marketing plan is implemented efficiently.

Effective administration requires attention to the firm's customers. Customers have needs that can require the attention of the international marketer. Assuring customer concerns and problems are adequately addressed and customers are satisfied is important to building relationships and securing ongoing purchases. Building customer relations and consulting with the firm's clients allows management to learn customers' uniqueness, which helps to guarantee that the international marketing program is fully implemented. Without effective administration, the international marketing plan will not work as envisioned.

INTERNATIONAL CONTROLLING PROCESS

The international marketing environment is dynamic and not static. Thus, conditions upon which the international marketing program was established will change. What was ideal when the international marketing program was implemented will not necessarily be ideal as time passes. As a result, the international marketing plan, no matter how well conceived, will not produce optimum results unless supplemented by an effective control process. The controlling process is needed to identify weaknesses in the international marketing plan as well as determine improvements in implementation. The international controlling process is depicted in Exhibit 17.8.

Controlling of the international marketing program starts by comparing what actually happened to what was expected to happen. The performance assessment made during the implementation process is compared with the marketing target (benchmark) established during the planning process. Any deviations indicate that the international

Exhibit 17.8 **Controlling for International Marketing**

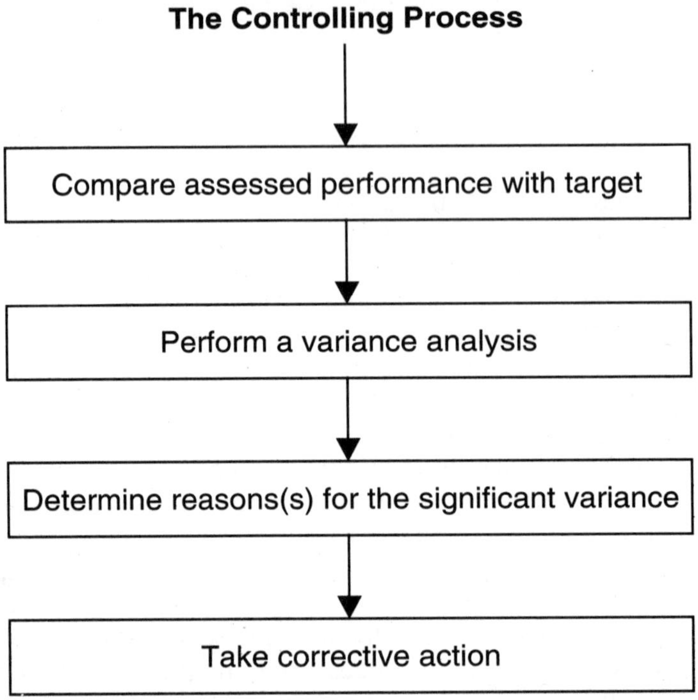

marketing plan is not producing the desired results. However, deviations that are too large at any particular time are unlikely to be due to natural causes and indicate that something is not operating as anticipated. For instance, changes in consumer spending and product availability can happen by chance. In other words, such deviations occur from month to month, even though the plan is operating as efficiently as possible. Expecting sales to be identical to the target every month is unreasonable, but on the average, the target should be achieved if the international marketing plan is operating effectively. However, if the deviations are too large at any particular time, such differences are not likely to be due to natural causes, but instead indicate something is not operating as anticipated. To make these determinations, a variance analysis is conducted. Appropriate variances between actual and anticipated require no action other than continuing measurement of performance. Unanticipated variances are an alarm bell that something is wrong.

When unanticipated variances occur, the international marketer will assess the situation and attempt to ascertain the reasons. More than one issue can contribute to the unanticipated variance. After the cause or causes of the unanticipated deviations are identified, corrective action is taken. Proceed carefully to assure the real reason for the unanticipated deviation is discovered. If an incorrect reason is identified, any corrective action directed toward that concern will be ineffective, because the real issue will still exist. This is an important aspect of the international marketing manager's controlling function since symptoms of the situation can mask the real reason.

Once the real reason is identified, the international marketer can evaluate alternative courses of action for correction. The objective of taking corrective action is to reduce the size of the deviation and bring the actual performance and benchmark closer together. Unanticipated deviation will fall into one of two categories: (1) The performance is poorer than the target—a negative deviation, or (2) the performance is better than the target—a positive deviation.

If the deviation is negative, the international marketer must pursue one of two courses of action. If the international targets (benchmarks) are judged to be appropriate, adjustments to the international strategy, marketing program, and tactics will be necessary to improve performance. If the international strategy, marketing program, and tactics are judged to be appropriate, lowering the targets will be necessary. In this case, the objectives were too ambitious, and since the international marketing plan is working well and performance cannot be improved, the only alternative is to reassess objectives. Of course, the real challenge for the international marketing manager is to recognize which situation exists. For example, the working relationship between the management at General Motors Corporation (GM), a U.S. firm, and AvtoVaz, Inc., GM's Russian joint venture partner for manufacturing cars in Russia, has become strained. The management of AvtoVaz has announced that the firm will build a new state-funded car plant, and the joint venture with GM might be closed. Therefore, GM's management is in advanced talks with Russian government officials to invest US$200 billion to build a new car factory near St. Petersburg. When things were not going as planned, GM's management decided to eliminate the possibility of losing access to the Russian market by changing the method of market entry.[10]

If the deviation is positive and performance exceeds the target, then the international strategy, marketing program, and tactics are working better than expected. Expectations were set too low, and possibilities were misjudged. In this situation, the international marketing manager will make an upward adjustment to the benchmark. Of course, the international strategy, marketing program, and tactics will be assessed to determine the efficiency of the operation and whether any improvements are possible.

Any changes to the international strategy, marketing program, and tactics may have implications for the international marketing objectives. Thus, the results of control will provide information that should be input for consideration in the ongoing planning process. Failure to consider this feedback could have an adverse effect on the direction of future marketing planning.

DEVELOPING AN INTERNATIONAL MARKETING STRATEGY

International marketing strategy guides management's marketing efforts in the foreign market. Therefore, developing appropriate guidance for the firm's international marketing program is an important activity. If done properly, the chances for success in the foreign market are greatly enhanced.

INITIAL MARKET ENTRY

Selecting the best market entry method is important to developing a good international marketing strategy. A simplified assessment of the market entry alternatives is shown in Exhibit 17.9.

Exhibit 17.9 **Market Entry Strategy**

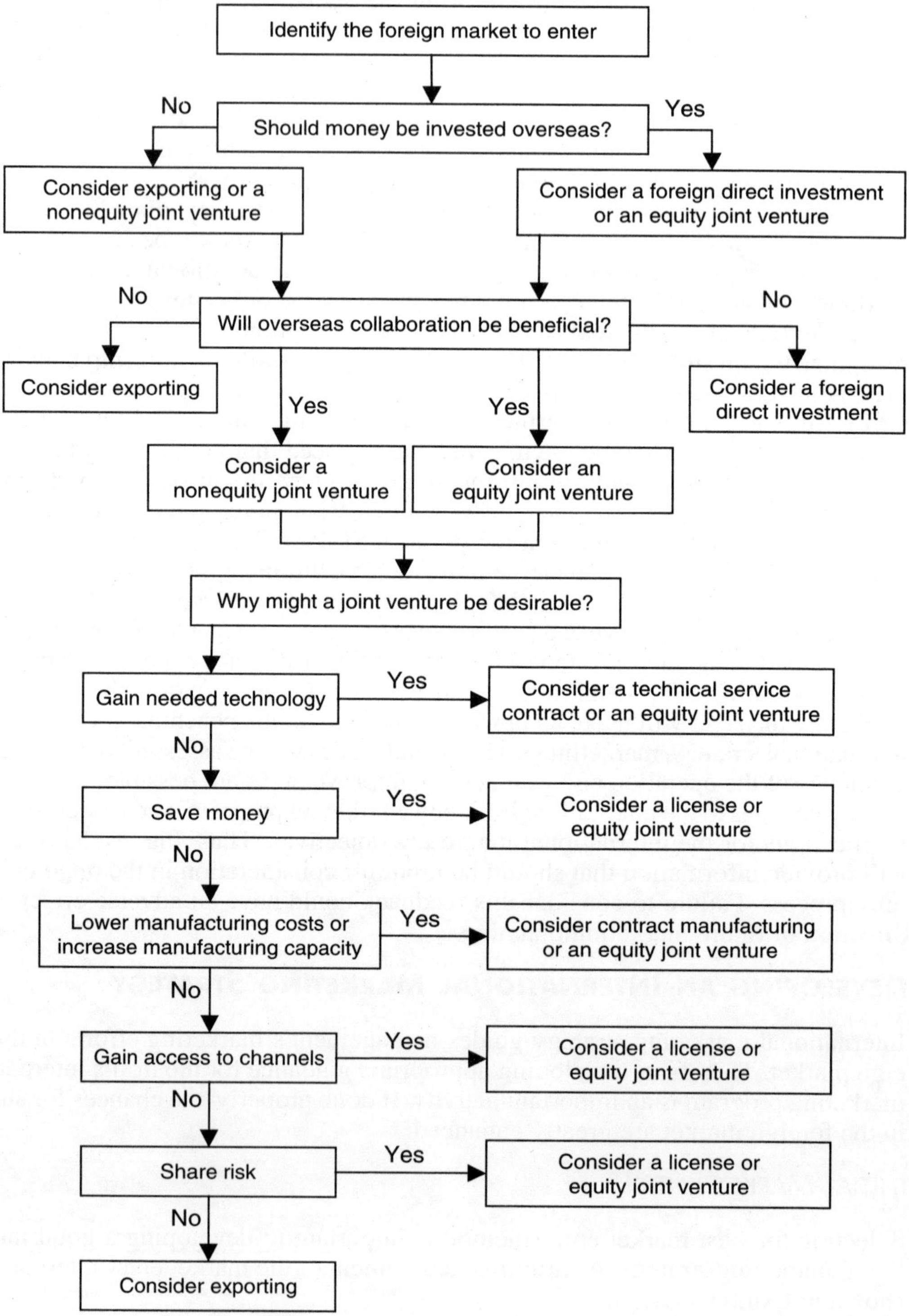

Once the market to enter has been selected, the international marketer will determine the appropriate market entry method. This will be influenced by the availability of money for investing overseas and whether doing so is desirable. If money is unavailable or not desired to be invested in the foreign market, exporting or nonequity joint ventures will be viable alternatives. If money can be invested, then equity joint ventures and foreign direct investments may be doable. Which option is selected will depend upon whether participation with foreigners is desirable. Of course, many business and marketing concerns will be involved in these decisions (see chapter 5 for a discussion of these factors). If collaboration with a foreign partner is considered necessary and desirable, various joint venture arrangements may be considered. The reason for the collaboration and whether or not money is to be invested will be considerations. For example, if manufacturing costs can be lowered through foreign production, a contract manufacturing nonequity joint venture or a contract equity joint venture are feasible options. Conditions in the foreign market and foreign laws can restrict the availability and desirability of any market entry method otherwise considered ideal. In those cases, an alternative market entry method must be sought if the market is to be developed. After the entry decision has been made, the planning process proceeds.

MARKET ENTRY EXPANSION

As has been explained previously, the market entry method will affect the development of international marketing strategy (see chapter 5). Since involvement in international marketing tends to be an evolutionary process, most marketing managers will elect to begin with the least risky and easiest method—indirect exporting. As international experience and involvement increase, management also tends to become involved in international marketing via joint ventures and foreign direct investments. Although this is the norm, special conditions (see Exhibit 17.9) may necessitate another market entry method being used for initial entry into the international market. When international marketing begins with a different market entry method than indirect exporting, entry expansion will of necessity progress differently. Regardless of the market entry method, the development of an effective strategy is required. Exhibit 17.10 shows the strategy development process for the three market entry methods as involvement in foreign markets increases.

Developing an international marketing strategy for any one of the three market entry methods involves careful assessment. However, as involvement in international marketing expands, market entry can involve any combination of the three entry methods. Not only must a strategy be developed for each individual entry method used, but also strategies for each entry method employed must be coordinated into one encompassing strategy. The impact of one market entry strategy on another market entry strategy must be considered when more than one market entry method is employed.

A final consideration in the development of an international marketing strategy is whether to use local managers or expatriates in any expansions that require a presence of personnel in the foreign market. Expatriate managers are least likely to be used in

Exhibit 17.10 **International Market Entry Strategy Development**

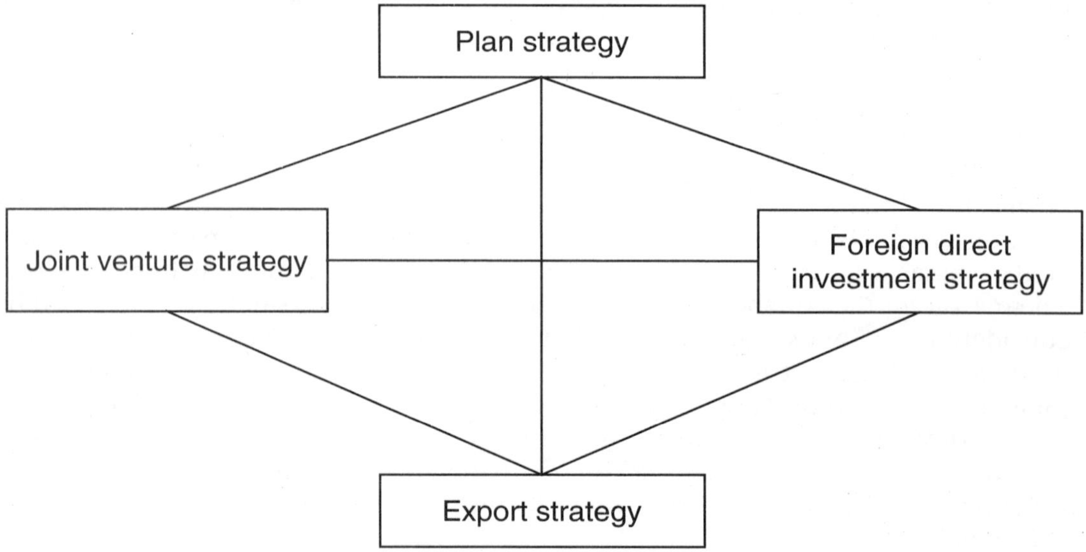

firms with limited international involvement and firms with extensive international involvement.[11] When beginning international marketing, indirect channels predominate, making use of local import agents and distributors. In firms with extensive involvement in international markets, management usually employs joint ventures and foreign direct investments that of necessity require the participation of local management.

Expatriate managers are used because of the following advantages domestic managers provide over host-country managers:[12]

- Expatriate managers are more likely to be familiar with the corporate culture and control system.
- Expatriate managers enhance the global mind-set of the organization.
- Expatriate managers provide better leadership in developing countries where local talent is limited.
- Expatriate managers provide more effective communication.
- Expatriate managers provide more effective coordination on marketing activities.

The use of expatriates is not appropriate for every situation because of the following limitations:[13]

- Adjustments in lifestyle may be difficult for the expatriate manager's family.
- Expatriates may have difficulty fitting into and adjusting to a distinctively different culture.
- Expatriates may not be accepted by foreigners as well as host-country managers.
- Relocating personnel can be costly.
- Training and preparation can be extensive and expensive.

Because of the problems associated with using expatriate managers, job dissatisfaction and poor job performance frequently occur.[14] Inadequate training and inability to acclimate to the foreign culture and environment are reasons often cited for the difficulties. Coming home after several years abroad can be difficult, and frequently expatriates are not sufficiently recognized for their achievements. Comparing the performance of expatriates with local managers may be inappropriate because of the vastly different conditions and working environment involved. The use of expatriate managers needs to be carefully considered as a component of international marketing strategy regardless of the method of market involvement employed. When expatriates are used, careful selection is mandatory to identify the appropriate person for the position. Adequate training and support will be required to assure the expatriate can do the work expected.

EXPORT STRATEGY

Since exporting is usually the first method of international market entry employed, a detailed understanding of the strategy involved is necessary. Developing an export strategy is a two-stage process.[15] In the first stage, the decision to engage in exporting and the market selection are made. The components of stage one are depicted in Exhibit 17.11. In stage two, the marketing mix is set. The components of stage two are depicted in Exhibit 17.12. Numerous decisions must be made in each stage of the process. A "yes" leads the international marketer toward completion of the overall strategy. A "no" to any decision thwarts the export strategy process and leads to a termination of the planning process, a decision not to engage in exporting, and no continuation of the strategy development process.

At each decision juncture in the strategy development process, risk may exist. However, the probability associated with the likelihood of proceeding or stopping is ultimately reduced to a "go/no-go" decision. Thus, decisions are always made under conditions of certainty, and a "maybe" or a "postpone" decision is not appropriate. A "maybe" or a "postpone" decision will cause strategy development to stagnate. A decision to do nothing now or to wait and see is indecision, and in reality is a negative decision that ultimately results in termination of the strategy development process.

The Decision to Engage in Exporting

The first stage of strategy development is the decision to engage in exporting. As can be seen in Exhibit 17.11, the first decision concerns whether or not management's attitude is favorable.

Is Management's Attitude Favorable? Management's attitude must be assessed. The attitudes of management influence international orientation and therefore affect the propensity of management to consider the export option. Management must have a favorable attitude toward the benefits expected before exporting options will be pursued. If the attitude toward exporting is unfavorable, further consideration of exporting opportunities will be forgone and strategy development never really gets started. If the attitude

Exhibit 17.11 **Developing an Exporting Strategy: The Exporting Decision**

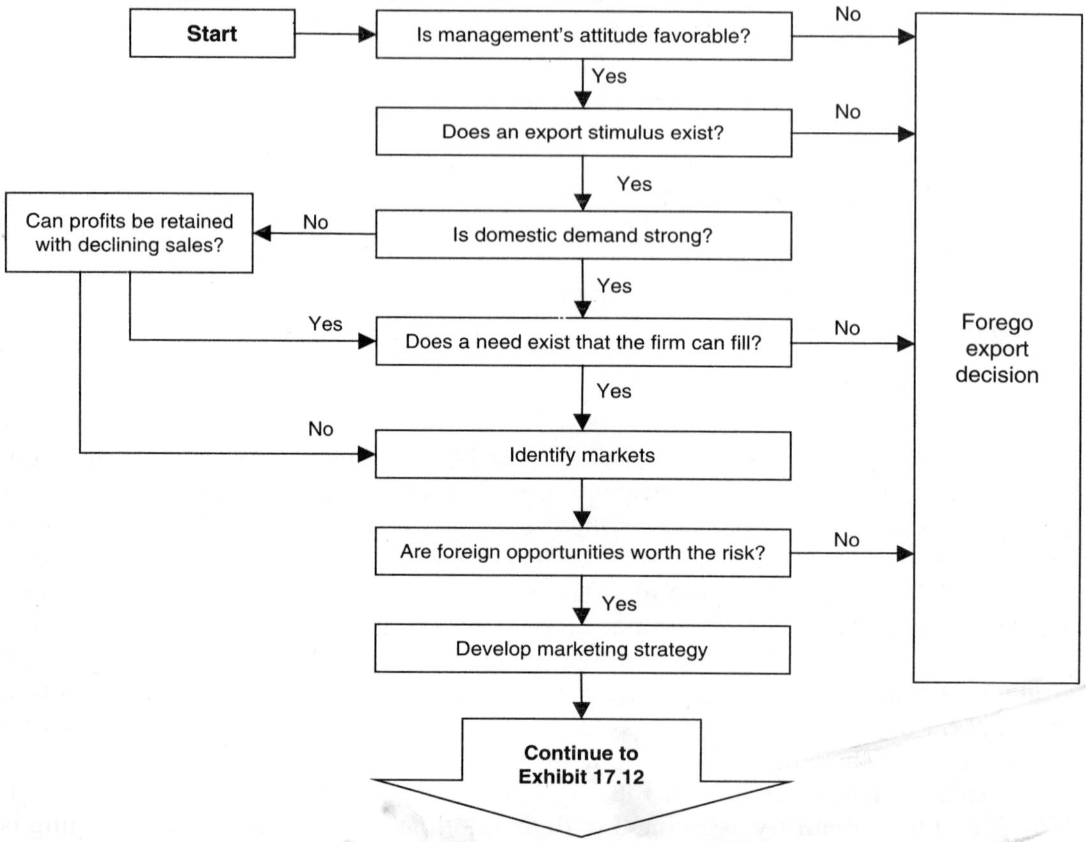

is favorable, the international marketer is inclined to export. At least the potential will be investigated. A "yes" decision leads to a consideration of the need to export.

Does an Export Stimulus Exist? Favorable attitudes do not necessarily guarantee export opportunities will be sought. Rather, favorable attitudes mean that if the attention of management is aroused concerning exporting, favorable consideration is given. The extent to which attention is stimulated depends upon the decision maker, the firm's environment, characteristics of the firm, and the interaction of those factors. A variety of attention evokers serve to arouse management's attention. These attention evokers are either exogenous or endogenous. Exogenous export stimuli consist of influences such as fortuitous orders from foreigners, and export stimulation from U.S. governmental agencies at the federal, state, and local level. Endogenous export stimuli result from business conditions within the firm that cause management to focus attention on export possibilities. If an export stimulus does not exist, the international marketer will not become aware of the potential, will respond negatively, and will forgo further strategy development. If a stimulus does exist, management will respond positively and continue strategy development by investigating export possibilities.

Exhibit 17.12 **Developing an Exporting Strategy: The Marketing Program**

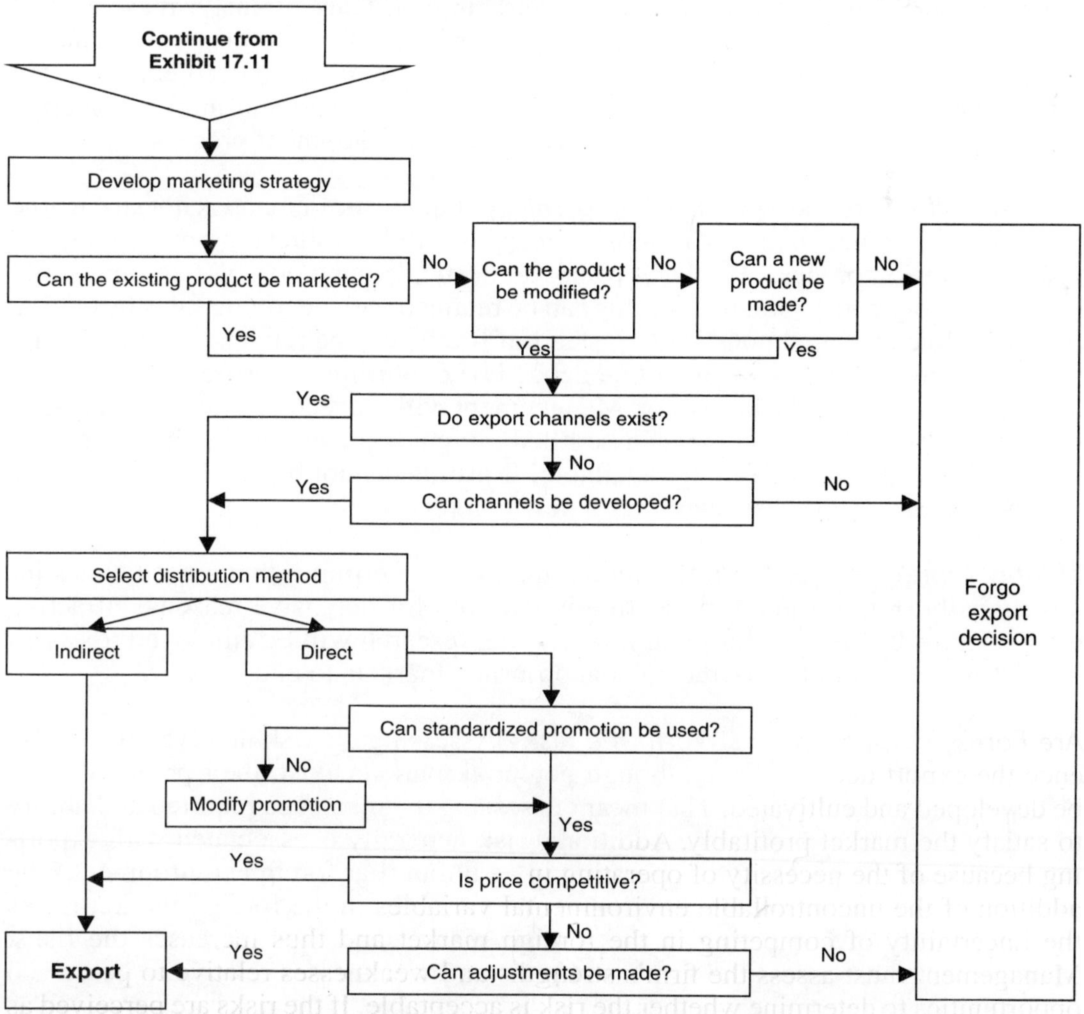

Is Domestic Demand Strong? Some export stimuli cause management to encounter pressures that draw or pull the firm into exporting. These pressures occur because of great or inviting opportunities perceived to be present in the foreign market. Such stimuli actually entice management into exporting. Other export stimuli cause management to encounter pressures forcing the firm into exporting. These pressures occur because of the lack of marketing opportunities domestically, and management feels compelled to consider exporting. Thus, the stimuli cause management to consider exporting for either offensive or defensive reasons. If the decision to investigate exporting is offensive, management is pulled by perceived opportunities; the justification is profit improvement. If the decision is defensive, management is pushed because of a lack of demand or need to protect market position; the justification will be profit retention.

Does a Need Exist That the Firm Can Fill? If domestic demand is strong and profit goals are being met, exporting is not particularly urgent. Thus, offensive reasons must exist to compel management to explore export opportunities. At this point, management will respond affirmatively and investigate whether or not a need exists for the firm's product outside the domestic market. Foreign demand and market selection decisions must then be made as part of the strategy development process.

Can Profits Be Retained with Declining Sales? If domestic demand is not strong, the response will be negative, and defensive reasons will be influencing management's strategy decision process. However, weak domestic demand does not automatically mean exporting will be pursued. Profits can be retained with declining sales by cutting costs and diversifying domestically instead. If profits can be retained with declining demand, then export sales may not be needed. If exporting is pursued, an offensive reason will have to be the motivator. Management will proceed to determine if a need exists in the foreign market that can be filled more adequately by the firm's product than by other offerings currently available. If profits cannot be retained while sales decline, management must search for a new market.

Identify Markets. Once the international marketer determines that a need exists internationally or that foreign marketing is required for defensive reasons, attractive markets must be identified for entry. Marketing research will be employed to assess the alternatives and identify the most appropriate markets to enter.

Are Foreign Opportunities Worth the Risk? Assessing the risk involved will influence the export decision. Even though potential markets exist, their potential must be developed and cultivated. That means assessing the resources required and ability to satisfy the market profitably. Additional risk generally is associated with exporting because of the necessity of operating in an unfamiliar foreign environment. The addition of the uncontrollable environmental variables in the foreign market raises the uncertainty of competing in the foreign market and thus increases the risks. Management must assess the firm's strengths and weaknesses relative to perceived opportunities to determine whether the risk is acceptable. If the risks are perceived as greater than the benefits, exporting will not be undertaken. If management perceives the foreign opportunities are worth the risk, exporting will be determined to be a desirable undertaking and an appropriate marketing strategy must be formulated.

The Export Marketing Program

The second stage of developing an export strategy, as shown in Exhibit 17.12 on page 337, involves formulating the correct international marketing program. This is an essential part of an effective exporting strategy. Although profit measures are the primary indicators used to assess the success of international marketing strategy, nonfinancial objectives such as maintaining or increasing market share or building image can drive strategy formulation.[16]

An appropriate international marketing program is formulated to assure the firm's offering can be successfully introduced in the foreign market and also to guide marketing efforts. How to be involved requires a determination of the target markets to be served, marketing expenditure levels (budgets), and the marketing mix. Standardization of as many elements of the foreign marketing strategy as possible is desirable because of resulting cost savings, and improved consistency of interactions and transactions with customers. However, adjustments are frequently required due to differences in the marketing environments between countries. Culture remains the most critical factor influencing international marketing strategy development.[17]

Product. Initially, management should carefully investigate the acceptability of the product in its existing form for meeting the identified need. When adjustments are needed, most likely to be affected are non-core elements, and even then preference is to keep changes to a minimum.[18] Most often changed are the following:

- labeling content, package design, and product names to meet legal requirements
- necessary parts of the product mix
- product instructions

In situations in which the product's national image is important, product modifications are undesirable and unnecessary. When product standardization is impossible, the international marketer must determine whether the product can be adapted to the tastes and economic characteristics of the foreign market. Product modification is desirable when this aids in achieving marketing objectives and contributes more to marginal revenue than marginal costs. Product modification may also be desirable because of differences in the stage of the country's economic development, the position of the product in its life cycle, and differences in culture.

If the existing product cannot be modified or if modifications are not economical, management may investigate the feasibility of reengineering and developing an entirely new product to meet the identified need. New products may be more easily introduced because no previous associations or prejudices have been established against the product. New product development may be appropriate and necessary for less developed markets where the standardized product is unaffordable. If introduction of a product in standardized, modified, or reengineered form is not feasible, exporting is not possible. If a product acceptable to the foreign market can be offered, an appropriate distribution strategy must be developed to provide availability when and where the customer desires.

Distribution. Obtaining distribution in a new market may be an obstacle to exporting. The international marketer should determine if the preferred export channel exists in the foreign market. Unfortunately, channel structures vary widely from country to country, and in general structures are influenced considerably by the foreign culture.

Because of differences encountered in channels among foreign markets, the preferred channel may not be available. It may not exist, or if it does exist, inclusion may be prohibited because of blockage. If the desired channel is available, incentives may occasionally be required to encourage participation. If the desired channel is not available, the feasibility of developing a new channel should be investigated. Exporting will be impossible if acceptable channels are not available or cannot be developed.

If channels are available or can be developed, management must select the most appropriate from direct or indirect alternatives. Risk is greater when direct channels are used, and thus, management inexperienced in exporting tends to begin with indirect methods. As experience in exporting is gained, management becomes more competent and tends to switch to direct channels when feasible. Management's attitudes toward the five salient factors discussed in chapter 11 tend to influence the channel alternative selected.

If an indirect channel arrangement is selected, exporting details are delegated to an export intermediary. The international marketer is relieved of further involvement with marketing strategy, and the export strategy development process is complete. The intermediary used will do the promotion required in the foreign market and will also set selling price. The international marketer will not be concerned with promotion or pricing strategy except as desired or arranged with the intermediary. The export process is completed for the international marketer when an indirect channel is employed and export strategy development is finished. If a direct channel is used, the international marketer must consider the remaining components of the marketing mix.

Promotion. Promotion strategy is the aspect of the marketing program with the greatest similarities from market to market, yet it may involve the greatest number of culturally related problems. The decision to standardize or individualize promotion is a controversial issue. Regardless, a decision is ultimately made whether to extend, adapt, or develop new communications and appeals in the foreign market. Themes are frequently standardized while the other aspects are individualized, as foreign market uniqueness requires. If standardization is not possible, modification is always possible. Care must be exercised, however, to ensure the modified promotions are acceptable to the foreign consumers.

Price. Price strategy can be an overlooked aspect of the foreign marketing program when decisions are based solely on costs. If demand and competition are ignored, price ceases to be a strategic element of the foreign marketing strategy and becomes static. Active pricing, on the other hand, is preferable because of its responsiveness to market conditions. Regardless, the selling price must be profitable and competitive. Both cost and market factors must be considered. Price escalation, if existent, needs to be carefully considered in the decision.

If price is not competitive, the market will need to have a preference for the product to pay a higher noncompetitive price. If the price is noncompetitive and the product has no special appeal to consumers, adjustments will be needed to make price more competitive. To accomplish this, costs must be lowered somewhere. This means adjustments will be sought in other parts of the marketing mix. Changes can be made in the distribution structure, the product and production process, or promotion so that costs can be reduced. Examples of product adjustments that result in cost savings include reducing material costs with substitutes, reengineering, simplification, cutting features, repackaging, cutting services, and reducing quality. Examples of distribution adjustments producing cost savings include endeavors such as shortening channels by eliminating intermediaries, cutting intermediary margins, changing agents, and identifying shipping efficiencies. Examples of promotion adjustments contributing to lower costs include activities such as changing media, reducing frequency of exposure, and increasing use of public relations and other free outlets.

The problem with trying to reduce costs is that optimum decisions have already been made for the marketing mix, and any changes may result in a suboptimum international marketing strategy. Since the components of the marketing mix are interrelated, changing one can affect the others. Therefore, any change made will require an assessment of the impact on the remainder of the marketing mix and the potential need to make other adjustments to compensate. If sufficient cost cutting were not possible to permit a competitive price, one final alternative would be to set a competitive price and accept a lower profit per unit. Managers valuing the opportunity to develop new skills, technology, and organizational capabilities are more likely to continue exporting, even when the immediate economic benefits are uncertain.[19] If adjustments to the international marketing program to make price competitive are not possible and accepting lower margins is not feasible, exporting cannot occur.

ETHICS IN INTERNATIONAL MARKETING STRATEGY

An important consideration influencing the development of an acceptable international marketing strategy concerns the appropriateness of behavior. Decisions and actions that the international marketer takes must be suitable and appropriate. The appropriateness of decisions is just as important as the accuracy of decisions. Overlooking the ethical aspects of decisions can result in problems that can lead to failure.

Ethics is the moral principles that guide conduct. The standards and mores that guide management's interactions with and treatment of others are paramount. Ethics involves right and wrong as related to the rules and standards for a set of guidelines that connects decisions to the overall well-being of society. The values one brings to a decision and how those values influence the decision are the essence of ethical or unethical behavior.

Almost all decisions contain an ethical component. Therefore, anytime a strategy decision is made, management can encounter a moral dilemma. So the question that must always be confronted is: How does one make correct judgments about what is morally right and wrong, that is, what is ethical? Ethical decision making involves three steps.[20]

1. Gather relevant factual information pertaining to the decision.
2. Determine the appropriate moral norms that relate to the decision.
3. Make an ethical judgment about what is right or wrong in the proposed decision.

Ethical judgments involve all kinds of considerations. Since ethics involves many considerations, following these steps will not always guarantee a moral decision. If relevant factual information is omitted or nonrelevant information is included; if the wrong moral principle is applied or the judgment decision flawed in some way, the

Exhibit 17.13

Ethical Considerations

Appropriate	Honorable	Respectful
Beliefs	Just	Responsible
Careful	Kind	Rules
Codes	Legal	Scrupulous
Compassionate	Moral	Social responsibility
Conscientious	Noble	Standards
Creeds	Precise	Suitable
Decent	Principled	Truthful
Doing right	Proper behavior	Upright
Fair	Respectable	Values
Honest	Respected	Virtuous

resulting strategy could be ethically inappropriate. A partial list of ethical considerations that may motivate and influence a decision or action is shown in Exhibit 17.13.

Ethical decisions do not result from following one's conscience. Letting your conscience be your guide will not guarantee ethical behavior. Basing decisions on conscience alone is an untrustworthy way to make ethical judgments. The problem is that consciences vary considerably among people and throughout time. Such things as religious beliefs, training, childhood learning, and circumstances influence conscience. Thus, what one person's conscience will permit, another person's may not. Since ethics are based on standards and universal codes of conduct, relying on conscience will not assure consistent decisions among different individuals facing the same situation.

Approaches to ethics fall into two different schools of thought:

- **Teleology**—whether a decision is ethical or not is completely dependent on the results or outcome of an action. The consequences of the decision are more important than the intent or means of achieving the decision.
- **Deontology**—whether a decision is ethically right or wrong is dependent on other factors instead of, or in addition to, the consequences. The means for achieving the results are the most important, and therefore, the duty or responsibility of how to behave is more significant than the outcome.

The school or orientation the decision maker embraces will influence the nature of the decision. Managers applying a teleological orientation are more concerned with the results of a decision than the means of achieving it. The ends justify the means. Managers using a deontological orientation are more concerned with the means employed than with the result of a decision. The means justify the ends. Thus, a teleological manager would tend to reward employees with an increase in salary based on their productivity. How the productivity is achieved is less important than

Exhibit 17.14

A Partial List of Popular Ethical Theories

Egoism
Justice
Relativism
Rights
Utilitarianism
Virtue

what the productivity is. A deontological manager would tend to reward employees with an increase in salary based on their effort and work ethic regardless of what that effort produced. What was achieved would be less important than the effort, energy, and good intentions employed. From a deontological perspective, employees would deserve a raise just because they exerted a lot of effort and worked hard even if they failed to fully achieve the desired goal.

A teleological manager rewards an employee who, for example, lands a large, profitable contract after one contact with the customer, even though little effort was involved and the business might be considered a windfall for the employee. A deontological manager rewards an employee who, for example, fails to get a large, profitable contract but cultivated the prospect, invested a lot of overtime, and made every appropriate effort to secure the account. For the teleological manager, the time involved and the effort invested are unimportant. The only important fact is that the account was obtained. For the deontological manager, what the employee does in an effort to secure the account is more important than what the prospect did. The important thing is that the employee tries very hard and does everything appropriate to try to acquire the account.

Various philosophical theories of ethical behavior have been advanced. Adhering to any one theory may or may not necessarily produce an ethical decision when viewed from the perspective of any of the other ethical theories. The international marketer should strive to embrace all or as many of the appropriate theories as possible when formulating a strategy decision to help assure the most ethical behavior is selected. Six commonly employed theories of ethics are listed in Exhibit 17.14, and discussions of each of these six follow.

EGOISM

According to the **egoism** theory the consequences for the decision maker are the only relevant considerations for determining whether or not something is ethical. Decisions are made on the basis of perceived self-interest. Others are considered only when they promote the decision maker's own well-being.

JUSTICE

Decisions that are fair, equitable, and impartial are ethical according to the **justice** theory. The decision maker must be evenhanded in terms of the benefits and burdens associated with a decision. The result of the decision must be appropriate for everyone. That is, a decision is just when those affected are treated comparably to how others would be treated under similar conditions. Rewards and punishments must be allocated equitably to all.

RELATIVISM

From the perspective of **relativism,** ethically right decisions are based on the unique conditions and facts involved in each and every circumstance. No single, universal standard or rule can be used in the decision process. All decisions must be determined on a case-by-case basis, because what may be considered unethical in one situation may be concluded appropriate in another based on circumstances. The decision maker looks at each situation as unique, and the decision is based on the merits of that situation alone. Relativism is also known as **situational ethics** and embodies the philosophy of "When in Rome, do as the Romans do."

RIGHTS

Ethical decisions require that the rights of those affected be maintained. **Rights** are entitlements that are not to be deprived by any decision. The decision maker must assure that decisions provide those affected with appropriate entitlements or do not deprive those affected of what is deserved. The management at Wal-Mart Stores has been accused of selling school uniforms that were purchased from JMS Garments Factory in Bangladesh and produced under sweatshop conditions. Workers at JMS Garments Factory worked up to nineteen-hour shifts, were made to stand for hours as punishment for arriving late to work, were subjected to verbal abuse, received beatings or kickings, and were paid as little as US$20 per month, an amount that is below the country's legal minimum wage.[21] Such behavior deprives people of their basic human rights.

UTILITARIANISM

According to the theory of **utilitarianism**, a decision is ethical when the results produce the greatest good for the greatest number of people affected. The optimum consequence that results from a cost/benefit analysis is the most ethical decision. Decisions that maximize good and minimize harm are ethical.

VIRTUE

A decision is ethical if the decision maker exhibits good character or **virtue**. Thus, the qualities of the decision maker and the motivation behind the decision are the most important factors. Admirable qualities possessed by the decision maker will influence the nature of the decision in a way that is ethically commendable and appropriate. For example, the Sun Products Corporation has been recognized by the People for the Ethical Treatment of Animals (PETA) for producing the "Best Cruelty-Free Personal

Care Product Line." The company was recognized through PETA's Proggy Awards, which distinguish animal-friendly achievements in commerce and culture. The firm's White Rain brand of shampoos, conditioners, hair sprays, mousses, styling gels, and body washes contain no animal ingredients and are never tested on animals.[22]

UNETHICAL DECISION MAKING

Egoism and relativism are two approaches to ethical decision making that probably are not credible and should, therefore, be avoided. Since the decision maker considers only himself or herself, decisions made under egoism are unlikely to be considered appropriate; the interests of others are subjugated. Decisions could become selfishly motivated and extremely immoral. Likewise, decisions made from a relativistic approach are unlikely to be good or right, only fitting. The decision maker can easily justify any position desired by applying only the standards favored. The decision maker simply decides to do whatever he or she believes is best. Thus, when the decision maker's belief system differs from that of others, whose beliefs are right? Relativism is an excuse for avoiding principles and will degrade to the lowest standard since differing views on morality should all be considered equally valid. However, relativism can be used to support an action or behavior in the foreign country that is considered appropriate there and not appropriate in another country. For example, DDT, an insecticide that was banned in the United States in 1972, is sold in third world countries for use in controlling malaria. A decision to sell DDT in foreign countries might also be considered ethical according to the utilitarian theory, because the benefits of controlling malaria are viewed to be more important than the environmental risks that result from spraying. However, from the rights and virtue perspectives, such behavior is likely to be considered inappropriate and unethical.

Another classic example of unethical behavior involves the decision of the management of Nestlé S.A. to sell infant formula in underdeveloped countries. Salespeople dressed as milk nurses distributed free samples of the formula to new mothers in the hospital, and tried to convince the mothers that formula feeding was superior to breast-feeding. Enough samples were given so the mothers who used the samples were unable to breast-feed. Because of illiteracy, ignorance, and poverty, the formula was misused. Mothers were not taught the correct way to prepare the formula, and as a result, bottles and nipples were not sterilized. Feedings were prepared in unsanitary conditions. Poorer mothers were unable to buy sufficient amounts of formula and added water to stretch the volume, causing nutritional value to be diluted. Misuse of the formula caused malnourished and sickly babies. Additionally, the production equipment developed a crack that allowed bacteria to get into the formula during manufacturing. Production of contaminated formula was allowed to continue after management became aware of the problem. No theory of ethics, except maybe egoism, could justify management's behavior. As a result of management's actions, a successful worldwide boycott was organized against Nestlé that had a significant impact on reducing the sales of Nestlé products.

Unethical behavior can have a negative impact on the firm's image and sales. Time and effort are required to build a firm's reputation and image. One careless, unethical act can quickly undo all of the goodwill that took years to build. Therefore, decision makers must take ethics into account so that marketing strategy decisions remain above reproach. Decision makers must strive to behave in a way that does not leave them or the firm open to criticism.

In some Middle Eastern countries, **baksheesh** is an acceptable way of doing business. Baksheesh is a small, under-the-table payment (bribe) that is requested by low-level government officials or businesspeople for the purpose of facilitating the business process. An example is a payment to customs officials to guarantee that paperwork is processed and not purposefully lost. Obviously, without paying the baksheesh, the shipment cannot be completed without considerable frustration and time. Initially, the Foreign Corrupt Practices Act of 1977 made such payments illegal under U.S. law. This law put U.S. businesspeople at a disadvantage when competing in countries where the practice is prevalent. The Omnibus Trade and Competitiveness Act of 1988 made lubrication payments like baksheesh legal to help ease processing and make clearing customs easier. Although legal, is bribery, regardless of the amount, ethical? Such practices could easily be justified via relativism. However, what might the impact be if customers or other citizens of the United States should learn about such activities? Just because an activity is legal does not necessarily make that activity ethical. All decisions should be judged as just, right, virtuous, and maximizing good before implementation. Otherwise, criticisms of unethical behavior might be raised. Marketing strategy alternatives must always be considered for ethical implications.

FREE TRADE ZONES

The use of a free trade zone can be an important component of an international marketing strategy. Some countries have created free trade zones as a method of encouraging and facilitating international sales. A **free trade zone** is a fenced-in area, usually at a seaport or airport, and is not considered to be part of the country as far as import regulations are concerned. Products can be freely moved in and out of the free trade zone without the firm paying tariffs or duties. Before the products are sold, the international marketer can engage in activities such as warehousing, processing, assembling, cleaning, sorting, repackaging, and light manufacturing in the free trade zone. The products can then be shipped to another location for sale, permitting the paying of tariffs to the country providing the free trade zone to be completely avoided. If the product is sold in the country in which the free trade zone is located, duties are paid only when the product leaves the free trade zone.

Using a free trade zone permits the international marketer to reduce some of the effects of price escalation so price can be more competitive. This is possible because labor and overhead costs incurred in the free trade zone during processing are not included in the total cost of the product and are therefore exempt from duties. When the product leaves the free trade zone and enters the country for subsequent sale, the taxable cost is the imported value before any processing is done in the free trade zone. An accompanying benefit is that tariffs are usually assessed at a lower rate on the import of unassembled components and parts than on the import of fully assembled products. The lower duties paid on the imported components and parts can also reduce the impact of price escalation, helping the international marketer control prices.

If a free trade zone is not used, duties on imported products must be paid at the time of import. When the product is exported to another country, the international marketer must apply for repayment of duties already paid when the product initially entered the country. A **drawback** must be processed in the foreign country to obtain repayment of previously paid tariffs. This represents an additional cost to management because forms must be processed for import and again for the drawback. Not only does management lose use of the money paid in duties until repaid, the processing of the drawback takes time and adds an additional administrative responsibility, all of which contribute to higher costs of doing business. By utilizing a free trade zone, the international marketer can reduce marketing costs.

CHAPTER SUMMARY

A successful international marketing strategy involves effective planning, assembling of resources, implementing, administering, and controlling. A good strategy is important if management wants to provide the greatest amount of satisfaction possible to the target market and stay ahead of competition. Effective international planning involves establishing objectives and developing an appropriate strategy, marketing plan, and tactics that will achieve that objective.

The market entry method will affect the development of an international marketing strategy. Most marketers begin via exporting, although joint ventures and foreign direct investments may also be used. Appropriate international marketing strategies are developed for each market entry method used. If more than one market entry method is employed, individual strategies must be coordinated into one encompassing strategy.

An effective exporting strategy involves numerous considerations that can be grouped into two stages. The first stage involves the reasoning process that precipitates the decision to engage in exporting. Management must be made aware of the potential offered by the international market by some export stimulus. If the appropriate stimulus exists, management will investigate the opportunities. Management can be enticed into exporting when an unfilled need is identified. When domestic demand is weak, management can be forced into exporting when profits cannot be retained in the domestic market. Possible markets to enter will be identified. Once the foreign opportunities in those markets are considered to be worth the risk, management will make the decision to start exporting.

The second stage is to develop an appropriate marketing program to satisfy customers in the selected countries. Product standardization or modification will be determined. An appropriate channel arrangement with intermediaries will be identified. A decision to standardize or customize promotion will be made. Finally, the price the customer considers appropriate will be set. The international marketer is now ready to enter the foreign market with the established export strategy.

The strategy developed must be ethical and appropriate to all people affected by it. Failure to consider the ethical impact of strategy decisions can adversely affect the firm's image and reputation. All strategy decisions must be just, correct in relationship to entitlements, virtuous, and appropriate to society. Management may need to subjugate financial concerns to ethical pragmatism to assure a successful international marketing strategy.

Using free trade zones can enhance marketing strategy. Free trade zones help reduce the cost of marketing by lowering tariffs paid. Effective use of a free trade zone can help provide price advantages.

KEY TERMS

Baksheesh	Justice
Deontology	Marketing strategy
Drawback	Mission statement
Egoism	Objectives
Ethics	Relativism
Free trade zone	Rights
International marketing plans	Situational ethics
International marketing strategy	Teleology
International marketing tactics	Utilitarianism
International marketing targets	Virtue

REVIEW QUESTIONS

1. How does planning affect international marketing strategy formulation?
2. Why is management's attitude influential in the decision to export and develop an effective marketing strategy? Review the material in the Management Orientation section in chapter 5 before formulating an answer.
3. What impact do domestic profits have on international marketing strategy formulation?
4. Explain how marketing-mix decisions can thwart international marketing strategy.
5. What is the difference between international marketing programs and international marketing tactics?
6. What is the role of control in the international marketing management process?
7. What is the difference between a teleological and a deontological orientation toward ethics?
8. List and define the six theories of ethics discussed in the chapter. Give a business example of each.
9. Do you consider the kinds of advertising done by Benetton Group, S.p.A., as described in the introductory vignette in chapter 15 ethical? Provide arguments, grounded in ethical theory, to support your position.
10. What is a free trade zone? How can the use of a free trade zone benefit international marketing strategy?

NOTES

1. PepsiCo, "Our Mission and Vision," http://www.pepsico.com/Company/Our-Mission-and-Vision.html; and PepsiCo, "Financial Information," in *2008 Annual Report,* http://www.pepsico.com/Annual-Reports/2008/financials/mda-01.html.

2. Ibid.

3. Ibid.

4. Robert Laing, "Pepsi's Comeback: Part II," *Mail & Guardian Online*, March 28, 2006, http://www.mg.co.za/article/2006–03–28-pepsis-comeback-part-ii.

5. Ibid.

6. Craig Morris, "AMD Is Investing 2.5 Billion US Dollars in Dresden," CeBIT, May 29, 2006, http://www.cebit.de/newsanzeige_d?news=24334&tag=1148857201&source=%2Fnewsarchiv_e&noindex=.

7. "2008 Annual Report," General Electric Company, 10, http://www.ge.com/ar2008/pdf/ge_ar_2008.pdf.

8. "2009 Annual Report," General Electric Company, 39, http://www.ge.com/ar2009/pdf/ge_ar_2009.pdf.

9. Stephanie E. Ponder, "A Work of Art," *The Costco Connection* 20 (2) (February 2005): 19.

10. "GM and Nissan Make Russian Move," BBC News, June 13, 2006, http://news.bbc.co.uk/2/hi/business/5075466.stm.

11. Meredith Downes and Thomas S. Anisya, "Knowledge Transfer through Expatriation: The U-Curve Approach to Overseas Staffing," *Journal of Managerial Issues* 12 (2) (Summer 2000): 131–52.

12. Linda Gorchels, Thani Jambulingam, and Timothy W. Aurand, "International Marketing Managers: A Comparison of Japanese, German, and U.S. Perceptions," *Journal of International Marketing* 7 (1) (1999): 97–106.

13. Ibid.

14. J. Stewart Black and Hal B. Gregersen, "The Right Way to Manage Expats," *Harvard Business Review* (March–April 1999): 52–60.

15. Donald L. Brady, "Toward the Development of a Normative Model of the Export Decision Process: Literature Analysis and Preliminary Findings," paper presented at the Northeastern Regional Meeting of the Academy of International Business, New York City, October 7, 1983.

16. Barbara Stottinger, "Strategic Export Pricing: A Long and Winding Road," *Journal of International Marketing* 9 (1) (2001): 40–64.

17. A. Coskun Samli, James R. Wills, and Laurence Jacobs, "Developing Global Products and Marketing Strategies: A Rejoinder," *Journal of the Academy of Marketing Science* 21 (1) (December 1993): 79–83.

18. Arnold Schuh, "Global Standardization as a Success Formula for Marketing in Central Eastern Europe?" *Journal of World Business* 35 (2) (Summer 2000): 133–49.

19. William J. Burpitt and Dennis A. Rondinelli, "Small Firms' Motivations for Exporting: To Earn and Learn?" *Journal of Small Business Management* 38 (4) (October 2000): 14–29.

20. Gerald F. Cavanaugh, *American Business Values with International Perspectives,* 4th ed. (Upper Saddle River, NJ: Prentice Hall, 1998), 71.

21. Pallavi Gogoi, "Wal-Mart Supplier Accused of Sweatshop Conditions," *Business Week,* October 9, 2008, http://www.businessweek.com/bwdaily/dnflash/content/oct2008/db2008109_219930.htm?chan=top%20news_top%20news%20index%20-%20temp_companies.

22. People for the Ethical Treatment of Animals, "PETA's 5th Annual Proggy Awards," 2008, http://www.peta.org/feat/proggy/2008/index.asp.

Glossary

Absolute advantage. A situation that exists when the firms in one country can better use the available resources to produce a product than can the firms of another country.

Ad valorem tariff. A fee assessed as a percentage of the value of the product.

Administered exchange rates. Occur when the rates at which currency is bought and sold are artificially set at a rate other than the free market rate; a form of nontariff barrier.

Administrative and legal barriers. Impediments intended to slow down or make exporting or importing the product difficult or impossible.

Advertising. All paid forms of impersonal communication from an identified sponsor.

Agent. Does not take title to the product, but brings the buyer and seller together to facilitate the sale, and earns income by charging a fee or commission for services rendered.

Air waybill. The consignment note for a product shipped by airplane; not negotiable.

American system. A system of measures used in the United States and some English-speaking countries.

Arms-length price. A price set for intracompany transfers that is defensible for tax purposes.

Arrival draft. Must be paid when the product arrives at the foreign port or the buyer's location (depending on what shipping terms are used).

Back translation. Translating from one language to a second language and retranslating the translated version back into the first language.

Baksheesh. A small bribe requested by low-level government officials or business-people for the purpose of facilitating the business process, which is often considered acceptable and necessary especially in Middle Eastern countries.

Balance of payments. A government's accounting of currency flows between its country and all other countries.

Balance of trade. Part of the current account; this considers only merchandise transactions and excludes services.

Bank credit countertrade. A form of countertrade in which a U.S. bank lends money to the foreign buyer to facilitate the transaction.

Barter house. Provides the services of a countertrade specialist who puts together countertrade contracts and is involved from negotiations to disposal of the countertraded products or services.

Benelux Customs Union. A free trade area formed in 1944 among Belgium, the Netherlands, and Luxembourg; the first modern-day attempt at economic integration.

Bilateral barter. The simplest form of countertrade, which occurs when the management in two firms agree to exchange products or services and no money is involved.

Bill of exchange. An unconditional written order from the seller to the buyer instructing the buyer to pay a specific amount of money to a third party, usually a bank or financial institution. Also called a draft.

Blocked channel. The international marketing manager is prohibited from using the desired channel.

Blocked currency. Occurs when foreign currency is nonconvertible. Also, a form of countertrade in which the domestic firm sells products or services to a foreign firm, purchases other goods or services from another firm in that country with the proceeds, and exports the goods or services.

Boycott. The refusal of a nation's citizens or government to purchase a product.

Brand. A word, name, design, or symbol that identifies the physical item visually, verbally, or in both ways.

Brand modifications. Changes in the brand mark or brand name.

Brand piracy. When foreign firms illegally use the firm's brand; usually occurs when the product is a status symbol, in short supply, or extremely expensive.

Built-in export department. Part of a direct international channel in which a firm's export sales are handled by members of the firm's domestic marketing department. The first phase of the international marketing evolutionary process, in which international orders are processed by the domestic marketing staff and no support for exporting is provided in the firm's organizational structure.

Burenstam Linder's theory. A theory of international trade that holds that great domestic demand for a product leads to increasing world demand, creating a large export market for excess capacity.

Buyback. Occurs when the management of the domestic firm sells capital products or services to a foreign buyer who repays gradually with an equivalent value of products manufactured with the purchased equipment or from the production process the expertise or technology helped establish.

Buying rate. The amount of the local currency that can be obtained for one unit of a foreign currency.

Canada customs invoice. May be required for shipments to Canada from the United States.

Capital account. The difference between the value of capital flowing into and out of the country for any reason other than for goods and services.

Carnet. A form used in foreign countries to avoid paying duty on product samples imported to those countries.

Cash in advance. Seller receives payment before the product is shipped.

Causal research. Research undertaken when the problem is clearly defined, cause and effect relationships must be identified, and management needs to make forecasts or projections.

Celsius. The fundamental unit of temperature in the metric system. The freezing point is 0°C, the boiling point is 100°C, and the distance between the two is divided into 100 equal units.

Centi. The prefix given to indicate 1/100. Ex.: a centiliter = 0.01 liters.

Certificate of origin. A form that specifies the origin of product content.

Code law. Law that is based on policies that have been placed in writing.

Cognitive knowledge. The ability to think and feel at home in the foreign culture in such a way that the factual knowledge can be understood and appreciated.

Collectivistic cultures. Cultures that tend to emphasize the importance of the group over that of the individual.

Combination tariff. A fee that combines a specific and an ad valorem tariff.

Commercial invoice. A statement of the merchandise sold describing essential facts about the shipment.

Common law. Law that is based on precedents set by previous court decisions.

Common market. The same characteristics as a customs union with the addition of free movement of labor and capital.

Comparative advantage. A situation that exists when the firms in one country produce a product more efficiently (with a lower opportunity cost) than firms in another country.

Comparative disadvantage. This occurs when the firms in a country produce a product less efficiently (with a higher opportunity cost) than firms in another country.

Concept of international exhaustion. A manufacturer's intellectual property rights (brands, trademarks, copyrights, and patents) end once the manufacturer distributes its product to the market.

Confirmed. A type of letter of credit in which the advising bank guarantees payment to the seller.

Construction and job performance contracts. Arrangements in which the domestic firm builds a physical plant and facilities for a foreign firm.

Consular invoice. Legalization that may be required by the foreign country's consulate located in the exporting country; a common practice in Middle Eastern, Latin American, African, and small Asian countries.

Containerized freight. A system of transport using metal box containers, known as isotainers, which can be easily loaded on and off truck trailer wheels, railroad cars, and ships.

Contract manufacturing. An agreement made with a foreign firm to transfer production expertise to the foreign country so a product can be produced there for the domestic firm, which retains marketing responsibilities.

Controllable variables. Those aspects of the marketing environment that can be manipulated or changed in the short run at the manager's discretion (referred to as the marketing mix).

Cosmopolitan marketing. Marketing between sovereign nation-states without a nationalistic frame of reference.

Counterfeiting. Occurs when a product is sold with an appearance that is the same as or similar to that of the real product.

Counterpurchase. Occurs when the domestic seller is required to purchase a given percentage of the contract value in other products or services from the foreign buyer.

Countertrade. The exchange of products or services for different products or services.

Credit. *See* open account.

Cultural electives. Behaviors that foreigners may observe but are not expected or obliged to respect.

Cultural empathy. Exists when managers put themselves in the foreigners' position so their perspective is understood and appreciated.

Cultural exclusives. Behaviors from which foreigners are excluded.

Cultural imperatives. Behaviors that foreigners must observe to be successful.

Culturally congruent strategy. A marketing strategy that is as similar as possible to the strategy of the local competition.

Culturally disparate strategy. A marketing strategy that deliberately ignores or opposes the prevailing cultural norms.

Culturally distinct strategy. A marketing strategy that remains culturally similar in most of the marketing program but introduces one or a few cultural dissimilarities.

Culture. A distinct way of life for an aggregate of people that encompasses things such as beliefs, habits, customs, morals, laws, religion, education, family, cuisine, work, and art.

Cumulative turnover tax. Assessed to the total selling price each time the product moves from one reseller to another.

Currency hedge. An arrangement that reduces the risk of a transaction by acting as a buffer against currency fluctuations.

Currency swap. The simultaneous purchase and sale of a foreign currency at a fixed exchange rate.

Current account. The difference between the value of the import and the value of the export of products and services for a country.

Customs union. Has all the characteristics of a free trade association, except member governments agree on a common set of external trade restrictions to be assessed against imports from nonmember nations.

Dated draft. Must be paid on or before the day, month, and year prescribed.

Dealer. An intermediary found in a direct international channel that acts as a principal in the purchase and sale of products.

Deca. The prefix given to indicate 10. Ex.: a decameter = 10 meters.

Deci. The prefix given to indicate 1/10. Ex.: a decimeter = 0.1 meters.

Deontology. An ethics that bases decisions about whether or not a behavior is right or wrong on factors other than the behavior's consequences. The means justify the ends.

Descriptive research. Research undertaken when the problem is fairly well understood and the manager needs only to describe characteristics or attributes.

Devaluation. The reduction in the value of one currency relative to that of another.

Developing countries. Countries that are striving to become industrialized. These countries are characterized by high growth rates of gross national income, limited population growth, increasing size of the middle class, and rapidly growing market economies.

Direct channel. A channel formed when the seller negotiates the sale with an intermediary or customer located in the foreign market.

Direct marketing. Specific messages that are tailored to communicate directly with targeted consumers in any way other than via a mass medium or in a face-to-face manner.

Distributor. An intermediary that is a type of wholesaler found in a direct international channel. It sells complementary, nonconflicting products to retailers and other intermediaries but not directly to the public.

Draft. *See* bill of exchange.

Drawback. Paperwork completed in a foreign country to obtain repayment of previously paid tariffs.

Dumping. Selling below cost to reduce unwanted inventory or gain market share in a foreign country; also producing a product in a low-cost area and selling in a high-cost area at a lower price than local suppliers.

Economic and monetary union. The same characteristics as a common market with the addition of a common currency.

Edge Act banks. Subsidiaries of U.S. banks that are permitted to make short-term and long-term loans to foreigners that can be used to finance international purchases.

Education. A type of factual knowledge that allows cultural behavior to be learned.

Egoism. An ethics in which decisions are made on the basis of perceived self-interest.

Embargo. Forbids or prohibits any exports or imports.

Emerging markets. Developing countries that exhibit rapid economic growth and present attractive business opportunities for the international marketer.

Equity joint venture. Also called a joint ownership, joint venture, it occurs when the owners of a domestic firm enter into a financial investment in the foreign country with one or more foreign partners.

Ethics. Concerned with the moral principles that guide conduct.

Ethnocentric. Home-country oriented and not acclimated toward international aspects of the business.

Eurodollars. U.S. dollar-denominated deposits held in foreign banks or branches of American banks. Banks holding Eurodollar deposits are a source of U.S. dollar loans for foreign business.

European Coal and Steel Community (ECSC). Formed by the Treaty of Paris in 1951; the members of the Benelux Customs Union joined France, Italy, and West Germany for free movement of coal and steel within the six member nations.

European Community (EC). Formerly known as the European Economic Community (EEC); now is the European Union (EU).

European Economic Area. Formed in 1994 for the purpose of allowing European Free Trade Association (EFTA) countries participation in the EU without the need to join.

European Economic Community (EEC). Formed by the Treaty of Rome in 1957 by members of the ECSC; eventually became the European Union (EU).

European Free Trade Association (EFTA). Formed by the Treaty of Stockholm in 1960 by European nations concerned with maintaining individual national sovereignty.

European Union (EU). The most successful and well-known economic integration of nations.

Exchange barriers. Restrictions that adversely affect foreign exchange transactions.

Exchange controls. Restrictions placed on the exchange of the country's currency to those of other countries.

Exchange rate. The amount of a country's currency that can be exchanged for one unit of another country's currency.

Expatriate. A person who is living in a country other than where raised or legally residing.

Experimental method. A primary data research method that determines the impact of systematically changing stimuli in a controlled environment.

Exploratory research. Research that is undertaken when the nature of the problem is not known or understood.

Export agent. A category of intermediaries found in indirect international channels. For a commission, they represent a number of noncompeting producers and locate foreign buyers for the products produced by those firms.

Export barriers. Any restrictions that will limit or make exporting impossible.

Export broker. An intermediary found in an indirect international channel that locates buyers for sellers and vice versa but is not a party to the sales transaction.

Export commission house. An intermediary that functions as a purchasing agent for one or more foreign buyers. Found in an indirect international channel.

Export department. An organizational structure characterized by the creation of a separate marketing function to accommodate international business.

Export house. An intermediary found in an indirect international channel that buys products from a domestic producer and engages in marketing efforts to locate buyers in foreign markets.

Export management company (EMC). An intermediary found in an indirect international channel that functions as an export department for various producers or provides services for a commission.

Export mechanics. The steps or procedures involved in exporting a product from one country and importing to another country.

Export merchant. A category of intermediaries found in indirect international channels that buy products from manufacturers or suppliers and resell them to buyers located in foreign countries.

Export trading company (ETC). An intermediary found in a direct international channel that sells the products of several competing firms, improves the availability of export financing, and is exempt from U.S. antitrust laws.

Export-Import Bank of the United States (Ex-Im Bank). Assists foreigners to buy U.S.-made products by making direct loans, guaranteeing loans, providing insurance, and discounting loans to U.S. commercial banks that lend to foreigners purchasing U.S. products.

Exporting. A market entry method in which the product is manufactured domestically and shipped to the foreign market.

Expropriation. The acquisition of the firm's property in the foreign country by the foreign government.

Factual knowledge. Knowledge about a culture that can be learned.

Feature modifications. Changes that are made to enhance the characteristics of the product so the number of real or fancied user benefits is increased.

Force majeure clause. A clause inserted into a contract that exempts the seller from nonfulfillment because of uncontrollable conditions such as floods, a ship's sinking, or war.

Foreign direct investment (FDI). A wholly owned international venture that is a subsidiary or branch of the domestic firm located in a foreign country.

Foreign factor. An intermediary found in a direct international channel that sells consigned or delivered merchandise for a commission.

Forward contract. A sale of one currency for another at a fixed rate on a specified future date.

Forward rate. The exchange rate at which a third party (bank) will agree to pay for a currency at a specified time in the future.

Franchise. An agreement in which the management of a domestic firm gives the foreigner firm permission to market a product or service according to the rules and procedures prescribed by the domestic management.

Free trade association. Member nations remove internal trade barriers for agreed-upon products but maintain individual trade barriers against nonmember nations.

Free trade zone. A fenced-in area, usually at a seaport or airport, that is not considered to be part of the country as far as import regulations are concerned.

Freight forwarder. An intermediary that specializes in the export process and the movement of products internationally.

Frequency. Refers to how often an ad appears on any given day or in any given medium.

General Agreement on Tariffs and Trade (GATT). Created in 1947 to reduce trade restrictions and promote free trade worldwide; replaced by the World Trade Organization (WTO) during the Uruguay Round in 1993.

General license. Used for all products exported from the United States that are not sensitive products or sold to sensitive countries; also known as open exporting.

Geocentric. A global perspective of marketing in which the world is seen as one big market and international markets are not necessarily considered separately from the domestic market.

Global marketing. Marketing in a worldwide perspective with no domestic references. Also called world marketing.

Gram. The basic unit of measure for weight in the metric system (equivalent to .001 kilogram).

Gross domestic product (GDP). The market value of all goods and services produced within a country in a year; equal to the sum of the values of consumption, investment, and government spending, and the difference between exports and imports. GDP = (consumption + investment + government spending) + (exports – imports).

Gross national income (GNI). The value of the total output of goods and services produced by a nation's firms in a particular year. GNI is GDP (the income from firms operating within the nation) plus the income from firms operating abroad.

Heckscher-Ohlin theory. Named for two Swedish economists, this theory holds that firms in capital-abundant countries will export capital-intensive products, and firms in labor-abundant countries will export labor-intensive products.

Hecto. The prefix given to indicate 100. Ex.: a hectoliter = 100 liters.

Idiom. A group of words that together have a different meaning than the dictionary definitions of the individual words.

Import agent. A category of intermediaries found in direct international channels that represent the firm's products. They may or may not hold inventory, are able sell in the name of the manufacturer, and function as a foreign sales branch for the firm.

Import broker. An intermediary found in a direct international channel that works with potential buyers and sellers, and assists them with the negotiation of the terms and conditions of their sales agreement.

Import jobber. An intermediary that is a type of wholesaler found in a direct international channel. It buys job lots of specific lines of products from producers and other wholesalers.

Import merchant. A category of intermediaries found in a direct international channel that includes foreign buyers at the wholesale and retail levels.

Import restrictions. Limitations placed on the ability of the international marketer to import raw materials, components, or parts.

Incoterms. Internationally accepted commercial terms specifying the transport responsibilities and obligations of the buyer and seller.

Indirect channel. A channel created when the seller negotiates with an intermediary or buyer who resides in the domestic country.

Individualistic cultures. Cultures that tend to emphasize the importance of the individual instead of the group.

Industrialized countries. The developed countries of the world that are characterized by high income per capita, slow growth in GNI, reliance on technology, and well-developed market economies.

International Bank for Reconstruction and Development (IBRD). The central institution of the World Bank Group that makes loans to those governments that can qualify under conventional terms.

International business. The study of firms that are involved in business-related endeavors in more than one country.

International channel of distribution. Consists of the organizations that facilitate the transaction and ownership flows.

International cross-cultural management. The comparative study of the management process in more than one country at similar points in time.

International Development Association (IDA). Makes loans to balance-of-payments-plagued nations that would not qualify for loans under conventional terms from the IBRD.

International division. An organizational structure distinguished by the existence of an international business function. It is located at a level in the firm's organization that is high enough to support a diverse and significant involvement in numerous international markets via any form of market entry.

International economics. The analysis of financial and trade policies that describe the movement of goods and investments among nations and help develop individual national economies.

International Finance Corporation (IFC). Helps promote the growth of the private sector by making loans to businesses and other nongovernment buyers.

International headquarters company. An organizational structure featuring the location of international business efforts in a separate company that remains affiliated with the domestic parent. International marketing operates independently of domestic marketing yet is structurally connected for business purposes.

International marketing. The performance of marketing activities that facilitate and expedite exchanges and build relationships with buyers in foreign markets.

International marketing plans. The essentials of policies and programs, not specifics, to be implemented to align marketing activities with the international marketing strategy.

International marketing strategy. A guide to the direction marketing efforts will take to effectively cultivate the foreign market.

International marketing tactics. The specific techniques required to implement the international marketing plan.

International marketing targets. The benchmarks or performance levels by which attainment of the international marketing objectives will be judged.

International product life cycle theory. A theory of international trade that holds that new products are developed and introduced first by firms in highly developed countries. Eventually, foreign demand increases sufficiently that production in a foreign market becomes attractive and economically feasible, and the product is exported to the developed nation that first introduced it.

International trade. The activities of firms relating to the production of products domestically for the purpose of shipment to buyers in foreign countries and the procurement of foreign-made products.

Intracompany transfer pricing. The price management charges itself for sales within the company, considered to be an arms-length or comparable industry price.

Intraterms. A set of standard shipping terms in simple and understandable language.

Invisible tariff. *See* nontariff barrier.

Irrevocable. A type of letter of credit in which changes are allowed only with prior approval of the seller, opening bank, and advising bank.

Islamic law. Based on the Quran.

Joint ownership, joint venture. *See* equity joint venture.
Joint venture. Any business association that involves collaboration of its participants over an extended period of time.
Jurisdictional clause. The clause in a contract that specifies which country's law should be applied in an international dispute.
Justice. An ethics that prioritizes fairness, equitableness, and impartiality.

Kilo. The prefix given to indicate 1,000. Ex.: a kilogram = 1,000 grams.
Kilogram. The fundamental unit of weight, or mass, in the metric system. Equal to the weight of the quantity of matter present in a cylinder of platinum-iridium alloy measuring 39 millimeters in diameter and height that is kept at the International Bureau of Weights and Measures at Sèvres, France.

Language. The primary means by which cultural awareness is communicated, and therefore defining of social life.
Legislative entity. A category of intermediaries found in a direct international channel. They are authorized by the U.S. Congress and provide some export incentive or benefit such as exemption from antitrust laws.
Less-developed countries (LDCs). The poorest countries of the world, characterized by low income per capita, agrarian populations, high birth rates, low GNI per capita, unstable governments, and low literacy rates.
Letter of credit. A document issued by a bank, which substitutes the bank's credit for that of the buyer and guarantees payment.
Licensing. A contractual arrangement in which the management of a domestic firm transfers production and marketing rights for a product to a foreign firm in return for royalties on each unit produced.
Lighter aboard ship (LASH). A form of shipping in which small flat-bottomed barges called lighters are sailed into the ship and stored on elevated racks.
Liner companies. Firms that operate cargo ships that sail on regular schedules to and from specified seaports by means of established sea routes.
Liter. The fundamental unit of volume in the metric system. The volume that is equal to one cubic decimeter or one thousandth (0.001) of a cubic meter.
Logistics. The commercial movements of products.

Maastricht Treaty. Formed the European Monetary Union and planned the creation of a common currency (the euro, in 1999). Signed in 1992.
Mail-order house. Part of a direct international channel in which a firm's export sales are generated via catalogs and e-commerce, rather than a sales force.
Management contract. An arrangement in which the management of a domestic firm supplies management expertise to a foreigner.
Managing agent. An intermediary found in a direct international channel that manages the export affairs of the producer in the foreign country. It assures contracts are fulfilled and all aspects of the export sale are correct.
Manufacturer's export agent. An intermediary found in an indirect international channel that acts on behalf of a domestic producer to develop a foreign market, representing its products to potential customers.

Manufacturer's representative. An intermediary found in a direct international channel. It represents a domestic producer in the foreign country by providing services the manufacturer requests to facilitate and assist with finalizing sales.

Market entry analysis. The investigation of foreign countries for the purpose of identifying appropriate expansion markets.

Marketing concept. A customer-driven management orientation in which business decisions are made with the objective of providing customer satisfaction.

Marketing environment. The totality of forces that surround the firm and affect the manager's ability to satisfy customers.

Marketing information system (MIS). An ongoing data collection activity gathering from internal and external sources.

Marketing mix. The controllable part of the marketing environment that can be manipulated at the manager's discretion.

Marketing research. The one-time collection of information that is not available from the MIS for the purpose of solving specific marketing problems.

Marketing strategy. A nonspecific, long-term plan of action that is intended to provide the procedures to be followed to accomplish marketing objectives.

Merchant. Takes title to the product, represents itself, and earns income based on resale ability.

Meter. The fundamental unit of length in the metric system. The distance between two lines engraved on a platinum-iridium bar that is kept at 0°C at Sèvres, France.

Metric system. A logical method of relating units of measure, based on units of ten and used in most of the world's countries.

Milli. The prefix given to indicate 1/1,000. Ex.: a milligram = 0.001 gram.

Mission statement. A general and brief declaration of the purpose of the organization.

Modifications. Made to individualize the product to the tastes, preferences, and specific needs of the target group in the foreign market.

Multinational banks. Intergovernmental organizations that provide banking services to a variety of buyers.

Multinational marketing. The conduct of business in foreign markets rather than between domestic and foreign markets.

Multiple exchange rate. More than one exchange rate is established at which a country will exchange its currency.

NAFTA certificate of origin. Required for shipments from the United States to Canada or Mexico.

Natural resources theory. A theory of international trade that holds that firms in countries richly endowed with a particular natural resource will tend to export that resource to countries that have a scarcity of it.

Newly industrialized countries (NICs). Emerging markets that are able to sustain rapid economic growth to the point at which the characteristics of an industrialized country are on the verge of being reached.

No export department. *See* a built-in export department.

Noncumulative turnover tax. Assessed on the value each channel member adds to the product.

Nondeliverable forward contract. A form of forward contract that can be used for emerging market currencies where a conventional forward market does not exist or is restricted.

Nonequity joint venture. A partnership arrangement that involves the sharing of anything other than money and ownership.

Nontariff barrier. Any nonfinancial impediment or restriction on exported or imported merchandise; also known as an invisible tariff.

Objectives. Broad statements of what the management of the organization wants to accomplish.

Observation method. A primary data research method in which the problem is simply viewed.

Ocean bill of lading. A receipt for the merchandise by the carrier; a freight contract that shows the carrier's obligation to ship the merchandise, establishes ownership, serves as a document of title, and is negotiable.

Open account. The product is shipped against the buyer's promise to pay at some future time; also called credit.

Opportunity cost. The exchange of resources from the manufacture of one product to the manufacture of another.

Option contract. An agreement that gives the international marketer the right, but not the obligation, to sell a specified amount of a foreign currency at a specified exchange rate within a specified period of time.

Organization for Economic Cooperation and Development (OECD). An organization that replaced the OEEC after the aid from the Marshall Plan was administered. It included all the countries that had been members of the OEEC plus Canada, Japan, Spain, and the United States and pursued freer trade through the harmonization of tax, fiscal, and related policies of member countries.

Organization for European Economic Cooperation (OEEC). An organization of seventeen Western European countries formed to administer and allocate the aid authorized under the Marshall Plan.

Overseas development banks. U.S. governmental organizations such as the Export-Import Bank and the Agency for International Development that have been established to support the export expansion programs of U.S. firms.

Package. The container or wrapper in which the physical item is stored.

Package modifications. Changes made to improve the nature, shape, and appearance of the package.

Packing slip. Specifies merchandise and packing information.

Parallel imports. The importing of products from a low-cost area to a high-cost area for the purpose of underpricing local sellers of the same product.

Parallel translation. When two people translate the same wording from one language into another language and compare translations to identify differences.

Parent company entities. A category of intermediaries found in an indirect international channel. They function within the firm, directing exporting activities.

Peg. A country fixes its exchange rate to that of another country. The value of the currency of the pegging country will fluctuate in proportion to the changes in value of the country's currency to which it is fixed.

Personal selling. Direct face-to-face communication with potential buyers by representatives of the seller.

Physical characteristics. The properties and attributes that identify and distinguish the tangible item as a particular product.

Phytosanitary certificate. Required by the U.S. Department of Agriculture for certain products shipped from the United States to assure those products were inspected or treated for insects or diseases.

Piggyback marketing. A method of marketing in which a seller arranges to have its product distributed through another international marketer's distribution channel.

Political union. Has all the characteristics of an economic and monetary union along with a supranational government.

Politics. A type of factual knowledge that prescribes what can and cannot be done legally.

Polycentric. Host-country oriented such that each country is viewed as unique and different, requiring individualized attention.

Precompensation. The same as counterpurchase in reverse. Products or services are purchased by a domestic firm and paid for in cash. The foreign firm promises to use the cash to buy products or services from the domestic firm.

Preferential trading agreement. A group of nations that agree to lower tariffs on selected products that are traded among members; the weakest form of economic integration.

Price controls. Constraints on the price management may charge for its product.

Price escalation. The need to raise price because of the added expenses of doing business internationally. These expenses are not encountered domestically, are beyond the international marketer's control, and include things like transportation, tariffs, taxes, and longer channels of distribution.

Price inflation. The slow loss of value of one currency relative to other currencies.

Primary data. Facts the manager or research team gathers by their own endeavors.

Product. Everything the customer receives in the exchange process. Consists of all tangible and intangible attributes embodied in the physical characteristics, package, brand, and services received.

Promotion. All methods the marketer uses to communicate with the target group of customers.

Public relations. Activities intended to influence the attitudes of people outside the firm in a positive way about the firm, its products, and the people working inside the firm.

Quality modifications. Changes made to improve reliability and durability.

Quota. A limit on the amount of a product that may be exported or imported.

Regiocentric. The standardization of marketing efforts within geographic regions of the world.

Regional development banks. Banks formed by nations located in the same geographic area for the purpose of facilitating economic growth in the region.

Relativism. An ethical theory, also known as situational ethics, in which no universal standards are considered to exist and ethically right decisions are based only on the unique conditions and facts involved in each situation.

Religion. A type of factual knowledge that entails beliefs about how to organize and interpret conditions over which control is lacking or which are not fully understood.

Rental agreement. When the management of a domestic firm provides equipment and maintenance to a foreign firm to equip its factory in exchange for usage or lease payments.

Representative. A category of intermediaries found in a direct international channel; an extension of the manufacturing firm in a foreign country.

Resident foreign buying agent. An intermediary found in an indirect international channel that serves as the purchasing agent for a foreign company. It purchases products for its foreign client and receives a commission for its services.

Retailer. An intermediary found in a direct international channel that is the final member in the marketing channel prior to the consumer.

Revaluation. An increase in the value of one currency relative to that of others.

Revocable. A type of letter of credit that the opening bank can invalidate or make changes in.

Rights. An ethical theory in which a decision is considered ethical when the rights of those affected are not violated.

Sales promotion. A variety of seller-initiated activities used to make advertising and personal selling more effective.

Sample. A small group of items drawn from all the items (population) that have the information the manager needs.

Secondary data. Facts that have been generated previously by another source.

Section 482. Section of the Internal Revenue Code that governs intracompany transfer pricing and states that no pricing procedure may be structured in such a way that results in evading the payment of appropriate U.S. taxes.

Self-reference criterion (SRC). Failure to adequately appreciate the foreign culture; making decisions in terms of your own cultural background.

Selling office. An intermediary found in a direct international channel that is located in the foreign country and functions as a sales office of the producer.

Selling rate. The amount of the local currency that must be given to a bank or money changer to obtain one unit of a foreign currency.

Service modifications. Changes made in the ancillaries that accompany the physical product.

Services. Tangible and intangible efforts and attributes that embellish the product and make acquisition and use easier or more enjoyable.

Shipper's Export Declaration. A document required if the value of the merchandise being exported from the United States is over US$2,500.00 (except to Canada) or is being shipped via a validated license regardless of the value; also the source of trade information and statistics reported by the government.

Sight draft. Must be paid immediately upon presentation to the buyer.
Single European Act. Established procedures for standardizing remaining impediments to free trade in 1986.
Situational ethics. *See* relativism.
Social relationships. A type of factual knowledge that prescribes appropriate and acceptable manners of behavior.
Solidarity theory. A theory of international trade that holds that managers in developed countries recognize their moral obligation to assist the developing and LDC nations to improve their economies.
Spacing. Refers to the sequencing of ads that appear during an advertising campaign.
Specific tariff. A fee assessed at a flat rate per physical unit.
Spot contract. An agreement to sell a foreign currency at the spot rate two business days after the spot contract agreement is reached.
Spot rate. The prevailing exchange rate at the time the contract is signed.
Standardization. Making components of the domestic marketing strategy part of the foreign marketing strategy without any changes.
Style modifications. Changes made in the product's appearance.
Subregional banks. Serve a limited area or region, and membership typically is limited to borrowing countries and excludes donors.
Supranational marketing. Considering marketing in terms of conglomerates of nations that provide harmony of business practices among participating countries. The European Union is an example.
Supply chain. The coordinated system of organizations, people, activities, information, and resources involved in moving products from supplier to buyer.
Survey method. A primary data research method, which involves the evaluation of information gathered from people by means of interviews.
Switch house. Also called an intermerchant. Helps management dispose of countertraded goods by locating buyers, arranging transportation, obtaining insurance, securing warehousing, and assisting with financing.
Switching. Helping the seller obtain money or other products or services for countertraded merchandise.

Tariff. A duty levied on exported or imported merchandise.
Tax haven. A country or municipality such as Liechtenstein in which little or no corporate income tax is charged.
Tax holiday. A period of time when low or no taxes are assessed.
Tax on value added (TVA). *See* noncumulative turnover tax.
Technical services contract. An arrangement in which technical expertise and process knowledge are provided to a foreigner firm to make high-tech equipment operational.
Technology. A type of factual knowledge that identifies the infrastructure system that is associated with what constitutes an appropriate way of life.
Technology theory. A theory of international trade that holds that firms in nations with a technological advantage will export their technology to countries needing that technology.

Teleology. An ethics that bases the decision about whether or not a behavior is ethically right or wrong on the result of the behavior. The ends justify the means.

Theory of comparative advantage. A theory of international trade based upon specializing in the production of products a country can make efficiently and trading those products with other nations to obtain products that cannot be made as efficiently as they can be made elsewhere.

Third-party logistics operators (3PL). A facilitating organization that provides a service such as hauling and storage and is focused on a company's international or domestic distribution requirements, or both.

Time draft. Must be paid before a prescribed number of days have passed after the draft is presented to the buyer.

Trade creation theory. A theory of international trade that holds that purchases of components will be made at the lowest possible price. As trade restrictions are reduced and eliminated, lower-priced foreign sources of supply are sought.

Trading company. An intermediary found in an indirect international channel. It buys products from manufacturers in different countries and markets them to buyers in a variety of countries.

Tramp vessels. Ships that are operated without fixed ports of call or sailing schedules.

Translation errors. Occur when the wrong word or words are selected, causing the message to convey an entirely different meaning than originally intended.

Transnational company. *See* world company.

Traveling sales representative. An intermediary found in a direct international channel. It travels to foreign countries for the purpose of locating wholesalers, retailers, and purchasing agents who are interested in the manufacturer's products.

Triangular barter. Similar to bilateral barter except that three firms are involved.

Turn-key operation. An arrangement in which a complete factory is built by a domestic firm for a foreign firm, workers are trained to operate it, and control of the whole operation is eventually given to the foreigner.

Turnover taxes. Assessed each time the product changes hands while moving through the channel of distribution.

Unconfirmed. A type of letter of credit in which the advising bank does not guarantee payment and can stop payment or change payment terms because of changes in the buyer's financial situation.

Uncontrollable variables. That part of the marketing environment that is beyond the manager's control in the short run and constrains marketing mix decisions.

United States Agency for International Development (USAID). Provides loans to friendly LDC governments for the purpose of buying U.S.-made products that will assist with infrastructure development.

Utilitarianism. An ethical theory that maintains that the most ethical decision is the one that produces the greatest good for the most people affected.

Validated license. Required for exporting all restricted commodities such as weapons, high-tech products with possible military applications, or other strategic items from the United States to any country, and for exporting any product to countries with which the United States does not have diplomatic relations; also known as closed exporting.

Value-added tax (VAT). *See* noncumulative turnover tax.

Values. A type of factual knowledge that acts as a screening device to determine priorities among alternative actions a person can take.

Virtue. An ethical theory that states that a decision is ethical if the decision maker exhibits good character.

Way Station Model. A six-step systematic approach to help management make the international market entry decision.

Webb-Pomerene Association. An intermediary found in a direct international channel that markets the products of competing manufacturers for the purpose of export sales and is exempt from U.S. antitrust laws.

Wholly owned. A 100-percent-owned subsidiary or branch of the domestic company.

Window forward contract. An agreement to sell a foreign currency at the spot rate within an agreed range ("window") of days.

World Bank Group. Formed in 1944 at the Bretton Woods Conference in New Hampshire and composed of the International Bank for Reconstruction and Development, the International Development Association, and the International Finance Corporation, which make loans to buyers in third-world countries for the purpose of developing infrastructures.

World company. An organizational structure that is distinguished by management that supports all foreign markets in the most efficient way possible, conducts business in most countries, considers all countries as potential markets, and has no domestic market.

World marketing. *See* global marketing.

World trade. Products that are produced in one country and shipped and sold in another country (exports).

World Trade Organization (WTO). The successor to the General Agreement on Tariffs and Trade (GATT); organized in 1993 at the Uruguay Round of the GATT.

Company Index

Subject Index

About the Author

Donald L. Brady is professor of marketing and chairman, Department of Business Administration at American University in Bulgaria. He received the Ph.D. degree in Business Administration from the University of Alabama in 1978, specializing in marketing.

Previously, Dr. Brady was on the faculty of Youngstown State University; Birmingham-Southern College, where he held the Elton B. Stephens chair of Marketing and Sales Management; and Millersville University, where he served as department chair and created and directed the university's Small Business Institute. Before entering academia, he worked in industry for Armstrong World Industries, Inc., Rust International, and the 3M Company. His teaching specialties include international marketing, sales force management, marketing research, research methods for business, and business ethics.

Dr. Brady's research interests include corporate international marketing strategy, marketing policy of small businesses, determinants of exporting success, and business ethics. His research has been published in numerous journals, including the *Journal of International Business Studies,* the *International Journal of Retailing,* the *Journal of Personal Selling and Sales Management,* the *Journal of Purchasing and Materials Management,* the *American Journal of Small Business,* the *Journal of Private Enterprise,* the *Journal of Business Education,* and the *Journal of Product and Brand Management.* He has also presented the results of his research extensively at conferences of various professional and academic organizations and published in their proceedings.

Dr. Brady studied in Europe; served as visiting professor of international marketing at Regents Business School, Regents College, London; and has accompanied students to Humberside University in the United Kingdom. He has been a frequent speaker and panel member in the areas of small business and marketing. He is a lifetime member of Sales and Marketing Executives International.

JAICO PUBLISHING HOUSE

Elevate Your Life. Transform Your World.

Established in 1946, Jaico Publishing House is the publisher of stellar authors such as Sri Sri Paramahansa Yogananda, Osho, Robin Sharma, Deepak Chopra, Stephen Hawking, Eknath Easwaran, Sarvapalli Radhakrishnan, Nirad Chaudhuri, Khushwant Singh, Mulk Raj Anand, John Maxwell, Ken Blanchard and Brian Tracy. Our list which has crossed a landmark 2000 titles, is amongst the most diverse in the country, with books in religion, spirituality, mind/body/spirit, self-help, business, cookery, humour, career, games, biographies, fiction, and science.

Jaico has expanded its horizons to become a leading publisher of educational and professional books in management and engineering. Our college-level textbooks and reference titles are used by students countrywide. The success of our academic and professional titles is largely due to the efforts of our Educational and Corporate Sales Divisions.

The late Mr. Jaman Shah established Jaico as a book distribution company. Sensing that independence was around the corner, he aptly named his company Jaico ("Jai" means victory in Hindi). In order to tap the significant demand for affordable books in a developing nation, Mr. Shah initiated Jaico's own publications. Jaico was India's first publisher of paperback books in the English language.

In addition to being a publisher and distributor of its own titles, Jaico is a major distributor of books of leading international publishers such as McGraw Hill, Pearson, Cengage Learning, John Wiley and Elsevier Science. With its headquarters in Mumbai, Jaico has other sales offices in Ahmedabad, Bangalore, Bhopal, Chennai, Delhi, Hyderabad and Kolkata. Our sales team of over 40 executives, direct mail order division, and website ensure that our books effectively reach all urban and rural parts of the country.

SINCE 1946